UNIX™
SYSTEM ADMINISTRATION

UNIX™
SYSTEM ADMINISTRATION

DAVID FIEDLER and BRUCE H. HUNTER

CONSULTING EDITORS:
Stephen G. Kochan and Patrick H. Wood

HAYDEN BOOKS
A Division of Howard W. Sams & Company
4300 West 62nd Street
Indianapolis, Indiana 46268 USA

This entire book was edited and processed under UNIX. The text was formatted using device independent `troff` (`ditroff`) with the assistance of `tbl` for the tables. The final layout was performed by Patrick Wood of PIPELINE ASSOCIATES INC., using `devlw` to convert `troff`'s output to POSTSCRIPT. An Apple LaserWriter was used for page proofs, with final output going to an Allied Linotype Lintronic 100 typesetter.

Acquisitions Editor: THERESE A. ZAK
Production Editor: MAUREEN CONNELLY
Cover art: LOU ODOR
Cover design: JIM BERNARD
Illustrations: JOHN McAUSLAND
Manufacturing: THE JOHN D. LUCAS PRINTING COMPANY

Printed in the United States of America

	2	3	4	5	6	7	8	9	PRINTING
86	87	88	89	90	91	92	93	94	YEAR

We would like to dedicate this book to our wives, Karen Hunter and Susan Fiedler. Without their encouragement, support, long hours of typing, and careful editing, we could not have finished — or even attempted — this book.

D.F. and B.H.H.

PREFACE

If you run a UNIX operating system or compatible, this book is for you.

It doesn't matter whether that system is a tiny IBM PC/XT running VENIX or XENIX, and you're the only user. It doesn't matter whether it's a VAX-11/780 under UNIX System V, with a user population of 75, and 8 modem lines plus 5 printers. *Every* UNIX system needs someone to take care of it, look after its needs, and sometimes give it love and affection. This someone is usually called the *S*ystem *A*dministrator (or SA) — a rather formal sounding title for such a caring position. This someone is probably you!

We'll show you how to do it all as painlessly as possible. Together, we've pulled SA duty on systems ranging from the tiny AT&T UNIX PC to giant Amdahl mainframes, including just about everything in between. We've experienced the challenge of running multiple systems simultaneously, and also the thrill of having them all *crash* simultaneously. Along the way, we've picked up quite a few tricks and shortcuts, and the realization that the job is both easier and harder than you might expect after reading the official documentation. Easier, because once you understand what the manuals are *trying* to say, your job is pretty straightforward. Harder, because no manual (or even book) can prepare you for the endless parade of unusual circumstances you'll have to face in what is sometimes referred to as "the real world."

Counting individual manufacturers' changes, there are literally dozens of variations of the UNIX system available on the market today, even though only about 10 official versions exist. These include the Sixth, Seventh, and Eighth Editions (often referred to as Versions 6, 7, and 8), PWB, System III, System V, System V Release 2, System V Release 3, Berkeley 4.1, Berkeley 4.2, and Berkeley 4.3. This list does not include variants of the above such as PC/IX, UniPlus+, Ultrix, VENIX, XENIX, or any of the UNIX look-alikes such as Idris or Coherent.

Due to the many variations in Bell Labs and commercial UNIX versions, your system may differ in its commands or locations of commands as presented in this book. Since we can't possibly cover everything, out of necessity we have to limit this book to descendants of the original AT&T Bell Labs UNIX System. We have used the AT&T System 5 and 5.2 manuals with occasional reference to other well known ports including Unisoft's. While you will undoubtedly learn enough here to be able to keep a Berkeley (BSD) system running, there are enough differences between BSD and AT&T UNIX that you could possibly get confused. If you *are* trying to run a BSD system using this book, keep an open mind and prepare yourself for a good number of files to be in different places.

This advice applies to almost everyone, actually. Because each implementation of UNIX is different (even when they're all ''standard''), minor differences between this book and your system will probably occur. We've tried to anticipate most of these, but some variations in spelling, file names, and locations are unavoidable. If you listen to the spirit of our words, and don't limit yourself to a literal rendition of each letter, you'll do fine. You learn to be flexible when using UNIX, and that will serve you well when running the system.

Which brings us to the anticipated audience of this book. We assume that you already know how to *use* the UNIX system; if you are still at the point where you don't know how to log in, look at files, edit them, redirect input and output, and send mail to other users, then you're not quite ready to run an entire system. You wouldn't want to run a nuclear power plant if you had trouble plugging in a radio without electrocuting yourself, would you? In this case, we recommend that you read a good introductory book or two on the UNIX system (see the *Bibliography*) before you start changing things around.

On the other hand, maybe you got this book because you've been told (or have told yourself) that a UNIX system is coming in and *you're going to run it*. Chapters 1 through 6 will get you past the hurdle of getting UNIX started up, but we strongly recommend that you learn how to use UNIX before going any further than that. You wouldn't want to risk a meltdown, would you?

You won't find long lists of UNIX commands and their options in this book. That's boring, and besides, you already have such reference material in your UNIX system documentation. This book is meant to be read with your system manuals by your side and your terminal in front of you. Try things out as you read them, and make notes as to how things work differently on your own system. We think you'll have fun exploring the system, once you realize that there are ways of doing that without the risk of blowing anything up.

Everyone Has His Own Style

Don't be afraid to do things your own way once you understand what you're doing. But we recommend that you keep to the general flavor of UNIX command naming and use. This way, it's easy for you to work on another UNIX system if necessary. When you write a program to put a new user on the system, whether you call it **newuser** or **adduser** isn't really important, as long as you don't call it **whiffenpoof**.

Certain UNIX traditions, such as leaving vowels out of command names, are not always for the best. Even so, using a traditional UNIX method to solve system administration problems is a good idea because it is almost always the best method, and it's usually easier to maintain afterward than other methods. Also, if everyone follows UNIX traditions, UNIX systems will continue to be relatively consistent.

Imagine the fun that would develop if you went to another machine and found that the SA there had changed all the major command names and directories. While the fact that this *can* be done shows the flexibility of the UNIX system, such a change would not be to anyone's benefit. Do we mean to say that UNIX is perfect as it is and can't be improved? No, but just make sure any change you make is a real improvement.

The UNIX system furnished with your machine is called the standard distribution. The system administrator's tools are always in **/etc**, major user commands in **/usr** and so on. The locations and names of files and commands are dictated by tradition, although UNIX, with its multiplicity of tools, is malleable enough to change this. Individualizing your system is one of the thrills of being a system administrator, but heed this word of warning. As you tailor your system, for the sake of consistency keep your user areas and homegrown commands away from the standard distribution. Tailor your system to suit your needs, but make it easier to get support from your software vendor and fellow administrators by keeping the standard distribution undisturbed. You will avoid confusion, make life easier on yourself, and have more time to enjoy the rewarding challenges of being a UNIX system administrator.

The authors would like to thank Tom Marshall of *tmmnet, Ltd.*, and Ron and Mary Ann Lachman of *Lachman Associates, Inc.*, for their many suggestions. Thanks are also due to Hayden Book Company staffers Maureen Connelly for her great patience and intelligence, and Juliann Colvin Hudson for a great job of copy editing. Jim Joyce of *The Gawain Group* and Les Hancock must be acknowledged for offering their valuable editing services, even though logistics did not permit this. In addition, we would also like to acknowledge Les and Chris Hancock and Sol and Lennie Libes for warning us about how much work is involved in writing a book. We did it anyway.

CONTENTS

1 The System Administrator's Overview of UNIX ▪ 1
2 Bringing Up the System ▪ 12
3 Checking the File System ▪ 30
4 Where Everything Is and How to Find It ▪ 48
5 Mounting and Unmounting File Systems ▪ 81
6 Shutting Down the System ▪ 97
7 Adding and Removing Users from the System ▪ 106
8 Backups ▪ 117
9 Security ▪ 145
10 Terminals ▪ 168
11 Printers on the UNIX System ▪ 183
12 Modems and an Even Bigger World ▪ 214
13 Shell Programming ▪ 251
14 Assorted Administration Tips ▪ 282
Appendix A Where to Learn More ▪ 295
Appendix B Talking to the Outside World ▪ 298
Appendix C A Typical UUCP Connection ▪ 307
Bibliography ▪ 313

C H A P T E R

1

THE SYSTEM ADMINISTRATOR'S OVERVIEW OF UNIX

What's So Special About UNIX?

UNIX is a very special operating system. It is not a manufacturer's system, steeped in hardware dependence and tied by a binary umbilical cord to the whims and fancies of one company. Neither is it limited in application — it is an ideal system for writing, programming, and communications. It is easily the most complete operating system in existence today.

Because UNIX is such a comprehensive system, a well-rounded approach to UNIX system administration is necessary. Remember the parable about the blind men who examined an elephant? One felt the trunk and concluded that an elephant was shaped like a serpent. Another felt the legs and determined that elephants were shaped like tree trunks. Both were partly right, but neither understood the whole elephant. In this chapter we're going to look at UNIX from a lot of different angles — UNIX past to UNIX present, a user's point of view and a system administrator's perspective, UNIX internals, and hardware and software considerations. In short, we're going to try to get an overall view of the beast.

What Is an Operating System?

The stock description of an operating system is that it is a large body of software that acts as a ''traffic cop'' and directs the flow of information to and from the hardware. While this is technically true, it brings us back to the elephant-as-serpent analogy. Any operating system, especially one as powerful as UNIX, is made of a number of different parts:

- *Device drivers*, or programs that stand at the lowest level and allow control of actual hardware devices. They negotiate between the kernel and the hardware bus.
- *A scheduler*, that decides which user programs are to be run, when, and for how long. On a primitive operating system such as CP/M-80 or MS-DOS, there is no scheduler because only one program runs under the control of the operating system at a time.
- *Memory management*, which determines how much memory to allocate to each program. If not enough memory is available to run a given program, it will move other programs (or parts of them) to temporary disk storage as necessary. This is known as *swapping* (or *paging*).
- *The file system*, a structure used to locate and store programs and files on disk.
- *System programs*, the software accessible directly by users to allow manipulation of files and devices in various ways for getting basic work done. These may include utility programs, text editors, language compilers, debuggers, and shells.

Shells

A *shell* is a command processor that is the actual interface between the UNIX kernel and the user. It is the shell that runs commands when you type their names, expands "wildcard" characters such as * and ?, and takes care of redirecting input and output. There are two common shells available. The first is the *Bourne shell* (written by Stephen R. Bourne), which is the "standard" shell supplied with most UNIX systems. Bourne shell command syntax is reminiscent of the Algol language.

The *C shell* was developed by William Joy at the University of California at Berkeley. As the name implies, command programs written in the C shell resemble programs written in the C language. Using the C shell can offer some advantages to the system administrator. One is its history mechanism, which permits the re-execution of complex commands and allows you to see the commands you executed during a login session. This last feature can save you when you get confused about what you did while working late at night. Another advantage is the ability to assign *aliases*, which permit commands to be "tailored" for the local system.

In spite of the advantages of using the C shell, we strongly recommend that all of your shell programs be written in Bourne shell. They will execute faster, use less memory, and be portable to *any* UNIX system.

The Kernel

What is generally referred to as the UNIX *kernel* includes the scheduler, memory management routines, and device drivers, as well as a large number of built-in system functions that are hidden from the casual user. These functions, known as *system calls*, are actually sub-programs or primitive functions that are accessible to user programs. The kernel is simply a program called **unix** (or **xenix** or **venix**) that is loaded in when the system is started and runs continuously until shutdown.

Portability

Portability is a significant feature because it signals the end of machine-dependent operating systems. Digital Equipment Corporation (DEC) has its VMS, Data General (DG) its AOS, and International Business Machines (IBM) has MVS. These all work just fine, but only on their own machines. The strengths and weaknesses of machine-dependent operating systems tend to reflect those of the hardware, not the system software itself.

UNIX, on the other hand, is system-independent. It is designed for portability, so it can run on numerous machines, from supercomputer to microcomputer. Should you need to change or upgrade machines, the **cd** command will still change directories on any size machine running UNIX — an AT&T 3B2/300, a VAX 11/780, an Amdahl 580, or a Cray II. Users can jump from supermicros to minis to mainframes with little retraining if they are all running versions of UNIX. Students coming right out of colleges and universities can enter industry and go to work almost immediately on UNIX because most have been exposed to UNIX at school. Portability is one of the UNIX system's most important and unique features.

▪ C — The Key to UNIX Portability ▪

The traditional view of UNIX is a set of layered spheres, each sphere representing a different level of the system. The outermost sphere represents the users; the innermost sphere, the system's hardware (see Fig. 1-1). Notice that the second layer surrounding the kernel consists of device drivers, which interface between the heart of UNIX (the kernel) and the hardware.

UNIX is portable because most of it is written in the high-level C language with only a small portion in native assembler code. A device driver is divided into two parts; the top end is written in C and the bottom end is written in both C and assembler. Surprisingly, 90% of the UNIX kernel is written in C. Assembler sections of the kernel are kept to a minimum, each module consisting of only a few lines of code called by a larger C module. Addressing registers, saving and restoring context (the CPU registers and immediate stack) is done from C, not assembler. C is the key to UNIX portability.

To illustrate how vital C is to UNIX, porting UNIX to a new processor (target machine) requires just three major steps. The first is writing a C compiler in that processor's assembly language, the most time-consuming part of the port (often this has been done already, due to the increasing popularity of the C language). The second step is taking an existing version of UNIX that is closest to the new processor's instruction set and modifying the assembler-level code and low-level device drivers accordingly. Once the system can read and write to disk satisfactorily, the C code for the UNIX system is cross-compiled on a development computer and brought to the target machine via serial port. As more and more of the UNIX system begins running on the target

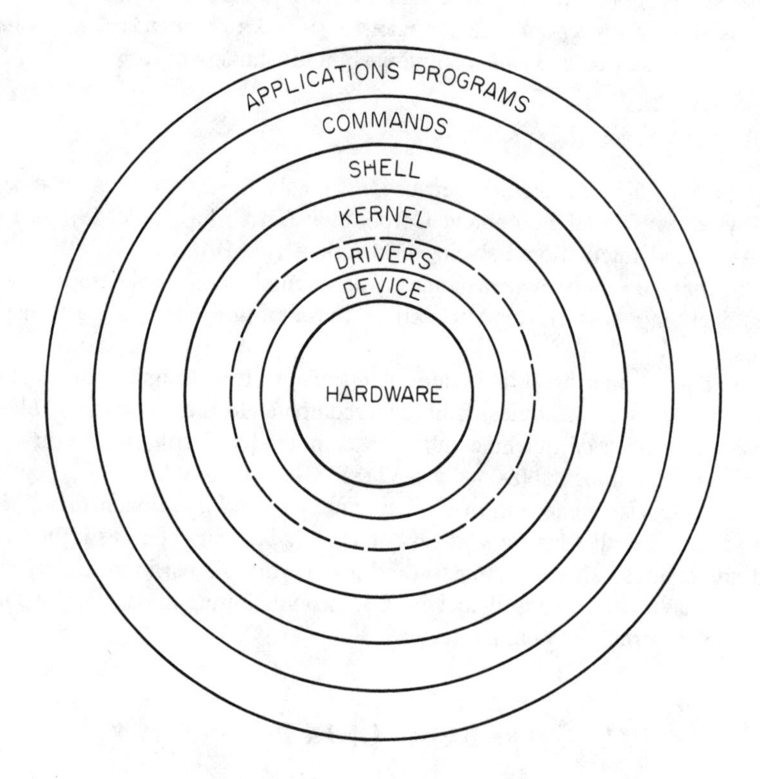

Fig. 1-1. The UNIX System

machine, development can continue directly on that machine until all the necessary code has been compiled and tested.

Originally, the only version of UNIX outside of Bell Laboratories was the DEC PDP-11 port. Now there are many AT&T-supported commercial UNIX ports, including the DEC VAX machines, the Motorola 68000 family of processors, the Intel 80286 family of processors, the National Semiconductor 16032 and 32032 family of processors, and Amdahl's UTS UNIX running on IBM architecture machines. At the small end of the scale is the little IBM PC and its army of UNIX derivatives, look-alike, and work-alike systems (VENIX, XENIX, and Idris, to mention three).

▪ UNIX Is a Self-Sufficient Programming Environment ▪

Some mechanical trades allow a craftsman to create his own tools, such as the blacksmith and the machinist. UNIX is like a machine shop, foundry, blacksmith shop, sawmill, and woodworking shop all in one. The variety of UNIX programming languages used in conjunction with its program development tools make it an ideal programming environment, powerful enough for developing almost any application. If a certain programming tool is not available, you have everything you need to create your own.

Today, most commercially viable business programs, even micro-oriented ones such as dBASE II, are developed in C under UNIX. Programs developed under UNIX take advantage of UNIX programming tools during the product's development. The tasks of preprocessing, compiling, and linking scores of header files, macros, and programs are kept simple and effortless with **make** (part of PWB, *The Programmer's Workbench*). **SCCS**, also part of PWB, keeps control of the project source code and keeps its documentation manageable and traceable with a minimum of effort. The **lint** program shows up errors before the code passes through the C compiler. UNIX debuggers find problems that **lint** misses. Additional UNIX utilities instrument, monitor, and trace the program to make it both fast and efficient. Tools to analyze a core dump (should the fledgling program fail), programs to examine the executable code, and programs to examine the data that the code reads and writes are all available as support tools.

Once a software package has been developed under a host UNIX system, it is ready to go out to any system where it is commercially viable. Since it is written in C, it is relatively easy to move it to a new processor or operating system. dBASE II has been ported to all major generic systems, UNIX included.

UNIX Is for Writers

UNIX's ability to handle text is well documented. From writing a simple letter to creating an entire book, UNIX gives you everything you need. UNIX formatting systems are universal. All are offshoots of a text system called **roff** and include **nroff**, **sroff**, and **troff**. There are commercial variants as well, such as **xroff**, to take advantage of special hardware such as laser printers. Thus, using UNIX you can write a book, typeset it, and send it to a publisher, ready for final printing.

There are a set of programs available on UNIX known collectively as *The Writer's Workbench*. They include programs that analyze text for readability, grammatical errors, and adherence to a particular style and level of writing. They can even determine whether text contains ''sexist'' words and phrases. A spelling checker is already standard on UNIX.

The Communicating System

UNIX is a chatty system. Users can **write** or send **mail** to each other internally or communicate from machine to machine. Networking software is built into the UNIX system. Remote mail, file transfers, and remote execution require a minimum of effort to install. Someone familiar with setting up a **uucp** network can get a new UNIX machine attached to a *LAN* (Local Area Network) in an hour or two. Hooking systems together using standard phone lines can take anywhere from 15 minutes to a day or more, depending on the cooperation of the machines involved and whether you read this book! Networking can be done either locally or over long distances, anywhere phone lines or satellite communications are available. Any UNIX system can be hooked up to another UNIX system with networking, either becoming a terminal on the remote system or allowing the remote system to become a terminal on it. Files and mail can be transferred immediately or stored and forwarded at a more convenient time.

The ability to network machine-to-machine (hardwire) opens new communications frontiers to computer users. It allows expensive peripherals such as typesetters, laser printers, plotters, high-speed printers, and mass storage devices to be shared by all machines within the network. It also minimizes the cost of software, since expensive software can reside on the machine for which it is legally purchased and still be used by all other machines and terminals within the networked system. File serving — keeping a single copy of all critical files on one machine — is a reality with networking. It cuts the cost of mass storage devices down to a small fraction of what it would be if every machine in the system had a private copy. This makes archiving easy and practical, and it helps prevent data loss.

Networked systems offer exciting opportunities. This book was written using six different UNIX machines in different parts of the United States. Two machines with radically different architectures were closely networked by hardwire, one doing duty as an external communications machine, the other a file server. A mainframe 40 miles away was used for bulk spelling correction and Writer's Workbench work using the **style** and **diction** programs. A fourth machine on the other side of the country kept in constant touch with **uucp** for electronic mail and sending the chapters back and forth for more editing. The manuscript was printed out using **nroff** on a dot matrix printer and sent to the publisher for review. Another pass for proofing was done using a laser printer and **troff**. After final approval, it was sent to yet another machine to be typeset, and the typeset galleys were sent to the publisher for printing.

Here is the power of UNIX in a nutshell. The two linked machines are a Codata 3300 (a 68000-based machine running UNIX System III) and an AT&T 3B2/300 (a WE32000-based machine running System V Release 2). The mainframe is an Amdahl 470 V7a running UTS, System V (UNIX 5.2). The fourth machine, a Cadmus 9790, uses System V Release 0 on its 68010 CPU. The fifth is an AT&T 6300 running XENIX System V, and the sixth is a 80286-based Altos also using XENIX. Without this ability to use different hardware while communicating easily and quickly, this book would have taken a lot longer to write.

The commercial applications of networking can already be seen today. UNIX's ability to network coupled with PC-DOS' growing similarity to UNIX resulted in the inevitable networking of PCs to UNIX machines. Companies have purchased hundreds of PCs for various uses, but networked, they become part of an overall computer system.

▪ UNIX Software ▪

UNIX has a lot of software built into its standard distribution, including several programming languages, program debuggers, and text manipulators. Just a few years after UNIX became a commercial product, a third-party software base emerged that fills hundreds of pages in AT&T's latest *System V Software Catalog*. Now you can have UNIX and your favorite applications software, too.

Most UNIX software is quite sophisticated. Database managers can be tied to applications generators which in turn are joined to applications packages like accounting systems. The power of UNIX enables firms with offices across the country to tie them all together through electronic mail and **uucp** capabilities, running the same software at each local machine and updating company-wide files automatically each night.

Third party UNIX software addresses a wide-ranging market because UNIX is ported to so many machines. Prices are usually proportionate to the size of the machine. A relational database manager that costs a few hundred dollars on a popular 68000-based machine, such as an NCR Tower, costs about $40,000 for a mainframe implementation.

UNIX Is Friendly

Controversies have raged over whether UNIX is easy to use, but the fact remains that only UNIX has the ability to be almost totally reconfigured. Its prompts and command names can be changed, user file trees can be moved around, and the entire user interface replaced if desired. UNIX may not be ideal for everyone, but it does not force you to to accept it "as is." While UNIX has been criticized for its complexity as compared to personal computer operating systems, most of these PCs add UNIX-like features as they mature.

▪ UNIX from Two Perspectives ▪

A user's perspective of UNIX is much different from a system administrator's. The user sees his own environment, his immediate user area, some libraries, and a few other user group areas. To him, UNIX seems moderate in size and complexity.

The system administrator is also a user. In fact, he frequently is his own best customer. But an administrator sees a much larger UNIX. There are hundreds of directories and thousands of files, and he must know where they are and how they fit into the larger whole. Whereas the user has executable commands searched automatically by his path as defined in **.profile** or **.cshrc**, the administrator must execute commands hidden in many strange places. First he has to acquaint himself with all the commands, and then he has to remember where they are. For example, **uucp** commands are one place, **lp** commands another, and standard administration commands somewhere else.

If a user loses a file, directory, or tree, he simply goes to the system administrator, tells his sad tale of woe, and his worries are over. All he has to do is wait for the system administrator to find the lost data from the previous night's backup tape. Users have the luxury of being able to make mistakes, but a system administrator does not. If system backups are not done adequately, and a user loses a file, the data can be irrevocably lost.

The Guru Is In

In time, users get used to relying on the system administrator for just about everything. She seems to have all the answers.[1] UNIX has traditionally been taught by word of mouth, and the teachers are usually the system administrator and fellow users. This is probably because the most vital UNIX system administration resources are the hardest to read — the manual sets. As system administrator, you also learn to rely on (and maintain!) the online manuals, **learn**, **help**, and any interactive commands available. The best way to learn is to take this book firmly in hand and prowl around your entire system. Draw yourself a map of all important files, and everything that "looks interesting." A few days spent this way pays large dividends later. And soon, you'll have a reputation as a UNIX *guru*, or someone who knows all about the system.

In this book we refer to small, medium, and large computer systems. These distinctions can easily be blurred, so they should be considered generalities.

A *small* system is one that supports 1 to 4 people. Such a machine might have up to 6 or 8 serial ports, 40 MB of Winchester disk, and perhaps 1 MB of RAM, with minifloppy or cartridge tape for backup. Many machines in this category have no system bus or backplane, and come "all-in-one" with the computer built into the system console terminal. Typical examples include the AT&T UNIX PC, Altos 586, Fortune 32:16, IBM PC/AT, and the Tandy 6000.

A *medium* machine (a "supermicro" or "small mini") generally is packaged in a system cabinet, with a backplane for plugging in expansion boards. Supporting up to 16 simultaneous users, it may have 24 serial ports, 200 MB of disk storage, and 4 MB of RAM. Backups are done on cartridge tape or 1/2 inch reel-to-reel tape. Typical examples include the AT&T 3B2/400, Cadmus 9790, Codata 3300, DEC MicroVAX 2, NCR Tower, and Plexus P/40.

Large machines usually have a special environment including their own air-conditioned room with a raised floor for cables. Rather than create even more categories, we are lumping together machines with capacities ranging from 17 to 500 users. They may have more than 1200 MB of disk storage and 16 MB of RAM, and backups are done using triple density 1/2 inch tape as well as removable disk packs. The one factor that separates this group from smaller machines is that the large ones *always* require a full-time system administrator. Such computers include the Amdahl 4070, AT&T 3B20, Cray II, DEC VAX 11/780, Gould PowerNode 9000, IBM 4300, and Pyramid 90x.

▪ The System Administration Workload ▪

Smaller, lightly loaded UNIX systems with built-in, menu-driven system administration programs, such as those found on an AT&T 3B2/300 or UNIX PC, are easy to run and take very little administration time. At the other extreme are large UNIX machines with a high level of user activity, loads of software coming and going, and little in the way of dedicated system administration routines. In any case, understanding what's going on is of paramount importance once the unexpected happens. Even if you're lucky enough to have a great set of canned menus or shell scripts left over from a previous

1 System administrators, like ordinary people, come in two sexes, male and female. Both are referred to in this book.

administrator, the day will come when the pressure will be on *you*. The administrator of an active system must be able not only to work without simplified administration menus, but create them if need be. Most people going into system administration by choice or chance find their workload somewhere in the middle. There is time to work as system administrator, system programmer, and user.

▪ Help and Where to Get It ▪

UNIX is still a maturing system, and it changes a bit with each new official release. Because any operating system is such a large concept, few people understand one completely. Even after trying **`help`**, the manuals, and the tutorials, from time to time you are going to need outside aid. It goes with the job.

Your primary source is the software support you purchased when you bought the system. Sometimes software support is part of the cost of the system, and sometimes you pay extra for it. Either way it is invaluable.

There is also free help available on the USENET network.[2] If you're not in a rush, post your problem in **`net.unix`** or **`net.news.sa`**, and with luck someone will return an answer to you in a few days.

In the long run, the greatest help is continuing education. Organizations that teach UNIX system administration are located all across the United States and Canada (see *Appendix A — Where to Learn More*). A good course is well worth the time and money. You get education and interactive experience as well as sharing your problems with sympathetic souls who have been in the same position. Some computer manufacturers also run excellent courses, such as Amdahl and DEC. They are especially designed for their specific brand of hardware and corresponding version of the system. Perhaps the best courses available today are from The Source itself, AT&T.

Naturally, not everyone has the time or the funds to attend courses. A number of periodicals on the market provide a consistent flow of quality information on keeping your UNIX system happy. And among the dozens of UNIX books around, we've picked out our favorites. All these invaluable sources are annotated in the *Bibliography*.

Finally, a good consultant who specializes in UNIX system administration is worth his weight in memory chips. If he has already done the kind of task you're looking for, especially on your hardware, he's probably worth twice what he's asking, considering the time he can save you. Good consultants rarely need to advertise. Ask around.

---

2 See *Chapter 12*.

▪ The Standardization of UNIX at 5.2 ▪

UNIX emerged commercially from AT&T as Version 7. It continued to develop, but other versions of UNIX quickly proliferated. Berkeley UNIX split away at Version 6. Some UNIX look-alikes stopped at System III. As a system administrator, you should be aware that there are many versions of UNIX out there at various stages of development.

At this writing, UNIX System V Release 2 (SVR2 or just UNIX 5.2) is the current AT&T standard. AT&T paid for ports to all major processors and architectures, and developed a standardization suite to assure uniformity. UNIX 5.2 is noticeably faster through the use of hashed searching, and it is the most robust version to date. It is also the only version AT&T supports!

AT&T has spent millions of dollars advertising System V as the standard for the UNIX system. There are thousands of older computers running the earlier versions of UNIX, and many others running Berkeley versions. While System V is not the only force in the market (as of this writing, there are more XENIX systems than any other), the AT&T campaign has given enough momentum to System V to convince other major players like Amdahl, IBM, and Microsoft to adopt it as well. So it pays to know about System V, without losing sight of the techniques needed to run older systems.

Where Do We Go from Here?

Commercial viability determines the ultimate success of an operating system, and UNIX is no exception. The push for standardization at UNIX 5.2 makes UNIX more homogeneous than ever. Implementations exist on supermicros on up to mainframes, and the increasing UNIX software library is addressing a wide market. We have just started seeing the networking capabilities of UNIX in the commercial marketplace. Where does UNIX go from here?

This is only the beginning. As disk and memory prices continue to fall, the next few years will see UNIX on smaller and more inexpensive hardware. It will be commonplace to have a multiuser, multitasking UNIX system with coprocessors that can emulate (or communicate transparently with) other operating systems such as MS-DOS, MVS, and VMS. Since it isn't tied to the volatile personal computer market as much as to the burgeoning business sector, UNIX has a bright future.

▪ Handy Shell Programs ▪

Towards the end of each chapter, we'll print a number of programs that you can type in and use. Most of these will be written in Bourne shell language, and some will be in C, but they should work on any UNIX system.

print_all

Some sites have the **dtree** program, which draws pictures of all the files and directories. While it is not as pretty, this command line prints out everything on your system by **find**ing everything and piping it to the printer through the **pr** program:

```
# find / -print | pr | lp
```

Use **lpr** if you are running pre-System V UNIX, and use **pr -w132 -2** instead of **pr** if your printer has wide (14 7/8 inch) paper. This will print the information in two columns, which will save paper.

mkcmd

Since you frequently will be creating shell programs, here's a shell program to help you create shell programs without even using the editor. To use it, give **mkcmd** the full path name of the program-to-be, then just type in the program itself, followed by Control-D:

```
# mkcmd /usr/local/print_all
find / -print | pr | lp
^D
# ls -l /usr/local/print_all
-rwxr-xr-x 1 root root  24 Sep 13 16:36 /usr/local/print_all
#
```

Here is the **mkcmd** program itself:

```
cat > $1
chmod +x $1
```

mkcmd simply takes its input from the terminal as you type it in (until you end it with the Control-D), stores it in the file you named, and makes that file executable so you can use its name as a command.

▪ Chapter Summary ▪

As a multifaceted, multiuser system with enormous quantities of built-in software, UNIX requires comprehensive administration techniques. Now that we've taken an overall look at the system, let's get down to some specifics. In the next chapter we'll go into the basics of getting your UNIX system running and keeping it that way.

C H A P T E R

2

BRINGING UP THE SYSTEM

Bringing Up the UNIX System

Every journey starts with the first step, and the first step in dealing with UNIX is knowing how to bring up the system. There are several basic steps:

1. Turn on system peripherals.
2. Turn on the computer.
3. Start the bootstrap program and load **/unix** (the kernel).
4. Set the date.
5. Go into single-user mode.
6. Check the file system.
7. Go into multiuser mode.

Turn It On

The first step is turning on the console, terminals, and any other peripherals that normally are attached to the computer such as printers, modems, and external disk and tape drives. You want these devices on so the computer recognizes them when it comes up. (The terminals have to be active so they respond to the **getty** put out by the computer — what the user sees as the **login:** message.) The next step is turning on the computer itself.

Booting the System

Once the computer is turned on, the operating system must be loaded in. This is called "booting" the system, from the expression "pulling yourself up by your own bootstraps."[1] This is appropriate, because the boot program reads in a very small program from disk, and its sole function is reading in *another* program from disk, which then loads and starts the kernel. Machines generally boot the system in one of two ways, either from a *PROM* program (*P*rogrammable *R*ead-*O*nly *M*emory) stored in a chip, or from a floppy disk. If the console terminal is not turned on first, the PROM program is not able to send a message to the console. Machines that "boot" from a floppy disk send a message to the console as soon as the boot floppy has been read or during the boot process.

If for any reason a message does not appear on the console when bringing the system up, do a manual reset. This usually involves pressing a little button on your machine's front or rear panel. Push that button, and your machine reads the bootstrap program from either the startup PROM or floppy disk. Don't push the power-off switch by mistake! This might erase your boot floppy and that is no way to start your day.

Loading UNIX into the Machine

Sometimes the primitive startup program requires something simple to load **/unix** into memory, such as pressing the *return* key. Other times, you have to give an entire command line to the boot loader. This usually tells where (on which device) to find the kernel, and what it's called. On most systems, the kernel is an executable file in the root file system called **/unix**. On VAX systems, it is sometimes called **/vmunix** (for *v*irtual *m*emory UNIX). Other times, it is named after the particular variant, such as **/venix**, **/idris**, or **/xenix**. Loaders that accept a human-entered kernel name are more flexible, because you can specify a "backup" version or test a different release:

```
BOOT: rh(0,1) /unix
Loading UNIX at 0x400000....
1,024,000 bytes of memory found.
Set the date:
```

It is always a good practice to wait 30 to 60 seconds before letting the computer start reading from the hard disk. If you try to read from a hard disk that is not yet up to speed, you can cause a disk read error. While such an error is generally harmless at this point, there's no sense in taking a chance. If your system boots and loads automatically, just sit back and wait for Step 4. Once **/unix** is loaded, the machine automatically starts the **swapper** (process 0) and **init** processes, the first two processes in UNIX.

As your users run their programs, the **swapper** makes room by moving these programs in and out of memory as necessary. **init** makes shells. Shells are spawned (created) early in UNIX, and **init** is the system's number one program, process 1, from which all other shells and processes are spawned. The shell provides the

---

1 If the computer refuses to come up at all, the authors sometimes give it a good boot in the side. This is merely a coincidence in terminology.

entire interaction between the user and the kernel. Refer to *Chapter 4* for further detail on **init** and **swapper**.

The machine then contacts the outside world, the console, and asks you for a date.[2]

Setting the Date

Once UNIX is loaded into the system, the first order of business is setting the date and time. Although setting the date may seem a trivial affair, its function within the system is not. UNIX needs an accurate date. If an erroneous date is entered, the wrong creation, access, and modification dates and times are attached to files.

Many modern computers have a built-in clock that functions even when the machine is off or being shipped. If you're lucky enough to have one like this, you'll know because the date will be correct when the system comes up (though the time may be set to the wrong timezone). In such cases, the date prompt will probably be omitted.

The **date** command has the following format in Version 7:

```
date yymmddhhmm[ss]
```

where **yy** is year, the first **mm** subargument is month, **dd** is the calendar day (number), **hh** is the hour (on a 24-hour clock), and the last **mm** subargument is minutes. The last argument is optional (that's why it's shown in brackets) and is used to set the exact number of seconds past the hour.

To enter January 3, 1986, at half-past six in the evening, you type this:

```
date 860103183000
```

You have the option of abbreviating it this way

```
date mmddhhmm
```

so you can also leave out the year and seconds and do this:

```
date 01031830
```

Leaving out the year causes the system to default to the year that was last set in the machine. If the system crashes in a peculiar way, using the default year can cause some interesting (and wrong) results.

Note that each element of the date is entered as two numbers, no more and no less. Entering the date like this

```
date 131830
```

won't work.

---

2 We told you UNIX was friendly.

After entering the date, the system responds with:

```
Fri Jan 3 18:30:00 PST 1986
```

Just to be different, the **date** command was changed starting at System III. Now the format is

```
date mmddhhmm[yy]
```

You can't set the exact seconds anymore, and the year field is now optional, though it still defaults to the year last set in the system.

On large systems that ask for GMT on startup, be sure to give the system what it asks for, Greenwich Mean Time, not local time! And this brings us to another peculiarity that you, as administrator, must understand. *All* UNIX systems operate internally on GMT, and only convert to "local" time when necessary for display. When you first fire up your machine, you will probably be confronted with a timezone, either EST (Eastern Standard Time) or PST (Pacific Standard Time), depending on where the computer was made. A shell environment variable called **TZ** (called **TIMEZONE** on some systems) is used to tell the system the local time. To convert the entire system to local time, you simply set the environment variable where it will be in effect for all users. The best place to do this is in a file such as **/etc/rc** or **/etc/profile**. Look in these two files for reference to the **TZ** variable. Sometimes, there is actually a file called **/etc/tz**, and if that's the way it's done on your system, change it there.

So what do you actually do? The **TZ** variable is generally set to a value in a command line like:

```
TZ=EST5EDT
```

The **EST** refers to the Eastern Time Zone, and the **5** refers to the number of hours that the Eastern Time Zone is *west* of Greenwich Mean Time. The **EDT** signifies that Daylight Savings Time is in effect during certain times of the year, when the time is officially EDT, or Eastern Daylight Time. The system knows when Daylight Savings Time goes into effect and changes itself automatically, so you only have to set this once. Therefore, in California you set **TZ** to **PST8PDT**, and in Chicago, to **CST6CDT**.

Coming Up into Single-User Mode

On pre-System V machines, you come up in single-user mode automatically. System V machines give you a choice, but the first few times you bring up UNIX System V, you should be in single-user mode. One way to do that is to use the **init** command at level **s**:

```
init s
```

Other System V machines may ask you

```
Enter init level:
```

and you simply respond with **s**. Some come up automatically into multiuser mode, forcing you to bring it back down to single-user with **init s**.

Checking the File System

Single-user mode is the time and place to do the kind of system administration tasks that require a quiescent machine, such as checking and repairing the file system or running backups. Whereas running **fsck** to check the file system is an optional task on many implementations of UNIX, you should know that running UNIX with a bad file system can quickly spread whatever maladies exist to far reaches of the disks, causing damage irreparable by any means other than a complete restore. In such a case, there is no room for error. It takes only about five minutes to check the whole system, but a restore can require many frustrating hours, even days. The simple solution is to type *yes* when UNIX asks you a question such as **Check file systems?**. The **fsck** program is generally easy to use, but we've given it most of a separate chapter by itself (*Chapter 3*) due to its importance.

When there are no more system administration tasks to do, the final step in bringing up the system is going multiuser.

Going Multiuser

Except for allowing the SA to log in at the console, UNIX will not accept users until it is in multiuser mode. Pre-System V machines are brought up into multiuser mode by a Control-D (*^D*), since you're literally logging out of the single-user shell. System V (and some System III) machines are brought up into multiuser mode by going to a numeric **init** level, usually level 2. The command line is

```
init 2
```

When the system comes up in multiuser mode, it sends a **login:** message to each active terminal including the console. In technical terms, a **getty** is spawned for each *tty*. At this point UNIX is officially up.

A Quick Review

1. Turn on the console, terminals, and other peripherals.
2. Turn on the computer.
3. Warm up the system for 30 seconds or more to let the hard disk come up to speed.

4. Start the bootstrap program and load **/unix**.
5. Set the date.

System V

6. Type **init s** for single-user mode.
7. Check the file system.
8. Type an **init 2** to go into multiuser mode.

Pre-System V

6. Check the file system.
7. Type a Control-D to go into multiuser mode.

Automating System Startup with /etc/rc

We've shown you the most general procedure possible for starting up UNIX. Don't be alarmed if your system acts a bit different. Once you've gotten to the stage where you feel confident enough to want to run the system instead of simply accepting whatever default behavior the manufacturer has decreed, you'll want to make some changes. These changes can be used to:

- speed up system startup
- check the file systems
- start system accounting and statistics
- run driver programs for special hardware
- recover files after a crash
- start the printer spooler

All of these, and more, can be best accomplished by automating the boot procedure. The place for this is a file in **/etc** called **rc**. **rc** is covered in *Chapter 4*.

▪ root and Super-User ▪

Root and super-user are sometimes confused by beginning system administrators, because the concepts they represent are so similar.

`root`

The UNIX system has an elaborate security system designed to let users protect their files and directories to any extent they desire. However, there is one user on the system who can circumvent all this protection. The name of this user is **`root`**. **`root`** has both user id and group id number 0, and can create or destroy anything on the system — files, directories, or processes — with just a few keystrokes. A user with the power of **`root`** is needed because some things are almost impossible otherwise, and someone with special powers and skill is needed when things go wrong.

When the system is up in single-user mode and you are at the console, *you* are **`root`**. This shouldn't scare you too much if you use the **`root`** login wisely. That's why we try to do things slowly in these first few chapters! Most of the time, when operating as system administrator, you will need **`root`** privileges. Even so, it's a bad habit to operate as **`root`** all the time. The eventual result will be either weakened security or making a mistake that would have been harmless had you not been logged in as **`root`**.

In some cases, your system will not come up automatically into single-user mode without a **`root`** login. This is to protect the system against unauthorized personnel being able to reboot the system and thus become **`root`**, as was possible before XENIX and System III. If this is the case, you get a **`login:`** prompt at boot time, to which you should respond **`root`**, followed by the **`root`** password when prompted. If this is the very first time the system is being brought up, the **`root`** password is generally either nonexistent or the word **`root`** itself. The whole sequence looks something like this:

```
Crosswind Computer X-15 with UniCom Version 5.2
login: root
Password: root
SINGLE-USER MODE
#
```

The special prompt **#** shows that you have **`root`** privileges. We will show this prompt in examples where it is necessary to become **`root`**. Get into the habit of never leaving your terminal when this prompt is active, so that system abusers won't have the chance to do sneaky things behind your back.

Super-User

The name "super-user" conjures up a mental image of some kind of super-hero, but this is not quite the case. The name super-user comes from the acronym **`su`** for *s*ubstitute *u*ser id. The **`su`** command allows a user to substitute his user id for another as long as he knows the user's logname and password. If a user needs to work on John Parker's files, and gets his password (and therefore permission to do so), she can use **`su`** to temporarily "become" John for working purposes. John can, of course, change his password later on so it is private once again:

```
$ whoami
emdall
$ su parker
Password: nicecoat
$ whoami
parker
$
```

If **su** is used without an argument, however, it takes on another meaning. The user invoking **su** with the proper (**root**'s) password takes on the identity of **root**, with all the rights and privileges thereof. That's how people started thinking that **su** stood for super-user, since **root**'s powers are so great!

The **root** password should be changed regularly. When anyone with **root** privilege leaves the company, it should be changed as well. The number of people who know the **root** password should be kept to an absolute minimum. We can guarantee that your system will become almost unmanageable if more than five people know it. If you work for a large company and you are system administrator, your boss is likely to be the head of data processing. Even your boss should not know the **root** password! Instead, write it down and place it in a sealed envelope in her desk. Then it should be used in an emergency only.

▪ Keeping the UNIX File System Healthy and Happy ▪

The UNIX file system is a little more complex than most because of its unique file tree structure. Although it's called a tree, it is an upside-down variety (see Fig. 2-1). As you can see, the very top of the tree is where everything else ''sprouts'' and for that reason, it's called the *root* directory (not to be confused with the *user* **root**). The root directory (written as **/**) is the top-level directory on the UNIX system. All second-level directories and files are located just under root, so their names (such as **/usr**, **/bin**, **/unix**) all begin with a single slash.

Each directory can have a large number of other directories and files under it. At the same time, an entire new disk drive (or section of a disk drive) can have a file system created on it, and ''mounted'' on any existing directory. This means that, theoretically at least, any UNIX file system tree can be expanded as ''deep'' and ''wide'' as you like, with the only real restriction being the amount of money you have for hardware.

It is imperative that this file system be kept in perfect order, and checking the file system frequently is the only way to ensure its health and safety. There are several ways to check the UNIX file system, but first you need to know some more details about how it works.

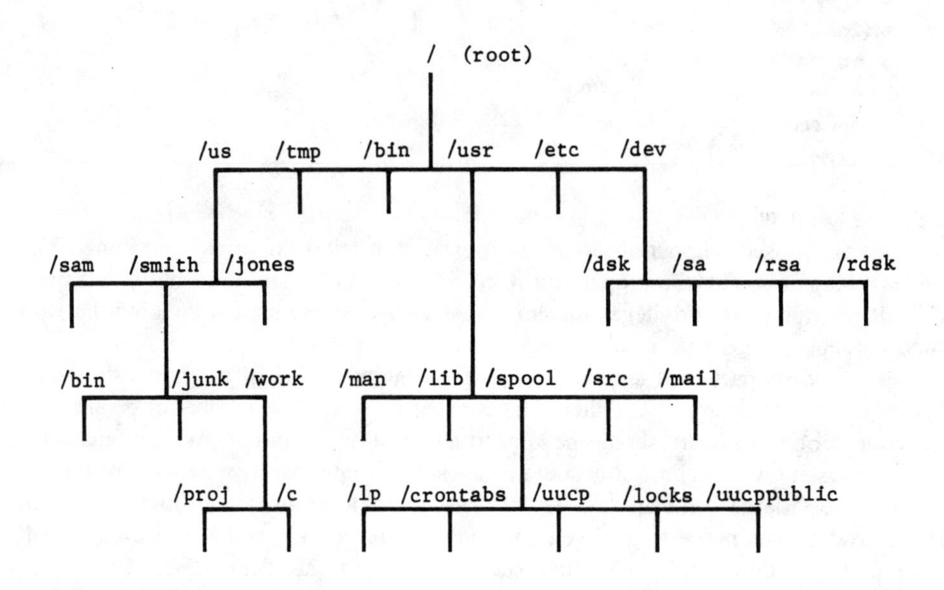

Fig. 2-1. The UNIX File System

▪ UNIX File Theory ▪

Blocks

UNIX files are measured in a unit (granularity) called a *block*. Block sizes vary. In general, System V systems have a block size of 1024 bytes and pre-System V systems have a block size of 512 bytes. Some UNIX systems use larger block sizes, such as UTS with its 4096-byte blocks.

The block exists because disk devices used to store files are most efficient when reading, writing, and storing large quantities of data at once. If it takes a disk drive 10 milliseconds to read one byte from the physical disk, it might take only 11 milliseconds to read 512 bytes, and 15 milliseconds to read 4096 bytes. Actually, the disk can't deal with any *less* than a block at a time, so only an integral number of blocks can be written or read at once. Block sizes on UNIX systems, then, tend to match the most common disk or hardware block sizes.

When a file is stored on the disk, it takes up as many bytes on the disk as it needs, plus whatever is necessary to fill to the end of the disk block (although nothing extra is stored there). Therefore, if UNIX is using a block size of 1024 bytes, then a 1023-byte file takes up 1 block, and a 1025-byte file takes up 2 blocks. Even a 1-byte file takes up an entire block.[3]

The fact that files smaller than a block nevertheless take up a full block is known as *block breakage*, and this may account for a large portion of disk space being totally wasted. If your file system consists mostly of many small files, then a large block size wastes more space because most of the files are less than a block. On the other hand, systems with a relatively small number of large files benefit from using large blocks, since the disk can read them more efficiently. In many cases, the computer manufacturer has already determined the block size to be used on your system based either on statistical analysis of the kind of files most of his customers use or whatever was most convenient.

Each file in the UNIX system has a name. Some files have more than one name. For example, the **mv** command is used to rename files. On many systems, **mv** is actually the same physical program as the commands **ln** and **cp**. If it is called by one command name, the program performs one function; if called by another name, it performs another function. This seemingly impossible feat is accomplished by *link*s. A link is a connection between a file name and the pointer that actually represents the file. Therefore, a single file with more than one name has several links.

Here's a trick using links that works on many UNIX systems. The **ls** command is often used as **ls -l** to find full details of directory contents. The source code for **ls** has sometimes been fixed so that if the program is called **ll** instead of **ls**, it becomes equivalent to typing **ls -l**. To see if this works on your system, go into the **/bin** directory as super-user and make a link to **ls**, then see if it works differently:

```
# cd /bin
# ll
ll: not found
# ln ls ll
# ll
total 3035
-rwxr-xr-x 1 bin     sys      36928 Dec  3  1984 adb
-rwxr-xr-x 1 root    bin        566 Dec  3  1984 as
-rwxrwxr-x 1 root    bin      60922 Dec  7  1984 awk
-rwxrwxr-x 1 bin     sys        903 Aug 30 01:04 calendar
-rwxr-xr-x 1 root    bin       7304 Dec  3  1984 cat
  .  .  .
-rwxr-xr-x 2 bin     bin      17418 Dec  3  1984 ll
-rwxr-xr-x 3 root    bin       8614 Dec  3  1984 ln
-rwsr-xr-x 1 root    bin      19082 Dec  3  1984 login
-rwxr-xr-x 2 bin     bin      17418 Dec  3  1984 ls
  .  .  .
```

3 The user never sees these details. To the user, a 1-byte file is one byte long, and a 1025-byte file is 1025 bytes long, because that is how the UNIX system presents it to him. On other operating systems, the user often has to take into account the number of blocks taken up by the file, which is unnatural and time-consuming.

```
-rwxr-xr-x 1 bin      bin       12420 Dec  3  1984 who
-rwxr-xr-x 1 bin      bin       15594 Dec  3  1984 write
-rwxr-xr-x 1 bin      bin        7034 Dec  3  1984 xargs
-rwxr-xr-x 1 bin      bin        8256 Dec  3  1984 xd
#
```

If this works, we've found other links that work with **ls**. **l**, **lr**, **lf**, and **lx** automatically activate the **-m**, **-r**, **-F**, and **-x** options, respectively. If no change is noted, simply get rid of the new link, and the old **ls** program will remain:

```
# rm /bin/ll
#
```

Inodes

Each file in a mounted UNIX file system is identified by the system with a unique pointer called an *inode* (for *i*ndex *node*) number. The basic rule of thumb is one file for each inode. The system keeps track of how many inodes are in use and how many are unused or free. The number of inodes in use plus the number of free inodes must equal the total available number of inodes. If not, this inconsistency points to potential trouble.

The directory entry for a file has only two pieces of information: the file's name and the inode number. The inode itself contains the balance of the information about the file. The inode tells about the file mode (permissions), file size, whether the file is a directory, where to find the data contained in the file, and other pertinent information such as if the file is a "special" file.

There is more to UNIX file theory, but it will keep. Armed with this rudimentary knowledge, let's examine some of the ways to keep the UNIX file system healthy and happy.

The fsck Program

fsck (for *f*ile *s*ystem *c*hec*k*) is designed specifically to test and repair the file system, pass after pass, until everything is checked. Each pass through the individual file systems is called a *phase*. The phases test blocks and sizes, path names, connectivity, reference counts, and the free block list. If inconsistencies are found or errors detected, **fsck** gives you the opportunity to repair the file system. **fsck** is so vital to system health that it should be incorporated into part of the regular routine of bringing up the system. The best time to do an **fsck** is on a quiescent machine, and running it in single-user mode before bringing the machine up to multiuser mode is ideal.

One of the most valuable features of **fsck** is that it allows you to check file systems interactively. When inconsistencies are found, **fsck** sends diagnostics to the console along with suggestions for repair of the damage. The administrator is then free to ignore or act upon the error.

fsck can be used with a variety of flags. The syntax as given in the manual is[4]

```
fsck [-y] [-n] [-sX] [-SX] [-t filename] [-D] [filesystem]...
```

We're going to discuss a few possible uses of **fsck** with flags.

In its simplest form

```
fsck -y
```

not only checks the file system but makes any necessary repairs automatically. It tells the system, "Check the file system and make any needed repairs without bothering to ask me whether I approve." This is convenient but dangerous. If major file system damage has occurred, you want to know about it. Intelligent human intervention is often better than a machine's, so do not use **fsck -y** exclusively. Rely on it instead as an occasional time-saver.

To see if there's anything wrong with the system without doing anything about it, use **fsck -n**. The **-n** option assumes a *no* response to **fsck** questions. It is useful for testing the file system without making any repairs.

The **-sX** option ignores the current free list and unconditionally makes a new one.[5] Its counterpart is the **-SX** option (note the capital letter). It does a reconstruction only if nothing is wrong.

These options can greatly speed up disk operations on busy file systems. They work because a newly created free list is more likely to have large contiguous chunks of free space, rather than single blocks scattered all over the disk.

The last **fsck** option, **-t**, is used on small memory machines. It uses a scratch (temporary) file to make up for lack of memory. This file must not be located in the file system being checked, so you would use an appropriate full path name (see below).

The **-D** flag performs extra consistency checks on directories. It only takes another 5 to 10 seconds per file system. Use it!

Here are some examples of how to run **fsck** when you want to check a particular file system:

```
fsck -t /tmp/junk /dev/hd07
```

This says, "Check the file system on **hd07** and put the scratch file in **/tmp/junk**."

```
fsck -y -D /dev/rhd06
```

This says, "Check the file system on **hd06**, using the raw character device for higher speed.[6] Check the directories, and do whatever you (the program) think is best."

---

4 Manual pages for system administration commands are most often found in a separate manual devoted to such commands, so when you do a **man**, the manual entry is not always (1) but often (1M).

5 The free list keeps track of all the blocks in the file system that are not being used to store any data.

6 See *Chapter 4*.

▪ Other File System Consistency Programs ▪

ncheck

The **ncheck** program is used to find the name of a file when you only have its inode number. The syntax is:

```
ncheck [-n i-numbers] [-a] [-s] [filesystem]
```

Everything is technically optional here because the default operation of **ncheck** generates a list of all file names on (usually) all file systems, which is not very useful. Most of the time, **ncheck** is used in the following way. Suppose you're running **fsck** to check the root file system and you get a message like this:

```
BAD/DUP FILE I=564 OWNER=root MODE=755
SIZE=14839 MTIME=Sat Mar  1 17:37:23 EST 1975
CLEAR?
```

You can tell that the size of the file is not zero (so the file might be important), and it's owned by root and executable (so it might even be a system command, especially with the date being as old as it is). You don't want to wipe out an important file like **/bin/sh** by mistake, so you answer **no** to **fsck** and eventually regain your shell prompt:

```
# ncheck -i 564 /dev/xt0a
/dev/xt0a:
564     /etc/temp.password
#
```

This way you find that the file in question is actually a backup copy of the password file you made a long time ago. Once you make sure the *real* **/etc/passwd** file still exists and is in good shape, you can rerun **fsck** and clear this extra file out.

Predecessors to fsck

fsck is a relative newcomer to UNIX. Other commands existed before **fsck**, and they either tested the file system or repaired it. We're going to talk about **dcheck**, **clri**, and **icheck**, though you should treat them as antiques because **fsck** tends to outperform them all.

dcheck reads through the directories in any specified system (defaulting to all available file systems) and tests the link count in each inode entry with the directory entries. Its syntax is:

```
dcheck [-i numbers] [filesystem]
```

and it is used this way:

```
dcheck /dev/dsk220
```

The optional **-i** flag may be used to specify one or a group of inode numbers about which you want more information.

Before the advent of **fsck**, one of the more reliable and commonly used file system repair programs was **clri**. **clri** clears inodes that diagnostics like **icheck** uncover as damaged. Once a "bad" inode is discovered, **clri** is invoked to zero out the inode. The syntax is:

```
clri file_system i-number...
```

and looks like:

```
clri /dev/dsk550 497 556
```

icheck is **fsck**'s predecessor. It is found on most UNIX machines and is still used on occasion by old-timers. Like **fsck**, it sends forth a fair amount of diagnostics to your terminal, including the number of regular files, directories, and block and character special files, the number of blocks used as directory blocks, the number of free blocks, and the number of missing blocks. **icheck** is also capable of reconstructing a new free list, if asked to, by using the **-s** flag.

The lost+found Directory

What happens if a file loses its link to its file name by accident?[7] Is it discarded and lost forever? UNIX is far too clever for that. When **fsck** checks a file system for connectivity (to see if there is at least one directory entry or link for each inode or file), and it discovers a file without a directory entry, it sends a notification to the console. The console message asks if you want to **RECONNECT**. If you elect to say *no*, the error condition is ignored and the file remains inaccessible. If, on the other hand, the answer is *yes*, the orphaned file is reconnected to a file in **./lost+found**. It is assigned a file name that is also its inode number.

The proper place for the **lost+found** directory is in the root directory of each file system. For instance, if you have two mounted file systems, **/usr** and **/own**, you should have *three* **lost+found** directories:

/lost+found	for the root file system — there should *always* be one for the root file system.

7 If you **rm** a file, of course, it *is* gone forever.

/usr/lost+found for the /usr file system.

/own/lost+found for the /own file system.

By this ingenious method, there is no need to lose a file even if the rug is pulled out from under the system before it updates the disk copy of the directory and super-block. As long as the system administrator takes the time to be sure that a directory exists for **lost+found** in every file system and that there is sufficient room in the directory to accommodate lost files, orphaned files can be recovered. It is always a good practice to check all **lost+found** directories from time to time for entries. This is particularly true if you use **fsck -y** often.

▪ What If the System Doesn't Come Up? ▪

This section is designed to help you quickly troubleshoot your system if you're having one of those days when *nothing* seems to work right.

Nothing on the System Works

If the console and the computer fail to communicate, examine the mechanical connections. Make sure that the cables are firmly attached to the proper ports. Is the console cable attached to the terminal's EIA (modem) port, or has someone made a mistake and attached the cable to its auxiliary (printer) port? At the other end: is the cable attached to the console port, or is it just attached to one of the *tty* ports?

The console port is the only way to get to the computer's main processor (CPU) at the initialization stage. The console port is generally labeled (on the back of the machine) *console*, *terminal*, *tty0*, or something similar. Remember, when all else fails, read the manual. If everything seems to be set up in accordance with the manual, it's time to get serious.

If you're covered by a service contract, the safest bet is to call your supplier and have him take care of things. After all, the system is supposed to work, right?[8] But if you're really on your own, here's what you can do. First, remove all media such as floppy disks or tapes, then turn off the power to the computer and peripherals. If your warranty is not voided by such an action, the best thing to do is a little exploratory surgery. Don't take apart anything you're not sure you can put back together. And whatever you do, don't open up any Winchester disk drives! Carefully open the computer's chassis (don't lose any of the little screws!) and test each board to be sure it is seated deeply into the (backplane) sockets. Also check that all internal cable connections are seated. Sometimes, simply removing and replacing a connection or board works. You'd be surprised how many malfunctions are caused by poor cable and board connections, especially after shipment. We also advise cleaning and lubricating the contacts with a recommended cleaning solution before replacing a board or connector.

8 Before you call for help, shut everything off for two full minutes, close your eyes, and try again. This has worked more times than it has failed.

The System Does Not Boot from the Boot Switch

If pressing the boot or reset switch (button) fails to bring up a boot message, there is a very good chance that the connection from the switch is not connected (or is poorly connected) to the CPU card. Test both ends of the connection and try to reboot.

The System Boots but Does Not Execute Commands

If the system fails to execute commands, it cannot reach a very critical directory called **/bin**. Your shell should always knows its search path. The only time you can get a command to execute is if it is directly located in your search path or if you have given a fully qualified path name. If the **PATH** variable set in your current root profile is not set to look in **/bin** and/or **/etc**, you'll have to change it. Refer to *Chapter 4* on configuring **rc**. Meanwhile, try resetting your search path with the following command if you are using the Bourne shell:

```
PATH=/bin:/etc:$PATH ; export PATH
```

or this line for the C shell:

```
setenv PATH "/bin:/etc:$PATH"
```

If this doesn't work, give full path names, such as **/etc/init**, **/etc/fsck**, and **/bin/sh**.

The System Does Not Go into Multiuser Mode

The trick is to have the right command for the right system:

System III	Pre-System III
init 2	Control-D

If neither of these works, the object is to kill the current mode. Try these keystrokes, in the following order, waiting 30 seconds between them to see if they've taken effect: Control-Z, Control-C, and the *delete* key. If those don't work, try typing **exit** or **logoff**. Or perhaps your **stty** status has been garbled, so try all the above again, this time followed by a linefeed (or Control-J) instead of a return. Once the system enters multiuser mode, all should be well.

▪ Handy Shell Programs ▪

create

Often you will find it necessary to initialize one or more empty files, or truncate them to zero length. This program does that for you quickly by simply copying nothing into every file named on the command line:

```
for i
do
        >$i
done
```

Once you have **create**, put it to use in scripts like **/etc/rc** or in your everyday work:

```
# create /usr/adm/pacct /etc/wtmp
# ls -l /usr/adm/pacct /etc/wtmp
-rw-r--r-- 1 root    root       0 Sep 14 13:46 /usr/adm/pacct
-rw-r--r-- 1 root    root       0 Sep 14 13:46 /etc/wtmp
#
```

mklost+found

lost+found directories must be "slotted," that is, they must have room in them for inodes to be stored while **fsck** is being run. The only way to do that is to create files and then delete them. This script does that nicely, and incidentally uses **create** (above).

```
for i in ${*:-.}
do
    cd $i
    mkdir lost+found
    cd lost+found
    create a1 a2 a3 a4 a5 a6 a7 a8 a9 a10 a11 a12 a13 a14 a15
    create b1 b2 b3 b4 b5 b6 b7 b8 b9 b10 b11 b12 b13 b14 b15
    rm a* b*
    cd ..
done
```

To use **mklost+found**, either go into the root directory of the *file system* that you want to create the **lost+found** directory in, or give as many of these root directories as parameters. The first line of the program figures out which you want:

```
# mount                                List root directories of mounted file systems
/           on /dev/xt0a read/write on Tue Sep 24 11:30:22 1985
/usr        on /dev/xt0c read/write on Tue Sep 24 11:30:28 1985
/usr/lib    on /dev/xt0e read/write on Tue Sep 24 11:30:29 1985
/usr/spool  on /dev/xt0f read/write on Tue Sep 24 11:30:30 1985
/own        on /dev/xt1c read/write on Tue Sep 24 11:30:31 1985
# cd /usr
# mklost+found
# ls -ld lost+found
drwxrwxr-x 2 root    root        512 Sep 14 14:29 lost+found
# mklost+found /usr/spool /own
#
```

▪ Chapter Summary ▪

The UNIX system is large, but it can be tamed. In the next chapter, we'll go over how to keep it from biting.

CHAPTER 3

CHECKING THE FILE SYSTEM

Why Check the File System?

Many computers have flat file systems: all files are in one directory or at one level. They are stable and straightforward, but finding a file can be a nightmare on any but the smallest system. UNIX has a hierarchical file system. It has a sort of database "manager" that you *perceive* as the file system. The entire directory structure is at your fingertips with the **find** command, a wonderfully convenient feature. However, if anything happens to the system before data are actually written to the disk (such as a system crash), the current, or memory, image of the directories (the true directory structure) is not saved properly on disk. Any files being written at the time of the crash run the risk of being lost or corrupted. As a result, the directories and files are not in agreement, and the file systems need to be repaired.

The most important part of a UNIX file system is the *super-block*. It keeps track of all the free space and inodes in the file system, as well as various internal parameters such as the size of the file system. There are at least two copies of the super-block *and* the disk buffers at any given time. One copy is in the computer's memory and the other is on disk, but the copy in memory is the most accurate because it is current. Don't count on the disk copy being up to date! Like any other disk data, if the super-block is not updated properly, you are asking for trouble. However, problems in the super-block can scramble an entire file system rather than just one or two files.

sync, update, and Peace of Mind

As we have seen, the super-block exists in both high-speed (core or RAM) memory and on disk. The disk version is "old" and reflects the current condition of the file system only if it has been updated in the last few seconds or if the machine is not being used. The mechanism for forcing the memory version of the super-block to be written to disk is the **sync** command.

The sync Command

All data, on its way to being written to the disk, are first stored in system disk buffers in kernel data space. These buffers are areas of fast RAM or core memory set aside to hold data until enough is accumulated to write out a full disk block (or several). Then the buffer is ''flushed'' by writing it to the disk.

If the system is brought down prematurely by a power failure or a crash, it is safe to assume that the disk copy probably does not accurately reflect the condition of the file system the way it's *supposed* to look. The **sync** command forces a write of the memory version of the buffers and super-block to the disk version. Many other operating systems do not put file data to disk until the file is closed. This is an obvious invitation to disaster in the event of a power failure or crash. UNIX avoids this potential disaster by issuing a **sync** call at regular intervals through either the kernel or a separate program, called **/etc/update**.

update

/etc/update causes a **sync** to be issued every 30 seconds, so that the disks are reasonably up-to-date in the event of a crash. **update** is normally executed with no arguments by **/etc/rc** at the time the system is brought up. However, there is an optional argument to **update** that allows an interval other than 30 seconds to be used. Theoretically, you can specify one-second intervals or even continuous **sync**s to make sure the system is always up-to-date, but this slows the system down to a crawl if any real work is going on.

Some systems don't run **update** as a separate program, but internally run the **sync** system call from the kernel every 30 seconds. The **sync** command simply makes this system call once when it is run. Here's a short version of **update** for you to compile and tuck away in your bag of tricks:

```
/*          update.c (simple version)          */
# define TRUE 1
main() {
        while (TRUE) {
                sync();
                sleep(30);
        }
}
```

The fsck Program

The **fsck** command consists of several file system reporting and repair tools. Any file system repairs should be done before bringing up the system for multiuser use, because when too many directories become corrupted, a mounted disk system unravels faster than a cheap sweater. In actual practice, large, busy machines stop running more often than small machines, so file systems should be checked frequently (daily) on this class of machine. Installations that run continuously should have regularly scheduled warm starts so file systems can be checked and repaired.[1] A lot of large installations do a warm start every morning precisely for this reason. You have the option of running **fsck** on the entire system with one command, or on individual file systems such as:

```
# fsck /dev/xt1a
```

System crashes can radically alter a file system, but don't wait for your system to fall down before you do an **fsck**! Even a small power glitch can make your system a little weird. Given enough time, files just sitting and rotating on disk day after day can degrade. Cosmic radiation striking impurities in the disk substrate can change any bit's value, and if one of the bits in the directory structure or inode gets flipped, your directory is corrupted. (No, we're not kidding.) As you can see, periodically checking and repairing your file systems is data insurance.

Most of the time an **fsck** yields no errors in the file system:

```
# fsck /dev/xt1a
/dev/xt1a
/dev/xt1a     File System: / Volume: xt1a

/dev/xt1a     ** Phase 1 - Check Blocks and Sizes
/dev/xt1a     ** Phase 2 - Check Pathnames
/dev/xt1a     ** Phase 3 - Check Connectivity
/dev/xt1a     ** Phase 4 - Check Reference Counts
/dev/xt1a     ** Phase 5 - Check Free List
/dev/xt1a     551 files 12260 blocks 3864 free
#
```

There are six possible phases in the **fsck** procedure. We're going to describe each phase, one at a time, along with its corresponding error messages. When there is something wrong, **fsck** starts asking you questions that require answers. While some of these error messages are scary, remain calm at all times. The worst possible error means only that you have to restore a file system from your backup tapes. If you allow panic to set in, you are setting yourself up for human error, known to have caused reformatted disks, erasing of backup tapes, and similar problems. Remember, if you get a particularly frightening message from **fsck**, the first thing you should do is *run it all over again*. On many occasions, when we prepare for the worst, a rerun allows **fsck** to fix all the problems on its own. Newer versions of **fsck** have constantly improved

---

1 *Warm start*: bringing the system down to single-user level and bringing it back up to multiuser without actually rebooting or powering down the system.

its ability to get you out of trouble! Be sure to write down any inode or block numbers that **fsck** tells you about, so you can repair them later.

Phase 1: Check Blocks and Sizes

The first phase deals with the file system's inode list. Phase 1 checks inode types, examines the inode block numbers for bad or duplicate blocks, and checks the inode format. Possible Phase 1 errors include the following:

Unknown File Type I=*1234* (CLEAR)?

The **unknown file type** error means what it says. An unrecognizable file type has been discovered on an inode (e.g., *1234*). The system can only deal with regular files, special files, and directory files. If you see this error, your only realistic option is to clear the inode and thus the file. This fills it with zeros, effectively wiping out the file forever. Clearing the inode causes an **unallocated** error to show up in Phase 2 for any directory referencing this file.

Link Count Table Overflow (CONTINUE)?

fsck maintains an internal table containing a list of allocated inodes with a link count of zero (files with no directory entries). If this table overflows, it generates the **link count overflow** error. A "no" reply terminates **fsck**. A "yes" reply has **fsck** continue but does not allow a complete check of the system. You should rerun **fsck** after encountering this error.

Can't [stat, open, read, write, seek, create] ...

A message similar to any of these phrases indicates that the disk is inaccessible in some way. You should check to make sure that the disk is physically online and not write-protected, and that you have permission to access it (look at both the character and block device entries for this disk in the **/dev** directory). Are you running **fsck** as super-user? You should be!

Size check: fsize *X* isize *Y*

The super-block has really gotten scrambled and the file system or inode sizes make no sense. Using great caution, you have to go into the super-block and correct these numbers (see the section on **fsdb**). If this cannot be done, you will probably have to reload this entire file system from your backups.

9999* BAD I=*1234

If a block number doesn't make sense to **fsck,** it lets you know. If block number *9999* in inode *1234* is out of range, it tells you. (This error condition also invokes a **BAD/DUP** error condition in Phases 2 and 4.)

EXCESSIVE BAD BLOCKS I=*1234* (CONTINUE)?

What if the **BAD** condition uncovers 10 blocks or more with a meaningless block number? A "no" reply to this error terminates **fsck**. A "yes" causes **fsck** to ignore the remaining blocks in the inode and go on to the next inode. Run a second **fsck** to recheck the system.

9999 **DUP I=***1234*

This means inode *1234* contains a block (*9999*) claimed by another inode. It causes Phase 1B to be activated, so you get the **BAD/DUP** indication in Phases 2 and 4.

EXCESSIVE DUP BLOCKS I=*1234* **(CONTINUE)?**

Ten or more **DUP** blocks are considered excessive. A "no" reply terminates **fsck**. A "yes" allows **fsck** to continue, but it is not complete. Run another **fsck**.

DUP TABLE OVERFLOW (CONTINUE)?

fsck's duplicate block table is full. A "no" reply terminates **fsck**. A "yes" causes **fsck** to continue. A second **fsck** is needed to make a complete check of the system.

POSSIBLE FILE SIZE ERROR I=*1234*

This indicates a disagreement between the number of blocks used by an inode and the size of the file. This is a warning only, because it is not considered a serious error. You will *always* get this error on named pipes (depending on your version of **fsck**), so be prepared when you check the file system containing **/usr/spool/lp**. Still, it is nice to have an error-free run of **fsck**, so here is how you can clear this error for ordinary files:

1. Finish checking this file system.
2. Keep the system in single-user mode (or bring it back down to that level).
3. **mount** the file system on which the error occurred.
4. Find the file in question using **ncheck -i**.
5. Copy the file to an unused file name temporarily.
6. **sync**! (You're in single-user mode, remember?)
7. Remove the original file.
8. Rename the temporary file to the original name.
9. **umount** the file system (this automatically does a **sync** so your work gets saved).

An example is always more illuminating than a list of rules:

```
# fsck /dev/xt0c
/dev/xt0c
/dev/xt0c       File System: /usr Volume: xt0c

/dev/xt0c       ** Phase 1 - Check Blocks and Sizes
                POSSIBLE FILE SIZE ERROR I=134
```

```
/dev/xt0c       ** Phase 2 - Check Pathnames
/dev/xt0c       ** Phase 3 - Check Connectivity
/dev/xt0c       ** Phase 4 - Check Reference Counts
/dev/xt0c       ** Phase 5 - Check Free List
/dev/xt0c       551 files 12260 blocks 3864 free
# mount /dev/xt0c /usr
# ncheck -i 134 /dev/xt0c
/dev/xt0c:
134     /adm/pacct
# cd /usr/adm
# ls
acct       cronlog.2  dtmp          msgbuf       sulog
aculog     cronlog.3  fee           pacct        usracct
cronlog    cronlog.4  lastlog       sa
cronlog.0  cronlog.5  messages      savacct
cronlog.1  cronlog.6  messages.old  shutdownlog
# cp pacct temp
# sync
# rm pacct
# mv temp pacct
# cd /
# umount /dev/xt0c
# init 2
```

Why don't you simply **mv** the file to a new name? The **mv** command doesn't actually do anything more than change inode information. Since the system is "confused" as to the actual length of the file, the file must be copied to give it another chance to get the length right.

DIRECTORY MISALIGNED (CLEAR)?

If you get this error message, you have a totally garbled directory. The algorithm testing for alignment divides the number of bytes in the directory by 16 (14 characters for the name, 2 bytes for the inode number) — in short, a mod 16. If there is a remainder, you have a problem, and clearing it is the only solution.

PARTLY ALLOCATED INODE I=*1234* (CLEAR)?

A wishy-washy inode (*1234*) has been discovered. It is neither allocated nor unallocated. The **CLEAR** prompt deletes the inode if it receives a "yes" reply; otherwise, the problem remains.

Phase 1B: Rescan for more DUPS

A duplicate block has been detected. The system is now rescanned to make sure there aren't any more that were missed in the first pass.

Phase 2: Check Path Names

Phase 2 is designed to clean up after Phase 1. It removes directory entries pointing to files or directories modified by Phase 1. Possible Phase 2 errors follow.

ROOT INODE UNALLOCATED, TERMINATING

Inode 2, the root inode, is out of allocation bits. This error is serious enough to cause the **fsck** program to quit, and you are in big trouble. You will probably have to restore the entire file system from backup media.

ROOT NODE NOT DIRECTORY (FIX)?

If the root inode is not a directory, a "no" reply terminates **fsck**, while a "yes" forces the root inode to become a directory. Prepare for an almost infinite number of errors if you type "yes".

DUPS/BAD IN ROOT INODE (CONTINUE)?

Phase 1 found duplicate inodes. A "yes" reply causes the error condition to be ignored. A "no" causes **fsck** to terminate.

I OUT OF RANGE I=*1234* **NAME=***core* **(REMOVE)?**

One of the files in the directory being checked has an inode number out of range (nonsensible). A "yes" reply removes the file; "no" ignores the condition.

UNALLOCATED I=*1234* **OWNER=***root* **MODE=***777*
SIZE=*64* **MTIME=***Fri Apr 1 00:00:00 EST 1988* **NAME=***tmp* **(REMOVE)?**

This error message means that a directory has entry been found that has no allocate-mode bits. A "yes" reply removes the directory; "no" ignores the condition.

DUP/BAD I=*1234* **OWNER=***root* **MODE=***777*
SIZE=*64* **MTIME=***Fri Apr 1 00:00:00 EST 1988* **DIR=***tmp* **(REMOVE)?**

Phase 1 or 1B has uncovered duplicate or bad blocks. A "yes" reply causes the entire directory to be removed; "no" ignores the condition.

DUP/BAD I=*1234* **OWNER=***root* **MODE=***666*
SIZE=*27* **MTIME=***Fri Apr 1 00:00:00 EST 1988* **FILE=***core* **(REMOVE)?**

Phase 1 or 1B has uncovered duplicate or bad blocks. A "yes" reply causes the file to be removed; "no" ignores the condition.

BAD BLK IN DIR OWNER=*root* **MODE=***777*
SIZE=*64* **MTIME=***Fri Apr 1 00:00:00 EST 1988*

This indicates a bad block has been found in the specified directory; usually caused by a file name that has no zeros after it. Correct by removing the directory or bad file name.

Phase 3: Check Connectivity

Phase 3 cleans up after Phase 2. Its main concern is connectivity — making sure that there is at least one directory entry for each inode and that multiple links make sense. Phase 3 also creates error messages for unreferenced directories and **lost+found** directories that are full or missing.

UNREF DIR OWNER=*root* **MODE=***777*
SIZE=*64* **MTIME=***Fri Apr 1 00:00:00 EST 1988* **(RECONNECT)?**

The directory inode has no connection to a directory. **fsck** does not tolerate an unconnected, full directory. A "yes" answer reconnects the inode in **lost+found**; "no" allows the error to continue.

SORRY, NO SPACE IN lost+found DIRECTORY or
SORRY. No lost+found DIRECTORY

If you forgot to run the **mklost+found** program we gave you back in *Chapter 2*, it's too late now. The file or directory will be lost.

DIR I=*1234* **CONNECTED, PARENT WAS I=***5678*

This shows that the inode in question (*1234*) has been successfully attached to the file system's **lost+found** directory.

Phase 4: Check Reference Counts

This phase is concerned with the link count and any alterations made in previous phases. Phase 4 lists errors resulting from unreferenced files, a missing or full **lost+found** directory, an incorrect link count, bad or duplicate blocks, or an incorrect sum for the free inode count.

UNREF FILE OWNER=*root* **MODE=***666*
SIZE=*27* **MTIME=***Fri Apr 1 00:00:00 EST 1988* **(RECONNECT)?**

A file (inode) exists without a directory entry. A "yes" reply connects the file to the **lost+found** directory. A "no" invokes a **CLEAR** error in this phase.

SORRY. NO lost+found DIR

No **lost+found** directory has been created. With this message it is a little late to make one (for this file) but early enough to make a **lost+found** for next time.

SORRY, NO SPACE IN lost+found DIR

No space has been found in **lost+found**. Check **lost+found** to see if it has any contents. It's probably full.

CLEAR?

If the file above cannot be connected to **lost+found**, this query appears. A "yes" reply zeros out the file.

LINK COUNT DIR=*tmp* **OWNER=***root* **MODE=***777*
SIZE=*64* **MTIME=***Fri Apr 1 00:00:00 EST 1988* or
LINK COUNT FILE=*core* **OWNER=***root* **MODE=***666*
SIZE=*27* **MTIME=***Fri Apr 1 00:00:00 EST 1988*
COUNT *3* **SHOULD BE** *1* **(ADJUST)?**

The link count for a file or directory is wrong. A ''yes'' reply corrects the link count, whereas a ''no'' ignores the condition.

UNREF DIR=*tmp* **OWNER=***root* **MODE=***777*
SIZE=*64* **MTIME=***Fri Apr 1 00:00:00 EST 1988* **(CLEAR)?** or
UNREF FILE=*core* **OWNER=***root* **MODE=***666*
SIZE=*27* **MTIME=***Fri Apr 1 00:00:00 EST 1988* **(CLEAR)?**

The file (inode) is not connected to a directory. A ''yes'' zeroes out the file. A ''no'' ignores the condition.

BAD/DUP DIR=*tmp* **OWNER=***root* **MODE=***777*
SIZE=*64* **MTIME=***Fri Apr 1 00:00:00 EST 1988* **(CLEAR)?** or
BAD/DUP FILE=*core* **OWNER=***root* **MODE=***666*
SIZE=*27* **MTIME=***Fri Apr 1 00:00:00 EST 1988* **(CLEAR)?**

Here we see the sins of Phase 1 revisited. Duplicate or bad blocks found in the first phase have yet to be dealt with. A ''yes'' reply clears the inode, while a ''no'' continues the error.

FREE INODE COUNT IN SUPERBLK (FIX)?

The free inode count in the super-block does not match the free inode count found by **fsck**. A ''yes'' updates the count, and a ''no'' leaves it incorrect.

Phase 5: Check Free List

UNIX is quite fastidious about maintaining a balance between the number of blocks allocated within a file system, the number in use, and the difference (known as the free block list). When **fsck** calculates a free block count that is not in agreement with the free block list (**FREE LIST**), Phase 5 reports it as an error condition.

EXCESSIVE BAD BLOCKS IN FREE LIST (CONTINUE)?

Too many — usually 10 — ''bad'' blocks have been detected. A ''bad'' block has a block address beyond the acceptable range established by the start and finish block addresses. **fsck** tests about everything testable to ensure the sanity of the file system. If you enter a ''yes'' reply to this, the rest of the free block list is ignored. A rerun of **fsck** is in order. A ''no'' terminates **fsck**.

EXCESSIVE DUP BLOCKS IN FREE LIST (CONTINUE)?

This error message tells you that too many inodes have been duplicated. The proper number is 0, and 10 is considered excessive. Answering ''yes'' to **CONTINUE** makes **fsck** ignore the rest of the list.

BAD FREEBLK COUNT

Another accounting upset. The number of free blocks in a free list block is too low or high (less than 0 or more than 50). This generates the **BAD FREE LIST** message.

N **BAD BLOCKS IN FREE LIST**

This is the final act of the **EXCESSIVE BAD BLOCKS** error message. It quantifies the number of bad blocks.

N **DUP BLOCKS IN FREE LIST**

This message quantifies the number of excessive duplicate blocks.

N **BLOCKS MISSING**

N unused blocks allegedly belonging to inodes were not found in the free list.

FREE BLK COUNT WRONG IN SUPERBLK (FIX)?

There is a disagreement between the free block count and the number in the super-block. A "yes" reply modifies the super-block into agreement; otherwise the error remains.

BAD FREE LIST (SALVAGE)?

This indicates a multitude of problems. There could be bad blocks in the free block list, duplicate blocks in the free block list, or blocks missing from the file system. In short, any of the above Phase 5 errors cause this message. A "yes" reply replaces the free block list with a new one, and "no" leaves the mess as it is.

X **Files** *Y* **Blocks** *Z* **Free**

This advisory message simply reports the total number of files, blocks in use, and blocks of free space in the file system.

******* FILE SYSTEM WAS MODIFIED *******

This advisory message simply means that an error was corrected by **fsck** and appears when **fsck** is completely finished with this particular file system (it appears after Phase 6, if a Phase 6 is required).

Phase 6: Salvage Free List

The last phase occurs only if something goes wrong in Phase 5, and you answer "yes" to the **BAD FREE LIST (SALVAGE)?** prompt. It reconstructs the free block list.

Special Note for Checking the Root File System

If any errors whatsoever were noted when running **fsck** against the root file system, you get the following message:

******* BOOT UNIX (NO SYNC!) *******

It means what it says. *Do NOT do a* **sync** *or an* **/etc/shutdown**. Do a cold start by pressing the reset button (or turning the key) and do it as quickly as possible before the next **sync**. The reason is that **fsck** fixes the file system by writing directly to the disk. If a **sync** is done, it writes the old incorrect information from memory to disk, undoing the work of **fsck** and requiring a new run. This is only necessary with the root file system.

▪ Administrative Tips for fsck ▪

When an error is detected by **fsck**, write down the error and note its location and address. You may decide to clear the error manually with **clri**. Manually fixing file system errors gives you the opportunity to check the directory entry associated with the inode. You may decide to notify the owner of the lost file. However, most of these files are either lost by clearing or sent to **lost+found**. Because they are usually temporary files, they are normally invisible to the user who invoked the program that created them. Had the crash not happened and the process completed, they would have been automatically erased.

In general, when you see **fsck** prompts that ask questions such as **SALVAGE? FIX? CONTINUE? RECONNECT?** or **ADJUST?** it is safe to answer "yes". Prompts that ask permission to **REMOVE?** or **CLEAR?** must be handled more carefully. Make a note of the disk id (**/dev/whatever**) and the inode number, so you know where you have sustained damage. If, for example, you find the disk in question is **/dev/dd0** and that is your **/tmp** directory, there is little to worry about. If the damage is on a user disk, you may have a restore job ahead of you. If for some reason you cannot restore (from backup media) a file that **fsck** wants to clear, you have nothing to lose by attempting to copy the file as mentioned above under **POSSIBLE FILE SIZE ERROR**.

If you're using a CRT terminal as the system console, one day your **fsck** messages will scroll right off the screen before you can read them. If your system supports a good many users, we suggest you ask management to buy an inexpensive, reliable printing terminal to use as the console. It will help pay for itself when logging system error messages that sometimes precede a crash.

▪ The fsdb Program ▪

If the file system or super-block is so garbled that even **fsck** won't touch it, you will have to go in by hand and patch things up a bit. This is the computer equivalent of open-heart surgery, and your scalpel is **fsdb** (*f*ile *s*ystem *de*bugger).

Since there are many ways you can get yourself in trouble during this process, we strongly advise you not to get too fancy using **fsdb**. Ninety-nine percent of the occasions on which **fsdb** is needed, it is simply to patch one or two locations in the super-block, called **fsize** and **isize**. The **isize** parameter tells UNIX how many blocks were allocated for file system inodes, while **fsize** tells the total number of blocks in the file system. In a properly operating file system, these are the values reported when you run **df -t**:

```
$ df -t /dev/xt1a
  /              (/dev/xt1a ):      3864 blocks     1497 i-nodes
                         total:    16384 blocks     2048 i-nodes

$
```

Here we are told the file system has a total of 16384 blocks and 2048 inodes allocated (**fsize** and **isize**), with 3864 blocks and 1497 inodes free. Let's run **fsdb** and see how it looks:

```
# fsdb /dev/xt1a
/dev/xt1a(/): 1K byte Block File System
FSIZE = 8192, ISIZE = 2048
```

Already we're running into some sort of trouble. According to **df**, we have 16384 blocks in the file system, but **fsdb** tells us there are 8192. But wait! **fsdb** also said that this is a 1K-byte file system. Could it be that **df** is talking about 512 bytes per block?

This system happens to use 512-byte logical blocks and 1024-byte physical blocks, and to keep "compatibility" with older software releases, reports things at "user level" in 512-byte blocks.[2] As system administrator, you're supposed to remember what's really going on.

Now that you understand that, let's dump the super-block in decimal and take a close look at it. On most machines, block 1 is the super-block, but since this one has already proved to be a bit strange, let's start from the beginning. The idea is to know what you're looking for, so turn to the entry for **filsys** in Section 5 of the *UNIX Programmer's Manual*, or the file **/usr/include/sys/filsys.h** on your system, and you'll see something like this:

2 Don't be annoyed at us for not using a "normal" system. There's *no such thing* as a normal system.

```
/*
 * Structure of the super-block
 */
struct filsys {
unsigned short isize;  /* size in blocks of i-list */
    daddr_t  fsize;    /* size in blocks of entire volume */
    short    nfree;    /* number of addresses in free */
    daddr_t  free[NICFREE];   /* free block list */
    short    ninode;   /* number of i-nodes in inode */
    ino_t    inode[NICINOD]; /* free i-node list */
    char     flock;    /* lock during free list manipulation */
    char     ilock;    /* lock during i-list manipulation */
    char     fmod;     /* super block modified flag */
    char     ronly;    /* mounted read-only flag */
    time_t   time;     /* last super block update */
    short    dinfo[4]; /* device information */
    daddr_t  tfree;    /* total free blocks*/
    ino_t    tinode;   /* total free inodes */
    char     fname[6]; /* file system name */
    char     fpack[6]; /* file system pack name */
    long     fill[15]; /* ADJUST so sizeof filsys is 512 */
    long     magic;    /* number to indicate new file system */
    long     type;     /* type of file system */
};

#define FsMAGIC 0xfd187e20 /* if magic = this, type is valid */

/*  valid values for type:  */
#define Fs1b    1               /* 512 byte blocks */
#define Fs2b    2               /* 1024 byte blocks */
```

The general idea is simply that the first number you're looking for is **isize** and the second is **fsize**. Unfortunately, we can't just look for a 2048 followed by 8192. Read a bit further in the **filsys** entry and you'll find that "the i-list is isize-2 blocks long." Look at the definition of **isize**: the size of the i-list in *blocks*. Since there are 1024 bytes per block, and 64 bytes per inode, there must be 16 inodes per block. Both **df** and **fsdb** agree that there are 2048 inodes here, so there must be 2048 divided by 16, or 128 blocks' worth of inodes. Add 2 (for the "isize-2") and you get 130. Look at hexadecimal addresses **200** and **204** in the dump, and what do you see? 130 and 8192! We can't say it's obvious, but at least it works:

```
0b.p0e
0000:      8   1024    918   1858   2047   2047      3    547
0010:      3  10178     24    913     31   8356  24628    552
0020:     63    324    168    377    261   6931  24948   7049
0030:    401   5507   8621   6468   8622   6469  25028   8498
```

```
0040:   499  9465 16921  7212   560  5679  8797  6202
0050:   640  1994 25228  7793   711  8973 25308  6482
0060:   738  2293   766  1923 13059  5261 25352  4165
0070: 17194  9735   819  4345 13112  6882 25404  2182
0080: 25404  5550 25411  3945   863 10268   864  8112
0090: 25490  4938 25490  7710 25491  7846     0     0
*
0200:   130     0  8192    33     0   232     0   230
0210:     0   228     0   226     0   224     0   222
0220:     0   220     0   218     0   216     0   214
*
0370:   129   128   127   126   125   124   123   122
0380:   121   120   119   118   117   116   115   114
0390:   113    31    12   112    11     0     0  7547
03a0: 31524     5   200     0     0     0  1932  1497
03b0: 12032     0     0 29552 24946 25856     0     0
*
03f0:     0     0     0     0  -744 32288     0     2
```

In the dump above, the asterisks represent lines that contain either all zeros or repeated data (addresses of blocks on the free list, which are not useful to us right now). 32-bit words are used with the most significant byte zero, which is why the numbering is two by two. Counting in hex, the top line therefore represents addresses of 0, 2, 4, 6, 8, a, c, and e.

Other information can be pried from this dump. See the contents of address **3ac** and **3ae**? Those are the number of free blocks and inodes (**tfree** and **tinode**) reported by **df** previously. Again, the value 1932 found at address **3ac** in the dump refers to the number of actual 1024-byte blocks free in the file system, which corresponds to 3864, the number of 512-byte blocks from **df**.

Now, let's play with **fsdb** a little. In the *EXAMPLES* section for **fsdb** in the *UNIX System Administrator's Manual*, we have this command listed:

```
2i.fd
d0:     2  .
d1:     2  .  .
d2:     3  u  s  r
d3:     4  d  e  v
d4:   202  b  i  n
d5:   260  b  i  n  .  c  a  d  m  u  s
d6:   299  b  i  n  .  s  y  s  5
d7:   359  b  i  n  .  s  y  s  3
d8:   430  b  i  n  .  v  e  r  7
d9:   515  x  f
d10:  516  e  t  c
d11:  571  l  i  b
d12:   15  u  n  i  x
```

```
d13:  383  . l o g i n
d14:  384  . p r o f i l e
d15:  385  . c s h r c
d16:  386  . s t d c s h r c
d17:  606  t m p
d18:  607  . t i p r c
d19:    0  c o r e
d20:  608  l o s t + f o u n d
d21:  605  u n i x . b a k
d22:    0  f 0
d23:  611  k
d24:  612  s t a n d a l o n e
d25:  614  . n e w s r c
d26:   43  o w n
d27:  105  n o h u p . o u t
d28:  110  i p s
d29:  109  d b
d30:    0
d31:    0
```

This displays the inode numbers and names of the contents of the root directory, just as the manual page says. Removed files and directories appear with the inode number set to zero (as in **d19: 0 core** above). Note calmly in passing that inode 2 points both to . and .., proof that this is indeed the root directory. Only the root directory can point to itself as its own parent.

Following the manual again, we change to the fifth inode listed, and dump the first 512 bytes in ASCII. This happens to be the directory **/bin.cadmus**, which contains some OEM-supplied commands:

```
d5i.fc
00731c00: \? \?  . \0 \0 \0 \0 \0 \0 \0 \0 \0 \0 \0 \0 \0
00731c10: \0 \?  .  . \0 \0 \0 \0 \0 \0 \0 \0 \0 \0 \0 \0
00731c20: \? \?  m  a  k  e  s  t  5  2  5 \0 \0 \0 \0 \0
00731c30: \? \?  b  a  d  b  l  k \0 \0 \0 \0 \0 \0 \0 \0
00731c40: \? \?  c  e  r  b  e  r  u  s \0 \0 \0 \0 \0 \0
00731c50: \? \?  c  o  n  n  e  c  t \0 \0 \0 \0 \0 \0 \0
00731c60: \? \?  d  i  s  k  f  o  r  m  a  t \0 \0 \0 \0
00731c70: \? \?  d  l  c  o  n  f  i  g \0 \0 \0 \0 \0 \0
00731c80: \? \?  d  l  s  u  p  p  o  r  t \0 \0 \0 \0 \0
00731c90: \? \?  d  l  u  p  d  a  t  e \0 \0 \0 \0 \0 \0
00731c90: \? \?  u  c  o  n  n  e  c  t \0 \0 \0 \0 \0 \0
00731ca0: \? \?  u  m  o  n  i  t  o  r \0 \0 \0 \0 \0 \0
00731cb0: \? \?  w  a  t  c  h  d  o  g \0 \0 \0 \0 \0 \0
00731cc0: \? \?  u  u  h  o  s  t  s \0 \0 \0 \0 \0 \0 \0
00731cd0: \?     u  u  q \0 \0 \0 \0 \0 \0 \0 \0 \0 \0 \0
  . . .
```

Now we'll demonstrate how you start at a particular address, which must be typed in decimal even though it is displayed in hex, and proceed one word at a time. If you type **0+256**, this gives you an offset of 256 *words* into the block, which is *byte* address hex **200**. Then by pressing *return* you go to the next word address sequentially:

```
0+256
0200: 00000082 (130)
0202: 00000000 (0)
0204: 00002000 (8192)
0206: 00000021 (33)
0208: 00000000 (0)
q
#
```

In each case, the contents of the address are displayed in hex (with the decimal equivalent in parentheses). To stop displaying addresses, press *delete* or Control-C.

Here's what happens if you actually change one of the values and then run **fsck**:[3]

```
# fsck /dev/xt1a
/dev/xt1a
/dev/xt1a        File System: / Volume: xt1a
Size check: fsize 4 isize 6313580
#
```

The **fsize** and **isize** are totally scrambled. This is the last thing you ever want to see from **fsck**! You will have to patch the super-block just to get **fsck** to run.

```
# fsdb /dev/xt1a
/dev/xt1a(/): 1K byte Block File System
FSIZE = 4, ISIZE = 2048
```

The first thing you notice is that **fsdb** isn't as upset about **isize** as **fsck** was, but it agrees that **fsize** doesn't look well. Let's do the dump:

3 Don't fool around with *your* root file system until you're ready to write a system administration book, too!

```
0b.p0e
0000:   8    1024    918   1858   2047   2047      3    547
0010:   3   10178     24    913     31   8356  24628    552
0020:  63     324    168    377    261   6931  24948   7049
*
0200: 130       0      4     33      0    232      0    230
0210:   0     228      0    226      0    224      0    222
0220:   0     220      0    218      0    216      0    214
```

It seems clear that **fsize** has been changed to a 4. Since we know it should read 8192, you have to change it. Start from hex address 200 as before:

```
0+256
0200: 00000082 (130)
0202: 00000000 (0)
0204: 00000004 (4)
```

You change the value by typing an equal sign and the desired value. Make sure you know what you're up to, since **fsdb** writes *directly* to the disk and does not wait for a **sync**.

```
0204: 00000004 (4)
=8192
0204: 00002000 (8192)
q
#
```

When **fsdb** verifies the change, type *q* to quit, and you're almost done. The safest action to take at this point is to reboot the system immediately, because this is the root file system we're dealing with. This would not be necessary if we were patching an unmounted file system, however.

If you are confused, there is another, easier method. The other way of fixing this problem is restoring the file system from a backup. We'll cover that in *Chapter 8*. But if we've only whetted your appetite for more fooling around with **fsdb**, think hard. Do you *really* want to fool around with your file system at that level, where one wrong key could blow the whole thing up? Having **fsdb** around is like having a parachute in an airplane: you may be a bit safer having it around, but using it can be pretty scary, too.

One more thing to remember: the only reason we know how to patch **fsize** to 8192 is that we know what it is supposed to be in the first place! Right now, go to your system, run **df -t**, and save the output somewhere safe in case you ever run into this kind of problem.

▪ Handy Shell Programs ▪

/etc/checkall

If you have the **dfsck** program on your system, you can use it to check two file systems simultaneously. This saves time, but you must watch the console carefully. Error prompts refer to only one system at a time, but other output is interspersed and hard to read. Don't use **dfsck** until you're comfortable with running normal **fsck**, and make sure you don't try to check two file systems on the same disk at the same time. The best way to do this is with a shell script:

```
fsck -D /dev/xt0a
dfsck -t /tmp/dfsck.chk $* /dev/rxt0[cef] - $* /dev/rxt1[acef]
```

/etc/checkall is generally called from **/etc/bcheckrc** or **/etc/rc** (see *Chapter 4*), like this:

```
/etc/checkall -D
```

This way, any parameters passed to **/etc/checkall** get passed to all file systems being checked, *except root*. The root file system should *never* be checked using **dfsck**, and *never* using the raw device.

▪ Chapter Summary ▪

Now that we have shown you how to bring the system up, check and repair it, you need to know the location of all the system administration tools and files.

C H A P T E R

4

WHERE EVERYTHING IS AND HOW TO FIND IT

▪ How Do You Find the Files You Need? ▪

As a novice UNIX system administrator, you have a big problem: How do you find out where everything is? The UNIX file system is a relatively complex tree hierarchy, with trunks, major and minor branches, and numerous intertwining sticks and leaves. It takes time to get to know your way around! Eventually, you will become intimately familiar with the UNIX file system as your system administration skills mature. You will develop daily, weekly, and monthly procedures to groom, curry, and clean the entire file system. You will also learn to rely on the **cron** to do many of these weekly procedures automatically. This chapter will save you a great deal of time prowling the system, and it will free your time to do more rewarding work.

Where the UNIX System Administration Files Are

You need to know the location of many files and directories in order to do your work well. The trick is learning where to look. Files and directories in UNIX proper are grouped by type.[1] Following is a list of some of the more important directories every UNIX system administrator eventually needs to know:

/bin	executable commands
/dev	the home of device files
/dump	a home for core dumps (not standard)

1 *UNIX proper* is the standard distribution copy of UNIX, before user-added files confuse the issue.

/etc	the system administrator's tool box
/tmp	for temporary files only
/usr/adm	some administration files live here
/usr/bin	executable commands not in **/bin**
/usr/include	header files for C programming
/usr/local	commands local to your system (not standard)
/usr/local/bin	commands local to your system (not standard)
/usr/lbin	commands local to your system (not standard)
/usr/lib	macros and specialized command groups
/usr/mail	mail directory for SVR2
/usr/src	source code for system commands
/usr/spool/at	spooling directory for **at** command
/usr/spool/cron	spooling directory for **cron** command (SVR2)
/usr/spool/lp	printer spooler directory (System V and after)
/usr/spool/lpr	printer spooler directory (System III and before)
/usr/spool/uucp	**uucp** job spooling directory
/usr/tmp	another repository for temporary files
/usr/ucb	Berkeley binaries (not standard)

Let's take a closer look at some of these directories and discover some of the ways you'll actually be using them and their contents.

▪ The /bin Directory ▪

In addition to keeping the system running, part of your job is user support. Occasionally a user will come to you and complain that a command doesn't work. It's up to you to remedy the situation, but where do you start? More often than not, the command won't work because, through some oversight, the directory of that command has not been placed in the user's search path.

One of the first places to look for commands is the **/bin** directory. As its name implies, **/bin** was originally intended to house *bin*ary executable files. Now it holds a few shell scripts as well. It holds many user commands and some system administration commands, but not all of them.

You also have to take the individuality of each machine into account when looking for commands. On most UNIX machines there are a few commands specific to a certain OEM's machine, and these commands are usually located in a

/usr/*OEM***/bin** directory. For example, UTS is Amdahl's mainframe version of UNIX. Many virtual UTS machines can run on one actual Amdahl or IBM computer, and the command **vmid** identifies which virtual UTS UNIX machine you are working on.[2] Obviously, this command doesn't apply to UNIX on a VAX, so **vmid** and a few other system-specific commands are located in a special directory called **/usr/amdahl/bin**.

When you customize your UNIX machine, you eventually create a few commands of your own. Both authors' machines have a directory called **/usr/local** that houses customized backup routines, modem control programs, and other specialized files.

Whether you call it **/usr/local**, **/usr/local/bin**, **/usr/lbin**, or even **/usr/allmine**, it's a good idea to standardize on one separate directory for locally added commands that are accessible to all users. If you keep adding things to **/bin**, for instance, they could be lost in the future. System software is usually upgraded all at once from a distribution tape, and anything in **/bin** is in the root file system and therefore liable to get overwritten when the new distribution tape is loaded onto your system. If all your own software is in one directory, you can always move it *en masse* to separate storage if necessary.

If you really need to find commands, you should look on your system for a command called **whereis** or **which**, a command that searches in known places for executable files.[3] In an emergency, you can always find a file called **lostagain** this way, no matter where it is:

```
# find / -name lostagain -print
```

▪ The /dev Directory ▪

UNIX is traditionally depicted as a series of concentric spheres with hardware at the center, users outside, and several spherical layers in between (see *Fig. 1-1*). The layer next to the hardware is usually designated as the kernel, but it is more accurate to assign that layer to device drivers, which are represented by the special files in the **/dev** directory. Device drivers are the software interface between UNIX and peripheral device hardware. Computers rely on devices like terminals, printers, modems, and plotters to make them complete machines. Without device drivers, computers can't talk to these devices, and a computer without peripheral devices is about as useful as an airplane without wings. Peripherals generally store, accept, or display input-output (I/O) data, and thereby allow people to interact with computers. System administrators deal with drivers indirectly, so let's first discuss what device drivers are. Then we'll look at how you can work with them.

---

2 Many virtual machines can timeshare on one mainframe as if they were physically separate computer systems, and each virtual machine can support multiple users.

3 We provide the code for a similar program, **where**, at the end of this chapter.

/dev Files Aren't What They Appear to Be

Little glory or credit has gone to the unsung heroes who write device drivers, and that is a shame. They are marvelous pieces of software. Each device driver has an upper half, written in C, that communicates with the kernel, and a corresponding lower half, written in C and assembler language, that talks directly to the hardware. The key to understanding device drivers is that the drivers are not located in **/dev** but actually compiled right into the kernel. The "files" in **/dev** are not ordinary files at all. In fact, they're empty. Their directory and inode information is used as an index or pointer to the drivers in the kernel. Obviously, the files in **/dev** are extremely specialized files. They are even referred to as *special files*.

People come in many different sizes, shapes and colors, and so does I/O data. There are two types of special files to handle I/O data — *block special* and *character special*. *Block special files* handle data in blocks. In a 1K-block size machine, typical on System V, each block is one kilobyte or 1024 bytes long. This is both buffer and disk-block size. All block data are buffered by the kernel. Typical block devices are disks (both hard and floppy) and tape. Block devices are used for the highest possible speeds, since one operation results in the transfer of a relatively large amount of data.

Character special files handle raw data streams, one character at a time. Typical character devices are printers, terminals, and modems. The actual hardware takes care of all the details of transforming bits into characters and back, so a "character" device can be attached to either a parallel or serial port. *Parallel* ports send data to a device (usually a printer) using 8 data wires in parallel to make a byte of character data. *Serial* ports send data over one wire, bit by bit, at a specific rate so that the receiving device can assemble the bits into a byte of character data. Serial ports are commonly used with terminals, modems, and some printers.

Do a long listing of the **/dev** directory:

```
$ ls -l /dev/*
```

Character special files look like this:

```
crw-rw-rw- 1 root       1,  0 Nov 19  1982 /dev/tty
crw--w--w- 1 bruce      4,  0 Mar 28 20:23 /dev/tty0
crw-rw-rw- 1 karen      4,  1 Feb  7 19:05 /dev/tty1
crw------- 1 root       4,  2 Feb  7 19:05 /dev/tty2
crw------- 1 root       4,  3 Feb  7 19:05 /dev/tty3
crw------- 1 root       4,  4 Feb  7 19:05 /dev/tty4
crw------- 4 root       4,  5 Mar 28 20:56 /dev/tty5
c--------- 1 root       4,  6 Mar 28 20:28 /dev/tty6
crw------- 1 root       4,  7 Feb  7 19:05 /dev/tty7
```

Block special files show up this way:

```
brw-r--r-- 1 root       9,  0 Dec 31  1969 /dev/cd00
brw-r--r-- 1 root       9,  1 Mar 23 10:03 /dev/cd01
brw-r--r-- 2 root       9,  2 Dec 31  1969 /dev/cd02
brw-r--r-- 1 root       9,  3 Oct 25 20:50 /dev/cd03
brw-r--r-- 1 root       9,  4 Dec 13  1983 /dev/cd04
brw-r--r-- 1 root       9,  5 Dec 13  1983 /dev/cd05
```

The first character in the permissions column indicates either a character (**c**) or block (**b**) special file.

Examining a single entry tells you even more:

```
crw-rw-rw 1 karen      4,  1 Feb  7 19:05 /dev/tty1
```

This 8-column entry tells a system administrator many things. The file permissions indicate that anyone on the system can write to it. There is exactly **1** link to the file — this means that the system knows it by only one name. The current owner is **karen**. The date and time of last access was **Feb 7** at **19:05** (7:05 PM). The file name is **tty1**, the **tty** (terminal) located on port **1**. So far, this is all pretty standard file information.

The numbers **4** and **1** located before the date are called the *major* and *minor* device numbers. Actually, these numbers are the most important information in this file entry. The major device number, **4**, points to a device driver, in this case device number **4**. This lets the kernel code access the device driver program that will control the correct device. The minor number, **1**, is the argument passed to that particular driver. When the device driver sees the **1**, it knows to act on the port labeled **1**. When dealing with asynchronous serial devices (anything that works over an RS-232 port), the minor number is often, but not always, the port number.

Just to confuse you, there are also *character special drivers* for *block special files*:

```
$ ls -l /dev/rcd*
crw-r--r-- 1 root      5,  0 Dec 31  1969 rcd00
crw-r--r-- 1 root      5,  1 Dec 31  1969 rcd01
crw-r--r-- 1 root      5,  2 Dec 31  1969 rcd02
crw-r--r-- 1 root      5,  3 Dec 31  1969 rcd03
crw-r--r-- 1 root      5,  4 Dec 13  1983 rcd04
crw-r--r-- 1 root      5,  5 Dec 13  1983 rcd05
```

These are frequently called *raw devices* because you can read them ''raw,'' or without the more sophisticated block access. Often when doing low-level I/O, it is faster to operate on the raw device. This is frequently the case when using commands such as **dd**, **fsck**, **cpio**, and **volcopy**.

Theory aside, how are you going to deal with the files in **/dev**? They may be *special files*, but you treat them the same way you treat any other UNIX file. One of the ways a system administrator uses the files in **/dev** is to send a data stream to a device by way of its **/dev** entry. Since a **tty** entry in **/dev** acts as both a device and a file, if you type

```
# echo "hello there" >/dev/tty3
```

the "hello there" message appears on an operating terminal attached to port 3 on our sample system.[4] Notice that the redirection symbol **>** must be used, rather than a pipe, because the message is not sent to a process but to a file, a *special file*. You can't do this unless you are the user on **tty3**, or you are super-user, or the permissions have been left open so anyone can write to it.

Devices can be read also. Although there's nothing in the special file itself, reading from any device shows you the actual data coming from the device. Try reading from kernel memory space. Since this is generally binary data, it makes sense to use the **od** command so you don't lock up your terminal by sending it the wrong combination of bits:

```
# od /dev/kmem
000 060000 001776 000000 000000 000000 002114 000000 002164
020 000000 002200 000000 002206 000000 002214 000000 002222
040 000000 002230 000000 002236 000000 002354 000000 004410
060 000000 002370 000000 002370 000000 002370 000000 002370
Interrupt
#
```

Unless you are an expert in UNIX internals, these data are close to meaningless. As super-user you can read from the tape drive, your raw disk, the modem, or any terminal. *Chapter 9* (Security) explains why it's important that a normal user not be able to read from all these places.

Our brief examination of **/dev** gives you a glimpse of the marvelous design behind the UNIX system. **/dev** files have no contents, because they are simply pointers to device driver programs. **/dev** files take or put data at one end and send data to or from a device at the other. The actual device drivers are compiled within the kernel. However, the creators of the UNIX system cleverly designated **/dev** entries as special files so they could be used in the same ways as other UNIX files.

Device Driver Source Code

What about the actual device drivers? When do you have to go into the kernel and modify device drivers or write new ones? Fortunately for the average UNIX system administrator, hardly ever. UNIX device drivers are extremely flexible. The drivers on an installed UNIX system, in combination with system commands and daemons, do just about anything you want them to do.[5] There is very little that cannot be done with the existing asynchronous serial driver in conjunction with **stty**. If changes need to be made, most standard UNIX systems have enough UNIX source code available either in **/usr/src** or from the supplier to modify I/O processes.

Naturally, in some UNIX environments, it is necessary to be able to either modify or rewrite a device driver. Writing a driver is kind of a "cookbook" affair. You find a driver that is close to the one you need for your application, then you copy it and

4 What would happen if a printer were on port 3 instead?

5 Daemons are discussed in *Chapter 11* on printers. They probably exist right now in your system, so show some healthy respect.

modify it to suit your needs. By "close" we mean another device that works similarly. For instance, interfacing a laser videodisk might mean using a driver for a hard disk as a model. Unfortunately there is very little information on this process because it is illegal to publish the kernel source code, since it is proprietary information.

▪ /usr — The Mystery Directory ▪

Don't make the mistake of approaching UNIX system administration with *too* much awe. (Convince the users you deserve some awe instead.) Brilliantly conceived, sublime operating system design notwithstanding, UNIX is still in the process of being refined, and some parts of it are a bit rough around the edges. Many directories such as **/usr** are like closets. They contain a lot of what you think they should, as well as a bunch of other miscellaneous stuff. **/usr/spool** is a collage of spooling devices, buffers, and associated commands. **/usr/lib** is a mixture of macros, header files, language libraries, and commands not found elsewhere. The only specific directory in **/usr** is **/usr/src**, which holds the system's source code. **/usr** directories seem to have one thing in common — they belong in **/usr** because they don't fit anywhere else!

/usr is actually a misleading name for this directory. In spite of the name **/usr**, it does not hold user files or directories. Most systems have some starter user directories in **/usr** when they are new, such as **/usr/guest** or **/usr/demo**. However, you should create a separate file system for your users' directories, since they grow quickly, and they are more easily backed up or moved when they are all together in one location. If you have no room for new file systems, we suggest making another tree under **/usr**, such as **/usr/own**, for your user directories.

There are also some user commands in **/usr/bin,** but most are found in **/bin**. What do **/usr** files have in common? The answer is subtle, and it lies in the realm of UNIX internals. While it is running, UNIX is divided into two parts, kernel (or system) and user processes. There is a distinct separation between kernel activity and what is broadly classified as user activity. Simply stated, the *user* classification encompasses any activity that is not kernel resident. You might think of **/usr** commands as those not strictly necessary for running the system.

The /usr/bin Directory

At one time, **/usr/bin** was a place for putting commands that were specific (local) to one machine. Now it contains some commands that overflowed from **/bin**.[6] Generally, these are nonessential to system operation, such as **BASIC, help**, **inews**, **look**, **postnews**, and **spell**, so they are still technically for the user's use. As mentioned earlier, OEM-installed commands have a **/bin** of their own. On UTS, **/usr/amdahl/bin** houses commands created by the OEM, Amdahl Corporation.

---

6 As a directory gets larger, it takes longer to search it. Directories of more than 10 blocks are inefficient. Do an **ls -ld /bin** to see how big your **/bin** directory is.

The **/usr/local** Directory

Programs peculiar to your UNIX installation should be put in the **/usr/local** directory. These are programs that you have written, begged, bought, or borrowed, including scripts for the system administrator, software like **kermit** (a file transfer system in the public domain) and various other bits and pieces of scripts and code that exist for your system alone. On some systems, the directory **/usr/local/bin** or **/usr/lbin** is used instead, so that all commands can consistently be found in a directory with the nomenclature "bin." Since you also find commands in **/usr/lib**, **/etc**, and other places (as noted elsewhere in this chapter), it's obvious that such attempts at consistency are thwarted by tradition.

The **/usr/lib** Directory

Most commands don't come in groups, but some do when they are related to one device or activity, such as the **uucp** programs and the printer commands, **lp** or **lpr**. Such grouped commands are generally found under **/usr/lib**. **lib** means libraries, which in UNIX terminology means archives of compiled program functions. The system administrator must access them to deal with printers and modems attached to the computer.

There is not a great deal of consistency here. For instance, the most important **uucp** files and programs are found under **/usr/lib/uucp**, but some of the printer programs are under **/usr/lib** itself, while others, such as the actual printer driver programs in System V, are found in a subdirectory of the spooler! Other things of interest in **/usr/lib**, aside from many function libraries, are miscellaneous help files, daemons, and reference files for Berkeley commands such as **whatis**, **whereis**, and **vi**. Some of the major directories under **/usr/lib** and their contents are as follows:

/usr/lib/acct	This is where you find the commands to run system accounting. The system accounting programs help you keep track of user logins, CPU usage, the number of times commands have been executed, and who has been using super-user privileges.
/usr/lib/font, **/usr/lib/fontinfo**	Here are the descriptions of the different typographical modes (bold, italic, and so on) used by **troff** and its various post-processors. (**/usr/lib/fontinfo** is used by one of the Berkeley post-processors.)
/usr/lib/macros	This directory contains the compressed and uncompressed document macro packages for use by **nroff** and **troff**.

/usr/lib/news	If your system is connected to USENET, this directory holds many of the files needed to keep track of the articles flowing in and out of your system.
/usr/lib/sa	Here may be found programs for recording the level of system activity for later analysis.
/usr/lib/spell	The programs and data files needed for the UNIX spelling checker reside here.
/usr/lib/struct	Contains the programs used for turning **f77** programs into **ratfor**.
/usr/lib/style	Data for the **style** and **diction** programs from Writer's Workbench is often kept here.
/usr/lib/tabs	This directory may be called **/usr/lib/tabset** on some systems. It holds ASCII files that are used to initialize tab settings on a variety of terminals and printers. Such files are generally referenced by entries in **/etc/termcap**.
/usr/lib/term	Source and binary files for **nroff** "terminal drivers" may be found here. When properly implemented, such terminal drivers allow emulation of **troff** using **nroff** for output on a given terminal.
/usr/lib/uucp	This directory has the program and data files needed to set up and run the **uucp** communications system.

/usr/lib/crontab

As administrator, you will get to know this file intimately. It enables consistent repetition of commands at any time or day you choose. Using **crontab** is almost like having digital timers on every appliance in your house. When the **cron** program starts up at system boot time, it reads the **crontab** file for instructions on what commands to execute, and when. After that, it checks the **crontab** file every minute to see if the file itself has been changed (presumably with new commands to execute). A different checking interval can be specified on some systems when **cron** is first started up. For example, running it as **cron 5** forces it to check the **crontab** file every 5 minutes. In System V Release 2, the **crontab** command must be executed to force **cron** to examine the appropriate file.

There are six fields in every **crontab** entry, separated by any amount of whitespace, so you can use tabs or spaces to line things up. Asterisks may be used to specify all legal values, and dashes can be used to signify a range of values. Counting from left to right, the first field controls at what time (after the hour) the desired command should be executed. The second field specifies the hour in 24-hour time (**2** or **02** means 2 AM, **14** means 2 PM). The third field can be used to specify a particular day of the month, useful if you want to run financial accounting on the 15th, or backup on the 1st.

The fourth field tells **cron** which month (1 through 12) to run your command, and the fifth tells which day of the week you want (where 0 means Sunday and 6 means Saturday). The sixth and last field is simply the command you want to run. The command is run as if typed into the Bourne shell, so asterisks here refer to file names as usual, and all shell constructs can be used. Here's a fairly complex **crontab** file taken from a working system, which we'll go through slowly:

```
# local stuff
00 * * * *          /bin/date
30 5 * * *          /usr/local/rmtrash
45 8 * * 6          /own/lev/gather_week
15 9 15 4 *         /bin/echo "taxes now late" > /dev/console
06 5 * * *          /bin/calendar -

# for at program and error logging
0,10,20,30,40,50 * * * * /usr/lib/atrun
5,15,25,33,45,55 * * * * /bin/dmesg - >> /usr/adm/messages
59 23 * * *          /usr/local/newcron

# for process accounting:
00 3 * * 1-6 /bin/su root -c  "/usr/lib/acct/dodisk"
00 4 * * 1-6 /bin/su adm -c "/usr/lib/acct/runacct \
    2> /usr/adm/acct/nite/fd2log"
00 8 * * 1-5 /bin/su adm -c "/usr/lib/acct/prdaily | lp"
03 * * * *   /bin/su adm -c "/usr/lib/acct/ckpacct 250"
15 5 1 * *   /bin/su adm -c "/usr/lib/acct/monacct"

# for uucp:
25  * * * * /bin/su nuucp -c "nice /usr/lib/uucp/uudemon.hr"
05 23 * * 5 /bin/su nuucp -c "/usr/local/pollall"
55 23 * * 6 /bin/su nuucp -c "/usr/lib/uucp/uusub -u 168 -r -l"
56 23 * * * /bin/su nuucp -c "/usr/local/uusum | mail nuucp"
57 23 * * * /bin/su nuucp -c "/usr/lib/uucp/uudemon.day"
10 05 * * 0 /bin/su nuucp -c "/usr/lib/uucp/uudemon.wk"

# for system activity statistics
3 8-17 * * 1-5 /bin/su adm -c "/usr/lib/sa/sa1 1200 3"
8 18-7 * * 1-5 /bin/su adm -c "/usr/lib/sa/sa1"
3    * * * 0,6 /bin/su adm -c "/usr/lib/sa/sa1"
11 18  * * 1-5 /bin/su adm -c "/usr/lib/sa/sa2 -s 8:00 -e 18:01\
    -i 3600 -A"

# for usenet news software
46 1       * * *    /bin/su news -c "/usr/lib/news/expire.sh"
45 2       * * *    /bin/su root -c "/usr/lib/news/trimlib"
45 3       * * *    /bin/su news -c "/usr/local/uuhosts -unbatch"
34 2,4,6   * * 1-5      find /usr/spool/news/junk -type f -print\
    | xargs rm
```

```
07 1,2,4,6 * * *    /bin/su news -c "/usr/lib/news/sendbatchnews"
07 09      * * 1-5  /usr/lib/news/news.off
07 20      * * 1-5  /usr/lib/news/news.on
```

This particular file has quite a few entries. Let's look at the first one, since it's probably the easiest to understand:

```
00 * * * *          /bin/date
```

This simply says, "at **00** minutes after every hour, no matter what day it is, run the **/bin/date** command". What use is this? Since a log of every command run is kept in the file **/usr/adm/cronlog** (**/usr/lib/cron/log** in System V Release 2), running the **date** command every hour serves to separate entries so you can determine when an event took place.[7] If your system isn't logging its **cron** entries here, make sure the file exists and that **cron** is actually running.

It's important to remember that any program run from **crontab** sends its output to **cronlog** unless otherwise specified. If you have a hardcopy console terminal and want to keep track of the system status to the nearest hour, you can change this entry to:

```
00 * * * *          /bin/date >/dev/console
```

and the date is written to the console as long as the system remains up and cron remains running.

Let's look at the next line:

```
30 5 * * *          /usr/local/rmtrash
```

Here **cron** is asked to run the **/usr/local/rmtrash** program every morning of every day, at 5:30. Since this program searches through the entire file system, it would slow down users' programs too much, so it's run when the system is quiet.

The next line is a little more specific:

```
45 8 * * 6          /own/lev/gather_week
```

This program gathers data from many different databases for collection and eventual transmission to another computer. Because it takes almost an hour to run, and it must be run while none of the databases are active, we decide to run it every Saturday at 8:45 AM.

The next line is a silly example of how the month and day fields can be used:

```
15 9 15 4 *         /bin/echo "taxes now late" > /dev/console
```

If you're sitting at the console, you'll see this message appear every April 15 at 9:15 AM. Note that the asterisk in the weekday field is still needed so the command will be run *no matter what day of the week* April 15 falls on.

---

7 On some systems, the **/usr/lib/atrun** program will also serve this purpose if it is run exactly on the hour.

Now look at the next section of the file for these two lines:

```
0,10,20,30,40,50 * * * * /usr/lib/atrun
5,15,25,35,45,55 * * * * /bin/dmesg - >> /usr/adm/messages
```

They show how programs can be repeated at specific intervals. The first line executes the **atrun** program (see the manual page for **at**) every 10 minutes, and the second line executes **dmesg** also every 10 minutes. By specifying the exact times to run each program and offsetting them by 5 minutes, we prevent the system from being loaded unnecessarily. This might happen if we ran both programs simultaneously every 10 minutes.

In fact, some administrators sort their **crontab** file by time (rather than by category as we have done) so they can easily keep track of what commands are being run at a particular time. This prevents inadvertently scheduling two large jobs for overlapping times, or running things in the wrong order. For instance, you can't run the **uusum** program — which summarizes the **uucp** log files — after the **uudemon.day** program, since **uudemon.day** effectively removes the log files! Our method is to sort by time *within* each category, because that focuses our attention on the actual programs to be run.

Note that the output from **dmesg** (which collects any possible system error messages) is redirected so as to *append* to the **/usr/adm/messages** log file, so that it accumulates error messages continuously.

One final entry will be examined:

```
00 4 * * 1-6 /bin/su adm -c "/usr/lib/acct/runacct \
                2> /usr/adm/acct/nite/fd2log"
```

This entry uses the **su** command to execute the **runacct** program as if the user named *adm* ran it. Since **cron** is normally started by the system at boot time, commands executed without **su** are effectively run as if *root* typed them in. This could cause a serious security breach. Just as you shouldn't run all your normal programs as super-user, it's safer to run programs that don't need the power of root with a more restricted ownership. In this case, executing **runacct** as *adm* also ensures that the accounting files and logs are actually *owned* by the *adm* user, so she will be able to do her job if she exists as a separate person.

This particular command runs system accounting at 4:00 AM every day but Sunday. It also introduces another technique: redirecting any *error* output to a different file from **/usr/adm/cronlog**. In this case, any errors encountered when running the **runacct** program are stored in **/usr/adm/acct/nite/fd2log**. If you want to save *both* normal and error output in the same file, create an entry like this one:

```
12 5 * * *    /usr/local/program >/usr/tmp/logfile 2>&1
```

Notice that the full path name of the command to be executed should be used in **crontab**. This makes sure that you're running the program you expect to, and not somebody else's program with the same name.

The /usr/src Directory

UNIX source code, whether restricted by "reconfiguration rights" or full (licensed) source, is located in **/usr/src**. Before you run out to buy a UNIX source license, you should know that the current cost is $43,000! Understandably, most systems have little in **/usr/src**. System administrators wishing to impress their friends can create files under **/usr/src** with names such as **ls.c**, **init.c**, **getty.c**, and so on, to appear as if they have a source license.[8]

The /usr/spool Directory

One of your first major system administration problems probably will involve a spooler file that is rapidly filling right before your very eyes, and you will have to figure out what on earth to do about it. Usually, you will be made aware of this by an error message appearing on the system console, such as:

```
Out of inodes on dev 9/4
```

followed shortly by telephone calls from users who want to know what is wrong and when will it be fixed? In this case, the notation **9/4** refers to the major device *9* and minor device *4*. Turn back to the section on the **/dev** directory, and you'll see that this notation refers to **/dev/cd04** on this system. *Chapter 5* explains that **cd04** refers to a specific file system.

Spoolers, and directories that act like spoolers, (such as buffers) have to be emptied periodically. (Spoolers, covered in detail in *Chapter 11*, allow many users to share a single device such as a printer.) Some files are created so quietly, neither user nor system administrator is aware of the file creation. Files created this way are particularly dangerous. For example, the **learn** utilities provide education and practice to new UNIX users, but they also leave unerased files behind that fill the **/usr/lib/learn** directory. They can keep filling the disk until the system comes down with a resounding crash, leaving you with a roomful of angry users and numerous broken inodes to deal with. Here are the locations of some of these files:

/usr/spool/mail (Berkeley), **/usr/mail** (System III and later)	Look (**ls -ltr**) for mail files that are never read and emptied. You'd be surprised how many users never read their mail.
/usr/spool/adm	Accounting files and directories accumulate and must be emptied.
/usr/lib/learn	Anyone who has been in this area using the **learn** facility has created files here.
/usr/lib/spell/spellhist	A collection of misspelled words (see *Handy Shell Programs* in this chapter).

---

8 If you really *do* have a source license, this procedure will wipe out your source files. This is not likely to impress anyone.

/usr/spool/cons	Console notes entered by the operators and error messages end up here. Like all notes, they should be read, then thrown out with the trash. Most of the time the system administrator ends up doing it (non-standard).
/usr/spool/news/net/junk	The USENET garbage can. If you are on USENET, delete everything in it regularly without fail!
/usr/spool/rdr	This is a graveyard of files transferred by fetch commands (UTS).
/usr/spool/uucppublic	A gathering place for wanted and unwanted files left by **uucp**. Refer to *Chapter 12*.
/usr/spool/uucp	Another **uucp** trash and treasure location.
/dump	This is the home for crash core dumps. It is created by **mkdump** and is large enough to store all of memory (nonstandard).
/tmp, **/usr/tmp**	A home for temporary files. These are supposed to be erased, but you have no guarantees.
/usr/adm	System accounting fills up this directory.

In addition to regular spooler areas, there are some other directories that must be emptied periodically, such as **/tmp**. **/tmp** is an interesting directory because it is reserved exclusively for temporary files. An amazing number of programs create temporary files, generally with names formed by the first few letters of the command followed by the process id:

```
$ ls -lt /tmp
total 396
-rw-rw-r-- 1 dave    staff     120 May 21 01:56 ctm8017885
-rw-rw-r-- 1 dave    staff    8998 May 21 01:56 ctm7017885
-rw-rw-r-- 1 dave    staff     634 May 21 01:56 ctm6017885
-rw-rw-r-- 1 dave    staff     634 May 21 01:56 ctm5017885
-rw-rw-r-- 1 dave    staff    5426 May 21 01:56 ctm4017885
-rw-rw-r-- 1 dave    staff    5426 May 21 01:56 ctm3017885
-rw-rw-r-- 1 dave    staff    2762 May 21 01:56 ctm2017885
-rw-rw-r-- 1 dave    staff   22347 May 21 01:56 ctm1017885
-rw-rw-r-- 1 dave    staff   12425 May 21 01:56 ctm0017885
-rw------- 1 susan   staff   63488 May 21 01:52 Ex17765
-rw------- 1 susan   staff   10240 May 21 01:52 Rx17765
-rw-rw---- 1 brenda  staff   54184 May 19 15:45 weekly13057
```

The files beginning with **ctm*** are created by the C compiler; the **Ex*** and **Rx*** files exist while a file is being edited with **ex** or **vi**, and the **weekly*** file is left by a locally-written program. It's plain to see that all system users create temporary files at one time or another. Such files are supposed to be removed after use by the program that created them, but "supposed to" is a phrase familiar to system administrators. Other programs make a valiant effort to remove unused files, but are thwarted by users who kill or suspend them.

By putting all temporary files in one or two directories, it is easy to clean them all out at regular intervals. For this reason, it's a good idea to encourage users to use **/tmp** for all files they need only a short while. Otherwise, their own directories (and therefore the system's available file space) gradually become filled. Good candidates for **/tmp** files include output files from **nroff** and **troff**, redirected output from commands, and short test programs. Educate your users to put such things in **/tmp**, and make sure all your locally written programs use **/tmp**, too. Depending on how your system disks are partitioned, you may find there is more free space in **/usr/tmp**, so that might be more convenient for your temporary files.

Each system also has local areas that must be emptied. For example, some systems have the **at** command that allow the user to define processes to be run at specific times. The leftover **at** files and logs that show what happened (usually found in **/usr/spool/at**) must be cleaned out. Use **rmtrash** (see the *Handy Shell Programs* section of this chapter) for this task.

▪ The /etc Directory ▪

While most user commands are in **/bin** and **/usr/bin**, most system administration commands are in another directory called **/etc**. **/etc** is a very special directory. It is the home of the tools and files that bring the system up. **/etc** programs are so specialized, they are no longer included in the standard UNIX user documentation. Instead, they are in a manual devoted to UNIX administration.[9]

A typical **/etc** listing looks something like this:

```
$ ls
checkall       getty    mklost+found  shutdown      ttytype
checklist      group    motd          termcap       update
cron           ident    mtab          ttys          utmp
ddate          init     passwd        ttys.2user
first.profile  lpset    rc            ttys.3user
$
```

Let's take a look at some of these files, starting with **/etc/passwd** and **/etc/group**, which are used to create logins and user shells. While we go into even more detail on these in *Chapter 7*, you should learn to understand their function as soon as possible.

9 Starting with System V, the administration commands in section 1 of the *UNIX User's Manual* (labelled *1M*) as well as all of sections 4 and 8 were moved to a new document, the *UNIX System Administrator's Manual*.

/etc/passwd

In time, the **/etc/passwd** file becomes downright familiar to system administrators, but at first glance it looks like Egyptian hieroglyphics:

```
root:hjbHWeEt2WORE:0:1:Super-User:/:/bin/sh
rootcsh:Dq2PskRl/PmBY:0:1:Super-User:/:/bin/csh
adm:VOID:2:1:User Administrator:/usr/adm:/bin/csh
sys:VOID:3:2:System Accounting:/usr/lib/sa:/bin/csh
bin:VOID:4:3:Owner of the System Commands:/bin:
nuucp:zL8wUerXUz/xM:5:6:UUCP Administrator:/usr/lib/uucp:/bin/csh
uucp:XLuM2jsr1tUb6:6:6:UUCP Login:/usr/spool/uucppublic:\
/usr/lib/uucp/uucico
bruce:5i4Vfgzhxs3I.:20:20:Bruce H Hunter:/us/bruce:/bin/sh
karen:MlNyd0pc7tgiE:21:20:Karen L B Hunter:/us/karen:/bin/sh
david:zCz.rpnUP1s22:23:20:David Fiedler:/us/david:/bin/csh
susan:/aik3QiekNOYU:24:20:Susan Fiedler:/us/susan:
who::50:25:The Who Command:/bin/who
```

Called a *password record*, each line deals with one user, and it contains all the information necessary for the system to create a login and user shell. There are seven fields in each password record, so let's take one password record apart and examine each field:

```
susan:/aik3QiekNOYU:24:20:Susan Fiedler:/us/susan:
```

The first field, **susan**, is the user login name. The second field, **/aik3QiekNOYU**, is the encrypted version of the password. The third field, **24**, is the *user id*, a unique integer. In UNIX terminology it is referred to as the **uid**. It is this number, not the login name, that the system uses internally to reference the user. The next field, **20**, is a group number or *gid*. It refers to **/etc/group**, the group file in which each named group has a (unique) number that associates its group name with a membership list. The next field, **Susan Fiedler**, is a comment field. It is used by programs like **whois** and **finger** to get user information including phone numbers and office locations. The following field, **/us/susan**, is the home directory of the user.

The last field can be varied. If blank, as in this case, the user gets the default shell, the Bourne shell. If **/bin/csh** is entered for this last field, the C shell is assigned to the user. It can also be the full path name of any executable program (even a shell script on some machines). **uucp** logins have the executable program **uucico** in their last field so that they may execute the **uucp** protocol at login time. If the last field is a single program, then the user is limited to that one program only, after which he is logged off. In the last line of our sample **/etc/passwd** file, this concept is illustrated with the **who** program.

/etc/group

/etc/group is the home of group information. This file is similar to **/etc/passwd**, but each record has fewer fields to contend with. Here is a typical **/etc/group** file:

```
root:VOID:1:root,rootcsh,daemon
sys:VOID:2:sys
bin:VOID:3:bin
uucp:VOID:4:uucp,nuucp
check:VOID:5:check
user:VOID:10:guest
edit:VOID:20:karen,bruce,david,susan
```

Like users, groups have an internal number associated with the group name. The first field is the group name (**check**, **user**, **edit**). The group number occupies the third field. And the fourth and last field is a list of the login names of the members of the group.

What about the second field, which contains **VOID** in all entries in this example? This is the password field, and an encrypted password may be present for each group. Some systems have a **group** command to manage the group memberships, the group files and passwords, but most systems do not. You can put passwords into **/etc/group**, (we show you how in *Chapter 9*), but it is not a good idea. The **newgrp** command lets a new user switch between groups if she knows the group password. Experience has shown, however, that while people tend to be very protective of their own personal password, they are not as careful with their group password. Since users often allow unlimited file access to others in their working group, this results in poor system security! For this reason we recommend that you put **VOID**, **NONE**, or the equivalent on every line in **/etc/group**. This prevents people from changing groups on their own, and serves as documentation to that effect. Then, the only way someone can join a group is if you, as system administrator, enter their name on the correct line in **/etc/group**.

▪ /etc/init ▪

init is a binary executable program found in **/etc**. When a UNIX system is booted, **/unix** (the kernel) is read into memory. When the kernel executes, it brings up the swapper, **swap**, and then **init**. **init** becomes the parent of all user shells. The dozens of programs and processes that make up the UNIX kernel are all extremely important, but none has as much impact on the system as **init**. It is the single most important process in the UNIX system because it creates the first human interface to the system, the shell.

Because there is a major difference in **init** between pre-System V and System V UNIX, we'll examine both separately.

Pre-System V **init**

In pre-System V UNIX, **init** creates itself in a single (root) user mode. It recognizes no terminals, only the *console*, the tty device the system administrator uses to bring up the system.

When you put UNIX into multiuser mode, you are actually signaling **init** to change its internal state (see *Bringing Up the System* in *Chapter* 2). **init** performs numerous tasks in multiuser mode. It goes into the **/etc/ttys** (teletypes or terminals) file (**/etc/inittab** on System III) and sends **login** messages (by spawning **getty**s) to all ports specified as active in the **/etc/ttys** (**/etc/inittab**) file.

In UNIX Version 7 and System III, **init** is almost invisible, although System III has a slightly more advanced **init**, approaching that of System V. Since it is not attached to a *tty,* it can be "seen" only by doing a **ps -x** or **ps -e**. It is highly visible in System V, as we shall see.

System V **init**

System V is a more mature, commercially viable operating system than earlier versions of UNIX, but it is also more complex. In early releases, UNIX (and **init**) ran in two modes, single-user and multiuser. Under System V there are seven levels, or modes, in which the system can run, two single-user and five multiuser. You must choose one of them to start up the system. Most system administrators need only be concerned with two levels, level **s** and level **2**.

The **s** mode is single-user mode. Level **2** is a general purpose, fits-all-does-all multiuser mode. These modes are controlled by a file called **/etc/inittab**. The entries in **/etc/inittab** are a list of processes that **init** calls at various initiation levels. UNIX System V gets all its process information from **/etc/inittab**.

Most **inittab** entries are a series of four fields in each record (line), separated by colons. Here is a complete **/etc/inittab** file:

```
is:s:initdefault:
su:s:respawn:/etc/slog </dev/console >/dev/console 2>&1
bl::bootwait:/etc/bcheckrc </dev/syscon >/dev/syscon 2>&1
bc::bootwait:/etc/brc 1>/dev/syscon 2>&1
rc::bootwait:/bin/sh /etc/rc 1>/dev/syscon 2>&1
pf::powerfail:/etc/powerfail 1>/dev/syscon 2>&1
co::respawn:getty console console
11:2:respawn:getty /dev/tty11 9600
12:2:respawn:getty -t 600 /dev/tty12 1200
13:2:respawn:getty /dev/tty13 9600
20:2:respawn:getty /dev/tty20 9600
21:2:off:getty /dev/tty21 9600
22:2:off:getty /dev/tty22 9600
23:2:respawn:getty -t 450 /dev/tty23 1200
```

Let's examine a single entry:

```
13:2:respawn:getty /dev/tty13 9600
```

Roughly translated into English, this says: "At id **13** under **init** level **2**, spawn a **getty** (create a **login**) on device **/dev/tty13** at 9600 baud."

Now let's take it one field at a time. The first field, **13**, is a mnemonic or label for the process or device that is about to be activated. The second field, **2**, is the process activation level, in this case level **2**. An **s** in the second field signifies single-user mode, and if it is empty, the entry is active at all levels. The third field, **respawn,** specifies what action to take. If the process does not exist, create it. If it already exists, go about the business of rescanning this table. The last field, **getty /dev/tty13 9600**, executes a **getty** on **/dev/tty03** at 9600 baud.

The timeout **-t 600** on line **tty12** means that if no **login** is received within 600 seconds (10 minutes) after the call is connected, hang up the line. This is especially useful on modem lines, which might otherwise sit around forever if a person, instead of a modem, called by mistake.

One of the benefits of this level of system initialization is that special levels can be set up. System V's various initialization levels allow classified processing to take place with ease. On a secured system at level **1**, for example, only the console and a terminal or two in the machine room are active, allowing classified information to be processed with no access to the system from the outside. At level **2**, only the terminals may be set up, no modem lines or hard-wired connections to other local computers. At level **3**, the modem lines become active. Here is an **/etc/inittab** listing that shows this kind of complexity:

```
is:s:initdefault:
su:s:respawn:/etc/slog </dev/console >/dev/console 2>&1
bl::bootwait:/etc/bcheckrc </dev/syscon >/dev/syscon 2>&1
bc::bootwait:/etc/brc 1>/dev/syscon 2>&1
rc::bootwait:/bin/sh /etc/rc 1>/dev/syscon 2>&1
pf::powerfail:/etc/powerfail 1>/dev/syscon 2>&1
co::respawn:getty console 1200 la180 # hardcopy console
bi:1234:respawn:getty bip0 9600 bip # secure CRT
11:234:respawn:getty /dev/tty11 9600 tvi950 #
12:34:respawn:getty -t 600 /dev/tty12 1200 h1500 #modem
13:234:respawn:getty /dev/tty13 9600 wyse #
20:234:respawn:getty /dev/tty20 9600 wyse #
21:6:off:getty -h /dev/tty21 2400 none #printer
22:6:off:getty -h /dev/tty22 1200 none #printer
23:4:respawn:getty -t 450 /dev/tty23 1200 h1500 #modem
```

There are a few extra fields shown in this example. The field immediately after the baud rate (**tvi950** on the **tty11** line, for instance) is used to pass the **TERM** environment variable to the user's shell. This clears the screen on some systems, so that the login message appears on the first line. As in most UNIX system files, comments may be placed on a line by preceding them with a **#** (pound sign).

Notice that the **getty** has a **-h** flag on the two printer ports. This keeps the line from "hanging up" or reinitializing to a default baud rate, since nobody ever logs in on a printer line! While the **-h** flag doesn't work on all systems, using it is good documentation and saves work if it becomes operational in a later software release. Using a setting of **off** prevents a process from actually being started on either of these lines. Actually, a process could not start unless **init 6** was run, in this case.

/etc/rc — The SA's Custom Shop

init is a binary executable program (*a.out* file). It cannot be altered except by recompiling it from source code, something most UNIX installations do not have. All by itself, **init** does not allow the flexibility that UNIX needs. The various **rc** files execute commands and scripts necessary to bring the system up in a condition suitable for a specific user community.

To customize UNIX and add some flexibility, **init** calls **rc** (for *r*un *c*ommands), an executable shell script, as the system comes up to multiuser level.[10] **rc** is a bare-bones program furnished by OEMs. VARs tend to add more to **rc** to suit customers' applications, such as initializing and automatic recovery of special databases. **rc** is very much like a custom shop, and by programming **rc**, you are in charge of the customization of your specific UNIX machine.

When modifying **rc**, make sure you don't alter any critical commands that might cause the system to hang up or loop without initializing. The safest way to add command lines to **rc** is to run them in the background (see the **/etc/lpset** line below), so if they fail to operate properly, the system will still come up.

rc is a system administrator's friend because it is relatively easy to use. It is written entirely in Bourne shell script, and can be a straightforward series of commands to execute. Because it is not written in C, you don't have to know that language to program **rc**. **rc** scripts can be short, eight-line scripts or they can run on for eight pages. After initializing a few files, **rc** generally starts up some critical process, such as setting port characteristics and mounting disks. Here is a very simple **rc** file taken from a Codata 3300 system running UNIX System III:

```
cp /dev/null /etc/mtab
cp /dev/null /etc/utmp
/etc/update
/etc/cron
/etc/lpset &
mount /dev/cd03 /us
rm -f /usr/spool/uucp/LCK*
rm -f /usr/spool/uucp/LOGFILE
rm -f /usr/spool/uucp/SYSLOG
```

The first two lines,

```
cp /dev/null /etc/mtab
cp /dev/null /etc/utmp
```

empty a pair of files called **mtab** and **utmp** by copying literally nothing into them. Those files are used by system accounting. UNIX has a number of files that should start out empty at each system startup, including these two. The **/etc/update** line below causes **update** to begin executing **sync**s at a specified interval. **/etc/cron** is a program that always runs in background, executing other programs at specified times from the cron tables. The next line executes a line printer device initialization script in the background:

```
/etc/lpset &
```

mount /dev/cd03 /us mounts logical disk 3 to the **/us** file tree. The next line removes all the lock files from the communication spooler:

```
rm -f /usr/spool/uucp/LCK*
```

Lock files must not exist at system startup; if they do, they prevent the desired activity from occurring. The last two lines remove a pair of log files for the communications system:

```
rm -f /usr/spool/uucp/LOGFILE
rm -f /usr/spool/uucp/SYSLOG
```

Here's a more complex example, from a Cadmus computer running System V with about 12 users:

```
TZ=EST5EDT
export TZ

if [ ! -f /etc/mnttab ]
then
        create /etc/mnttab
        devnm / | grep -v swap | grep -v root | setmnt
fi

        echo "Doing mounts"
        /etc/Mount

# recover vi files:
        /usr/lib/ex3.6preserve /tmp

# code for the printer ports:
        echo "Setting printers"
        nohup /usr/local/set_diablo_bd &
        nohup /usr/local/set_oki_baud &
```

```
# process accounting:
        rm -f /usr/adm/acct/nite/lock*
        /bin/su - adm -c /usr/lib/acct/startup
        echo process accounting started

# system activity:
/bin/su sys -c "/usr/lib/sa/sadc /usr/adm/sa/sa`date +%d` &"

        create /usr/adm/cronlog /usr/adm/sulog
        nice -19 cron

        rm -f /usr/spool/uucp/LCK*
        rm -f /usr/spool/mail/DELIVERING
        rm -f /usr/spool/lp/SCHEDLOCK
        /usr/lib/lpsched &
exit 0
```

First, the **TZ** variable is set, and takes effect here for the entire system:

```
TZ=EST5EDT
export TZ
```

The following four lines create the **/etc/mnttab** file if it doesn't already exist, then initialize it with information for the root file system:

```
if [ ! -f /etc/mnttab ]
then
        create /etc/mnttab
        devnm / | grep -v swap | grep -v root | setmnt
fi
```

The **grep -v root** is required on some machines to prevent the device on which the root file system is mounted from being included in the mount table. Notice that a different file name and technique is used from the System III example. All user file systems are then mounted with the **/etc/Mount** command:

```
echo "Doing mounts"
/etc/Mount
```

These mount-related files will be covered in detail in *Chapter 5*.

Saving Editor Files

Assuming that the system is coming up from a crash, the next command

```
# recover vi files:
        /usr/lib/ex3.6preserve /tmp
```

runs a special program — part of the **vi** package — that does the following:

- goes to the specified directory (in this case, **/tmp**)
- finds all **Ex*** and **Rx*** files left there by **vi** or **ex** when the system crashed
- reconstitutes them into editable form
- puts them in the **/usr/preserve** directory
- sends a mail message to their owner, notifying her that she can recover her files

Let's go through this process, so you can explain it to your users. Running the **preserve** program happens quietly enough, but the user gets a mail message like this one the next time she logs in:

```
$ mail
From root Tue Sep 24 18:53 EDT 1985
A copy of an editor buffer of your file "etc"
was saved when the system went down.
This buffer can be retrieved using the "recover" command
of the editor.
An easy way to do this is to give the command "ex -r etc".
This works for "edit" and "vi" also.
? q
$
```

The user must know what directory she was in last, unless the full path name was given on the original **ex** or **vi** command line. The best thing to do is proceed to that directory, and carefully examine the current version of the file in question. Then determine whether that, or the recovered version, is the one you want to keep:

```
$ ls -l etc
-rw-rw---- 1 susan   staff     16905 Sep 24 18:25 etc
$ ex -r etc
"etc" [Dated: Tue Sep 24 18:45:06] 704 lines, 18232 characters
:wq
"etc" 704 lines, 18232 characters
$
```

Here Susan determined that the older (and shorter) version was the one actually in her directory, and that 20 minutes' worth of work had been saved by the **recover** program. Writing the file out from **ex** gets rid of the old version. If you aren't sure which one is better, write the file out using a different name, then use **diff** to see which one to keep.

Notice the special message **[Dated: Tue Sep 24 18:45:06]** from **ex** that means you are working on a recovered file. Since **ex**, **vi**, and **edit** (as well as **e** and **view** on some systems) are all links to the same program file, using this technique works with any of them.

/etc/rc Continued

Because of an annoying bug that exists on many UNIX systems, you cannot set a serial port to a constant baud rate unless there is a process running on that port. Since this usually involves printer ports, it is explained in *Chapter 11*. The next part of our **/etc/rc** file deals with that problem by running special programs to fool the system. Because these programs never exit, they are run in background with the **nohup** command, which keeps them going "forever":

```
# code for the printer ports:
        echo "Setting printers"
        nohup /usr/local/set_diablo_bd &
        nohup /usr/local/set_oki_baud &
```

The next set of commands removes lock files, and initialize the process accounting system:

```
# process accounting:
        rm -f /usr/adm/acct/nite/lock*
        /bin/su - adm -c /usr/lib/acct/startup
        echo process accounting started
```

If the system activity programs are desired to be run, the next line initializes their logging file. These programs, run regularly from **crontab**, keep track of how heavily the system is loaded at different times of the day, and are ideal for determining when it's time to upgrade hardware:

```
# system activity:
/bin/su sys -c "/usr/lib/sa/sadc /usr/adm/sa/sa`date +%d` &"
```

Here two main logfiles are reinitialized, and **cron** is started at low priority. Then the lockfiles for **uucp**, the **mail** system, and the printer spooler are removed. Finally, the printer spooler program itself is started:

```
        create /usr/adm/cronlog /usr/adm/sulog
        nice -19 cron

        rm -f /usr/spool/uucp/LCK*
        rm -f /usr/spool/mail/DELIVERING
        rm -f /usr/spool/lp/SCHEDLOCK
        /usr/lib/lpsched &
exit 0
```

If your system keeps its mail in **/usr/mail** instead of **/usr/spool/mail**, the fourth line from the bottom should read:

```
rm -f /usr/mail/*.lock
```

/etc/brc

On System V, there are two additional files used at system startup. **/etc/brc** is a very simple shell procedure that simply removes the previous **/etc/mnttab**. This function is performed by the first few lines in the **/etc/rc** file just shown, so if you copy ours, your **brc** can be empty, or you can use this one:

```
if
        [ -f /etc/mnttab ]
then
        rm -f /etc/mnttab
fi
```

/etc/bcheckrc

The other new System V file is used to handle all the file system checking before **/etc/rc** is called. If you have a program to set the date or timezone, it can be run from here as well. Your **bcheckrc** can be fancy, with prompts requesting whether you want the file systems checked, but we prefer to do that all the time:

```
TZ=EST5EDT; export TZ
/etc/checkall -D
exit 0
```

/etc/getty and /etc/login

getty is called by **init**. **getty** is the process that sets the baud rate, asks for a login name, then executes the actual **login** program (generally found in **/etc/login** but sometimes in **/bin/login** instead). **login** then comes back and asks for a password, turns off echo while getting the password, encrypts it, validates it (retrying if necessary), and finally gets around to giving the user a login. The arguments passed to **getty** in normal usage are the *tty* number, the baud rate (transmission speed), and the time it should allow for an entry before "going away" or timing out.

System V **getty** must deal with **/etc/gettydefs**. Without going into agonizing detail yet, **gettydefs** provides a series of **stty** and **ioctl** settings to **getty** (these will be explained in *Chapter 10*). One of its many purposes is to retry serial asynchronous lines (**tty**s) for different baud rates until it can successfully get login data. After control is passed to the **login** program, **login** must do other tasks, such as changing the ownership of the **tty** to root, and then, on success of the login, change the ownership to that of the user.

▪ Handy Shell Programs ▪

Like the files and directories we've examined in this chapter, the mix of shell programs we have for you is somewhat eclectic:

morning

Here's something you should run when you first log on in the morning, either as a matter of habit or through your **.profile** or **.login** file. Customize it to your liking; the commands we provide are only a starting point:

```
( who ; df -t; tail -24 /usr/adm/messages ) | ${PAGER:-more}
```

type

You won't appreciate this until you use it a few times, but it's perfect for prowling around places like **/usr/lib**. To use it, you have to be familiar with the shell construct **`program`**,[10] which lets you run an arbitrary program and send the output to the shell command line. It's sort of like a sideways pipe. Here's an easy example:

10 Notice we're using the single backwards quote, not the single forwards quote. See *Chapter 13* for more details.

```
$ cat chapter
All
bin
dev
etc
shellprogs
summary
usr
where
$ ls -l `cat chapter`
total 90
-rw-rw---- 1 dave    staff       142 Sep 15 01:02 All
-rw-rw---- 1 dave    staff      2968 Sep 15 00:59 bin
-rw-rw---- 1 dave    staff      9896 Sep 17 00:06 dev
-rw-rw---- 1 dave    staff     16371 Sep 15 01:22 etc
-rw-rw---- 1 dave    staff       180 Sep 17 01:30 shellprogs
-rw-rw---- 1 dave    staff       977 Sep 15 01:01 summary
-rw-rw---- 1 dave    staff     11548 Sep 17 01:08 usr
-rw-rw---- 1 dave    staff      2123 Sep 15 00:59 where
```

Notice that the **ls** program got the names of the files to display by running **cat chapter**. In this way, the output of one command can be used as the arguments to another command. Anyway, here's the **type** program:

```
file * | grep $1 | sed 's/:.*$//'
```

Here's how you use it. Go into **/usr/lib** and try to look at the contents of every file with **cat**, **more**, or even **head**. What you will get is headaches, as your screen fills with binary garbage. You only want to look at ASCII text files, to see what's inside. The **file** command tells you what kind of file you're looking at:

```
$ file /usr/lib/*
/usr/lib/accept:     shareable executable with symboltable
/usr/lib/acct:       directory
/usr/lib/acctcon:    shareable executable with symboltable
/usr/lib/atrun:      shareable executable with symboltable
/usr/lib/crontab:    ascii text
/usr/lib/ctextlib.a:        archive
/usr/lib/deroff:     shareable executable
/usr/lib/dict.d:     commands text
/usr/lib/dprog:      shareable executable
/usr/lib/edwhatis:   ascii text
/usr/lib/eign:       ascii text
  . . .
/usr/lib/whatis:     roff, nroff, or eqn input text
/usr/lib/whereis.dirs:      English text
/usr/lib/winlib.a:   archive
```

Since you only want to see text files, notice that such files always have the word **text** in their description from running **file**. This is how **type** determines what to do.

```
$ cd /usr/lib
$ type text
crontab
dict.d
edwhatis
eign
  . . .
whatis
whereis.dirs
$ head -3 `type text`
==> crontab <==
# this crontab file assumes that the system runs day and night
# the # is a comment character
# min hour day-of-mos(1-31) mos(1-12), day(0-6, 0=sun)

==> dict.d <==
ing behavior
 ability to
 a great deal of
==> edwhatis <==
g/\\-/s//-/
g/\\\*-/s//-/
g/ VAX-11/s///

==> eign <==
the
a
and

  . . .

==> whatis <==
A.OUT 5       a.out \- assembler and link editor output
A68 1         a68 \- MIT assembler
ABORT 3C      abort \- generate an IOT fault

==> whereis.dirs <==
WHEREIS LOOKS INTO THESE DIRECTORIES
  This file is read out line by line.
    1. Commentary, Format: free
```

Aside from exploring, you can also use **type** for system administration tasks. For instance: removing symbol tables from programs can save a surprising amount of space. Since **strip** won't disturb files that aren't in the correct **a.out** format, the lazy way is to do something like this:[11]

```
# strip /usr/bin/*
strip: /usr/bin/append not in a.out format
strip: /usr/bin/basic already stripped
strip: /usr/bin/checknews already stripped
strip: /usr/bin/hdial already stripped
strip: /usr/bin/help not in a.out format
strip: /usr/bin/indent already stripped
strip: /usr/bin/inews already stripped
strip: /usr/bin/initmodem not in a.out format
strip: /usr/bin/pick already stripped
strip: /usr/bin/postnews already stripped
strip: /usr/bin/readnews already stripped
strip: /usr/bin/rmtrash not in a.out format
strip: /usr/bin/rnews already stripped
strip: /usr/bin/scomp not in a.out format
strip: /usr/bin/spell not in a.out format
strip: /usr/bin/today already stripped
```

See all the error messages? The right way to do it is to strip only the files that have unwanted symbol tables:

```
# cd /usr/bin
# strip `type symboltable`
#
```

This avoids error messages and also assumes that **strip** never acts on the wrong file by mistake. On some systems, the message from the **file** program may say **executable not stripped** instead of **executable with symboltable**, so you could run the following instead:

```
# cd /usr/bin
# strip `type stripped`
#
```

findbig

Large directories are inefficient, and you should keep track of very large files. This program mails you the details about each one:

11 Do not strip files that may produce core dumps if you want to analyze the dumps.

```
find / -type d -size +5  -print | xargs ls -ld | mail root
find / -type f -size +$1 -print | xargs ls -l  | mail root
```

While only directories greater than 10 blocks long are a problem, reporting them when they reach 5 blocks alerts you to directories that are growing. **findbig** should be executed from **crontab** once a week with an argument to specify the minimum size of the ordinary files to report. Remember that the default operation of **find** uses the number of blocks, not bytes:

```
07 03 * * 0   /usr/local/findbig 500
```

This reports all files larger than 256,000 bytes (for 512-byte block systems) or 512,000 bytes (for 1024-byte block systems).

rmtrash

Not only do certain directories fill up, but files with certain names keep popping up all over the system, no matter how useless they are. This program, which should serve as a model for your own version, should be run every night in the wee hours to clean things up:

```
find / \( -name core -o -name dead.letter \) -mtime +1 -print \
        | xargs -t /bin/rm
find /tmp /usr/tmp /usr/preserve -type f -mtime +1 -print\
        | xargs -t /bin/rm
find /usr/spool/uucp /usr/adm/acct -type f -mtime +3 -print\
        | xargs -t /bin/rm
```

The first line shows you how to find and remove several different file names in a single pass through the file system. It removes all **dead.letter** and **core** files more than one day old. (You don't want to remove someone's **core** file while they're running **adb** or **sdb** on it!) The syntax is tortuous but effective. (See *Chapter 13* for more details on **find**). Notice that in this and the previous example, we use the **xargs** program available on most systems. **xargs** collects the output from the **find** with the **-print** option and executes its command argument just *once* on each file named by **find**. This avoids the alternative:

```
find /tmp -type f -mtime +1 -print -exec /bin/rm {} \;
```

which executes **/bin/rm** every time a file is to be removed, slowing the system down unnecessarily.[12] The **-t** flag for **xargs** prints the file names as they are removed; they will be left in **/usr/adm/cronlog** as an audit trail.

---

12 Thanks to Fred Yankowski of AT&T Bell Laboratories for pointing this out.

spellcount and dospell

This handy one-liner shows you the words misspelled most often by users of the **spell** program on your system. Since the output of **spellcount** shows the most frequent ones first, these words are probably correctly spelled words that do not appear in the dictionary:

```
sort /usr/lib/spell/spellhist | uniq -c | sort -nr
```

After running **spellcount**, you can create a file containing the correct words, and add them to the dictionary by whatever process works on your system. Would we leave you without a program to do that? Call it **dospell**:

```
cd /usr/lib/spell
cp hlista hlista.old
sort -u $1 | hashmake > newhash
hashcheck <  hlista   > oldhash
sort -u newhash oldhash > sorthash
n=`wc -l sorthash | sed "s/^ *//" | sed "s/ .*//"`
spellin $n < sorthash > hlista
rm newhash oldhash sorthash
```

Of course, you run this by typing

```
$ dospell new_words
```

where **new_words** is the name of the file you created after running **spellcount**.

newcron

Once you start using the **cron** seriously, the **/usr/adm/cronlog** file rapidly fills up. You could clean it out regularly, but it's often useful to review the entries for a particular day. This program helps you manage **cronlog** by splitting it up into smaller daily files. You can extend this idea as far as you like if you prefer to keep logs even longer than a week:

```
cd /usr/adm
mv cronlog cronlog.last
create cronlog
uniq cronlog.last cronlog.`date +%a`
rm cronlog.last
chmod o-r cronlog cronlog.???
```

The construct **`date +%a`** tacks on a file suffix (such as **.Sun** or **.Mon**) that indicates which day of the week the log covers. This only works with the **date** program versions that allow **date**'s output to be formatted. And make sure to run **newcron** every night at 23:59!

where

This highly useful C program is one you will use often. **where** looks in your **PATH** for executable files named the same as the arguments on the command line, and shows you their full path names if found:

```
$ where spellcount vi where
/usr/local/spellcount
/bin/vi
/usr/ucb/vi
/usr/local/where
$ where foobar
No foobar in :/bin:/usr/bin:/bin.cadmus:/bin.ver7:/bin.sys3:
/bin.sys5:/usr/ucb:/usr/games:/etc:/usr/local:/own/lev:
/usr/lib/news:/usr/lib/uucp:/usr/lib/acct:/usr/lib/sa:
/own/stat/bin:/usr/lib:/usr/lib/spell:.:
$
```

Although **where** doesn't look for commands in obscure places the way the Berkeley **whereis** program does, it's much faster than its almost-equivalent **which**. Even if you have **whereis** or **which**, you'll love **where** even more:

```
/*
 *      where.c
 *
 *   by Larry Barello, Teltone, Bellevue, WA
 *   ..!uw-beaver!{tikal,teltone}!larry
 *
 */

#include <stdio.h>

char *getenv();
char *index();     /* use strchr() on System III and later */

main(ac,av)
char **av;
{
     char *origpath, *path, *cp;
     char buf[200];
     char patbuf[512];
     int quit, found;

     if (ac < 2) {
        fprintf(stderr, "Usage: %s cmd [cmd, ..]\n", *av);
        exit(1);
     }
```

```
        if ((origpath = getenv("PATH")) == 0)
           origpath = ".";

        av[ac] = 0;
        for(av++ ; *av; av++) {
           strcpy(patbuf, origpath);
           cp = path = patbuf;
           quit = found = 0;

           while(!quit) {
                cp = index(path, ':');
                if (cp == NULL)
                   quit++;
                else *cp = '\0';

                sprintf(buf, "%s/%s", (*path ? path:"."), *av);
                path = ++cp;
                if (access(buf, 1) == 0) {
                   printf("%s\n", buf);
                   found++;
                }
           }
           if (!found)
                printf("No %s in %s\n", *av, origpath);
        }
        exit(0);
    }
```

▪ Chapter Summary ▪

In the past, most operating systems had flat file systems. Modern multiuser operating systems use a hierarchical file system starting with Multics and currently present in UNIX, AOS, and MVS. A hierarchical file system has a significant advantage: it allows the system's users to deal with a large file system in an organized way. But there is a price. The file system hierarchy must be maintained. Next we examine how to mount and unmount these file systems.

CHAPTER 5

MOUNTING AND UNMOUNTING FILE SYSTEMS

UNIX — A Divided System

UNIX is not a homogeneous entity — it is divided into several working parts. The smallest UNIX system deals with a minimum of three separate file systems. One is the standard UNIX distribution (**/unix**: the kernel, **/dev**, **/etc**, and **/bin**), another is for the swapper (to swap executable binaries back and forth as needed), and the other is for a user file system. Each of these file systems is stored on its own separate section of the disk called a *disk partition*. The **swap** area is not mounted and is actually not a file system.

Larger UNIX systems have huge disk capacities and thus many more mounted file systems. In fact, on very large UNIX systems, not only are there many separate user file systems, even UNIX proper may be divided into smaller partitions on hard disk. There is more than one way to partition a UNIX system, depending on the size of the system and the implementor's fancy.

When you come up in single-user mode (**init s** in System V), you are working with disk partitions — UNIX proper and the swap disk. These are already created when you receive your UNIX system. However, when you go into multiuser mode (**init 2 - 6** in System V), **init** calls **rc**, and **rc** mounts any other file systems it has been told to mount. Here's where you, the system administrator, enter the picture. In order to get **rc** to mount a file system, first you need to create a disk partition for it on one of your disks. Then you create the file system (by using **mkfs**) and **mount** it. Finally you edit the appropriate file in **/etc** to add the **mount** command so it will be mounted automatically as the system comes up multiuser. In this chapter we are going to discuss how to do all of those things plus explore some UNIX file theory in the process. We're also going to learn how to unmount a file system. But before getting in any deeper, let's back up a bit and discuss some essential concepts.

▪ What Is a Mounted File System? ▪

First of all, what is the difference between mounted and unmounted file systems? Each mounted UNIX file system is a user file tree that has its own root, not to be confused with *the* root (UNIX proper). The file system is attached to the UNIX file tree, and consequently it is accessible for the usual UNIX operations — reading files, writing files, and so on. An unmounted file system, on the other hand, is *not* attached to the UNIX file tree. Unmounted, a file system can be created and formatted by the system administrator, but it is noninteractive and essentially useless for system use. Once mounted, it officially becomes part of the working UNIX system.

A Little UNIX File System Theory

Although the actual process of mounting and unmounting file systems is straightforward enough, the theory behind it is not. You are far more effective as UNIX system administrator if you not only know what to do, but why you do it. So let's take a brief moment to discuss some elementary UNIX file system theory.

UNIX is a multiuser system, capable of being quite large indeed. Mainframe UNIX implementations deal with billions of bytes of data and hundreds of users. Regardless of the actual number of users, it is essential for an operating system to maintain data integrity, no easy task on multiuser systems. Hence, file systems are kept not only separate, but inviolate. UNIX is extremely particular about crossing the boundaries of mounted file systems. Each file system has its own separate disk partition, and communication between file systems is rigidly controlled by UNIX proper. If you try using the **ln** (link) command from one file system to another, you quickly find out that the system refuses to allow links across disk boundaries. By selectively isolating data in this manner, not only is data corruption prevented, but data security is also facilitated.

In order to adapt to the demands of a busy, multiuser system, system administration is much more effective if you have the freedom to mount and unmount file systems to suit specific needs. UNIX gives you this freedom. On small UNIX systems, although system administrators seldom need to create more than a few mounted file systems, having the ability to do so makes even the smallest UNIX system much more versatile and expandable. For example, if you run out of room on your hard disk, you get the additional space you need for more user file trees by simply purchasing another disk drive and mounting it as a separate file system.

In addition, as we mentioned in earlier chapters, the reason for doing most system administration tasks in single-user mode is because user file systems are unmounted at this time. On occasion, even the system administrator of a small system may find it necessary to manually unmount a user file system in order to prevent inadvertent data damage during crucial system administration operations. Fortunately, UNIX makes unmounting file systems an easy task.

Naturally, the larger the UNIX system, the more variables involved in system administration, and the greater potential for creativity. File systems can be mounted to UNIX proper one at a time, or they can be stacked one on top of another.[1] On the

---

1 **/usr/spool**, **/usr/src**, and **/usr/man** are typical stacked file systems. On very large machines, **/usr** is mounted as one file system to which **/man**, **/src**, and **/spool** are attached as separate file systems.

largest systems, the system administrator may create duplicate file trees as an alternate backup strategy for critical areas. On systems heavily loaded with users, the system administrator often has to create custom-sized file trees to manage existing disk space. Your system supplier usually provides you with a layout of the disk partitions available on your system, looking something like that in Fig. 5-1.

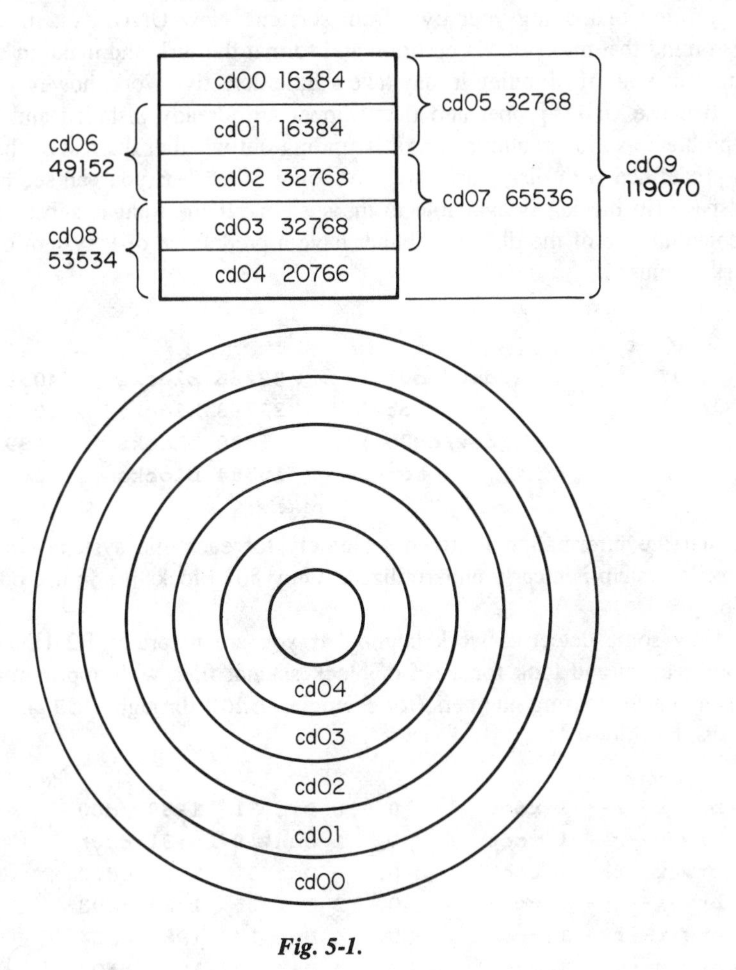

Fig. 5-1.

These partitions are simply entry points in the device driver code that tell the driver where each partition begins and ends on the disk. By using partitions **cd02** and **cd03** separately, you get two reasonably sized file systems of 32768 blocks each. But by addressing them jointly as **cd07**, you have one large 65536-block file system if you need one. Similarly, the *entire disk* may be used as a giant 119070-block file system by simply calling it **cd09**.

Now that you know a little bit of the theory behind mounting user file systems, let's find out how to actually do it!

▪ File System Creation and Implementation ▪

First things first. Before you can create a file system, you have to set aside a special area for it on the hard disk. This area is called a *disk partition* (or predefined disk subsystem). The birth of every file system starts with two possibilities: using an existing disk partition or making your own from scratch. New UNIX system owners need to bear in mind that most OEMs partition and format the disk and make (**mkfs**) a file system to start you off. Finding it may take a little detective work, however.

Because UNIX proper and the swapper are already installed and mounted, your first problem as system administrator is finding out whether the rest of the hard disk has been predefined with disk partitions. By doing a **df -t** you can see how much total disk space (in blocks) is available to the system. If the total is substantially less than the potential size of the disk, you either have a predefined disk system or a large block of disk is unused:

```
$ df -t
/usr            (/dev/cd01 ):    32266 blocks     4059 inodes
                       total:    32768 blocks     4096 inodes
/               (/dev/cd00 ):     3888 blocks     1489 inodes
                       total:    16384 blocks     2048 inodes
```

Note that the information is given separately for each file system. In this case, the **/usr** file system is clearly underutilized. Only 502 blocks are in use out of a possible 32768.

Now some detective work begins. If you are in pre-SVR2 UNIX, go into the **/dev** directory and look for a set of block special files with approximately the same file name but increasing numbers (for example, **cd00** through **cd37**). These are your hard disk partitions:

```
brw-r--r-- 1 root      0,  0 Dec 31  1969 cd00
brw-r--r-- 1 root      0,  1 Jun  9 20:31 cd01
brw-r--r-- 1 root      0,  2 Dec 31  1969 cd02
brw-r--r-- 1 root      0,  3 Oct 25  1984 cd03
brw-r--r-- 1 root      0,  4 Dec 13  1983 cd04
brw-r--r-- 1 root      0,  5 Dec 13  1983 cd05
```

Now find a corresponding set of character special files with a similar name and the same set of numbers. These are "raw" disks (**rcd00** through **rcd37**). They are there to handle tasks requiring character I/O, such as formatting:

```
crw-r--r-- 1 root      5,  0 Dec 31  1969 rcd00
crw-r--r-- 1 root      5,  1 Dec 31  1969 rcd01
```

```
crw-r--r-- 1 root       5,  2 Dec 31  1969 rcd02
crw-r--r-- 1 root       5,  3 Dec 31  1969 rcd03
crw-r--r-- 1 root       5,  4 Dec 13  1983 rcd04
crw-r--r-- 1 root       5,  5 Dec 13  1983 rcd05
```

Now go to **/** (root) and nose around for a directory that looks like a match.

```
# ls -l /
total 359
drwxr-xr-x 2 root        3040 Oct 14  1984 bin
-rw-rw-rw- 1 root       14336 Jun  1 12:29 core
drwxr-xr-x 2 root        1856 Feb 24 11:59 dev
drwxr-xr-x 2 root         480 Feb 11 14:46 etc
-rwx------ 1 root          49 Nov 19  1982 fdload
drwxr-xr-x 2 root         496 Jan  1  1970 lib
drwxr-xr-x 2 root        4608 May 22 20:31 lost+found
drwxrwxrwx 2 root          32 Dec 31  1969 mnt03
drwxrwxrwx 2 root         208 Jun 11 21:08 tmp
-rwxr--r-- 2 root       77656 Aug 13  1984 unix
-rwxr--r-- 2 root       77656 Aug 13  1984 unix.cd.dm.i
drwxr-xr-x16 root         336 Feb 17 18:44 usr
```

Can you find the directory in question? It's **mnt03**, an OEM-created directory. It is empty and located in the root directory, a natural place to mount a new file system.[2] If the disk partition is made into a file system, it shows its size when the **df** command is used. When you mount **/dev/cd03** to **mnt03**, you have the beginning of a file system.[3]

```
# mkfs /dev/cd03 16384
# mount /dev/cd03 /mnt03
#
```

If you want to change the name of the file system to something more human, say from **/mnt03** to **/us**, use the **mv** command to do it, and then you can mount **/dev/cd03** on **/us**:

```
# mv mnt03 us
# mount /dev/cd03 /us
#
```

2 Any directory with a displayed size of 32 bytes is empty. Since you need 16 bytes per file name (14 for the name and 2 for the inodes), there are always a minimum of 2 entries in a directory: 1 pointing to itself (**.**) and 1 pointing to its parent (**..**).

3 On System V Release 2 the disks have their own directory in **/dev** called **/dev/dsk**.

▪ If You Have to Create a Disk Partition ▪

If no predefined subdisk is available, you have to make one. At this point, those of you not trained in operating system theory may be surprised to find out that normally UNIX does not do this task. Disk partitions must be created using special partitioning and formatting utilities. This varies from machine to machine.

UNIX relies upon a host operating system to bring it up. The host operating system may be something as sophisticated as VM/SP (Amdahl and IBM), or as primitive as a simple PROM-based monitor with no purpose other than providing minimal facilities to support UNIX. With few exceptions, this host system provides the means of partitioning and formatting disk subsystems for UNIX. Some hardware support systems, like AT&T's 3B2 firmware, are quite sophisticated. Very large systems such as UTS UNIX under VM/SP even allow partitioning ''mini-disks,'' or partial disks, by absolute addressing. Check your manual to see what needs to be done on your machine. Sometimes, all of these functions can be performed directly from within UNIX.

Formatting is also done from the host system. Small 68000-based machines format from the boot PROM system. Exceptions include UTS UNIX, which formats from UTS itself. There is no standard method. Each system is different. Great care must be exercised when either formatting or making a file system (**mkfs**) as both are highly destructive of any data already existing within that area. As one manual puts it, ''data will be mercilessly destroyed.''

format is not a standard UNIX command for hard disks, but it is commonly used for floppy diskettes. When found on UNIX systems, it is supplied by the OEM as an extension of UNIX proper. **format** allows hard disks to be formatted from UNIX rather than by the boot operating system. This is much easier for the system administrator because she is working with UNIX more often than not.

Formatting prepares the disk for a file system. It zeros out old data and creates a disk format that is compatible with the host UNIX system. Don't confuse this process with **mkfs**, which creates the inode and file structure necessary for a UNIX file system. And don't forget that *either* process wipes out all data on the section of disk you are dealing with!

Creating a File System with mkfs

Before the actual mounting process takes place, you need two necessary ingredients — a file tree or system ready to mount, and a directory to mount it on. You make a file system with the **mkfs** command, and you make a directory with the **mkdir** command.

mkfs creates a UNIX file system. UNIX demands that a file system have its super-block and inode information initialized before it even *thinks* about putting a file or directory on disk. UNIX goes to a default formula unless the system administrator specifies otherwise, but you must specify the size of the file system. With UNIX System V, you have the additional option of being able to specify the number of inodes desired as well as the most efficient disk block spacing.

Being able to control file system size is handy if disk space is at a premium. File systems vary in flavor and texture, depending on their purpose. If you have lots of small files, such as data files for an accounting system billing operation that are seldom more than a few hundred characters each, the number of inodes should be close to the number of blocks. On the other hand, if you are dealing with massive text files such as book chapters or reports, the number of inodes should be substantially less than the number of blocks. Remember, at least one inode is needed for each file, no matter how small, but large files may contain many blocks. Even inodes take up disk space.

If unspecified when running **mkfs**, the number of inodes defaults to the number of physical blocks in the file system divided by four. Experience has proved that this is more than sufficient in most cases. The file system used to hold USENET news files (generally **/usr/spool**) should have twice this many inodes, however. Actual usage and continuous checking (**df**) will show you the best ratios.

Don't continually reformat or re-**mkfs** your disks. One day you will forget to back something up, and wipe out several months' work. Unless the data are very unusual — from USENET on one extreme to large graphics bitmap files on the other — stick with the default formula.

You create a file system with the **mkfs** command:

```
# mkfs /dev/cd03 1000
```

where **/dev/cd03** is the block special file, and **1000** is the number of blocks in the new file system. In System V Release 2 the command line looks like this:

```
# mkfs /dev/dsk/cd03 1000:500
```

where 500 is the number of inodes desired.

More Than You Ever Wanted to Know about Disk Drives

In the manual page for **mkfs**, two other parameters are listed: *gap* and *blocks*.[4] These refer to the actual physical disk you are using, and are really quite simple.

All data on a disk are written and read in blocks of 512, 1024, 4096, or some other multiple of bytes at once for efficiency. The disk is constantly spinning, and the read/write head moves backward and forward to go from track to track (see Fig. 5-2).

Let's say that the head stays in one place for awhile; all the data on a track eventually will pass underneath it to be read. As the desired data (perhaps block 5 of track 0) passes under the head, it is read and transferred to a buffer area in the disk controller. This takes a short but significant amount of time, during which several other blocks of data pass under the head. If the blocks are numbered sequentially on the disk as shown above, and block 6 is wanted, the disk has to spin around an entire turn before block 6 comes up again. So system designers measure the time needed to transfer data, and calculate the number of blocks skipped when reading or writing. Then by starting at block 0, and skipping two blocks before assigning block 1, the head is ready to read data immediately. Then the block numbering is as shown in Fig. 5-3.

---

4 There is also a procedure mentioned for automatically creating an entire file system, including a boot program, from a specification file, but this is so tricky, we don't advise using it.

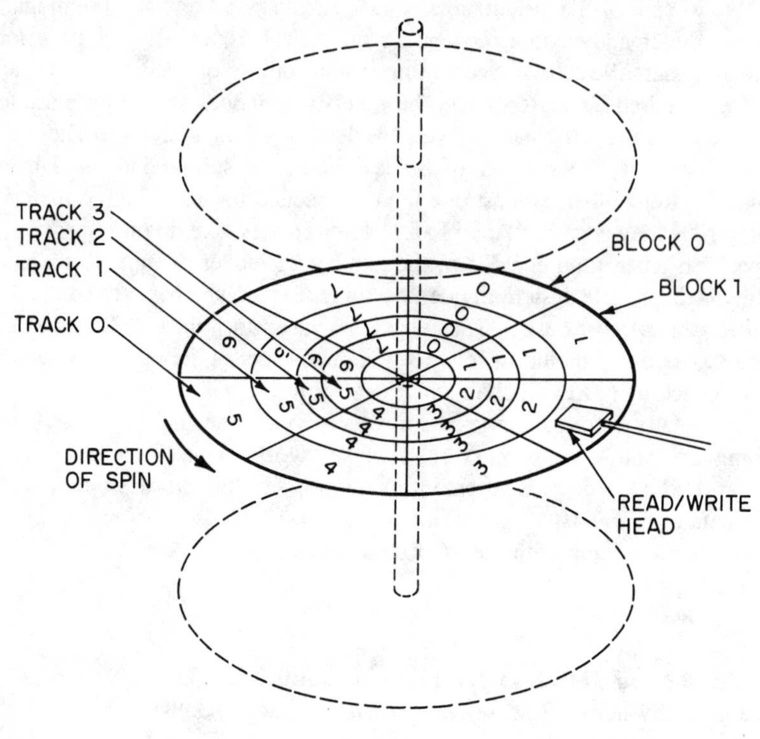
TRACK 3
TRACK 2
TRACK 1
TRACK 0
BLOCK 0
BLOCK 1
DIRECTION OF SPIN
READ/WRITE HEAD

Fig. 5-2.

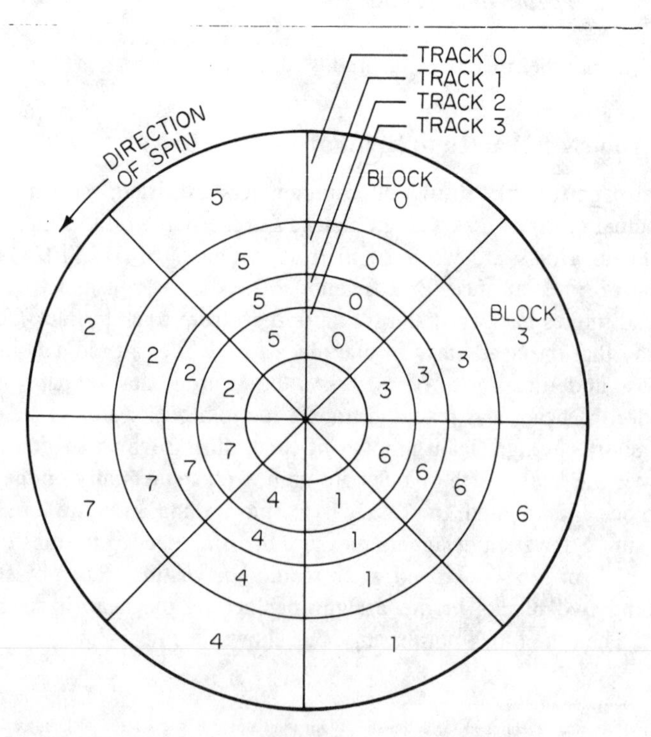
TRACK 0
TRACK 1
TRACK 2
TRACK 3
DIRECTION OF SPIN
BLOCK 0
BLOCK 3

Fig. 5-3.

This is known as "sector skewing" or "interleaving", and the *gap* is simply the number of blocks skipped, in this case 2. Disk operations are speeded up considerably by using interleaving.

The quantity *blocks* is the number of blocks per *cylinder*. A cylinder is an imaginary vertical slice of disk comprising all tracks of the same number on each usable disk surface. Cylinder 1 contains all track *1*s on all disk surfaces, cylinder 2 all track *2*s on all disk surfaces, and so on as in Fig. 5-4.

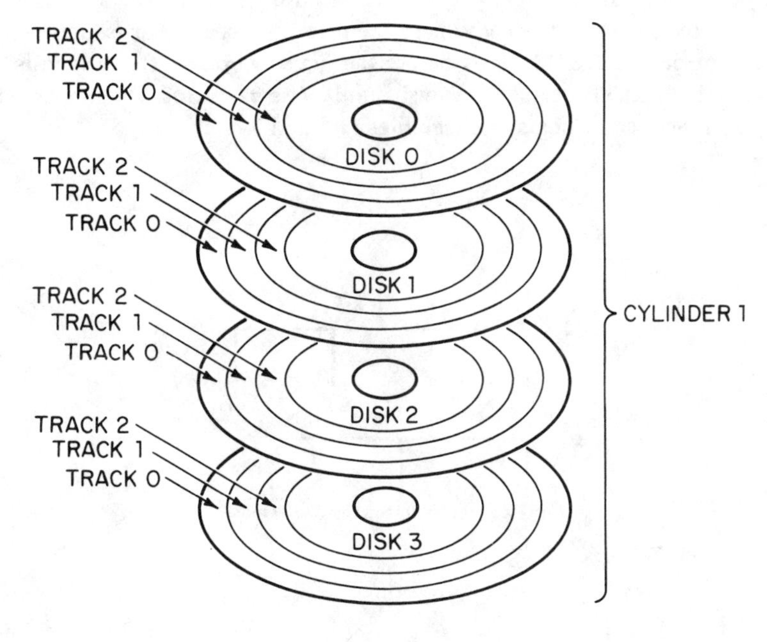

Fig. 5-4.

For example, if a disk has 6 "platters" of which only 4 are actually usable (on both sides), there are 8 usable disk surfaces. If there are 20 blocks per track, then there are 20 * 8 or 160 blocks per cylinder.

Both gap and block figures should be specified to you by the system supplier, or else **mkfs** should have been modified by them so that it automatically supplies the correct values. If not, you should now have enough information to figure the values out yourself, if necessary, from the disk drive specification sheet.

Once the formatted subdisk is prepared and you make the file system with **mkfs**, the groundwork is completed. Now a subdisk exists that is defined and formatted and has all the file and inode structures needed to make a system run once it is mounted.

▪ Mounting a File System ▪

A file system or tree is attached to another file system by mounting it. The command to mount a file tree is **mount**:

```
# mount /dev/xt0f /usr/spool
```

Any data on the special file **/dev/xt0f** are now part of the file system **/usr/spool**. Be careful when you do this because when one file system is mounted on top of another, any files already there seem to disappear! For example, if the text file **/usr/spool/README** exists before the **/usr/spool** file system is attached, **/usr/spool/README** seems to vanish until **/usr/spool** is unmounted. However, it is still there and using space (see Figs. 5-5 and 5-6).

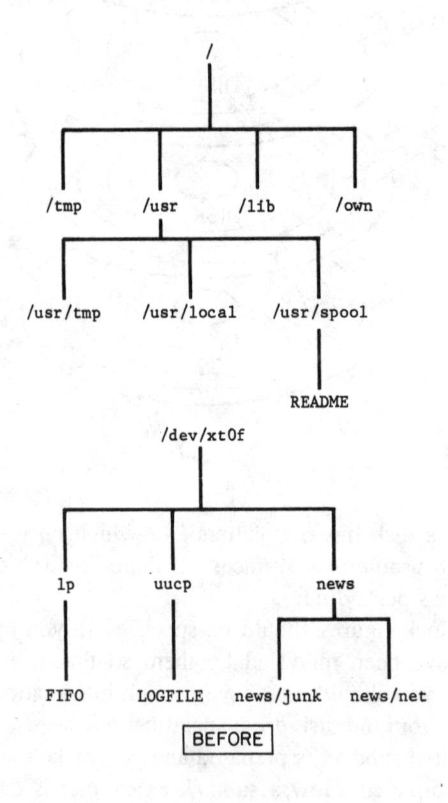

Fig. 5-5.

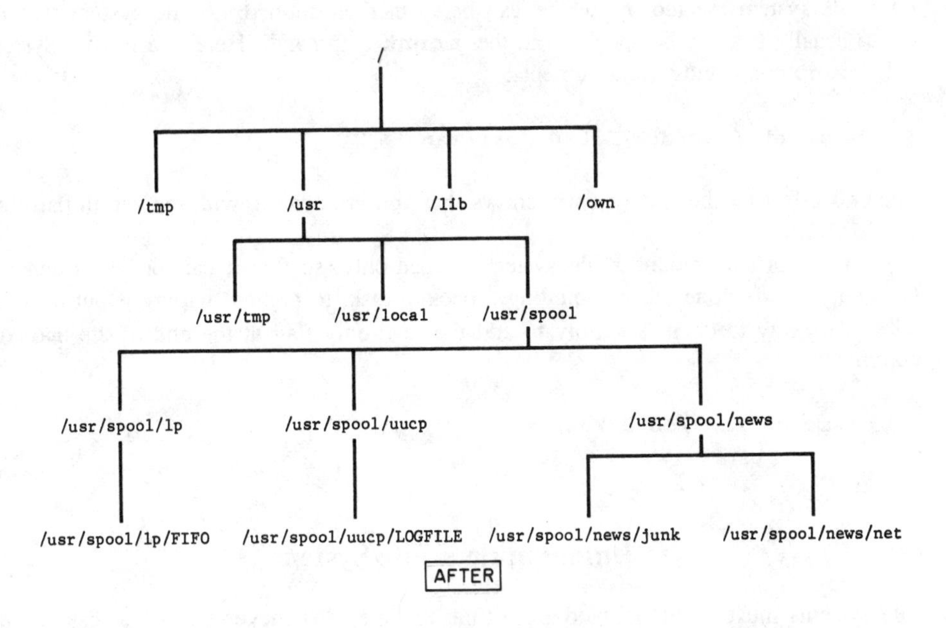

Fig. 5-6.

A **df** shows whether the system is mounted:

```
$ df /dev/xt0f
(/dev/xt0f ):    21554 blocks     7801 inodes
```

The **df** command displays free disk space, showing that the **/usr/spool** system is not only mounted, but has 10+ megabytes free (21554 blocks of 512 bytes divided by 2). The **mount** command without arguments also shows all mounted systems:

```
/           on /dev/xt0a read/write on Tue Sep 10 17:19:03 1985
/usr        on /dev/xt0c read/write on Tue Sep 10 17:19:07 1985
/usr/lib    on /dev/xt0e read/write on Tue Sep 10 17:19:08 1985
/usr/spool  on /dev/xt0f read/write on Tue Sep 10 17:19:09 1985
/tmp        on /dev/xt1b read/write on Tue Sep 10 17:19:23 1985
/own        on /dev/xt1c read/write on Tue Sep 10 17:19:10 1985
/ips        on /dev/xt1e read/write on Tue Sep 10 17:19:11 1985
/db         on /dev/xt1f read/write on Tue Sep 10 17:19:12 1985
```

Mounting a file system under System 5.2 is a little more complex, but not much. Each file system created by **mkfs** can be further partitioned. A file system starting point, usually 0, must be specified in the **mount** command. Here is a typical System 5.2 **mount** command with arguments:

```
# mount /dev/dsk/330s0 /usr/man
```

The **s0** offset on the **/dev** entry shows that you are dealing with the zeroth partition of **/dsk330**.

You can also mount a file system as read-only, so that it cannot be written on. Generally this is done when mounting a backup disk, to prevent wiping it out by mistake.[5] The way to do it is simply to add the read-only flag at the end of the **mount** command:

```
# mount /dev/cd03 /us -r
```

▪ Unmounting a File System ▪

File systems must be unmounted from time to time. Whenever you do a disk frontal lobotomy (a **format** or a **mkfs**), you've got to unmount the system. **fsck** is best done on a quiescent system, and an unmounted system is even safer. Fortunately, the **umount** syntax is simple. It takes only one argument — the name of the special file (device) to be unmounted:

```
# umount /dev/cd03
```

Whatever **/dev/cd03** was attached to is now a free directory, and **/dev/cd03** is unreachable by the users.

You will not be able to **umount** a file system if any of the following conditions are true:

- You don't have write permission on the device the system is mounted on. You must have super-user privileges to unmount a file system in almost all cases.
- Anyone is using it. This includes you! Generally, you must be in the root file system to **umount** other file systems.
- *Anyone* is using it. This means that if any user has a file open on the file system in question, even the super-user will not be able to unmount it.
- *Anyone is using it.* This means if the *system* has a file open on that file system, you will also be blocked from unmounting it.

---

5 Of course, people who wipe file systems out by mistake also usually forget to mount it read-only in the first place.

How can the system have a file open? Let's say someone is editing a file with **vi**, and you're trying to unmount the **/usr** file system. Since **vi** is located in the **/usr/ucb** directory (on most systems), as long as **vi** is being executed, the system has the binary file **/usr/ucb/vi** open! The user must get out of **vi** for you to be able to unmount **/usr**. Or, for an even trickier example, you won't be able to unmount **/usr/lib** until you kill the printer daemon (**lpdaemon** or **lpsched**), because the daemon's home directory is **/usr/lib**.

/etc/mnttab

The system keeps a binary record in the **/etc/mnttab** file of what file systems are mounted, and when they were mounted. As we've seen, executing the **mount** command with no arguments prints this information out in human-readable form. When the system is brought up after a crash, **/etc/mnttab** still exists, and if it is not reinitialized, the data are there several times over, and you get the following sort of nonsense:

```
$ mount
/        on /dev/xt0a read/write on Mon Oct  1 14:02:38 1984
/usr     on /dev/xt0c read/write on Mon Oct  1 14:02:43 1984
/usr/lib on /dev/xt0e read/write on Mon Oct  1 14:02:43 1984
/xf      on /dev/xt0f read/write on Mon Oct  1 14:02:44 1984
/usr     on /dev/xt0c read/write on Thu Jan 31 17:35:31 1985
/usr/lib on /dev/xt0e read/write on Thu Jan 31 17:35:32 1985
/xf      on /dev/xt0f read/write on Thu Jan 31 17:35:32 1985
/usr     on /dev/xt0c read/write on Thu Jan 31 22:39:50 1985
/usr/lib on /dev/xt0e read/write on Thu Jan 31 22:39:50 1985
/xf      on /dev/xt0f read/write on Thu Jan 31 22:39:51 1985
```

If this is the case on your system, make sure **/etc/mnttab** is being properly erased on each reboot. The simplest way to do that is to put these lines in your **/etc/rc** file:

```
> /etc/mnttab
devnm / | setmnt
```

▪ Handy Shell Programs ▪

/etc/Mount

The idea behind **/etc/Mount** and **/etc/Unmount** are similar. Try to isolate the details of your normally-mounted file systems in a pair of command files. Then, when you're in single-user mode and want to test a program, you can mount all file systems by simply typing:

```
# Mount
```

This eliminates the common error of forgetting to mount one, especially important in this case, because two file systems are mounted *on top of* **/usr** and therefore order is important. This program can also be used in **/etc/rc** when mounting all file systems. Naturally, you must substitute the commands to properly mount *your* file systems on *your* devices. Don't copy ours!

```
mount /dev/xt0c /usr
mount /dev/xt0e /usr/lib
mount /dev/xt0f /usr/spool
mount /dev/xt1b /tmp
mount /dev/xt1c /own
mount /dev/xt1e /ips
mount /dev/xt1f /db
```

/etc/Unmount

The same program in reverse, of course. You wouldn't get far if you tried to **umount /dev/xt0c** before **/dev/xt0f**, so now you won't do that by accident.

```
umount /dev/xt1f
umount /dev/xt1e
umount /dev/xt1c
umount /dev/xt1b
umount /dev/xt0f
umount /dev/xt0e
umount /dev/xt0c
```

free

The **df** command lets you know how many free blocks you have on each file system. Some systems, like XENIX, UTS 2.x, and 4.2 BSD, tell you what *percentage* of free space you have left. This can be more useful, because having 4,000 blocks free may be either good or an imminent disaster, depending on how big your system is. The following little program (a combination of **awk** and **shell**) tells you the number of kilobytes, blocks, and percentage free on any or all file systems:

```
while true
do
        echo ${1:-Total}"\t\c"
        df -t ${1:-} | awk '{
                if (( NR % 2 ) == 1)
                        bl += $4
                else total += $2
                }
        END { kb = bl / 2 ; avg = 100 * (bl/total) ;
        printf "%d KB (%d blocks) free or %d%% of usable space\n"\
                ,kb,bl,avg}'

        if test $# -gt 1
        then shift
        else exit 0
        fi
done
```

If no parameters are given, **free** automatically totals the information for all file systems; otherwise it works for the file systems named on the command line:

```
$ free
Total  28341 KB (56682 blocks) free or 28% of usable space
$ free / /usr /tmp
/       1910 KB (3820 blocks) free or 23% of usable space
/usr    1239 KB (2478 blocks) free or 7% of usable space
/tmp    7349 KB (14698 blocks) free or 89% of usable space
```

Note that this program was written for older (pre-System V) systems, where 512-byte blocks were used, so some arithmetic is done to figure out the number of free kilobytes. If you use 1K blocks, change the line beginning with END to:

```
END { kb = bl ; avg = 100 * (bl/total) ;
```

If you use 4096-byte blocks, change it to:

```
END { kb = bl * 4 ; avg = 100 * (bl/total) ;
```

Also, the system on which this program was written returns **df** output like this:

```
/           (/dev/xt0a ):      3822 blocks    1491 i-nodes
```

If yours has no whitespace between the name of the device and the closing parentheses, change the line reading

```
bl += $4
```

to

```
bl += $3
```

▪ Chapter Summary ▪

In the next chapter we're going to look at one of the most vital system administration tasks — how to shut down the system gracefully (and carefully).

C H A P T E R

6

SHUTTING DOWN THE SYSTEM

How to Be Nice to Your System

Stopping the system "cold" by simply cutting power is not only an invitation to disaster but almost guarantees damage to the UNIX file system. Bringing down the system nicely is an absolute necessity. Since the file system's directory and inode information exists in RAM as well as on disk, it is imperative that the disk version matches the one stored in RAM when the system comes down. You must also have provisions to prevent additional users from logging onto the system after the shutdown warnings have gone out. There are many factors to consider, but first let's examine the basics of a voluntary system shutdown.

Shutdown Fundamentals

In the simplest terms, you shut down a UNIX system by updating each disk's file system information with a **sync** command and doing a *soft kill* on **init**. (A soft kill is an interrupt number 15 or **SIGTERM**, generally done by a command such as **kill -15 1**.) Most systems, though, have a shutdown script created by the computer supplier. It is usually in **/etc/shutdown** and must be performed from the root login and on the system console. This procedure is best done after all users have logged off and all background processes have been stopped.

The system administrator should develop procedures for bringing the system down in an orderly fashion with as little discomfort to the users as possible. If the system is brought down nightly, the system should remain up during normal working hours and be brought down at a reasonably consistent time every night. If the system is normally up around the clock, it is necessary to bring it down from time to time for maintenance. These shutdowns should be scheduled, and the users should have ample warning. As a general rule, never go more than a week without throwing out excess baggage, testing the file system for consistency, and making general repairs.

Since **/etc/shutdown** starts out as a canned shell script, we recommend that you gradually develop your own **shutdown** script. This is not as hard as it sounds. Use the original script as a pattern and add to it as you develop scripts for your particular installation. For example, you'll be adding mounted file systems as your system expands. You're going to want to unmount them before shutting down the system (killing **init**), and what better place than in **/etc/shutdown?** Use the **/etc/Unmount** script from the last chapter as a guide and make things easier.

Don't be afraid to customize your own system. UNIX is uniquely plastic. It was created to be readily programmable, so no two UNIX systems need to be exactly alike. In fact, a good UNIX system administrator molds her machine to fit the needs of her particular installation.

Warn Your Users Ahead of Time

Unless all of your users are within shouting distance, you should place a message in **/etc/motd** (the *m*essage *o*f *t*he *d*ay file that users normally see when they log in) warning users of the scheduled shutdown. Also, **wall** (*w*rite *all*) the users at reasonable time intervals before the shutdown, and once more immediately before initiating the shutdown procedure. Give at least a five-minute "grace" period before shutdown begins. System administrators usually put all this in **/etc/shutdown**. In the simplest form, it looks something like this:

```
echo starting shutdown
/etc/wall<<!
Please log off.  System coming down in 5 minutes.
!
sleep 300
/etc/wall<<!
System coming down now!!
!
sleep 15
cd /
/etc/Unmount
sync; sleep 1
sync
sleep 5
sync
sleep 5
kill -15 1
```

Remember, once the shutdown procedure has started, make sure that you have made provisions to exclude users from logging on. Some systems have a file called **/etc/nologins**, or **/etc/maxusers**, which prevents new logins simply by being on the computer (it is usually created by **/etc/shutdown**). On other systems, you physically turn off all incoming modems. If someone logs on while the system is coming down, they get logged off immediately.

Scheduled shutdowns are the most desirable, but panic shutdowns are inevitable, particularly on large systems. Hanging logins, unsuccessful mount requests, and runaway processes can confuse the system so much that your only hope is to bring it down and restart it again. When doing this, give as much notice as possible, even if it's only a few seconds. The fewer people left stuck in editors, the less work you have when the system comes back up. As a general rule, when things start acting funny, type **sync** from the nearest terminal.[1] Let the users close their files and log off if possible.

Recovering from System Catastrophes

The system administrator must jump into the heat of battle when system catastrophes occur. They can range from minor problems such as hung-up terminals or processes to major disasters such as a head crash. You must keep your head while the world around you comes unraveled.

Your first step to to ascertain exactly what happened. The next step is to carefully formulate a recovery plan. Make too hasty a move and you may find yourself picking up the shattered remains of your system.

▪ About Processes ▪

Each program that runs on your system, no matter how small, is run as a *process*, or separate program with its own input, output, and ''parent'' program that can control it. The user who starts a process is the *owner* of that process and all subsequent children. The owner of a process can terminate (kill) it at any time. Root has the power to kill any and all system processes.

To get information about the processes on the system, you use the **ps** (process status) command. **ps** takes a ''snapshot'' of the system's process table at the instant it's executed. When run without arguments, **ps** shows you information about all your own processes:

```
$ ps
   PID TTY TIME CMD
 25371 12  0:14 -csh
 26023 12  0:14 vi shutdown
 26054 ?   <defunct>
 26055 12  0:00 sh -c ps
 26056 12  0:02 ps
$
```

The leftmost column, labeled **PID**, displays the individual *p*rocess *id*entification numbers: the unique numbers that UNIX assigns while processes exist in the system. The count starts over again after 32767. The **TTY** column tells you which **tty** (or terminal line) the process was initiated from, in this case **/dev/tty12**. **TIME** is simply the total amount of system CPU time that has been used by each process.

1 Any user can **sync** the system; you do not have to be root.

In the **CMD** column, **ps** attempts to print the command line used to start the process. At this point, we are logged in under **csh**, editing a file with **vi**, and we are running the **ps** command under the Bourne shell. This last Bourne shell is actually a subshell created expressly to run the **ps** command while in **vi**, which is why it shows up as a separate **sh -c ps**. **<defunct>** marks a process that ended its existence just before **ps** could determine any information about it aside from its **pid**.

Let's look at a more complex report. **ps -elf** (or **ps -ax** on Berkeley UNIX) shows a great deal of information about all processes running in the system, not just your own. This is what you will usually run as system administrator:

```
$ ps -elf
  S UID   PID  PPID PRI NICE  SZ  WCHAN TTY TIME CMD
  S  0      0     0   1   20   0 12b094 ?  129:38 swapper
  S  0      1     0  39   20  40 200000 ?    3:05 /etc/init
  S   0 21224     1  28   20  36 128a22 co   0:02 getty console console
  S   0 20781     1  28   20  36 128a74 11   0:02 getty /dev/tty11 9600
  S   0 19024     1  39   39  24 200000 12   2:02 cron
  S  12 25371     1  39   20 124 200000 12   0:14 -csh
  S   0 20783     1  28   20  36 128b18 13   0:02 getty /dev/tty13 9600
  S   0 22697     1  28   20  36 128b6a 20   0:02 getty /dev/tty20 9600
  S  12 26023 25371  26   20 260 1119d2 12   0:39 vi shutdown
  S   0    63     1  26   20  56 111502 ?    0:07 /usr/lib/lpsched
  R  12 26047 26040  65   20  88        12   1:15 uucico -r1 -swhuxcc
  S  12 26037     1   0   20  44 115bd8 12   0:01 poll whuxcc
  S  12 26040 26037  30   20  44 115c40 12   0:00 poll whuxcc
  Z  12 26101 26023  20   20   0  10000 ?    <defunct>
  S   0 22927     1  28   20  36 128f42 bi   0:01 getty bip0 bip bip
  S  12 26102 26023  30   20  44 115f7c 12   0:00 sh -c ps -eLf
  R  12 26103 26102  70   20  28        12   0:04 ps -eLf
```

Looks marvelous, doesn't it? All the gory details are written up in the manual, so we won't repeat them. The important columns for you are **S**, **UID**, **PID**, **PPID**, **NICE**, **SZ**, and **WCHAN** (some other columns have been excised due to width restrictions).

The **S** column shows you what process is running at the exact moment of executing **ps**, which always shows **ps** and perhaps something else as well (only one process actually runs at a time, but even **ps** isn't perfect). The **S** column is useful for spotting problems. In this case, the process noted before as being **<defunct>** has the flag **Z**, known colloquially as a *zombie* because it has been killed but refuses to die. When this happens to a process, you should become super-user and attempt to kill it. If you can't kill it as super-user, it is destined to haunt your system until the next reboot, which may be sooner than you think if the process is large and growing. Sometimes zombies die when a device they are waiting for changes state, such as a tape drive or printer. Other letters that are likely to appear here, as detailed in the manual, include **R** (for a running process), **S** (for a sleeping process, which will run when its turn comes or it stops sleeping), and **T** (for a process that has been stopped, usually by someone using the C shell).

The **UID** column shows you who owns the process (by user id number). We know what **PID** means now, and **PPID** is the *previous* process ID, or the "parent" of the process. If the parent process is killed, all child processes started by the parent should also die. Note that in this longer listing, you can trace the evolution of the various processes started from the original **csh** with **PID 25371**.

The **NICE** column shows the "niceness" of a process (default 20). This is related to the priority number because when a program is run with **nice**, its priority number goes higher. A high priority number means a lower actual priority. So just think of the priority number as its place in line: a higher number means it has longer to wait. If you know you will be running a large or long program, you run it at lower priority to be "nice" to other system users. As super-user, you can also start processes off at negative niceness to get them done as quickly as possible:

```
# nice --30 nroff important.file
```

If you have the Berkeley program **renice**, you can change the priority of a program after it has already started (as super-user only):

```
# renice 26023 10
```

This raises the niceness of the **vi** process to 10, making response time faster for editing.

The **SZ**, or size column, shows how much actual memory each process takes up. If you add up all the process sizes, you can get a good idea how much memory is being used. If the total is more memory than you actually have available, your system will slow down because the swapper has to move processes in and out of memory to run them. If you are lucky enough to have a virtual memory system, then only "page"-sized chunks (usually 4 KB) of program get moved out, greatly speeding system operations.

On most systems, programs have *shared text*. In other words, if the same program is being run more than once (even by different users), its "text," or program area, is shared by all processes running it.[2] So even though there are several processes listed as running **getty**, each taking up 36 KB, the *actual* amount of memory in use from all of these is still only 36 KB, plus a bit extra for nonshared space specific to each process. To check this, you can run the **file** program on system programs:

2 Process = text (shared) + data area + context + stacks (user and kernel) + user structure.

```
$ file /bin/*
/bin/adb:       shareable executable
/bin/as:        commands text
/bin/awk:       shareable executable
/bin/calendar:        c program text
/bin/cat:       shareable executable
/bin/cc:        shareable executable
Interrupt
$
```

Since the binary executable files are marked shareable, you have the shared text feature. On other systems, **file** may return a string saying "pure text" or another phrase that means the same thing.

The total memory usage, as reported by the above **ps**, is 744 KB. If you find your processes often add up to more memory than you have available (as reported by the kernel at boot time), you may want to buy more memory for maximum speed.

The last column to discuss is **WCHAN**. It tells what device, or ''channel,'' each process is waiting for. On most systems, what appears in the **ps** listing is a number that is the kernel address of the device driver in question. To use this, you need an address map of your kernel. Some enlightened suppliers have added a routine to the **ps** that prints the actual name of the device being waited for, such as **/dev/lp**.

Hung Processes

A hung process usually manifests itself in a terminal that echoes whatever you type, does nothing useful whatsoever, and cannot be killed or stopped. Like a mad dog, when a user's process becomes hung, it must be destroyed. The proper method is to kill the user's process. It takes three steps.

The first step is running the **who** command to get the *tty* number of the process. The next step is to find the process id number by executing the process status command **ps -a** (**ps -e** in System V). Look for all processes attached to the **tty** the user is logged on to. The last step is to kill the hung process. It may also be necessary to kill other processes owned by the user that may also be affected. In fact, sometimes when you want to be absolutely sure that the hung process is destroyed, you kill all of the user's processes including his login shell, then let him log back on again. If the user is hung in **kermit** (a communications program), the only way to kill the process and free the user is to kill the user's shell.

Imagine that one of your users, Chad, comes to you with his editor hung. No amount of coaxing to **vi** will get it to do anything, so it is time to play Grand Exalted Process Executioner. First, figure out where Chad is logged in:

```
$ who
karen    console Mar 18 19:08
bruce    tty0    Mar 18 18:54
chad     tty1    Mar 18 18:56
```

Next do a **ps -a** to find Chad's process numbers:

```
$ ps -a

PID TTY TIME CMD
212 co  0:07 -sh
250 1   0:07 -sh
213 0   0:07 -sh
298 1   0:19 vi mor.let
342 0   0:02 ps -a
317 co  1:32 vi adm.rep
```

Finally, issue a *sure kill* to all of Chad's processes. Do this by becoming super-user and issuing the **kill -9** (terminate with extreme prejudice) command followed by the process numbers.

```
$ su
Password:
# kill -9 298 250
```

Chad's CRT should complain righteously with a ''killed'' message, followed by a polite new login.

The quick and dirty method to accomplish the same thing: simply turn off the terminal (if it is hardwired with proper modem control) and turn it back on. This logs him off and kills all his processes in most cases. Never do this on IBM and IBM-type (Lee Data) synchronous terminal equipment, however. It upsets the hardware controllers.

Hung Devices

Computers and their peripheral equipment are a long way from perfect. The combination of imperfection talking to imperfection often results in a peripheral getting hung. Hung terminals go deaf and dumb, neither taking nor displaying data. Modems get hung sending data to themselves or sitting off hook without doing anything to recover. Printers go schizophrenic typing crazy graphics. All of these devices have the same problem — they can no longer communicate intelligently with the computer.

Normally two steps are required to bring your peripherals back to sanity. The first step is a hardware reset. Most devices are reset by shutting them off for about 15 seconds and then turning them back on. Some, such as IBM 3270 terminals, have a reset key. If resetting the device fails to return it to its senses, kill the process associated with the device. If you have the **fuser** command, it comes in handy here:

```
# fuser -k -d /dev/tty3
```

This command line does an automatic ''seek and destroy'' on all processes using **/dev/tty3**.

Killing a process related to a device is not without its repercussions. A killed printer process, for instance, can leave a lock file that prevents further printer activity until it is removed (see *Chapter 11* for more details). A terminal that is reset may have the opposite problem — no activity can occur until the process using it has been killed, which then allows a new login message to be displayed.

Paradoxically, modems are hung when they refuse to hang up! Here a little skill goes a long way. Talk to the port that the modem is on by accessing it with the **cu** command. Send the modem its hangup sequence. In the case of a D.C. Hayes or compatible modem, try the following sequence:

```
$ su
Password: KissMe
# cu -l /dev/modem
Connected
ATH
~.
#
```

or the direct approach:

```
# echo "ATH" > /dev/modem
```

Either sequence attempts to send the letters ''ATH'' to the modem, which should cause it to hang up the phone. If neither works, turn off the modem and then turn it back on. As with the printer, lock files may still have to be removed (see *Chapter 12*).

▪ System Crashes ▪

Small UNIX systems seldom crash. They core dump at the drop of a hat, but they don't crash. The tri-nightly crashing of microcomputers went away with MMUs (*M*emory *M*anagement *U*nits prevent wild pointers from bringing the system crashing down like a falling redwood tree). Large systems are more sophisticated, so they seldom core dump, but they do crash with painful regularity. Getting a million dollars worth of silicon, copper, gold, aluminum, and steel to play the same song is not possible at all times and under all circumstances. When a large system gets confused, it only has one action left to defend itself — it crashes. Elegant systems do a great deal of precrash juggling, such as closing files and writing open editor files out to error files to be recovered later. They then attempt to log the cause of the crisis.

But even the most sophisticated systems seldom do that final **sync**. The last **sync** puts a good copy of the directory and inode information on disk. Because many crashes occur so quickly, nothing gets updated, no files get closed, and the total result is a disaster. As a result, the file system becomes the major victim of the crash. Broken inodes lay scattered around the system, and the system administrator is left with the cleanup job.

A crash is *imminent* when the system begins slowing down precipitously, when people start getting logged off mysteriously, when almost every command yields a core dump, or when garbage starts appearing on people's terminals. At this point get as many people as possible logged off, and head for the console. If you have a chance, type **sync** a few times for luck. If time is really tight, remember that **sync** works from any terminal — you don't have to be super-user to run it.

A crash is *complete* when everything stops. Sometimes your terminal echoes characters but nothing runs. Sometimes the disk makes a repetitive sound of seeking but not finding anything. At this point you're safer rebooting than letting strange broken programs run. They might erase your disk! Note to advanced administrators: if the system hangs you may want to force a dump as the final act of the crash so you can analyze it with the **crash** command later.

To recover from a system crash, your first step is to bring the system back up into single-user mode and leave it there while doing an **fsck** (or equivalent). Do *not* get in the habit of relying on the **-y** option. As broken inodes appear, make note of the disk partition and location of the node that has to be cleared, if possible. Expect to see many temporary files irrevocably lost. These files are normally invisible to the user and their loss will not be mourned.

The two areas most subject to damage are the root and spooler areas. If damage is severe you will have to reboot UNIX, perhaps a number of times, while doing an **fsck**. Some lost files are saved in **lost+found** directories. Files that are lost ''forever'' have to be restored from the previous evening's backup tape (or disk). System crashes are the best argument for regular system backups.

▪ Chapter Summary ▪

We have seen how to bring up a UNIX system and shut it down. Mounting and unmounting file systems is no longer a mystery. With the basics behind us, now it's time to take a longer view of the day-to-day running of a UNIX system.

C H A P T E R 7

ADDING AND REMOVING USERS FROM THE SYSTEM

Adding New Users

A user leaves his mark all over the UNIX system. He has an entry in the password file (**/etc/passwd**), another in the group file (**/etc/group**), a mail box in **/usr/spool/mail** (pre-System V) or **/usr/mail** (System V), and a home directory where he lives containing at the very least a profile (**.profile**) that instructs UNIX about his environment. All of these must be created by the system administrator to officially add a new user to the system.

How do these entries and files fit together when a user logs in? The **login** program goes to the **/etc/passwd** file to get information about the user. **/etc/passwd** gives **login** the user's home directory and tells it which shell to execute, Bourne shell, C shell, or restricted shell. Armed with this information, **login** moves to the user's home directory and starts up his shell, which then executes his **.profile**. The profile executes a series of commands initializing the user's environment, such as his prompt, the type of terminal he is using, the settings for his editor, and his search path. As you can see, information critical to a user's environment is also critical to create the files needed for the login process.

Although UNIX system administration tasks vary a little from machine to machine and installation to installation, most tasks, such as adding and removing user logins, are common to every UNIX machine.

Keep It Simple, SA

Imagine that it is 3:30 Friday afternoon. You are an average user, busily completing an intensive programming project. Putting the final touches on your intricate program, you relish the thought of getting it all done today so you can enjoy the first peaceful weekend in months without the project on your mind. Suddenly you notice the response time on your terminal slows to a snail's pace. Although you try to go on with your project, the response time becomes intolerably slow, and your blood pressure starts to rise. Impatiently you do a succession of

```
$ ps -a
```

commands to see what is slowing up the system, revealing what you suspected all along — one user is hogging the system with a CPU-and disk-intensive task (usually **nroff** or one of the language compilers). Time drags on as you wait for the user to finish, but he or she continues to hog the system, oblivious to the needs of other users. If you don't find out who that user is, you can throw your peace of mind out the window. By doing a **who** command, you have access to the current users (by login name), terminals, and login times:

```
$ who
susan      tty10      Sep  2 14:15
david      bip0       Sep  2 12:39
pecos      tty14      Sep  2 15:27
```

If the login names are clearly descriptive, such as last names, it is easy to locate the user in the company's phone directory and yell at him or her for hogging too much CPU and disk space. The user (hopefully) yields his piggy process, you can finish your project on time, and our little story will have a happy ending. But what if that user's login name is ''wizard'' or ''mouse''? Finding that user is not only going to waste a lot of your time, it's going to waste even more of the system administrator's time. Your project won't be completed on time, and our story will have an unhappy ending.

The moral of this story is to keep user login names simple and straightforward. It's better for you and for your users. If the most efficient system administration possible is your prime directive, even pedestrian tasks like adding users to the UNIX system requires some forethought. Reliable and clearly descriptive login names make life easier for everyone, especially in large systems with hundreds of users. Enough said.

Some UNIX systems provide a self-explanatory, menu-driven, screen-mapped utility to add users to the system, frequently called **adduser**. It is found in **/etc**. On other UNIX systems you must do the job manually with **root** privilege. We'll first show you the slow, manual way to do this, then give you an **adduser** program you can type in and use.

Entering Users to the /etc/passwd File

First things first. The manual entry of new users starts at the password file, requiring super-user privilege. Start by opening **/etc/passwd** with an editor.[1] Before you enter any data to **passwd**, be sure to do a search on the new user's last name to make sure she won't get mixed up with someone else. **grep** or a simple search within the editor does this very nicely.[2] Even more important is making sure the new user-id

1 Do not hold **/etc/passwd** open for very long. It can be fatal to your system.

2 Sophisticated **adduser** utilities do this for you automatically.

number does not match one currently on the system. If two users have the same user-id number, only the first one (as you read the **/etc/passwd** file) is the official owner of any files created by either one.

Once you have established the uniqueness of the new user's proposed login name and user-id number, you are ready to enter data. **/etc/passwd** entries have the following fields:

- login name
- encrypted password
- user-id number
- group-id number
- comments
- home directory
- login shell

A typical **/etc/passwd** entry, when completed, looks something like this:

```
khunter:bm%q4Bc03A?:12:14:Karen Hunter:/us/khunter:/bin/csh
```

Let's examine each field at a time.

khunter is the name under which Karen Hunter will log in as user. It is good practice not only to use a straightforward login name such as the user's first initial and last name, but to be consistent with your other login names as well. Inconsistencies are easier to pinpoint that way.

The second field, **bm%q4Bc03A?**, is the password field, unintelligible because it is stored in encrypted form. There are several ways to install user passwords. One method is to leave the password field empty, depending on the user to add his own password voluntarily. To do this, you type in every field but the password field, like this:

```
khunter::12:24:Karen Hunter:/us/khunter:/bin/csh
```

The empty password field is a "null password." Now the user can enter her password into the system with the **passwd** command. Of course, you have to be prepared to go back and check the password file to verify that a password was added. The user may try to duck out of entering a password so she can log on directly! On pre-System III UNIX, you can stop our user from doing this by adding anything to the password field to prevent her from logging on. The word VOID does very nicely, and is also clearly visible:

```
khunter:VOID:12:.....
```

Karen Hunter will not be able to log in until she sees you. Then you can make sure she enters a password.

System III and later UNIX lets you handle the user password installation another way. It gives you an elaborate series of password aging commands. To make sure our user enters her password, one option is adding a comma and two periods to the password field when making a new user entry in **/etc/passwd**:

```
khunter:,..:12:...
```

This makes the null password obsolete immediately by telling the **login** program that the password is aged. A new password will be requested from the new user the moment she logs on.

Yet another way to enter a password is to use the **passwd** command as super-user. When you run the **passwd** command as an ordinary user, UNIX responds by asking you for your old password to be sure that you are who it thinks you should be. It then asks you for the new password twice. When the super-user uses the **passwd** command, it takes on a different flavor. Although the super-user can't read another user's password, he can change any password on the system using the **passwd** command with the name of the user as an argument:

```
# passwd jsmith
New password: tribble
Retype new password: tribble
#
```

The super-user will not be asked the old password name. He only needs to enter the new password name twice. If a password is entered that the system feels is too short, it asks repeatedly for a new one that is long enough. Many systems insist on a 6- to 8-character alphanumeric mix.

The third field, **12**, is the **user_id** field. It must be an integer less than 65535, and it is usually the next available sequential user number. This *uid* number is used internally by the system to designate all file and directory ownerships. If you are entering users manually, sometimes the addition of a new user-id number requires visually scanning the list and taking the next available number. On larger machines, employee numbers might be your best bet (especially handy if, in the future, you ever need to merge machines). Each uid must be unique or two login names will refer to the same files. The user's employee or badge number is a good candidate for a unique uid number.

The fourth field, **14**, is the group-id number, taken from the **/etc/group** file. Use the number of the specific group required. (For example, if the system has an editing group designated as group number 12, each member of the editing group has 12 as the group number in his or her **/etc/passwd** entry.) Even if you don't need groups right away, it's a good idea to indicate an **other** category for this field with an arbitrary integer, such as 100, because later on it's easier to search and replace a specific number. Naturally, you also have the option of leaving this field blank.

The fifth field, **Karen Hunter**, is a comment field. Usually the user's full name is inserted here to positively identify the user with her login name. Other data such as department name and phone extension are also helpful.

The sixth field, **/us/khunter,** is the user's base or **HOME** directory. When the user logs in, she is automatically placed in this directory. It also is the directory defined as **HOME** in the user's **.profile** file.

The last field, **/bin/csh**, is the shell assigned to the user when logging in.[3] It is usually **/bin/sh** for the Bourne shell, **/bin/csh** for the C shell, or **/bin/rsh** for restricted shell. If the shell field is left blank, most systems default to the Bourne shell.

There are two places you can specify that a certain shell be used at login time: the last field in the **/etc/passwd** file and in **.profile**. The **/etc/passwd** file is a much better place to do the job. When **/bin/csh** is found by **login** in the **/etc/passwd** file, the C shell becomes the user's shell immediately. Then all it needs to do is search for **.cshrc** and **.login** in the user's HOME directory. However, if **/bin/csh** is executed from **.profile,** an extra process is spawned needlessly, which makes the login process slower.[4] Therefore, specifying shells in **/etc/passwd** entries is more efficient.

Any executable program can be used as a shell. If you have a user who only wants to work with the **wondercalc** program, simply put the path name **/usr/local/wondercalc** instead of **/bin/sh**.

Here are some typical **/etc/passwd** entries with various shells in the last field:

```
bruce:jlc4EEKiPwiRw:20:20:Bruce H Hunter:/us/bruce:
karen:MlNyd0pc7tgiE:21:20:Karen L B Hunter:/us/karen:/bin/sh
david:zCz.rpnUP1s22:23:22:David Fiedler:/us/david:/bin/csh
susan:/aik3QiekNOYU:24:22:Susan Fiedler:/us/susan:
chad:Vzqv.YMBLNDe2:27:30:my kid:/us/chad:/bin/rsh
```

If you're going to designate the Bourne shell, you might as well leave this field blank, because **login** gives you the Bourne shell first.

A final warning: don't keep the password file open for longer than necessary. If **/bin/passwd** or any other program that writes to **/etc/passwd** is called, the system will get confused. One day on a UTS machine, an expensive UNIX consultant we brought in left the **passwd** file open for over an hour. The system got terribly confused, losing track of **root**'s uid. Finally the system crashed (a major disaster on a mainframe), putting two hundred users (and the consultant) out of business on the spot. We had to rebuild the entire machine from the bits and pieces that were left.

Adding the New User to the /etc/group File

Once the user has been entered to the **/etc/passwd** file, you need to add her to **/etc/group**. The **/etc/group** entry is similar to the **/etc/passwd** entry. They both use the colon as a field separator. Each group entry has the following form:

---

3 **csh** is found in various places on different systems. Since it is considered an add-on, it is frequently found in **/usr/ucb**. You may have to use **find** or **where** to locate it.

4 Unless **login** is told otherwise, the user's shell automatically becomes the Bourne shell. If the C shell is specified when **.profile** is executed, it is necessary to create another process to accommodate the change to C shell before it goes to the user's **HOME** directory to look for **.login** and **.cshrc**.

```
group_name:encrypted_password:group_id_no:user1,user2,user3
```

As super-user, enter the data with an editor. A typical entry looks like this:

```
edit:VOID:12:hogan,singer,weaver
```

When a new member needs to be added to the group, you simply append the name to the end of the **/etc/group** entry.

Notice that the **encrypted_password** field is VOID. Group memberships are usually determined by the system administrator. This prevents people from crossing groups, since no password will work.[5] When a group has an encrypted password field and directories restricted to that group, the group's files and directories cannot be entered by nonmembers.

Creating a Directory for the User

Now you need to create the home directory for the user. To create and give Karen Hunter ownership of her home directory, go to the directory above the intended home directory and follow this command sequence:

```
# cd /user
# mkdir khunter
# chown khunter khunter
# chgrp khunter edit
# cd khunter
# cp /usr/local/stdprofile .profile
# chown khunter .profile
```

The **mkdir** command is used to create the directory, and then the ownership of the directory is given to Karen Hunter by the **chown** (*ch*ange *own*er) command. A **.profile** is created using the **cp** command to copy **/usr/local/stdprofile**, already created earlier by the system administrator as a standard profile for new users. A typical **stdprofile** might look like this:

```
PATH=:/bin:/usr/bin:/usr/ucb:/usr/games:/usr/local:.:
EXINIT='set shell=/bin/sh noai redraw bf opt wm=12 scroll=22'
PAGER=more -c
EDITOR=/bin/vi
TERM=wyse
export PATH EXINIT PAGER EDITOR TERM
```

Ownership of the file is given to the user by the command line **chown khunter .profile**. The user is now free to modify her **.profile** further to suit her personal needs.

---

5 See *Chapters 4* and *9* for more information.

Creating a Mail File for the New User

Now go to **/usr/spool/mail** (**/usr/mail** in System V) and create a mail file for the new user. To give a mail file to Karen Hunter, do the following:

```
# cd /usr/spool/mail
# create khunter
# chown khunter khunter
# chgrp mail khunter
# chmod 660 khunter
```

Once this new user has an empty file in **/usr/spool/mail**, she can receive mail. Changing the file mode to 660 prevents anyone else from reading her mail.[6] The line **chown khunter khunter** gives her ownership of that file.

The End Result

All of these operations result in a complete computer work environment for the new user. She has a password file entry in **/etc/passwd** that locates her *HOME* directory and assigns her a shell. She has a *HOME* directory, a profile, a group file entry, and a mailbox. Karen Hunter is ready to start work on the UNIX system. If she chooses, she is free to add to or modify this computer work environment to suit her needs.

▪ Removing Users from the System ▪

Removing users from the system is also a day-to-day administration task involving two essential steps: saving all the user's files on offline backup media and removing the user from the system. Sophisticated UNIX systems have utilities (usually called **rmuser** or **deluser**) to remove the user's file tree, password entry, group entry, and mailbox. If these utilities are absent from the system, you need to do the job ''from scratch.''

Back Up Data Before You Remove It

Before removing anything, copy the user's entire tree to tape or floppy disk. A user's contribution to a company represents a significant company investment. Perhaps a new user will come in expecting to start up where the former user left off. An efficient backup system allows you to present new users with all the information they need to breathe new life into old projects. It's always a good idea to back up data before you destroy it. You might need it again! For this special case, the fastest way to back up is to use **find** with the **-cpio** option:

```
# find /usr/khunter -user khunter -cpio /dev/tape
```

---

6 See section on permissions in *Chapter 9*.

If the new user is starting work right away, simply change the old user's login name and home directory in **/etc/passwd**, change the password and you're done. No **chown** commands have to be issued because the actual user id number is the same (unless employee numbers are used).

Look Before You Leap

After copying the user's file tree, you need to go just above the user's home directory. Because you are doing a mass deletion, be sure that you remove only what is necessary. Always use the **ls** command before removing any files so you know exactly what you are removing.

To remove Karen Hunter from our system, we do the following:

```
# cd /usr
# ls -al khunter
total 125
drwxr-x--- 12 khunter        576 Sep  8 05:13 .
drwxr-xr-x 27 bruce          512 Jun 28 05:13 ..
-rw-rw-rw-  1 khunter        455 Aug 28 03:16 .cshrc
-rw-rw-rw-  1 khunter         76 Jun 20 00:41 .login
-rw-rw-rw-  1 khunter          8 May  6 20:50 .logout
-rw-r--r--  1 khunter          0 Feb  6  1984 .news_time
-rw-rw-r--  1 khunter        899 Sep 10 17:07 .newsrc
-rwxr-xr-x  1 khunter        326 Feb 27  1985 .profile
drwxrwxrwx  2 khunter        176 Oct 18 20:42 C
drwxrwxrwx  2 khunter         32 Oct 10 16:19 Doc
drwxrwxrwx  2 khunter        160 Oct 15 19:52 HCR
drwxrwxrwx  2 khunter        224 Oct 18 19:23 Letter
drwxrwxrwx  2 khunter         80 Oct 17 21:45 Sysad
drwxrwxrwx  2 khunter         64 Oct 15 18:36 bin
-rw-r--r--  1 khunter      18737 Oct 17 10:03 chron
-rw-r--r--  1 khunter      18666 Oct 14 13:50 chron.bak
-rwxr-xr-x  1 khunter         37 Oct 15 19:28 dsp
```

All 16 **khunter**-owned files and directories can easily be seen and inspected.

Search and Destroy

Now the **rm** command can quickly remove all **khunter**-owned files and directories in this area:

```
# cd /usr
# rm -rf khunter
```

Using **rm** rather than **rm -r** or **rm -rf** adds an extra cushion of safety, because it forces you to go into each subdirectory, one at a time, to remove the contents, until you finally end up at the base directory. Remember, the **rm** command with the **-rf** option does a no-questions-asked recursive removal of all files and directories so you have to be extra careful when using it.

After the directories and files are removed from **/usr/khunter**, go to **/etc/group** in an editor and do a global removal of the user's login name:

```
# ed /etc/group
247
1,$s/[\,,:]khunter//g
w
231
q
#
```

In this command line you are substituting the null string (or nothing) for the string **khunter**. Now go to **/usr/spool/mail** and remove the **khunter** mailbox from the system:

```
# cd /usr/spool/mail
# rm khunter
```

Finally, when you remove the user's entry from **/etc/passwd**, she is gone from the system. Should you fail to complete each one of these steps, you will leave bits and pieces of trash all around the system to clutter and confuse you later. To make sure there are no extra files lying around, check with the **find** command:

```
# find / -user 12 -print
```

Any file that is still owned by userid **12** (**khunter**'s old uid) will be reported.

▪ Changing Passwords ▪

Passwords have a limited lifespan. After awhile it's natural for some users to get careless. It's not uncommon to mistakenly type in a password instead of a name in response to the **login** prompt. Now any one who happens to be standing near the terminal can see what the password is! You also have to be on the alert for the usual system mischief by system abusers. Your users may fall victim to the old Trojan horse technique, a shell script written by a curious system abuser that sneakily emulates the login and password sequence for the purpose of capturing user lognames and passwords. Determined system abusers often pick up passwords by glancing over the shoulder of a user entering his password. So it is good insurance to change passwords fairly often. We'll delve into this in the chapter on system security.

▪ Handy Shell Programs ▪

fickle_finger

While not as fancy as Berkeley **finger** or UTS **whois**, this program makes it a bit easier to find information about a user from the password file. Naturally, the more information stored with each entry, the better:

```
grep $1 /etc/passwd | cut -d: -f5
```

Why not call it **finger** (or **whois)** if you don't have a program by that name already?

sortpw

If you keep adding users by hand, your password file will eventually start looking confusing, even if it really isn't. While this won't do anything for the system, it will make your job easier. It sorts the password file by user id, leaving a backup copy in **/tmp** just in case. Since it modifies the password file, it should only be run when you're the sole user on the system:

```
cp /etc/passwd /tmp
sort -nt: +2 /etc/passwd -o /etc/passwd
```

adduser

Here's a simple little **adduser** program. It doesn't even look in the password file to find the next user id, preferring to let the administrator make that determination. But it gives you an easily understandable starting point for your own modifications.

```
USERBASE=/own     # where all your user directories will go
if [ $# -lt 1 ]
then
        echo "Login Name: \c"
        read NAME
else NAME=$1
fi
echo "Userid Number: \c"
read UID
echo "Group number: \c"
read GRP
echo "Extended Finger Information: \c"
read FINGER
echo "Login shell (enter /bin/sh (default) or /bin/csh): \c"
```

```
read SHELL
echo "Updating /etc/passwd..."
if mkdir /etc/ptmp   # fails if passwd command running
then
      cp /etc/passwd /etc/pw$$
      echo "$NAME::$UID:$GRP:$FINGER:$USERBASE/$NAME:$SHELL" \
            >> /etc/pw$$
      ln /etc/passwd /etc/opasswd
      ln /etc/pw$$ /etc/passwd
      rmdir /etc/ptmp
else
      echo "/etc/passwd file in use, try again later"
      exit 1
fi
echo "Now set initial password..."
passwd $NAME
echo "Initializing Home Directory"
mkdir $USERBASE/$NAME
chmod 775 $USERBASE/$NAME
echo "Initializing mail directory"
cp /dev/null /usr/spool/mail/$NAME
chmod 660 /usr/spool/mail/$NAME
echo "Initializing default .profile"
cat >>$USERBASE/$NAME/.profile <<!
HOME=$USERBASE/$NAME
TERM=
MAIL=/usr/spool/mail/$NAME
export TERM MAIL HOME
!
echo "Initializing .cshrc"
cat >>$USERBASE/$NAME/.cshrc <<!
source /.stdcshrc
setenv HOME $USERBASE/$NAME
setenv MAIL /usr/spool/mail/$NAME
!
echo "Changing ownership..."
chown $NAME $USERBASE/$NAME
chgrp $GRP $USERBASE/$NAME
chown $NAME /usr/spool/mail/$NAME
chgrp mail  /usr/spool/mail/$NAME
chown $NAME $USERBASE/$NAME/.profile $USERBASE/$NAME/.cshrc
chgrp $GRP  $USERBASE/$NAME/.profile $USERBASE/$NAME/.cshrc
```

▪ Chapter Summary ▪

Now that we have the new user comfortably on the system, let's examine how to best preserve the data he or she creates. In the next chapter we discuss how to back up the system.

CHAPTER 8

BACKUPS

An Introduction to Backup Philosophy

Computers exist to create, store, and disseminate data, the heart of a business. Backups preserve that precious data and keep you in business. There are many ways to back up data in UNIX, but whatever the method, the reason you back up a system is so you can put it all back together should the system come crashing down or data be lost or corrupted. All files, directories, and file systems can be restored fully *if* your system is properly backed up. It's more useful and inexpensive than a complete DP center insurance policy.

Data loss is far more common than you might think. Often it is due to accidents and just plain carelessness by users, but it's not confined to users alone. When those with super-user power lose data, they generally do it in a big way, such as losing an entire file system! Data loss also occurs when the system crashes. Small single-user machines seldom crash, but large ones do with frightening regularity. The more users you have, the more potential you have for crashes. UNIX system administrators on large machines need to be prepared to restore the system, piece by piece, at the drop of a hat.

Fortunately, UNIX is a versatile operating system, so there are numerous backup and archive commands that allow you to back up all of the system or part of it, from one file to an entire file tree. Some of these include **cpio**, **dd**, **dump**, **find**, **tar**, and **volcopy**.

Although you can use these directly on a command line, you probably will opt to choose the commands you want for your system and incorporate them into your own customized backup shell scripts. This keeps backups consistent, an important point when you want to restore data.

Determining the best backup technique for your system depends on many factors. The time you decide to spend on backups must be balanced by the time it takes to do a restore. In other words, a quick, easy backup scheme will backfire on you when you end up spending hours restoring the system. Small UNIX systems can get by with a nightly, cyclic backup approach, but larger UNIX systems require a more sophisticated set of overlapping backup programs to protect data adequately in the event of a hardware crash. Two hundred users working on 4 completely different projects require a different backup technique from 20 users working on 1 project. Data processing installations are data intensive and require specific backup approaches that are not necessary on program development installations. And so on.

As you can see, in order to devise the best backup strategy for a machine, a system administrator needs to be armed with more than just a list of UNIX backup commands. She needs to be able to make intelligent choices. So before we look at the backup commands, let's delve into some behind-the-scenes backup strategies.

▪ A Little or a Lot? ▪

There are two basic backup options available to you — you can back up all of the system or part of it. Following are those schemes and common variations:

Full: Full (unqualified) system backups back up everything on the system, including UNIX itself.

Partial: Partial system backups are anything less than a full system backup. These include:

- Qualified system backups back up all file systems other than root, along with some UNIX files and directories that are subject to frequent modification, such as **/etc/passwd**, **/etc/group**, and **/etc/inittab**.
- Incremental backups are a specialized form of partial backup, copying files based on the last time the file was modified, written, or read.
- Walking backups copy different parts of the file systems on different nights.

Because of the flexibility of the UNIX system, you can perform each backup method in a variety of ways. Consider the full backup. If you do a **tar** dump from the root file system, you can do a full backup of the entire system, but you'll probably run out of tape first! However, full backups can also be made up of a series of partial backups. On mainframes and superminis, the magnetic media is reel-to-reel tape. Full backups could never fit on one tape, so they are done in sections, each section sized to fit comfortably on a single tape.[1] On smaller machines, you may find yourself using

---

1 We assume that you are using triple-density (6250 bytes per inch), 2400-foot tape reels, which are a mainframe standard. Each reel holds about 170 megabytes. An average working mainframe for non-DP use requires about a dozen reels (more than 5 miles of tape) to fully back it up!

cartridge tapes or even floppy diskettes for backup. Let's go into some of these approaches in a little more detail.

Full Backups Versus Partial Backups

Full backups are *unqualified*. This means that they copy everything, UNIX proper and all user areas — something like eating a watermelon whole: rind, seeds, and all. Full backups are often done to checkpoint and document the system status at particular points in time. On the average, they can be done every month for systems with over 36 simultaneous users and every 3 to 6 months for smaller systems.[2] Some SAs choose to do one a day. It's up to you and the management to decide what is best for your site. Of the two major backup approaches, a partial backup is more practical for most types of everyday work. It gives an up-to-date copy of all the rest of the system, including parts of UNIX that are modified frequently, such as **/etc/passwd**. One thing even a full backup won't do is copy the system so that it can be reloaded if your disk is completely erased. A restore from the distribution tape is necessary to get UNIX running again so a file system restore can be done.

▪ Partial Backups ▪

Partial backups are the most versatile backup method open to system administrators. They are one of the many ways SAs begin customizing and optimizing their system operations.

What if you have a system with two user areas, each around half a backup tape in size? Should you try to cram them both on one tape with a "best-fit" algorithm or should you go ahead and use two tapes, one for each file system?

It is always best if partial backups are separated along mounted system divisions. Best-fit algorithms that cram as much data on tape as possible have their uses, but not in this case. Should the system go down, it is much faster and easier to restore when each file system is on its own clearly labeled tape. Otherwise you waste a lot of time sifting through directories, then cutting and pasting your file systems back together. Tapes are cheap compared to the time wasted by you and all the other users while the computer is down.

Incremental Backups

Incremental backups are selective partial backups. The modification date of a file is the date the file was made or modified (touched), and this is the date on which incremental backups are based. A Tuesday evening backup covers all files touched on Tuesday. An incremental backup on Monday evening should cover three calendar days (Saturday, Sunday, and Monday) to take care of the work performed by weekend workers. Be sure to run backups that cover holiday periods, too.

---

2 If all else fails, don't forget that you can restore UNIX proper from the original distribution tape, instead of from a full backup. The distribution tape is neither tired nor degraded from constant use.

Incremental backups save tape and time, and at first they seem to be a tremendously appealing backup method. You only copy what has been touched or modified, thereby preserving a constant file update. Why not rely on nightly incremental backups supplemented with monthly permanent backups? While this is a common practice, you must be aware of potential hidden pitfalls.

Picture a user coming in to you with a tale of woe about a lost directory. You look for it on yesterday's incremental backup and it is nowhere to be found. Interrogation of the user reveals that he doesn't remember when he accessed the directory last, but it was a very long time ago. Now you have a big problem. How many permanent monthly tapes are you going to have to go through before you finally find the darned thing?

This story is far from unusual. The larger the system, the greater the incidence of user carelessness such as forgotten passwords and misplaced directories. Qualified backups take longer, but they work better. If your system falls down, it is faster and easier for you to restore with qualified backups. In the event of a head crash, the worst disaster of all, a qualified backup along with the UNIX distribution tape will have you back in business as soon as a replacement disk can be found. If your system has enough hardware redundancy (a spare disk on hand), you can be back in business in a few hours, even on the largest systems.

▪ Backup Schedules ▪

In an ideal world, with an unlimited supply of free tapes and an infinite storage area, backups would be no problem whatsoever. Unqualified backups of the entire system would be done every night and stored permanently! In the real world, backup media cost money, and you quickly run out of storage space. So, you fudge a little.

An overlapping backup strategy is always the safest way to go, even on small machines with only one to eight users. Combine two or three backup techniques, and you increase your chances of being able to rebuild your machine. Most backup schemes combine regularly scheduled qualified backups with one or two supplemental partial backups. In addition, one current set of full backup tapes should *always* be stored off premises in case of a fire or major disaster. We use the word *tape* in this context to refer to any removable backup media including tapes and floppies.

Let's examine two hypothetical backup schedules in detail, one for a small UNIX system and one for an extremely large one.

Backing Up Smaller UNIX Systems

Small UNIX systems have about 32 megabytes of disk with about 1 megabyte of memory. Systems of this size generally have 1 to 10 active users. A safe, minimum backup schedule involves 4 backup steps:

Nightly:	Partial backups done nightly and reused week to week.
Weekly:	Incremental backups covering the previous week and stored off premises until the end of the month, when they may be reused.
Monthly:	Incremental backups done monthly and stored off premises until the next full backup.
Quarterly:	Full backup stored off premises.

A nightly backup is done each day of the week to ensure that all new files are captured. At the beginning of a new week, you tape over your old tapes (on Monday, you write over the previous Monday's backup, and so on). To reinforce the weekly backups, you have another set of permanent backups, done monthly, and stored off premises for an indefinite period. The weekly tapes allow you to recycle the daily tapes without worry.

As long as your system is stored on removable media away from the physical system, you are safe from disaster. You can re-use monthly tapes after 3 to 6 months or so, depending on the value of the media and your site's needs. Naturally, you should do a full backup at that time. Assuming that you do the full backups after 3 months, you will need 12 tapes altogether: 5 for the dailies, 4 for the weeklies, 3 for the monthlies, plus however many tapes (usually 2 or 3) it takes to make the full backup, *times 2*.[3] Why? What happens if your system crashes while making the full backup (it's happened to us)? So you make the *new* full backup on the extra tapes, after which you can recycle the monthlies and the old full backup tapes. Buy 20 tapes when you get your system, and you'll not only get a quantity discount, but you will also have enough for emergencies. Remember, *don't* reuse your *old* full backup tapes until you have verified that the new ones are readable.

You can replace your hardware with a check from the insurance company, but once your data files are lost, they are lost forever! Incidentally, it takes all day to do a full floppy backup of a small machine, but it takes less than an hour on one extended length tape cartridge.

Backing Up a Very Large UNIX System

Large UNIX systems are another animal altogether. Mainframe UNIX systems with more than one bank of disk drives are not uncommon. Administrators on large UNIX installations must stay alert to keep data safe. A minimum backup schedule for one mainframe UTS UNIX system with about 200 users runs something like this:

Nightly:	Partial backups done nightly and reused week to week.

3 So if it takes 3 tapes for a full backup, you will need at least 12+(3*2) = 18 tapes for 3 months' worth of backups.

Weekly: Partial backups stored until next month and then recirculated.

Monthly: Full backups stored permanently off premises.

These are *supplemented* with some kind of specialized backups of the user file systems, such as incremental backups. On systems with overlayed operating systems like V-VM (UTS/VM), a byte-for-byte copy technique is often employed in addition to a standard UNIX copy technique. The VM **DDR** copy command copies a disk pack verbatim. The boot track on these machines is not in UNIX format, so it has to be **DDR**ed in order to copy it. It takes about 12 tapes and a little longer than 1 hour, including mounting and unmounting tapes, to do a partial backup of a mainframe UTS UNIX system.

Other Systems

Between the extremes of small and large systems are the minicomputers. Their backup methods are the same, but the tape quantities and speed vary with system size. Most minis use 1600 bpi tapes, good for storing about 40 MB.[4] Since a typical mini has anywhere from 80 to 1,000 MB of disk storage, it takes between a half hour to 2 hours for a full backup. This time also depends on how fast the tape drive is.

▪ Backup Media ▪

The size of your computer system generally determines what type of backup media the manufacturer provides. Small systems typically come with one floppy drive or cartridge tape drives. If you have the option (and the money), we recommend reel-to-reel tapes for any computer system serving over 16 simultaneous users. Available backup media are:

- 1/2-inch reel-to-reel tape
- floppy diskette
- tape cartridge
- removable disk pack
- removable cartridge disk

Let's discuss the pros and cons of each.

---

4 BPI (bytes per inch) stands for the byte density stored on tape. If it is a 1600-bpi tape, then 1600 bytes can be stored on one linear inch of tape. As of 1985, mainframes have adopted 6250-bpi as the default density. Still, 1600 bpi is your best guarantee of portability.

Reel-to-Reel Tape

There are two types of reel-to-reel tape, conventional (start-stop) and streamer. The difference is in the way they operate. A start-stop tape writes a buffer's worth of data at a time, leaving gaps between the blocks of data. A streamer sends data in literally a constant stream to the tape. The ''best'' UNIX backup media is conventional (start-stop) 9-track, 1/2-inch reel-to-reel tape at 1600 bpi. 1600 bpi is the only tape density that is guaranteed to be universally readable from one machine to another. Streamers might be better for your application because they are faster and can store more data per tape, but *only* if they can also function in conventional mode for portability.

Tapes run quickly and quietly in the background with no attention required from the system administrator or system operators except mounting and unmounting. They are very fast. IBM and Amdahl mainframes read in tape at 200 feet per second. Tape-to-tape copies can be made in 5 minutes. Tape is the cheapest magnetic medium available — at $23.00 a tape (2400 feet long), a dollar's worth of tape can store over 7 megabytes! Unfortunately, the hardware for these tapes is very expensive, with a decent unit costing at least $10,000. For this reason, reel-to-reel tapes are used only with larger computers.

Floppy Diskette

The slowest, most inconvenient backup method uses floppy diskettes. Floppies cost only about $2.00 each, but hold about 100 kilobytes per dollar. They are much more expensive than any other backup medium. They require constant attention, and it takes several *cartons* of floppies and hours of time to do an unqualified backup of even a small UNIX system. Their only saving grace is that floppy disk drives are the cheapest backup hardware available at a few hundred dollars. Therefore, they are commonly used on small systems. However, diskettes are generally incompatible if you try to take them from one computer to another, sometimes even if the computers are from the same manufacturer.

Cartridge Tape

Cartridge tapes are a good compromise between reel-to-reel tape and floppy diskettes. Each 4-by-6-inch cartridge easily slips into the drive slot like a video cassette. They are reasonably fast, and a standard size tape holds anything from 10 to 60 megabytes. You can back up a standard distribution 30 megabyte system on one extended-length cartridge tape. Because each cartridge costs $30.00, at 25 MB of data, the cost is about $1.00 per MB. The drives cost about $3000 each and are also available in streamer and start-stop models. Since virtually all cartridge drives at this writing have their own format, try to get the fastest kind available if you have a choice.

Removable Disk Pack

Disk packs are the *de facto* standard type of storage on most large minicomputers. While much more expensive than Winchester drives, they compensate by their extremely high speed and the fact that the entire disk medium may be removed from a drive in seconds. Full disk-to-disk copies are done in a few minutes, greatly simplifying backups.

Disk packs require constant attention from system operators because the packs must be changed. All packs for a given drive look exactly the same, so you have to be alert when handling them. They also are rather heavy and easy to damage, not an inconsequential problem when you consider the $1,000 price tag per pack. Disk packs look like 6 or 8 LP records stacked on top of each other while the drives themselves closely resemble top-loading washing machines.

The term **/usr** comes from the days when UNIX was run on machines with such removable disk packs. Most of UNIX proper (kernel, **/bin**, **/etc**...) was kept on a fixed disk. The **/usr** file system was kept with all user files. Even though the machine didn't have enough storage for all the user files, you could change disk packs. One set was for accounting, another for engineering, and so on.

Cartridge Disks

Cartridge disks are a cross between Winchester (sealed) disks and (open) disk packs. They consist of several disk platters encased in plastic (the whole assembly resembles a pizza in a traveling case), and they can be removed and changed in a minute or so. Cartridge disks were popular on minicomputers several years ago, but are almost obsolete there now due to the low cost of Winchesters. One particular cartridge disk (called the *Bernoulli Box*) is popular as mass storage and fast backup on IBM Personal Computers.

Comparative Cost Analysis

The following information is based on list prices from a computer supply catalog. If you actually *pay* these prices, you're either not trying hard enough or are in a big hurry. There are many discount houses offering quality brand-name media (don't buy any other kind) at a bargain. Find a brand that works well on your machine and then stock up at quantity prices. It usually is cheaper to buy tapes in quantities of 5 or 10.

Media	Cost Each	Capacity (MB)	Cost Per MB ($)
Reel-to-reel 1/2-inch tape, 2400'	23	40	.58
Cartridge tape, 600'	35	67	.52
Cartridge tape, 300'	24	23	1.04
Floppy diskette, single density	2	.3	6.66
Floppy diskette, double density	2	.6	3.33
Floppy diskette, octal density	7.50	1.2	6.25
Disk cartridge, RL02	279	10	27.90
Disk cartridge, RK07	879	28	31.39
Disk pack, RM03	455	80	5.69
Disk pack, RP03	725	200	3.63
Disk pack, RM05	1095	300	3.65

Note: costs for error-free media are used where available.

At these prices, for a small, 30-megabyte UNIX system, a weekly backup set of cartridge tapes (5 tapes, 67 MB capacity) costs about $175, and a weekly backup set of floppies costs $100 to $200. A 100 MB UNIX system with 1/2-inch tape can be backed up for the entire week for just $69. As you can see, reel-to-reel tape is the best bargain in flexible media, and floppies are the most expensive by 10 to 1.

Write Protection

There are various methods of physically write-protecting magnetic media to prevent accidental erasure of information. This differs slightly from protecting the data via software under UNIX (using permission bits or mounting a file system read-only). Physical write-protect prevents writing unless actual damage is done to the unit, whereas software protection is not as secure.

It's important to note that although these methods prevent writing over data using the computer hardware, *any* magnetic medium can be erased at any time using a permanent magnet or strong magnetic field (such as those found near motors, terminals, and fluorescent light ballasts).

Reel-to-reel tapes cannot be written on unless the soft plastic "write ring" is present on the back of the reel hub. These rings are generally a bright color such as red or yellow, and are used by system operators on the night shift for impromptu games of ring toss during backups.

Mini-floppy disks (the 5 1/4-inch square variety) are write-protected by putting a sticker on the write-protect notch cut on the side. Floppies of the larger size (8 inches) are write-protected by taking the sticker *off* the write-protect notch. This is one of the greatest mysteries in computer science.

A cartridge tape has a little slot on top at the left that can be turned with a screwdriver or your finger toward the word *SAFE*, which then prevents the drive from writing on it. Disk packs have a write-protect switch on the drive itself. If you get a write error when trying to make a backup, always make sure the appropriate write-protect has not been activated.

▪ Archive Versus Copy Programs ▪

Technically, there's a small but important difference between an *archive* program and a *copy* program. Copy programs, such as **dd**, copy data, plain and simple. Archives store all critical data for reference, and the information is filed so that the archive can recreate the entire data structure. **tar** and **cpio** are both excellent archivers, and they are excellent for backups as well.

It's best to incorporate a dual copy and archive scheme on your system to really be safe. If you do, you'll have a 100% reliable method of restoring lost files. A copy program stores the data, but archivers keep track of data. Archives are necessary when moving users to another machine or file system (doing a "rollover"). They also are necessary to do a file system compression (gaining back disk space by taking data off the machine and putting it back on by recursive copy).[5]

Restoring Data — A Reminder

Shortly we're going to examine a few UNIX backup and archive commands in detail. But before we do, remember that backup and archive commands are used for two purposes, to read data out onto magnetic media (back it up) and to read data from the magnetic media back into the machine (restore it). Whenever anyone loses or corrupts a file, directory, or tree, you will have to find it on the backup tape and read it back into the system. *The trick is to read in only what you want so you don't overwrite good data.*

Imagine that a careless user, Mr. A, loses a two-block file, his third one this month. He is reluctant to tell the system administrator he lost another file, because he will get yelled at. However, he convinces his friend, an operator on the machine, to find the file for him. The operator, Mr. B, is new at his job, but he is a loyal friend, so he mounts yesterday's **tar** backup tape on the machine and does an unqualified extract:

```
tar x
```

This reads the entire contents of the tape back into the machine, overwriting all the file systems. As a result, all the work for the last 24 hours is wiped out! Mr. A and Mr. B have to hide behind the tape drives to escape the wrath of the system administrator and 200 angry users!

5 Recursion, in programming, is a process calling itself. In a recursive copy, as each directory is copied, all the files within it are copied. Each subdirectory in that directory is **cd**ed to, all the files within it are copied, and so on.

If you backup and restore your data in a thoughtful, methodical way, you should have few problems.

Wear a Belt and Suspenders, Too

While it's probably not necessary to keep duplicate copies of your backup tapes, it never hurts to have a healthy suspicion of all your backup media. Especially when using media that must be formatted (i.e., all floppy disks and many cartridge tapes), it pays to verify that you'll be able to read your precious backups at a later date. The safest way to do this is to read the entire blank tape or disk after it has been formatted. This shows that the formatting was done correctly.

As an example, the Cadmus 9790 uses a Cipher ST525 streaming cartridge tape drive for backup. This particular drive (also used on the AT&T 3B2 series) actually emulates a floppy disk interface, so that it must be formatted before use. To read the entire tape for checking purposes, we use the following command line:

```
# dd if=/dev/rst525 of=/dev/null bs=17k count=1470
1470+0
1470+0
#
```

The output from the **dd** command shows that the full 1470 blocks (corresponding to the 25,589,760-byte capacity of the tape) were read from this tape. A defective tape would have had an **I/O error** indication and an incorrect block count.

The same method can be used for any media if you know the exact capacity. Use a block size (**bs=17k** in this example) that matches the hardware buffer size of the device for best efficiency. If you really want to be careful, do the same check again *after* you have made the backup onto the tape. This makes sure the data itself is readable. If you've ever been unable to read a backup when you needed it, you will be completely paranoid, so check the *logical* data as well to be on the safe side. We not only demonstrate this separately for each command, we highly recommend this procedure for all weekly, monthly, and full backups.

▪ UNIX Archive and Backup Commands ▪

tar — The Tape Archiver

tar copies just about anything you want to tape, floppy disk or hard disk. It once was the number one UNIX tape archiver, but it is currently being phased out in favor of **cpio**, which was introduced with System III. Pre-System V machines are set up so that **tar** defaults to the largest removable storage device. If the system has 1/2-inch reel-to-reel tape, **tar** defaults to **/dev/rmt0** (**rmt** stands for raw magnetic tape). If the only medium available is floppy diskette, then that is the default medium. Such default behavior applies only when the system has already been set up by the supplier.

Some **tar** Flags

This command line copies all of UNIX, tape quantities permitting:

```
# tar c /
```

The **c** flag means start the copy from the beginning of the tape. Other flags, such as **r**, copy to the end of the tape, but you may run out of tape if you're not careful. For this reason, the **c** flag is safest for backups. For archives of a large file tree, it is particularly important to rewind the tape and start the copy from the beginning.

Often, you want to watch the progress of the copy operation. **tar**'s **-v** flag is the *verbose* option, and it writes everything to the standard output as it is copied. The following command line copies the entire **/us** file tree, starting at the beginning of the tape, and sends the path name of each **/us** file to the terminal:

```
# tar cv /us
```

tar's syntax is simple enough, but *where* you start your **tar** copy is critical. If you start from root, the file paths on the archive also start at root. Thus, the file names will be fully qualified, as in

```
/usr/system/hunter/monitor/monitor.dat
```

If you start at the base of the file structure, **/usr/system/hunter/monitor**, the archive also starts there, and the file is stored as **./monitor.dat**. When reshuffling data (moving data from system to system or tree to tree), you definitely want the shortest path. This allows you to move the data without having to create extra directories.

tar is fully recursive. It climbs its way down each file tree, from the base directory given as an argument, and copies everything all the way to the bottom. Because **tar** is an archiver, it insists on putting each file back where it came from, even if it has to make up directories as it goes along to do so. Don't be surprised when you occasionally find a set of directories that you never (deliberately) created.

For example, if you want to use **tar** to archive a file tree such as **/5650/accounting/jones** so you can transfer it to another machine as **/us/jones,** doing a **tar** copy from root or **/5650** will be a disaster. This command sequence on the target machine

```
# cd /
# tar x /5650/accounting/jones/*
```

forces **tar** to make the directory

```
/us/jones/5650/accounting/jones
```

or die trying. The trick is to **cd** to the base of Jones's HOME directory (**/us/jones**) on the old machine and start the copy from there. There will be no qualified path name to deal with, and the transfer will go smoothly.

A Bourne Shell Script Using **tar**

Below is a Bourne shell script that backs up all user files plus critical UNIX system files that are subject to frequent change:

```
cd /etc
tar cvf /dev/rmt0 /us /usr/local passwd rc ttytype ttys group
exit
#    backup
# backup script for Hunter's UNIX system
# B H Hunter
# Nov 4, 1984
```

Notice the three flags:

```
tar cvf /dev/rmt0 ...
```

We've covered the **c** and **v** flags, but the **f** flag is new. It means that the argument following is the file or device where the archive is being written, in this case **/dev/rmt0**, the raw magnetic tape. The last arguments are the names of the trees and files to be copied.

Notice that by keeping your users' files away from **/usr** or any other file systems in the standard distribution, it is easier to copy pertinent system files. If you have **/usr/tom**, **/usr/dick**, and **/usr/harry**, the only way to get a copy of each to tape or diskette without copying everything else in **/usr** is by specifying each directory individually. This is not convenient, so it invites data loss by oversight. If all users are in a separate directory (tree) just below root level, like **/us/tom**, **/us/dick**, and **/us/harry**, you need only specify **/us** to copy all of them, and no users will be left out by mistake.

On systems that require more than one tape to do a backup and on those with floppy disks (using **tar**), a separate copy script is necessary for each tape or floppy:

```
tar cf /dev/floppy /usr
echo change floppy, press return when ready
read $ready
tar cf /dev/floppy /own
```

Restoring Data with **tar**

Restoring a file from a **tar** archive or backup tape is perhaps the easiest of all restoration methods. The syntax is

```
tar x file.name
```

Imagine that a novice user (Jones) comes up to you with a sad tale. He was in his home directory thinking he was in **$HOME/junk**, did a

```
rm -r *
```

and lost everything. Now you have to restore him. Mount last night's **tar** backup tape (or diskette) and read back his lost file tree with

```
tar xv /us/Jones
```

x is for extract, removing data from the tape. In this example you will also see all the files that are being restored because of the **v** flag.

tar's **t** flag is used to get names of the files on tape and then put them out to the standard output. The following verifies that all the files you wanted are on tape, and it puts them out to the printer as well:

```
# tar t | lp
```

The lack of an argument means everything and is better than the equivalent of

```
# tar t * .* */* .*/* .*/.* */*/* .......
```

Adding the **v** flag enables you to check all logical data in the tape and get even more information than is available with just the **t** flag:

```
# tar tv | lp
```

dump and restor

dump is the old, standard all-purpose backup command. It doesn't have the simplicity of **tar**, but it's simpler than grappling with the redirection and syntax of **cpio**. **dump** has a lot going for it. It is excellent for straight backups, especially incremental backups. The command line that follows does a backup of the file system mounted on disk device **/dev/cd0** at incremental level 4 using a floppy with a capacity of 2300 blocks:

```
# dump 4ubf 2300 /dev/floppy /dev/cd03
```

"Dump levels" consist of a series running from 0 through 9. The maximum level, 0, causes the entire system to be dumped. The minimum level is 9, catching only the most recently changed files. Because the manual is confusing, here's our simple version of how to use **dump** for the recommended series of daily, weekly, and monthly backups:

1. First, realize that the dump level numbers are totally arbitrary as well as relative. We pick mnemonic dump levels:

   0 full dump (done each quarter)

   3 monthly (3 months per quarter)

   4 weekly (there are about 4 weeks per month)

   7 daily (7 days per week)

2. Every day, do a level 7 dump.
3. Every week (on a Friday afternoon), do a level 4 dump.
4. Every month, do a level 3 dump.
5. Every quarter, do a full level 0 dump, and after checking that the backup is correct, recycle the monthly tapes.

No command is perfect, and **dump** definitely has its drawbacks. First of all, it is not usable for archives. But its major failing is that it is too dumb to recognize the end of the tape until it is too late. We have seen **dump** grind its way through a tape for nearly an hour only to fail when it passed the end of the tape! For this reason **dump** is becoming obsolete, and may not appear in future releases of UNIX.

restor is **dump**'s counterpart command. Don't use it to get back an individual file or directory, because you'll have a heck of a time. Used without a great deal of forethought and planning, **restor** can easily put back the entire contents of the dump backup tape onto the file system, sending your system backward a full day, or worse, and losing all the work put in for the current day. That's because this is how **restor** is usually used — to restore an entire system. Be careful with this one.

The dd Command

As all-purpose data copy programs go, **dd** is one of the most useful. With **dd**, you can not only copy data, but also convert it from ASCII to EBCDIC (what they use on IBM mainframes) and back, convert uppercase to lowercase, skip a given number of records, and even read blocked records from other operating systems.

For backup purposes, however, **dd**'s uses are limited to making exact (byte-for-byte) copies of tapes, floppies, disks, or even disk partitions. With a little imagination, **dd** can still be an extremely handy program to have around.

For example, let's say you have a precious boot floppy that you would very much like to have a backup of, but you only have one floppy drive, so there's no way of copying the disk. Just use **dd** to read the *entire* floppy into a temporary file, then write the data back out to a backup floppy. It doesn't matter what the format of the floppy data is, as long as your equipment can physically read and write it:

```
# dd if=/dev/fdsk of=/tmp/floppy.image
dd read error: I/O error
1900+0 records in
1900+0 records out
# ls -l /tmp/floppy.image
-rw-rw---- 1 root  staff  972800 Nov 4 19:16 /tmp/floppy.image
#
```

The I/O error shouldn't startle you. Since we didn't specify to **dd** how many blocks it should read, it simply read until it reached the end of the floppy. Reading past the end of most block devices causes a harmless I/O error, because you're asking the hardware to do something it can't. Now we have the information necessary to make our backup. Simply put a clean, formatted floppy in your drive and type:

```
# dd if=/tmp/floppy.image of=/dev/fdsk count=1900
1900+0 records in
1900+0 records out
#
```

You can speed up the transfer if you know the number of sectors per track on your floppy. If you have 12 sectors per track, and 1024 bytes per sector, a 12 KB buffer allows an entire track to be transferred at once. You could use this command line instead:

```
# dd if=/dev/rfdsk of=/tmp/floppy.image bs=12k count=80
80+0 records in
80+0 records out
#
```

How did we know to use a count of 80? Partly by dividing (972800, the file size, divided by (12 times 1024) equals 79.166, so we have to round up), and partly by the fact that there are 80 tracks on a double-sided, 5 1/4-inch floppy disk. If you miscalculate, do it again.

Notice that we had to use the *raw* floppy device (**/dev/rfdsk**). Disk drivers are accessed by a driver that utilizes blocking. Blocking groups its output into blocks of data, each data block consisting of a certain number of bytes. The block size depends on the system. Old UNIX systems (Version 7) use 512-byte blocks. System V uses 1024-byte blocks. UTS UNIX systems use 4096-byte blocks. However, all block devices also have a raw or character interface that allows a system administrator to perform little magic tricks like this.

Because we're specifying to **dd** exactly how much to read at a time, we can't let the block device feed us data at one rate and try to read at another. Actually, we can, but it would take a lot longer. In a practical test, it took about 75 seconds to read a floppy using the raw disk and 12 KB blocks, almost 2 minutes using the default (512-byte blocks and the block device), and 6 1/2 minutes using 512-byte blocks and the raw device. This shows that you shouldn't bother fooling with the raw device unless you know how to use it!

In a similar way, you can back up an entire disk with **dd**. This is commonly done with disk packs or cartridges, which can be removed and stored safely. Here is how it might be done on a DEC RK07 cartridge drive:

```
# dd if=/dev/rhk07 of=/dev/rhk17 bs=22*512 count=2575
```

The block size, 22*512, corresponds to a full track of data (22 blocks of 512 bytes), and the count to the number of total blocks on the disk (53636) divided by the number of tracks. This kind of information is available for most drives on the appropriate manual page in Section 4 of the *UNIX Programmer's Manual*. For example, we found it for the RK07 on the page called **hk(4)**, since the device is known as **hk** on the system.

A disk partition can also be backed up with **dd** to another disk or tape. Using **RK07** again as an example, we can copy the first partition of the disk to the corresponding part of another cartridge:

```
# dd if=/dev/rhk00 of=/dev/rhk10 bs=22*512 count=438
438+0 records in
438+0 records out
#
```

or to a tape:

```
# dd if=/dev/rhk00 of=/dev/rmt0 bs=22*512 count=438
438+0 records in
438+0 records out
#
```

Again, the information regarding the size, partitions, and number of the disks are taken directly from the manual. Notice that using a different device number refers to a different partition: when copying the entire disk, **rhk07** signified disk 0, partition 7 (meaning the entire disk), and now using **rhk00** means disk 0, partition 0 (just the root file system).

cpio

cpio made its appearance on System III. It is also present in XENIX. Its name stands for "*c*o*p*y *i*nput to *o*utput," and it does just that while archiving everything passing through. It ingeniously makes the most of the attributes of UNIX by using the standard input as its source of file names and the standard output as the archive output. The list of file names to be copied comes from **stdin**.

Watch how cleverly **cpio** takes advantage of the existing attributes of UNIX. Using either **ls** or the **find** command to get a list of file names, you can use a pipe to direct the results to **cpio**:

```
# ls | cpio -o > /dev/floppy
```

or

```
# find . -depth -print | cpio -o > /dev/rmt0
```

There are several possible options, and the first two are used for archiving purposes:

- **-o** for copy out
- **-i** for copy in
- **-p** for "pass" mode (in and out in one operation). This is very versatile, but not an archive command.

Using **find** as a source of the file list gives more control than **ls** because **find** can be selective, qualifying by size, date, and so on. In this case we are working from the current directory ("."). Using **find** with the **-depth** flag causes a descent of the directory hierarchy to be done so that all entries are acted on before the directory itself. (System III, System V, XENIX, and BSD 4.2 do not support the **-depth** option.) This gets around the problem of copying directories without write permission, and is handy when you're in a hurry. Redirection and pipes are used both to get the list of files into **cpio** and to send the archived output to a device.

Backups and Recovery with cpio

Here's an example of how to use **cpio** for selective backups. The following backup script is used on one of the authors' systems for nightly, weekly, and monthly incremental backups. It finds and archives all files that have been modified in the number of days specified on the command line, with one day as the default:

```
days=$1
echo "backing up last ${days:=1} day(s) -- kill if wrong"
sleep 10
cd /
find . -type f -mtime -$days -print | cpio -o > /dev/tape
#       backup
#       incremental backup script for infopro machine
#       by D. Fiedler
```

On some systems, the **find** command itself has a **-cpio** option, so that the last line of the **backup** script could be written this way:

```
find . -type f -mtime -$days -print -cpio /dev/tape
```

With this syntax, the program is more efficient, saving memory and an extra process while doing the same thing. We consistently use the **-type f** flag; otherwise, **cpio** will back up FIFOs (named pipes) and device special files. This is just a waste of good backup media, and there's no reason to chance clobbering one of your device files during a restore.

The **backup** script can be used in any of the following ways:

```
# backup
./usr/lib/crontab
./usr/lib/news/sys
./usr/lib/news/active
./usr/lib/news/history
./usr/lib/news/seq
./usr/lib/news/log
./usr/lib/news/ohistory.Z
./usr/lib/news/moderators
./usr/lib/news/backbone
./usr/lib/news/mapsh
    . . .
#
```

Or you can specify the number of days to back up:

```
# backup 7 >/dev/null
#
```

Here, the list of file names was thrown away (**>/dev/null**) rather than watching it on the terminal. When running monthly backups, it's a good idea to save the names of all files being backed up. The easiest way is to just pipe the output of **backup** to the printer spooler:

```
# backup 31 | lp
#
```

Those interested in saving paper can do this instead:

```
# backup 31 | pr -3 -w132 | lp
#
```

To verify that you have all logical data on a **cpio** tape, you only have to read it back in with the correct flags. Here's what we do when running important (monthly or full) backups using **cpio**:

```
# backup 31 >/tmp/tape.out
# cpio -itv </dev/tape >/tmp/tape.in
# tail /tmp/tape.out
./ips/book/ch13/All
./ips/book/ch13/ideas
./ips/book/ch13/create
./ips/book/ch13/extra
./ips/book/ch13/misc
./ips/book/ch13/philos
./ips/book/ch13/storage
./lpinterface/diablo
./lpinterface/oki
./.stdlogin
# tail /tmp/tape.in
100660 dave    46 Oct 25 18:59:01 1985 ips/book/ch13/ideas
100666 dave  6295 Oct 25 18:59:01 1985 ips/book/ch13/create
100666 dave  3031 Oct 25 18:59:01 1985 ips/book/ch13/extra
100666 dave  5466 Oct 25 18:59:01 1985 ips/book/ch13/misc
100666 dave  9163 Oct 25 18:59:01 1985 ips/book/ch13/philos
100666 dave  9757 Oct 25 18:59:01 1985 ips/book/ch13/storage
106751 root   463 Oct  6 15:42:34 1985 lpinterface/diablo
106755 root   859 Oct  6 15:42:34 1985 lpinterface/oki
100644 dave    28 Oct  3 10:20:57 1985 .stdlogin
48072 blocks
# pr /tmp/tape.in | lp
#
```

Running the **tail** program on the log files shows that what was read in from the tape matches what was put on the tape in the first place. Then, printing the **tape.in** file gives us a hard copy record of not only the file names, but also their sizes and times of modification. The extra time spent is worth it.

Those log files come in most handy when it's time to recover a file. All you have to do is determine the file name or names you want, and use our handy **recover** script:

```
cd /
cpio -ivdmu $* < /dev/tape
#       recover
#       selective file recovery script
#       for use with backup program above
#       D. Fiedler
```

Use it like this, leaving off the initial slash (/) of each path name:

```
# recover etc/passwd etc/*rc usr/lib/crontab
etc/passwd
etc/bcheckrc
etc/brc
etc/rc
usr/lib/crontab
48072 blocks
#
```

Notice that file name substitution (a la the shell) can be used to match names of files. And that brings us to the one major problem with **cpio** for a backup method: if the file to be recovered is not named, it won't be pulled off the tape. So if you lose an entire directory (or even a file system), you will either have to know the name of every file to be recovered, use file name substitution (very carefully), or recover the entire system (by specifying no argument at all). For this reason, it's good to supplement incremental **cpio** backups with qualified backups of each file system on a regular basis. These qualified backups can be done with **cpio**, **tar**, or **volcopy**. A quick example of how to do a qualified backup of the **/usr** file system with **cpio**:

```
# cd /usr
# find . -type f -print | cpio -o > /dev/tape
```

Notice that we always **cd** to a directory before running the backup. Keeping all path names relative proves useful if you ever have to move an entire file tree unexpectedly, or even restore to a different disk.

tar Versus cpio

Each UNIX command has its unique advantages and disadvantages, and you find this out with use. It's hard the beat the simplicity of **tar**'s syntax. On the other hand, although **cpio**'s syntax is a little clumsy, it is far more versatile.

To make a long list of files to be copied with **tar**, you go to the directory in question and make a file of the file names. In the following example, all file names in **/usr/doc** are appended to **file.list**:

```
$ ls /usr/doc >> file.list
```

When the file list is complete, you go into it with an editor and remove any unwanted files before you copy. To copy all those files with **tar**, the syntax is:

```
# tar cv `cat file.list`
```

The argument **`cat file list`** supplies each file name to **tar** as if it were a list of names entered on the command line (whitespace included). If the list is too long for **tar**, it fails with the complaint "list too long." The list will be too long if the number of files causes the name buffer to fill.

cpio does the same thing, but better. Below a file list is being read into **cpio** by a pipe. The file list can be any length — you won't get a "list too long" error:

```
# cat file.list | cpio > /dev/rmt0
```

There is no default other than standard input for a file list or standard output to archive. Because of this you have to specify the tape as a device (as in **/dev/rmt0** above). Another advantage of **cpio** is that it will often retry automatically if a tape error is encountered while attempting to recover files.

volcopy

volcopy copies an entire file system (or **volume**) to tape or another disk (generally a disk pack). It is very fast, because it uses a large internal data buffer and deals with raw devices. Another advantage of **volcopy** is that it can check machine-readable labels of the tape or disk, preventing an error when backing up or restoring.

The main disadvantage of **volcopy** is that a separate tape must be used to back up each file system. If you have partitioned your disk into many small file systems, using **volcopy** will be expensive in terms of media — even if you could fit all your data on one tape, you will still have to use one for each file system. Another problem is that if **volcopy** fails while restoring data from tape, you might end up with a scrambled file system and be in even worse trouble. Finally, single files or groups of files cannot be recovered with **volcopy**: it's the whole file system or nothing. One way of getting around this problem is to restore the file system onto a spare section of your disk, then just copy the files you want.

Running **volcopy** without a script can be frustrating, as the manual is not completely clear about what arguments are expected where. Here's our handy guide to **volcopy** arguments:

```
volcopy filesystem raw-device-from vol-from raw-device-to vol-to
```

filesystem: The file system you want to copy, such as **/usr**, **/usr/spool**, or the root file system, **/**. This can be confusing, since you are *not* expected to enter the exact name (such as **/usr**). Rather, you're supposed to make up your *own* name for the file system of less than six characters, which must be done *beforehand* and entered using the **labelit** command (don't worry, we'll show you how).

raw-device-from: The raw device (generally, a disk partition, if you are making a backup) that you wish to copy *from*.

vol-from: This should uniquely identify the particular volume involved, especially if it's removable media. On fixed disks, use the device name of the partition. For disk

	packs and tapes, use the last few digits of the serial number (if there is one), or number each one uniquely with permanent markers. Daily backup tapes or packs can use the day as the volume name, so that the wrong backup isn't used by mistake.
raw-device-to:	The raw device you want to copy *to*. Usually a tape drive.
vol-to:	Again, your own unique name for the volume being copied to. If a tape, use the serial number or other identifier.

Now let's see how this all works:

```
# volcopy root /dev/rxt0a xt0a /dev/rxt1a xt1a
```

In this simple example, the first partition (**a**) of disk 0, containing the **root** file system, is being copied to the corresponding partition of disk 1. We are dealing with fixed (Winchester) disks, so each volume is the name of the corresponding partition.

Let's try something a bit more complex, but realistic: a complete backup of the root file system onto tape. First, we'll check the machine-readable labels on the disk and tape to make sure they correspond, using **labelit**:

```
# labelit /dev/rxt0a
Current fsname: root, Current volname: xt0a,
Blocks: 16384, Inodes: 2048
FS Units: 1Kb, Date last mounted: Wed Oct  2 20:08:31 1985
```

Well, that looks reasonable. How about the tape?

```
# labelit /dev/rst525
Current fsname: 626Qmo, Current volname: d.rec.,
Blocks: 1949199727, Inodes: 29464
FS Units: 512b, Date last mounted: Thu Sep 24 12:08:05 1998
```

A few strange pieces of information, eh? It turns out that the last time this tape was used, it was for a **cpio** backup, so we have to write a new tape label:

```
# labelit /dev/rst525 root tape01 -n
Skipping label check!
NEW fsname = root, NEW volname = tape01 -- DEL if wrong!!
#
```

Giving the new file system name and volume name on the **labelit** command line, followed by the **-n** flag, forces a new tape label to be written (that's what the **Skipping label check!** message means). **labelit** echoes what it thinks you are trying to do, and delays 10 seconds to allow you to kill the command if anything seems incorrect. Nothing is, so we can let **labelit** run to completion. Now we'll check the new tape label:

```
# labelit /dev/rst525
Volcopy tape volume: tape01, reel 0 of 0 reels
Written: Wed Nov  6 02:21:42 1985
Current fsname: root, Current volname: tape01,
Blocks: 0, Inodes: -16
FS Units: 512b, Date last mounted: Wed Nov  6 02:21:42 1985
#
```

The negative inode count **Inodes: -16** might seem alarming, but inodes mean nothing on tapes because they are not mounted file systems. Now it's time to run **volcopy**:

```
# volcopy root /dev/rxt0a xt0a /dev/rst525 tape01
You will need 1 reels.
(The same size and density is expected for all reels)
From: /dev/rxt0a, to: /dev/rst525? (DEL if wrong)
#
```

Again, **volcopy** gives you a chance to stop before it starts writing all over your output device. This is a handy feature if you suddenly discovered you have switched input and output by accident!

By prompting, **volcopy** will also lead you through if anything important doesn't match. You will be able to override almost any incorrect combination of label or file systems this way. This gives you the option of continuing if something was typed badly, but it also allows you to make serious mistakes. We recommend starting over with the correct information, since overriding changes the labeling on the output device, possibly causing more and bigger errors.

To restore a **volcopy** backup from tape, simply use the tape as the input (volume-from) device and the appropriate disk partition as the output (volume-to) device. This is the time when you will appreciate **volcopy**'s insistence on the correct label. If you've heeded our warnings about how to choose your volume names, you won't make a mistake and restore onto the wrong disk.

▪ Backup Shell Scripts ▪

We're going to take a look at a few backup scripts for an Amdahl mainframe (IBM 370 architecture) running UTS UNIX. There will be a few nonstandard UNIX commands in these. This is unavoidable when dealing with a bay of tape drives. But essential UNIX commands are the same.

Backing Up a Mainframe in Three Easy Steps

Backing up a UNIX mainframe system can be done in three quick scripts: **tape_mount**, **tape_copy**, and **tape_print**. The first script causes a tape request to go to the system's main console. It also sets the parameters for having the tape mounted with a write ring and run at maximum density:

```
tape -w -d 6250 -b tape.utsa
exit
#         tape_mount
# tape mounting command
# bhh  3/22/84
```

tape must be used since the drives must be mounted from VM, not UTS. The **tape** command line says "mount a tape called **tape.utsa** as writable **(-w)** at 6250-bpi density **(-d 6250)** and bypass label processing **(-b)**". The reason for making a script out of a one-line command invocation is to guarantee that the mount request is done properly. Then the operator need only type the name of the command:

```
tape_mount
```

The next script causes the actual copy to occur:

```
tar c tape.utsa /ddf /491 /idf /pas /rdf /system /etc/passwd
exit
#        tape_copy
# copy user file trees to
# UTSystem administrator nightly backup tape
# bhh 3/33/85
```

There it is in its beautiful **tar** simplicity. The system creates a file known as **/dev/tape/tape.utsa** and to it writes all the specified file trees (**/ddf** through **/system**) as well as the password file. When the **tape_copy** script is completed, the tape is not rewound.

The last script, **tape_print**, rewinds the tape, extracts every file name from it, and sends the names out to the system printer:

```
tm tape.utsa rew
tar t tape.utsa | pr -3 -w132 | lp
tape -u tape.utsa
exit
#         tape_print
# make a listing of the files on the backup tape created by
# mount and copy
# bhh 3/22/85
```

tm, the tape manipulator, is instructed to rewind (rew) the tape so that it can be reread.

tar uses the **t** option to get the file names from the tape. This is used instead of the **v** to verify that the files have indeed been copied. The **-u** option with **tape** is used to logically dismount the tape.

These three scripts guarantee that a good set of backups are done consistently. The listing is usually made on wide green bar paper in three columns for a total width of 132 characters. It is left on the system administrator's desk at night, and in the morning he has visual proof that the file systems are backed up. The listing is also available for users. They can look for files to verify that their work is on last night's tape. These listings are usually kept for no less than 7 days.

tapefit

Any storage medium is finite. Imagine spending 30 minutes writing to a tape on a slow system and then finding out that you have so much data, you have run off the end of the tape. This is a common backup problem. Yesterday's data distribution may not work today, especially after someone has just imported a few megabytes of text in **mm** format, processed it, and left the formatted output in a file! So what do you do?

Most of your shell scripts will be pedestrian and straightforward, but occasionally you will come up with something stunningly elegant. The following **tapefit** shell script was written by Brett Robblee to predetermine the number of tapes required and file distribution for backups. The script takes advantage of the **df** (disk free) command with the **-t** option to display both the number of blocks used as well as the total blocks available. This program is worth its weight in core memory when it comes to tape fitting:

```
# NAME
#       tapefit - report file system block usage
# SYNOPSIS
#       tapefit [ file-system ... ]
# DESCRIPTION
#       tapefit reports the number of blocks used for all
#       or selected mountable file systems. also displays
#     the device name, file-system name, and what
#     percentage of a tape(s) the file-system will use up.
# FILES
#       tapefit uses "pipelining" throughout. No intermediate
#     files are created.
# SEE ALSO your UNIX manuals on the following:
#       ascii(1), awk(1), df(1m), echo(1), printf(3s), sed(1),
#     sh(1), sort(1).
# NOTES
#       tapefit doesn't know if arguments passed to it are
#     valid file systems.  It blithely passes all arguments
#     to "df" which, in turn, handles all error reporting.
# VERSION
#       bpr  6/29/85  version 1.0
```

```
echo "Report Number of 512-byte Disk Blocks Used"
echo "Version 1.0    6/29/85 bpr"
echo
echo "blocks used      device name      file system  tapes needed"
echo

df -t ${*:-} | grep -v vio0 | grep -v src |
awk 'BEGIN { TAPEBLOCKS = 60000 }
    {
        if ((NR % 2) = = 1)
        {  tree[NR] = $1
           special[NR] = $2
           used[NR] = $3
    }
        else
        {  sum[NR-1] = $2
    { printf "%6d\t\t%17s\t%-12s\t%4.3f\n", \
  ((sum[NR-1]-used[NR-1]) * 8), special[NR-1], tree[NR-1], \
(((sum[NR-1]-used[NR-1]) * 8) / TAPEBLOCKS )}
    }
}' | sort +0nr -1
exit 0
```

tapefit takes shell programming to an advanced state, cleverly using **awk**'s ability to create arrays. The name of each file tree, its special file name (in **/dev**), the number of blocks used, and the total number of blocks for each file system are stored in single-element arrays called vectors. The modulus operator ("%") is used to test each line in the **df** output to see if it is even or odd. The even-numbered lines contain totals and require a different assignment than odd-numbered lines. A constant, **TAPEBLOCKS**, is defined to store the number of 512-byte blocks on the tape. Here the program is set up to deal with 2400-foot tape running 6250-bpi density. There are eight "UNIX blocks" (of 512 bytes) per system hardware block (4096 bytes). These numbers have to be changed to meet your system's parameters. Remember, System V uses 1024-byte blocks, Version 7 uses 512, and UTS UNIX for mainframes 4096. On most systems the blocks are the same size so no multiplier is needed. Look at **BSIZE** in **/usr/include/sys/param.h** to find the value for your system.

Note that two file systems have been deliberately filtered out — **/src**, which is illegal to copy, and **/dev/vio0**, a memory device used by **/tmp**. The final output is sorted in the first field so that the output is from the largest file system to the smallest.

Typical **tapefit** output looks like this:

```
Report Number of 512-byte Disk Blocks Used
Version 1.0     6/29/85 bpr

blocks used      device name        file system  tapes needed

109416        (/dev/dsk/318s0):      /d5           1.824
 40448        (/dev/dsk/560s0):      /5460         0.674
 36584        (/dev/dsk/520s0):      /5520         0.610
 28640        (/dev/dsk/220s0):      /             0.477
 26784        (/dev/dsk/802s0):      /5802         0.446
 18496        (/dev/dsk/540s0):      /sysgrp       0.308
 13464        (/dev/dsk/544s0):      /system       0.224
  4256        (/dev/dsk/5a0s0):      /sys          0.071
  3504        (/dev/dsk/530s0):      /5530         0.058
  2896        (/dev/dsk/599s0):      /ds           0.048
  2032        (/dev/dsk/542s0):      /pass         0.034
  1856        (/dev/dsk/502s0):      /project      0.031
   152        (/dev/dsk/300s0):      /5300         0.003
   144        (/dev/dsk/740s0):      /5740         0.002
   136        (/dev/dsk/502s0):      /pdl          0.002
   128        (/dev/dsk/512s0):      /ids          0.002
   128        (/dev/dsk/dd0s0):      /dump         0.002
```

As you work with your system, you gain insights about the needs of the machine and the needs of your users. Gradually you will develop backup and archiving routines of your own. The scripts to run them need not be fancy, only effective.

▪ Chapter Summary ▪

If you forget to back up just *once*, you'll be in a world of trouble! Remember, we warned you.

Now that we've dealt with preserving and backing up the system's data, we need to learn how to protect the data on the machine from mischief, espionage, and theft.

C H A P T E R

9

SECURITY

The Running System

An important, but often overlooked, feature of running a computer system is maintaining its security from outside intrusion, internal sabotage (known as "mischief" outside of the commercial environment), and just plain user stupidity. In this chapter we cover the basic information you need to understand and make use of UNIX security features.

Multiuser systems need security features. Since the system is potentially open to anyone who walks by a terminal or has a terminal and a modem, it must be protected from intrusion by unauthorized individuals. System security features must be flexible to be universally useful. Otherwise, they are so specialized that nobody can use them. UNIX security features accomplish this without too much difficulty.

We go into great detail about security holes in this chapter. While some of the techniques and advice may seem overly paranoid at first reading, all of them have been used to break into UNIX systems at one time or another. Underestimating the cleverness of a "bad guy" is a poor mistake, and so is assuming he won't decide to wipe out your system once he becomes **root**. Few systems can be totally secure, so your best chance is knowing exactly what the problems are and knowing your users.

Be as careful about security as you want, but if you have an incoming modem, we hope you also have a full, current set of backups. The minute you run an outside line into the machine, the potential for mischief increases dramatically.

Security Basics

The ability to access files or go through file systems is called *privilege*. The permissions of a specific file show not only who has the privilege of accessing that file but also the degree of access. Permissions also indicate whether a file can be executed or a directory traversed. There are three types of privilege usable in three different areas:

- *r*ead (to read a file only)
- *w*rite (to create and modify a file)
- e*x*ecute (to run a program)

These can be applied to three different types of users:

- owner (of the file, called *u*ser)
- members of a *g*roup (who share privilege for this and other files)
- all *o*thers (any current and potential system user)

These two categories are combined to form the various privilege designations we see whenever a long listing is performed:

```
$ ls -lg /bin/ls
-rwxr-xr-x  3   bin     adm  21108 Jan 23 16:22 /bin/ls
```

This is a long listing of the **ls** command as it resides in **/bin**. The string **-rwxr-xr-x** showing the settings of the *protection bits* is broken down into 3 three-letter segments:[1]

User	Group	Other
rwx	r-x	r-x

meaning that the owner, **bin**, has *read*, *write*, and *execute* privilege while members of the **adm** group and all others on the system have *read* and *execute* privilege only. A hyphen signifies that a privilege is denied; in this case, *write* privilege.

Changing Ownership of Files and Directories

If a person has neither group nor ownership rights to a file, the system will not allow him access. This is as it should be, but when we, as administrators, create files and directories, how are we going to assign ownership to the intended user? The command to change ownership is **chown**. The syntax is

 # chown *logname filename*

and it is used like this:

```
# chown david bruce.file
```

We have now changed **bruce.file**'s owner to **david**. In another case, we copy a

---

1 The leftmost character does not relate to security. It is set to **-** for ordinary files, **d** for directories, **c** for character special files, **b** for block special files, or **p** for FIFOs.

.profile to a new user's HOME after creating the HOME directory while acting as super-user. Both the home directory and the profile now have **root** as the owner. The user can neither execute the profile nor change it. **chown** rectifies the problem in seconds:

```
# chown singer .profile /us/singer
```

On some systems, the use of the **chown** command and system call is restricted to **root** to avoid the **sushi** security hole described later in this chapter. On other systems, **chown** has been fixed to prevent this problem. On most, you are left wide open.

Changing Group Ownership

Analogous to the **chown** command and system call is **chgrp**. This allows you to change group ownership of files, directories, or devices. Normally, the group ownership of files created by a given user is that of his group as assigned in **/etc/passwd** (or his effective group if running under the **newgrp** command):

```
$ whoami
david
$ grep david /etc/passwd
david:TDDc8H8ZFlA9I:12:7:David Fiedler:/own/dave:/bin/csh
$ grep david /etc/group
staff:VOID:7:susan,brenda,debbie,unique,root,david,chris
$ cp /etc/passwd /tmp
$ ls -lg /etc/passwd /tmp/passwd
-rw-r--r-- 1 root    root    3673 Dec  7 17:33 /etc/passwd
-rw-r--r-- 1 david   staff   3673 Dec  7 21:47 /tmp/passwd
$ chgrp other /tmp/passwd
$ chgrp other /etc/passwd
/etc/passwd: Not owner
$ ls -lg /etc/passwd /tmp/passwd
-rw-r--r-- 1 root    root    3673 Dec  7 17:33 /etc/passwd
-rw-r--r-- 1 david   other   3673 Dec  7 21:47 /tmp/passwd
$
```

Protection Bits

The **chmod** command uses file protection bits to establish protection levels. They are expressed in octal (base 8). Each octal number has its own individual meaning, and the sum of the bits incorporates all of the meanings associated with each octal number.

Read	4	4	4	4			
Write	2	2			2	2	
Execute	1		1		1		1
Sum	7	6	5	4	3	2	1

Octal **4** means read, octal **2** means write, and octal **1** means execute. Thus, octal **7**, when applied to permissions, means that the file can be read, written to, and executed. You generally use three octal digits when changing the permission bits with **chmod**, one each for user, group, and other. This set of bits is called the *mode*. With the bit system, permissions are quickly set with the **chmod** command using the following syntax:

chmod *octal-bits file-name*

so that

```
$ chmod 751 my.file
```

gives read, write, and execute privilege to the owner, read and execute privilege to the group members, and just execute privilege to all others. **root** may use **chmod** to modify privilege on any files, while a user may only modify the protection on her own files. The resulting listing from the above command might look like this:

```
-rwxr-x--x 1 penny        128 Apr 18 my.file
```

Most people do not like to fool with octal bits. On most systems, you can also use *symbolic modes* with the **chmod** command. Symbolic modes let you add or remove permissions using letters (such as **u** for user, **g** for group, **o** for other, **a** for all (user, group, and other), and of course **r**, **w**, and **x**). Using symbolic modes is simply a matter of first specifying *who* should get their permissions changed (the default is the **a** flag), then either a plus or minus sign (for giving or taking away permission), then the specific permission you're referencing. As usual, it's easier to show than to tell:

```
$ chmod o+r my.file    # add read permission for others
$ ls -l my.file
-rwxr-xr-x 1 penny        128 Apr 18 my.file
$ chmod g-x my.file    # take away group execute permission
$ ls -l my.file
-rwxr--r-x 1 penny        128 Apr 18 my.file
$ chmod a+w my.file    # give everyone write permission
```

```
$ ls -l
-rwxrw-rwx 1 penny        128 Apr 18 my.file
$
```

Symbolic modes are useful for turning a specific permission on or off without having to calculate octal numbers, but as administrator, you will gradually learn to use octal.

Permission bits work a little differently for directories, since a directory is actually just a file with with special data in it about other files.

- *Read* permission for a directory means you can look at the file names in the directory, even if you can't actually **cd** to it.
- *Write* permission for a directory means you can alter the contents of the directory. Therefore, you can wipe out files in the directory, even if you have no write permission for those files!
- *Execute* permission means you can **cd** to the directory or use it as part of a path name.

As you can see, directory permissions can permit security breaches if they are not understood. If a directory is set this way:

```
drwxr-x--x   root   bin 56 May 27 05:30 /usr/lib/src
```

then even a lowly user can type something like:

```
$ cat /usr/lib/src/secret.c
```

and look at any file within that has read permission for **other**, as long as he knows its name. If you do not want others in a directory, set the mode accordingly:

```
# chmod o-wx /usr/lib/src
# ls -ld /usr/lib/src
drwxr-x---   root  bin 56 May 27 05:30 /usr/lib/src
#
```

umask

Most people do not like running **chmod** every time they create a file, so it is nice to be able to set default permissions. This is done with the **umask** command. **umask** is sometimes difficult to understand because it implies a *logical inverse*. The easiest way to calculate the **umask** is to think of it *taking away* permission. Let's say you want your files set to mode 660, and your directories to the equivalent 770. Think of ''taking away'' as subtraction, so 777 minus 770 equals 007. Figuring this out relative to *directory* permissions allows both files and directories to be created with appropriate modes:

```
$ umask
007
$ > zero
$ mkdir nothing
$ ls -l zero nothing
-rw-rw---- 1 david   staff         0 Nov 23 15:07 zero
-rwxrwx--- 2 david   staff        32 Nov 23 15:07 nothing
$ umask 002
$ > one
$ mkdir another
$ ls -l one another
-rw-rw-r-- 1 david   staff         0 Nov 23 15:08 one
-rwxrwxr-x 2 david   staff        32 Nov 23 15:08 another
$ umask 000
$ > two
$ mkdir pair
$ ls -l two pair
-rw-rw-rw- 1 david   staff         0 Nov 23 15:09 two
-rwxrwxrwx 2 david   staff        32 Nov 23 15:09 pair
$
```

The best place to set **umask** is in your **.profile** or **.cshrc** so it is always in effect. The most common settings are:

Umask	Yields	Purpose
077	-rw-------	most restrictive and private
	-rwx------	(directory and executable)
007	-rw-rw----	working with groups in sensitive environment
	-rwxrwx---	(directory and executable)
002	-rw-rw-r--	working with groups in academic environment
	-rwxrwxr-x	(directory and executable)
022	-rw-r--r--	a reasonable default
	-rwxr-xr-x	(directory and executable)
000	-rw-rw-rw-	for people who trust everyone
	-rwxrwxrwx	(directory and executable)
277	-r--------	for people who don't trust themselves
	-r-x------	(directory and executable)

To set the default **umask** for everyone on the system, put the setting you want into **/etc/profile** and **/.stdcshrc**. Anyone who cares can change their **.profile** themselves.

▪ Some Very Special Modes ▪

Besides read, write, and execute bits, there are three remaining permission bits. They are:

- Set-User-Id (*setuid* or *SUID*)
- Set-Group-Id (*setgid* or *SGID*)
- the "sticky" bit

The first two solve an otherwise unsurmountable problem, and the last can speed up system response time.

The Set-User-Id Bit

How does the system deal with a command like **passwd**? **passwd** allows the users to change their password. It lets them write a new encrypted password to the file **/etc/passwd**. Yet, **/etc/passwd** cannot be modified (written to) except by **root**. The trick is that when the **passwd** command is executed, the user is given the same privilege as the owner of the **passwd** command, **root**. When a user uses **/bin/passwd**, the system acts as if **/etc/passwd** is being modified by **root**. This trick is accomplished with the set-user-id bit. Look at the permissions of the program file itself:

```
$ ls -l /bin/passwd
-rwsr-xr-x 1 root          17136 Nov 19 1982 /bin/passwd
```

The listing looks normal except for the strange **s** in the **x** field of the owner's permissions. The **s** shows the set-user-id bit is active. It was set by **chmod** in the following way:

```
# chmod 4755 /bin/passwd
```

The 4000 bit sets the user id to the same *effective* user id as the owner (**root**) of the program file, *but only while the program is being run*. In other words, while the program is running, it acts as though its owner (**root**) was running it, rather than an ordinary user. This wondrous bit of magic (pun intended) is the brainchild of Dennis Ritchie and is actually patented (U.S. Patent #4,135,240). The **chmod** program is written so that only **root** or the owner of a program may make it SUID. Thus, any user can create an SUID program.

What is most dangerous, of course, is a program that is SUID and owned by **root**, especially if that program is general purpose, rather than specific in nature. For instance, **passwd** only operates on the **/etc/passwd** file, but an editor that is SUID and owned by **root** lets anyone edit **/etc/passwd** or any other file.

A Bit of Sushi

The first thing any bad guy will do if he gains access to the **root** login, even if only for a minute, is execute these commands:

```
# cp /bin/sh /own/badguy/sushi
# chmod 4755 /own/badguy/sushi
```

Now he logs off from being **root**, and goes back to his original identity. The copy of the shell he just created is SUID and owned by **root**, so merely executing it gives him untraceable **root** privileges. Any time he wants, he can become **root**:

```
$ pwd
/own/badguy
$ sushi
#
```

sushi (*s*uper-*u*ser *sh*ell, *i*nteractive) illustrates how careful you must be with SUID programs, as well as with the **root** password. Here are some rules that protect you from dangerous sushi:[2]

1. Never let anyone else use your **root** password or login. Even close supervision is not good enough.
2. No program that is SUID **root** should be writable by anyone but **root**. If you fail to guard against this, someone will copy the shell onto that program quicker than you can say ''Chopsticks, please.''
3. Don't use any SUID shell programs. Some versions of UNIX allow even shell programs to be SUID, and for various technical reasons, these can be compromised no matter how the permission bits are set. They can not be traced with the accounting either, making them hard to monitor!
4. Don't expect to protect yourself by looking for programs named **sushi**! When testing the security of various systems, one of the authors would move the stolen shell to a file called **.profile** or **junk**. Even if the administrator found this file, he would tend to ignore it due to the name. The only safe method is to run a program similar to **checksecure** (at the end of this chapter) on a regular basis.
5. The only programs that should be SUID **root** are those that are delivered this way with the system and are documented as needing SUID **root** privilege. When a user comes to you with a program that he says must be SUID **root**, assume that he has hidden a security hole inside unless he can prove otherwise by going over it line-by-line, with the best system programmer you know (and trust).

---

2 If you get caught, you will join the ranks of *fugu*: *f*ooled *U*NIX *g*urus *u*nited.

6. Only single-purpose programs (like **passwd**) should be SUID **root**. Anything with a shell escape — especially, any interactive program — will give you a problem.

7. To ensure that only the owner of an SUID file has write permission on it, always use the command **chmod 4755** rather than the symbolic equivalent **chmod +s** when creating it.

8. If the **chown** command and system call are accessible to normal users on your machine, test them to make sure the old security holes have been fixed. After setting a test program to mode 4755, **chown** it to **root** (while a normal user). The mode should be reset automatically to 755 to prevent unexpected raw fish dinners.

Watch Your crontab

The **/usr/lib/crontab** file (and its System 5.2 equivalent, **/usr/lib/cron/crontabs/***) is very useful, but you must use it wisely. A dedicated bad guy can find many holes by studying it. First of all, if anyone besides **root** can read it, you are running the risk that a bad guy may write a program to look at the modes of every program executed through **cron**, and copy his own code on top of any he finds that are writable. Most **cron**s execute their commands as **root** (even 5.2 has a **cron** file for **root**) and as such are extremely dangerous.

An even bigger problem relates to the **at** program found on many systems. This facility allows the average user to schedule execution of programs at a later time. To accomplish this, a daemon called **/usr/lib/atrun** is started by **cron** every 10 minutes or so. When the user runs **at**, a file is created in the **/usr/spool/at** directory containing the commands to be executed. Since the daemon has to be able to execute any program, it is SUID **root**. The bad guy has several options:

- Run the commands to create the **sushi** program using **at**.
- Run a harmless program with **at**, but edit the spool file (the one **at** puts in the **/usr/spool/at** directory) to add the **sushi** code.
- Make a copy of the spool file, add the **sushi** code to this copy, and give the copy a name that tricks **atrun** into executing it at a particular time.

Whichever approach he picks depends on what holes have been left open. Sometimes changing the ownership of the spool file to **root** is enough to fool **at**. To guard against an **at** attack, make sure the **/usr/spool/at** directory is owned by **root** with mode 755. Now log in as a normal user, and try all of the above methods. If any of them work, the only solution is to disable the **atrun** daemon, or remove its SUID status. Naturally, a complaint to your system supplier is also in order.

The Set-Group-Id Bit

Just as the set-user-id bit allows a user to have the same power as the owner of a file, so the set-group-id (SGID) bit allows a user to have the same power as any member of the group the file belongs to. An example of the use of the SGID bit is the creation of a special program to allow an otherwise restricted user to access certain files in a predetermined way.

For instance, a system operator might be given an SGID program that would allow him to copy all of a particular group's files to tape for backup, and nothing more. If written correctly, the program would not permit him to print or even examine the files. Here, the SGID feature allows greater access (to all files belonging to the group) without greater risk. The alternative would probably be giving the operator root privilege through a SUID program, so SGID limits the potential for danger in case there *is* an undiscovered security hole in the program.

The Sticky Bit

The third special case of permission bits is the sticky bit or ''save text image after execution'' bit. To understand the sticky bit, you have to remember that the program files are normally loaded into system memory by reading them from the file system. To do this, the system must find every block of the file (which may be randomly scattered all over the disk), load them all into memory, and then begin executing it.[3] This could take a noticeable amount of time, especially for large files. When not enough memory is on the system to hold all active processes simultaneously, a process ''text'' (program) area is ''swapped out'' by writing it *sequentially* to a special area on the system disk.

The sticky bit is used only on large executable programs (**a.out** files) that are called constantly, like screen editors, the C compiler, and the shells. It tells the system to leave the program's text on the swap area permanently (or until the system is rebooted). Next time someone tries to execute it, the system will load it from the swap area much faster than it could be loaded from the file system. Also, the system will only swap the text *out* once — after that, it knows that the copy is out there and doesn't have to be copied out again.

To make a file sticky, you should use the symbolic mode **+t** of the **chmod** command, to avoid changing any other permission bits:

```
# ls -l /usr/ucb/vi
-rwxr-xr-x 3 bin     sys     131078 Sep 28 13:26 /usr/ucb/vi
# chmod +t /usr/ucb/vi
# ls -l /usr/ucb/vi
-rwxr-xr-t 3 bin     sys     131078 Sep 28 13:26 /usr/ucb/vi
#
```

Now, on a quiet system, type **vi** and time how long it takes before your screen is set up, then exit **vi** and time it again. It should load noticeably faster. If it does not, you might as well remove the sticky bit.

3 On some systems with virtual memory, execution can begin before the entire file has finished loading.

With the sticky bit, the main thing to avoid is getting carried away and making too many programs sticky. If that happens, you could run out of swap space, which would crash your system. As a general rule, the total size of your sticky programs should not exceed 25% of your available swap space.

Sticky Memory

Because of the decrease in size and price of RAM chips, many UNIX systems, especially small ones, have more RAM available than disk swap space. To take advantage of this, *VenturCom*, the supplier of the VENIX operating system, developed the concept of *sticky memory*.

A program that has its sticky memory bit set (denoted by an **m** instead of a **t** in column 10 of a **ls -l** listing) will be kept in RAM as long as there is sufficient room for it. This allows virtually instantaneous reloading of the program and enables a VENIX system to have all the advantages of the RAM-disk concept (used on personal computers) without having to set aside a fixed amount of memory for the RAM disk.

▪ Passwords ▪

Security is impossible without passwords. In UNIX, a password is the key to otherwise locked doors. The first password a user sees is his own login password. When a user attempts to log on the system, he must enter his login name, then his password. The password is encrypted and compared to the encrypted version stored in **/etc/passwd**, and the user is allowed to log in if they match. Since only the encrypted version is stored in **/etc/passwd**, it is safe to allow all users to read it.

The biggest problem with passwords is human frailty. Given a choice, the average user selects a password that is easy to remember and type in. It is also easy for an intruder to guess such a password. Studies have found that, on almost every system tested, *someone* uses his first or last name, his friend's or pet's name, or another easy-to-guess password.

A person who uses his own name for a password is called a *joe*. Running under your usual login, test other people's passwords on a regular basis to see if they qualify. The authors have a program called **joetest** that automatically checks all logins for this and similar problems (such as using last name, department name, etc.), but **joetest** is too easily abused to publish.

The **passwd** program tries to encourage people to use longer passwords than just a few letters. Remember, though, that only the first eight characters of a password are actually used by the **passwd** program. You should go further and encourage people to use more complex, but still easy to remember, passwords. Some good methods are:

- Use two short words with a space or underscore between them: **kiss me** or **darn_it**.

- Replace letters by mnemonic digits. For example, if your name is **david**, use **dav1d**, or **r00t** instead of **root**.
- Throw in extra punctuation, such as **whosez?** or **egg;roll**.
- Capitalize letters within the words: **hIlda** or **gArbAge**.
- Use several methods at once: **y0u T00!**.

Aging

Some systems allow password *aging*, so that a password expires after a certain number of weeks. This is not a bad idea in theory, because eventually even the best password may be guessed soon or otherwise compromised. Unfortunately, the UNIX password aging implementation requires the administrator to manually edit the the password field for each user. Errors are almost inevitable because of the complex series of obscure codes used by aging.

Another problem is that aging forces you to select your new password at login time (once the old one has expired, of course). Since most people are in a big hurry to log in, they tend to select an ''easy'' password at this point, negating all your careful planning. Or, they select two passwords and switch back and forth between them at expiration time. This is called password toggling and is a common practice.

We suggest a regular program of gentle reminders to users, rather than forced aging. Use the **mall** program (at the end of this chapter) or **/etc/motd** to alert people to change their passwords. Do this with **crontab**, and you won't even have to think about it again.

Groups

The concept of groups extends the usability and versatility of UNIX. With properly set group privileges, members of a group may share files with some people while excluding all others from them. A group called **edit** can set up privileges such as:

```
-rw-rw-r-- 1 susan    edit 9870 Apr 18 20:56 chapter9
```

so that the owner, **susan**, and any member of the group **edit** can *read* and *write* to the **chapter9** file. Anyone else may only read it. Group privilege is meaningful only when the group file, **/etc/group**, is carefully edited to be sure that only the members of the intended group are attached to the group and that the group entry is protected. Here are some typical group entries:

```
edit:876cAt07dbeh:20:bruce,karen,david,susan
people:3hqE02n1Md33:30:bruce,karen
dragons:4hQ83zO3Fm9A:40:david,susan
```

Here, **20** is the unique number assigned to the group **edit**. The **edit** group privilege becomes valid for a user only when her login name is entered into this file.

Only when a person (**susan**) is part of an active group (**edit**), or uses **newgrp** (with the correct password) to temporarily join the group does the group permissions for the members' files (**chapter9**) become functional.

The group number assigned to a user in her **/etc/passwd** file entry is the default group for that user. If she is listed as a member of several groups in **/etc/group**, she may switch between those groups at will by simply executing the **newgrp** command with the name of the desired group. If she is *not* listed as a group member (for group **people**, let's say) she may only **newgrp** to **people** if she knows the group password associated with **people**:

```
$ whoami
susan
$ create test
$ ls -l test
-rw-rw-r-- 1 susan     edit        0 Apr 18 20:56 test
$ newgrp dragons
$ whoami
susan
$ create another
$ ls -l another
-rw-rw-r-- 1 susan  dragons        0 Apr 18 20:57 another
$ newgrp people
Password: foobar
$ whoami
susan
$ create yetanother
$ ls -l yetanother
-rw-rw-r-- 1 susan   people        0 Apr 18 20:59 yetanother
$
```

A Note on Group Passwords

There is still no consistent way to apply group passwords. Older UNIX systems had no provision for group passwords whatsoever. Some later UNIX systems have group commands that encrypt the group password in **/etc/group** just as **passwd** encrypts the login password. Others simply allow an unencrypted password to be placed in the password field in the **/etc/group** file, but in cases like this care must be taken to prevent anyone other than **root** from reading the group file. If an encrypted password is needed in **/etc/group** and no command supports it, here is how to add one:

1. Make a dummy entry in **/etc/passwd**:

```
# ed /etc/passwd
751
$
a
dummy::999:999::::
.
w
770
q
#
```

2. As **root**, create an encrypted password for dummy:

```
# passwd dummy
# New password: eggn0g
#
```

3. Look at the new dummy entry in **/etc/passwd**, and carefully copy the encrypted password on a piece of paper:

```
# tail -1 /etc/passwd
dummy:2ux8ha#4%bc:999:999::::
#
```

4. Edit the **/etc/group** file, and enter the encrypted password there:

```
# ed /etc/group
58
/edit/
edit::20:bruce,karen,david,susan
s/::/:2ux8ha#4%bc:/p
edit:2ux8ha#4%bc:20:bruce,karen,david,susan
w
74
q
#
```

5. Delete the dummy entry from **/etc/passwd**:

```
# ed /etc/passwd
770
$
d
w
751
q
#
```

For best security, you should disable the group passwords completely. As we pointed out earlier, people do not protect group passwords as vigorously as their own personal account. If group passwords are disabled, then only **root** can assign people to groups. This means more work for you, but also a much more secure system. On most systems, simply having *no* password for a group in the **/etc/group** file disables passwords and prevent people from switching groups with **newgrp**. But we recommend, if only for the sake of reminding yourself, that you put the word **VOID** or something similar in the password field of the group file.

▪ The Restricted Shell — rsh ▪

While most users feel that they are heavily restricted when it comes to security administration (compared to **root**), the average user has enough privilege to get into plenty of trouble. The ideally secured machine has no lines outside of the console and no users other than the administrator. However, such a machine is incapable of producing much work. To tighten up a machine's security and prevent damage either from those who lack expertise in UNIX (or those who have too much), a restricted shell is available.[4] It acts very much like the standard Bourne shell with several exceptions. The person confined to a **rsh** cannot:

- change directory
- reset his search path variable **PATH** or **SHELL** environment variable (depends on version)
- use the "**/**" character in a path name, thus effectively eliminating trips outside the home directory
- redirect output because the **>** and **>>** forms of redirection are unavailable
- **exec** a program (depends on version)

On some machines, a companion editor **red** is provided to give similarly restricted use in editing.

---

4 If there is no **rsh** file on your system, make a link from **/bin/sh** to **/bin/rsh**, and execute **rsh** to see if it works as we describe.

The administrator can further restrict an **rsh** user by making a special restricted directory **/usr/rbin**, copying in only those programs needed by the restricted user, and setting the **PATH** for that user to **/usr/rbin**.

Does this sound like a lot of trouble? As time goes on, a restricted user will probably ask for more commands than you have given him. At this point, your options are:

1. Refuse. This will be safe but might get you in trouble with management.
2. Give in. Put the desired commands in **/usr/rbin**. Each new command is a potential security hole. Do you have time to check them all?
3. Give up. Giving the restricted shell user a normal shell may open a can of worms, but it is likely to force the issue. If he is a bad guy, you will probably find out fast.

Unfortunately, the security goals of the system administrator are not always in line with the goals of management. In fact running a tight system may put you at odds with both the user community and management. Taking any privilege away once granted makes you a bad guy with management. It is tempting to compromise security to avoid run-ins with management, but these compromises leave the system open to all sorts of potential security breaches.

One method of providing restricted access to a single program is to use that program as a user's shell, as in this **passwd** entry:

```
joe:hsdfkyeiuky:59:100:Joe Editor:/own/joe:/usr/ucb/vi
```

Joe can now use only **vi**. Or can he? By typing **:sh** from within **vi**, Joe gets a regular shell, and can then do whatever a normal user can. A better way is to execute **vi** from a restricted **rsh**:

```
# grep joe /etc/passwd
joe::hsdfkyeiuky:59:100:Joe Editor:/own/joe:/bin/rsh
# cd /own/joe
# ls -la
total 3
drwxr-xr-x  2 root    bin         64 Mar  9  1984 .
drwxr-xr-x 27 root    bin        512 Nov 22 19:18 ..
-r-x--x--x  1 joe     bin        223 Mar  7  1984 .profile
# cat .profile
PATH=/usr/rbin
SHELL=/bin/rsh
export PATH SHELL
/usr/ucb/vi
exit
#
```

Now even if Joe figures out how to escape to the shell, all he will get is **rsh**. Notice that Joe can execute his own **.profile**, but can't change or erase it.

One thing you should know is that the restricted shell available on your system may not be truly restricted. New holes are found periodically, and new versions of the restricted shell are written to deal with them. There's no guarantee that even the newest **rsh** doesn't have a way out, so it should never be used to contain a potentially hostile user.

▪ Data Encryption ▪

Another way to prevent data from being read is to make the data unreadable to anyone accessing it. This is done by coding or encrypting it. The **crypt** command is a software version of the old German Enigma code machine used in World War II. It uses a single rotor with 256 elements. Although it is not impossible to break a coded file made with **crypt**, it is difficult enough to keep all but the most serious intruder at bay.[5]

crypt is a filter that encodes or decodes as it takes in data. It relies on the use of a **key**, like this:

```
$ cat no_code | crypt passwl > coded
```

where the file **no_code** is passed to **crypt** with the key **passwl** and encoded. The output is then redirected to the file **coded.** To decrypt the file, you reverse the process:

```
$ cat coded | crypt passwd > no_code
```

There are several problems with this, however. The first is that both the encrypted text (the file called **coded**) and the clear text (the file **no_code**) are left on the system. This makes it much easier for a potential spy to decrypt any future messages, because almost everyone who uses **crypt** tends to use the same key over and over again.

The solution to this is never keep the clear text on the system. This can be done by using the editor (**ed** or **vi**) with the **-x** encryption option, so that the file is always stored encrypted and can be decrypted whenever it is again edited or examined:

---

5 You should be warned, however, about an article in a recent issue of the *AT&T Bell Laboratories Technical Journal* (see the *Bibliography*) that, while terse, does discuss a method of attacking **crypt**.

```
$ ed -x coded
Key: bigjohn
a
Hello there everybody.
.
w
23
q
$ cat coded
bcx5@fuoiwe47h139po9803
$ cat coded | crypt bigjohn
Hello there everybody.
$
```

Another problem with the way we have been using **crypt** is that the key is given on the command line. Any good spy can simply run **ps -af** and see your key. To prevent this, force **crypt** to prompt you for your key:

```
$ cat coded | crypt
Key: bigjohn
Hello there everybody.
$
```

Encryption seems to be a nearly perfect solution to the security problem. The super-user can access any file and directory in the system, but even she cannot ordinarily read the contents of an encrypted file. A problem arises if a user's files are encrypted and he leaves the company or forgets the key. His files are inaccessible! For this reason the **crypt** command is restricted on some machines.

The last security flaw of **crypt** is that a dishonest super-user could compromise it by modifying it so that it secretly writes the user's name and key to a hidden file. This can even be done without the source code, although we won't mention how. Since it is hard for the average user to determine whether this has been done, truly top-secret material should not be trusted to a multiuser system.

▪ High Security ▪

The foregoing will generally prove sufficient for end-user populations. If you have C programmers (especially systems programmers) on your machine, or sensitive material, you cannot afford to be complacent.

Each of the techniques presented here has been used successfully to break into a UNIX system. While some of them require great technical skill, others do not. By presenting the details, we intend to shock you into action, rather than making it easier for the bad guys. Most of these methods are well-known already, though we know a few more than aren't (unfortunately beyond the scope of this book).

Exploring the Limits

A bad guy has all the time he wants to crack your security at leisure. Some try to find system limitations in order to exploit them. For example, in UNIX Version 6, a bad guy could open so many files that there was room in the system's file table for only one more to be opened. Opening the final file made him **root**, automatically. In another case, the **su** program was written so that entering a very long password (even though incorrect) would write over an internal buffer, forcing the long password to "match."

While both these system bugs have been fixed, you can never be certain that a new one has not been introduced, or that an old one hasn't been found yet. Method of protection: none!

Device and Conquer

The **/dev** directory is a potential gold mine for bad guys with enough knowledge. All devices should be as fully read and write protected as possible. Let's start with a simple example. Suppose you have carefully protected your source code directory (as you should, since you might be held liable if someone stole the code). We examine the permissions and the disk partitions involved:

```
$ mount
/    on /dev/xt0a read/write on Sat Dec  7 20:34:09 1985
/usr on /dev/xt0c read/write on Sat Dec  7 20:34:13 1985
/src on /dev/xt1b read/write on Sat Dec  7 20:34:15 1985
$ ls -ld /src
drwx------15 bin     sys        1104 Nov 22 02:04 /src
$ ls -l /dev/*xt1b
crw-r--r-- 1 root    bin      84, 17 Dec  4  1984 /dev/rxt1b
brw-r--r-- 1 root    bin      73, 17 Nov  8 20:33 /dev/xt1b
$
```

While the ownership and permissions of the **/src** directory have been carefully set, the device that this file system is mounted on is readable by anyone. Therefore, *anyone* can write a program to read the device, extract the inode information, and read any file he wants! If the disk device is writable by anyone, then *anyone* can do what he wants to the entire file system. This can range from wiping it out to changing permissions and SUID bits on any file. Method of protection: all entries in **/dev** pertaining to disks should be mode 600 and owned by **root**.

Overly Intelligent Terminals

Modern CRT terminals are able to do much work on their own. A short sequence of control characters can be sent to a terminal to make it delete or insert a line, position the cursor, and so on. This makes it relatively easy to write screen-oriented text editors and other programs.

Unfortunately, many such terminals also make it easy for bad guys. For example, the following command line forces a Wyse 50 terminal to transmit the command

```
rm -r *
```

to the computer:

```
echo "\0338rm -r *\0339\033s"
```

If this command is typed in by a bad guy and *redirected to your terminal*, the computer will think that *you* typed the **rm** command and will merrily begin removing all your files. The bad guy can even send the "lock keyboard" command to your terminal, preventing you from halting the runaway command. Instead of removing your files, he can send a series of commands that give him a **sushi** program owned by you.

Naturally, if you are **root** when this trick is sprung on you, the results will be that much worse. Method of protection: if you use a terminal that can be forced to transmit information to the host computer by a code sequence (most can), the only defense is to disable other users and processes from writing to your **tty** line. The simplest way to do this is to execute the command:

```
mesg n
```

when you log in (from your **.profile** or **.cshrc** file). This has the unfortunate side effect of preventing interterminal communications via the **write** command.

▪ Handy Shell Programs ▪

checksecure

This should be run by **cron** as **root**, as often as you think necessary for your installation. It will send you information by **mail** on **setuid** programs owned by **root** and programs in **root**'s execution path that may be written by others:

```
find / -user root -perm -4000 -exec ls -l {} \;              \
        | mail root # setuid
find `echo $PATH | tr ":" " "` -perm -0002 -exec ls -l {} \; \
        | mail root # writable
```

Sample output:

```
From root Tue Sep 24 23:06 EDT 1985
-rwsr-xr-x 2 root  bin    14488 Oct 13  1983 /usr/lib/lpd
-rwsrwsr-x 1 root  bin    15490 Mar 15  1984 /usr/lib/atrun
-rwsr-x--- 1 root  news    9012 Sep 14 00:57 /usr/lib/news/mapsh
```

```
---s--s--x 1 root  uucp   28012 Mar  8  1984 /usr/lib/uucp/xqt
-rwsrwxr-x 1 root  bin    16838 Dec 16  1983 /usr/lib/jobdaemon
-rwsrwsr-x 1 root  bin    38234 Jul 23  1984 /usr/lib/lpadmin
-rwsrwsr-x 1 root  bin    13020 Jul 23  1984 /usr/lib/lpshut
-rwsrwsr-x 1 root  bin    29790 Nov 28  1984 /usr/lib/lpsched
-rwsr-xr-x 1 root  bin    23928 Jun 28  1984 /usr/lib/ex3.6recover
-rwsr-xr-x 1 root  bin    17468 Jun 28  1984 /usr/lib/ex3.6preserve
---s--x--x 1 root  bin    14804 Mar  7  1984 /usr/bin/uulog
-rwsr-xr-x 1 root  bin    22512 Mar 10  1984 /usr/bin/mail
-rwsr-xr-x 1 root  bin    19082 Dec  3  1984 /bin/login
-rwsr-xr-x 1 root  bin     5768 Dec  3  1984 /bin/mkdir
-rwsr-xr-x 1 root  bin    12078 Dec  3  1984 /bin/passwd
-rwsrwxr-x 1 root  bin     6170 Dec  3  1984 /bin/rmdir
-rwsr-xr-x 1 root  bin    15588 Dec  3  1984 /bin/su
-rwsr-sr-x 3 root  uucp   29974 Dec  4  1984 /bin/mail
-rwsrwsr-x 2 root  sys    22176 Dec  4  1984 /bin/lp
```

The output can be saved in a hidden file owned by **root** with mode 600, and run through **diff** with each new invocation of **checksecure** to look for changes, which will probably be real threats.

sticky

Similar to the above program, **sticky** finds all files on the system with the sticky bit set:

```
find / -perm -1000 -exec ls -l {} \;   \
      | mail root # sticky bit
```

```
From root Tue Sep 24 23:06 EDT 1985
-rwxr-xr-t 3 bin     sys      131078 Feb 15  1985 ex
-rwxr-xr-t 3 bin     sys      131078 Feb 15  1985 vi
-rwxr-xr-t 3 bin     sys      131078 Feb 15  1985 view
-rwsr-sr-t 2 news    news      63558 Dec 22  1984 inews
-rwsr-sr-t 2 news    news      63558 Dec 22  1984 rnews
```

Note that only two programs were actually found, since each link shows up separately.

mall

This is a cute one-liner. As **wall** writes a message to everyone on the system, **mall** mails a message to everyone on the system:

```
mail `ls /usr/spool/mail`
```

You will have to change the directory to **/usr/mail** on AT&T's UNIX versions. In addition, System V's **mail** program deletes null mail files, so the following line is more reliable there:

```
mail `cut -f1 -d: /etc/passwd`
```

Unfortunately, this also has the side effect of generating mail for every separate login entry, including **uucp** logins and administrative logins that are generally forwarded to **root**.

syssnoop: Tracks User Accounting and Disk Usage

syssnoop monitors user activity. It executes once a week, getting the system's (System III) user accounting and disk usage data:

```
#
#                           syssnoop
#   a program for weekly system usage statistical gathering
#                      bh hunter 12:12:83
#
> /tmp/tmp.$$
df >> /tmp/tmp.$$
echo >> /tmp/tmp.$$
disku -ams | sort -rn >> /tmp/tmp.$$
echo "                         BLOCKS / USER" >> /tmp/tmp.$$
disku -adtsm >> /tmp/tmp.$$
echo >> /tmp/tmp.$$
disku -ams  | awk '{sum = sum + $1}
END {print "total system file blocks ", sum}' >> /tmp/tmp.$$
echo >> /tmp/tmp.$$
echo "                         USER ACCOUNTING" >> /tmp/tmp.$$
echo "user   dept   connect   #commands   cpu   records" \
      >> /tmp/tmp.$$
echo "id     no     time      issued      time  r or w'tn" \
      >> /tmp/tmp.$$
au | sort -nr +5 -6 >> /tmp/tmp.$$
echo >> /tmp/tmp.$$
ac >> /tmp/tmp$$
lpr /tmp/tmp.$$
rm /tmp/tmp.$$
exit
```

The data output provides the system administrator with valuable disk usage and user information he needs to plan his system administration activity for the following week.

By the way, a seasoned system administrator also can catch system abusers by reading the output of this script. Normal activity shows a balance of CPU time and disk I/O.[6] If you find a correlation between high CPU time and high file activity, you probably have a busy user. If there is a disparity, the user is may be making unauthorized or time-wasting use of the system. He merits watching.

▪ Chapter Summary ▪

Despite the many security features on UNIX, some quite elaborate, we have seen that there are ways around most of them. Since UNIX was originally designed to help programmers share work together, this should not be too surprising.

When all is said and done, UNIX probably isn't any more insecure than other multiuser operating systems. No system is totally secure; it just has holes that have not been found yet. Knowing the security problems of UNIX gives you a head start on the bad guys. It is up to you — with the understanding and cooperation of your users — to keep your system safe.

---

6 Activity such as calculating *pi* to 10^6 places does not involve disk writes. Therefore, this activity shows as high CPU tasks with no disk I/O.

CHAPTER 10

TERMINALS

All about Terminals

Terminals, the source of nearly all original data, are the windows to the system from the outside world. But quiet, polite CRT terminals were unknown to the original UNIX. It had a Teletype instead. This slow, indestructable, oil-dripping, noisily clanking escapee from the Smithsonian was the only terminal available for most early computers, including the little PDP-7 that Ken Thompson used to give birth to his MULTICS variant, UNIX. In those days programmers had to live with any terminal device that could be scrounged, begged, or borrowed. As a result, UNIX has a versatile terminal interface second to none, with provisions for all sorts of **tty** (*t*ele*ty*pe) oddities such as delays for formfeeds, tabs, carriage returns, and linefeeds.

This UNIX past affects us today. Imagine that you bought a terminal to attach to your UNIX system that emulates a VT100. All you have to do is attach it by cable and "make it run." On most operating systems this can be a trauma. Sometimes it involves writing an addition to the computer's Input/Output system in assembly language and recompiling the entire thing. Making a terminal talk to UNIX is nowhere near that difficult.

Few operating systems have as much versatility as UNIX in dealing with asynchronous serial devices (ports). For normal everyday devices, such as terminals, teletypes, printers, and modems, UNIX provides device drivers that are so versatile, it is seldom necessary to write special drivers. UNIX also provides a way to reset a device's characteristics dynamically. You can change characteristics "on the fly" if you have to.

▪ Initializing the Ports ▪

Before any data can pass through a serial port, a few parameters must be set. There are two main parameters required to initialize a port. The first parameter is whether the port spawns a **getty**.[1] If the port is going to be used by a device that logs into the system, such as a terminal or a modem, it must be prepared to spawn a **getty**. If it is going to be used for output, such as a printer, no **getty** can be present on the port. The second parameter is the transmission speed (baud or line rate) of the device.

Beyond these two parameters there are many other characteristics that can be set as well, such as **xon/xoff** protocol, tab expansion, upper/lowercase, and folding and character delays, to mention a few. Fortunately, the defaults generally work just fine.

/etc/ttys

Older UNIX (Version 7 and before) and XENIX III are simple and forgiving. Setting a port is a one-line entry to the **/etc/ttys** file:

```
$ cat /etc/ttys
1dtty0
1dtty1
0dtty2
0dtty3
0dtty4
19tty5
1dtty6
09tty7
```

Let's dissect a few of the entries:

Getty?	Speed	Address
1	d	tty0
0	d	tty2
0	9	tty7

The first section of each entry is a **1** (yes) or **0** (no) to indicate whether to spawn a **getty**. The questions it answers is "Getty?" The characters in the address section are the file name (base name) of the special file (port) as it is known in the **/dev** directory. Line speed (baud rate), the second character in the **/etc/ttys** entry, requires a little translation table to help you see what's going on:

1 The **getty** (get tty) is the process that lurks about a port waiting for someone to log on. The word *spawn* refers to the way that **getty**s are continually created by the system.

Code	Baud Rate
1	50
2	75
3	110
4	134.5
5	150
6	200
7	300
8	600
9	1200
a	1800
b	2400
c	4800
d	9600
e	Ext A and 19200
f	Ext B
d e f g	300 / 1200 / 150 / 110
h i	1200 / 300

Now, armed with all of this information, let's put a 300 baud modem on port 4. The current entry for port 4 is **0dtty4**, a 9600-baud port with no **getty**. So right now this port is good for little more than filling a space in the **/etc/ttys** file, but it does remind you that the port exists on your system. The modem you want to attach is an auto-answer device you purchased to take incoming logins from your pesky cousin Freddie, the hacker. Your modem can be set to either 300 or 1200 baud, but because you hate to hear from him, you set it at the slowest rate, 300 baud, to discourage him from sending too much mail. The disadvantage to you is having your phone line tied up. The answer to "Getty?" is **1** (yes), and the port is **tty4**. Three hundred baud in the chart is a **7**, so the entry in **/etc/ttys** should be changed to:

```
17tty4
```

The last two entries in the above table refer to speeds for dial-up lines. Most modern auto-answer modems change speeds automatically to match the calling modem, so a 300/1200 baud modem could be logging in a call at either speed. The **tty** driver is written so that when a BREAK or NULL character is detected, it switches to the next speed in the sequence.[2] The effect is that if you attempt to log in at the wrong speed on a port that uses **h** or **i** in its **ttys** entry, sending BREAK or NULL cycles it through the other speeds. Choosing **h** or **i** (or **d**, **e**, **f**, **g**, in the other case) selects which speed UNIX tries first. This should be the most likely dial-up speed (probably 1200 baud).

---

2 BREAK is actually not a character but consists of sending a solid 500 ms. burst of 1's. It is usually generated by a special key on your terminal. NULL is simply ASCII 0 hex (*not* the ASCII code for numeral zero), and can be generated by typing Control-@.

/etc/inittab

inittab is new UNIX (System III and above). **inittab** is not quite as cryptic as **/etc/ttys**, but it is a bit more complicated to use. Typical **/etc/inittab** entries for ports look like this:[3]

```
co:1234:respawn:/etc/getty console 9600
11:2:respawn:/etc/getty -t 60 tty11 1200
12:2:off:/etc/getty tty12 9600
13:2:respawn:/usr/lib/uucp/uugetty -r -t 60 tty13 1200
14:2:respawn:/etc/getty tty14 9600
```

The entries are separated into fields with colons as the field delimiters.

The console (**co**) and port 14 are terminal ports. Ports 11 and 13 are modem ports, and port 12 is a hardwired, null-modem port (a direct connect with pin 2 wired to 3 and 3 to 2) to another computer. Let's examine the entry for port 14 more carefully:

Id	Init	Action	Command
14	**2**	**respawn**	**/etc/getty tty14 9600**

Like its **/etc** "cousins" (**passwd** and **group**), **inittab** uses the colon "**:**" as a delimiter. The first (id) field is a unique number identifier, usually the port number. Port 14 is specified as "port one four" (*not* "port fourteen") signifying board 1 port 4.

The second (init) field is the **init** level at which the device becomes active. If there is no entry in this field, the device is **always** active. Use **init** level 2 to make the device active when running multiuser on most systems. However, as we showed earlier, you can do far more than designate one number for the entire system's multiuser operation. You can use **init** level 2 for your local lines, 3 to add remote lines, and 5 to activate lines attached to the PBX (phone lines). Be creative — it's your file and your machine.

The third field is an action field. The most important actions for use with terminals are:

respawn	Start up the process (in the next field) if it isn't already running.
off	If the process in the next field is running, kill it. If it is nonexistent, ignore it.
wait	Start the process and wait for it to terminate.

The last field is the command that you want to execute in conjunction with the action in the third field. The most frequently used command is **/etc/getty**. Even if you don't want anything on the port, you can't leave the field blank. It is traditional in that case to use a **getty** in the fourth field and **off** in the third. This guarantees

3 The System III **inittab** is similar to System V's, except that **c** is used instead of **respawn** and **k** is used instead of **off**.

no **getty** will be on the port. This "no-**getty**" technique is used for printer ports and outgoing modem ports like **tty12**. AT&T systems (System V Release 2 and later) have a **uugetty** program available that allows one modem to work for both incoming and outgoing calls; this is shown on port **tty13**.

It is important to know that the speeds given as arguments to **getty** are not actually baud rates; they are really labels for lines in the **gettydefs** file (System V and later). That means you could use descriptive words such as **fast** instead of **9600**, although it could be confusing.

/etc/gettydefs

The **gettydefs** file eliminates the **/etc/ttys** problem of being "stuck" with the predefined switchable baud rates and also lets you "customize" your login ports. Here is a sample **/etc/gettydefs** file:

```
1200# B1200 SANE # B1200 HUPCL SANE IXON TAB3 #login: #300

300# B300 SANE # B300 HUPCL SANE IXON TAB3 #login: #1200

9600# B9600 SANE CLOCAL # B9600 SANE #infopro login: #9600
```

The fields are separated by a pound sign (**#**) instead of the usual colon (**:**). The first field, as we have noted, is the label corresponding to the speed in an **inittab getty** entry. The second field is called *initial-flags*, and is used to initialize the port.

The "flags" referred to are actually collections of bit patterns used in the **termio(7)** interface package of System V. Looking at the manual entry for **termio** in Section 7 shows that the flags are written in all CAPITAL letters, and that there are literally dozens of them. Luckily, all you really have to do here is specify a baud rate (which always begins with a capital **B**) and the catchall value **SANE**, which keeps things "normal." Another flag used often is **CLOCAL**, which specifies that a terminal is directly attached, rather than through a modem.

The next field is *final-flags*, and it is used to set up the port with the parameters that will be used throughout the login session. While these can be changed by the user at will using **stty**, it is a good idea for you to properly set up all ports at login time. Like *initial-flags*, this field needs the actual baud rate. As a minimum, we recommend the flags **SANE**, **HUPCL**, **TAB3**, and **IXON**. For dial-up lines, **HUPCL** allows the phone line to be hung up automatically once the user logs off (if the hardware was designed correctly). **TAB3** expands tab characters to spaces and ensures that your screen displays properly. **IXON** allows you to temporarily stop output with Control-S, and resume it with Control-Q.

After this, things are simple. The next field is the prompt the user will see. Here it's important to enter exactly what you want, and be sure to leave a space after the colon (the colon after the prompt is the reason this file uses a **#** to separate fields). Most people like to add the name of their machine (see our 9600 baud entry) to their prompt. Even so, it's a good idea to *always* use the word **login:** as the last word of your prompt, because that is what other computers will scan for when they attempt to log in automatically (see *Chapter 12*).

The last field is called *next-id*, and is used to point to the next speed to use when a BREAK or NULL character is received during the login process. As you can see in this sample, if the end of the 1200 baud line is reached, the 300 baud line is tried, then back to 1200 again. You can create your own merry chase through any sequence of baud rates you want. Note that here, 9600 baud terminals are hardwired (the CLOCAL flag shows this) and so the entry simply loops around back to 9600 in all cases.

Two last things to remember about the **gettydefs** file: there *must* be a blank line between entries, and the *first* entry is taken to be the default line speed if no speed was specified for the line in **inittab**.

To check the entries in **gettydefs**, you can run **/etc/getty** with the **-c** (check) option:

```
$ /etc/getty -c /etc/gettydefs

**** Next Entry ****
1200# B1200 SANE HUPCL # B1200 SANE IXON TAB3 #login: #300

id: 1200
initial flags:
iflag- 0 oflag- 0 cflag- 2651 lflag- 0
final flags:
iflag- 12446 oflag- 14005 cflag- 651 lflag- 73
message: login:
next id: 300

**** Next Entry ****
300# B300 SANE HUPCL # B300 SANE IXON TAB3 #login: #1200

id: 300
initial flags:
iflag- 0 oflag- 0 cflag- 2647 lflag- 0
final flags:
iflag- 6446 oflag- 14005 cflag- 647 lflag- 73
message: login:
next id: 1200

**** Next Entry ****
9600# B9600 SANE CLOCAL # B9600 SANE #infopro login: #9600

id: 9600
initial flags:
iflag- 0 oflag- 0 cflag- 6255 lflag- 0
final flags:
iflag- 12446 oflag- 14005 cflag- 655 lflag- 73
```

```
message: infopro login:
next id: 9600
$
```

The check option shows you how **getty** interprets each entry of the file when it runs. The flag values are listed numerically for programmers who might want to check them that way. Making an error in the **/etc/gettydefs** file might mean you would be prevented from logging in (although 300 baud can be used at the console in an "emergency"). So it's prudent to copy a working **/etc/gettydefs** to a temporary file, edit the new copy, and test it with **getty -c**. Here's some sample output of such a run using a file with two typical misspellings and an extra field:

```
$ /etc/getty -c /tmp/newgetty
**** Next Entry ****
300# B301 SANE # B300 TAP3 #login: #1200 #300
Undefined: B301
Undefined: TAP3
Parsing failure in the ''next id'' field
300# B301 SANE # B300 TAP3 #login: #1200 #<—error detected here
$
```

stty

Once you've made the entries in **/etc/ttys** or **inittab**, the remaining port characteristics may need to be set with **stty**. **stty** is not a file to be changed but a dynamic command. It has many options that can set or reset a port to suit your needs.

stty is a handy command for user and administrator alike. Let's say you have installed a new terminal and you find out that the erase character is still set as the old pound sign (**#**) character rather than the *backspace* key. **stty** allows you to reset the erase character dynamically without having to bring the system down. You type in

```
$ stty erase ^h
```

where **^h** can be either the *up-arrow* (caret) followed by **h**, or the actual *backspace* key (Control-H). On some systems you will have to precede the **^h** by a backslash (\). Typing an **stty** without an argument confirms that *backspace* is indeed the erase character:

```
$ stty
speed 9600 baud; evenp hupcl
erase = ^h;
brkint -inpck icrnl -ixany onlcr tab3
echo echoe echok
```

As a general rule, for changes such as this one, you don't want to do them every day, so you should put it in all affected users' **.profile**s, or in **/etc/profile**.

From this example, you should see the flexibility of **stty** when initializing a port at system startup. In Unisoft UNIX ports there is a file called **lpset** called by **rc**, that initializes the printer port and can initialize any other port as well. Here is an excerpt from that file where you can see **stty** in action:

```
stty 300 -raw -echo -nl tabs nl2 cr2 ff1> /dev/lp
stty 1200 -raw -echo -nl -tabs nl0 cr0 >/dev/modem
chmod 666 /dev/tty5
chown nuucp /dev/tty5
```

The printer initialization sets the baud rate at 300 baud, shuts off raw mode (which is useful only during screen-oriented programs), allows carriage return/linefeed pairs, preserves tabs, and sets maximum delays for returns, linefeeds, and formfeeds. This is set up for an ancient printer that needs all the time it can get to output its file.

Only **root** can use the **stty** command with ports other than the ones she owns, unless permissions otherwise indicate. Redirecting **stty** to a port other than the terminal you're on in order to change the settings is a versatile feature of UNIX. Note the syntax:

```
# stty 1200 > /dev/tty7      # pre-System III UNIX
```

which forces **/dev/tty7** to be set to 1200 baud. In System III and beyond there is a difference:

```
# stty sane < /dev/tty7
```

Here we are redirecting *from* the device to be operated on and forcing the terminal line to take on a ''normal'' (sane) value. By not entering any arguments to **stty**, you merely ''read'' what the current settings are on the other port, analogous to just typing **stty** on your own port. As a rule, you must have root user id or effective user id of root (by invoking **su**) to use the **stty** command on another port. Other **stty** options on almost all versions of UNIX include:

raw	raw mode input (no erase, kill, interrupt, quit, LF, EOT; parity bit passed back)
-raw	negate raw mode
cooked	same as ''**-raw**''
-nl	allow carriage return for newlines
-tabs	replace tabs by spaces when printing
tabs	preserve tabs as single characters

ek	reset erase and kill characters back to normal **#** and **@**
erase *c*	set erase character to *c* (default usually Control-H)
kill *c*	set kill character to *c* (default **@**)
intr *c*	set interrupt character to *c* (default *delete*)
quit *c*	set quit character to *c* (default Control-\)
eof *c*	set end-of-file character to *c* (default Control-D)

stty is closely tied to the system call **ioctl**(2). This, and the **termio**(7) entry (Section 7 of the *UNIX System Administrator's Manual*) should be considered mandatory reading for systems programmers.

Most other operating systems have nothing like **stty**. It is usually necessary for a system programmer to develop a stock driver to access devices that require interpretation of characters such as newlines, returns, and formfeeds.

Tabs present a particularly sticky problem maintaining tight columnar control. The flexibility of **stty** eliminates the need for such drivers and output filters in UNIX. If your terminal supports hardware tabbing (it sends eight spaces in response to the tab character), you can speed things up a bit by setting:

```
$ stty tabs
```

which turns tab expansion off.

▪ Screen Control ▪

UNIX loves dumb terminals. The primary editor, **ed**, does not care what your terminal looks like, nor does **vi**'s parent editor, **ex**. On the other hand, people are not as fond of dumb terminals. People like Teletype 5420s, DEC VT101s, TeleVideo 950s, and just about everything else that costs more than $1,000 a tube. We also prefer visual editors like **vi** and software that requires character-mapped screens. All of this requires that the user's environment understand exactly what kind of terminal is being used or emulated. **termcap** is one special type of software that allows this information to be passed into the user environment.

termcap

termcap is one of Berkeley's finest contributions to UNIX. It lets programs requiring screen control have the information necessary to put the characters where you want to see them. To help a new user set up her initial environment, you need to put a statement in her **.profile** or **.login** script telling the shell what the terminal is. First find out what **termcap** calls the terminal. Because you can spend all afternoon wading through the voluminous **/etc/termcap** file, put UNIX to work and have **grep** filter the information out for you:

```
$ grep vt100 /etc/termcap

d0|vt100|vt100-am|vt100|dec vt100:\
        :rf=/usr/lib/tabset/vt100:ku=\EOA:kd=\EOB:kr=\EOC:
d1|vt100|vt100-nam|vt100 w/no am:\
        :am@:xn@:tc=vt100-am:
        :al=99\E[L:dl=99\E[M:ip=7:dc=7\E[P:ei=\E[4l:
di|vt100-23|vt100 for use with vt100sys:\
        :li#23:is=\E[1;23r\E[23;1H:tc=vt100-am:
dt|vt100-w|dec vt100 132 cols (w/advanced video):\
        :co#132:li#24:rs=\E>\E[?3h\E[?4l\E[?5l\E[?8h:tc=vt100-am:
dt|vt100-w-nam|dec vt100 132 cols (w/advanced video):\
        :co#132:li#24:rs=\E>\E[?3h\E[?4l\E[?5l\E[?8h:vt@:
vt100am:tc=vt100-am:
vt100nam:tc=vt100-nam:
vt100s:tc=vt100-s:
vt100w:tc=vt100-w:
```

You see? There is more than one way to skin a DEC.

Needless to say, **termcap** makes even the **/etc/passwd** file look simple. Essentially, **termcap** entries consist of coded actions or descriptions, followed by sequences of ASCII characters necessary to get the terminal to perform those actions. For example, here is a complete entry for a Cadmus graphics tube emulating a "normal" 24x80 terminal:

```
bi|bip|pcs bitmap:\
      :li#24:co#80:cl=\f:ho=\EH:sf=\ES:sr=\Es:\
      :sg#0:ug#0:pt:cm=\EM%r%+ %+ :\
      :so=\ER:se=\Er:us=\EU:ue=\Eu:cd=\EJ:ce=\EK:\
      :nd=\EC:do=\EB:up=\EA:bs:am:al=\EO:dl=\EX:
```

The first two entries show the number of lines and columns respectively (24 by 80, remember?). The next (**cl**, for clear screen) tells a program that sending a formfeed character (Control-L, often written as **\f**) will clear the screen. Following this is **ho** (home cursor, or move it to the top left position), which can be performed by sending *escape* code (notated as **\E**) followed by **H**. And so on.

There has been at least one entire book written about creating and maintaining **termcap** entries (see the *Bibliography*), so we can just begin to give you a flavor of what is involved.

If all this looks too complex, try to get a programmer to do any necessary **termcap** maintenance for you. Try to avoid extra work whenever possible. If a new terminal appears on your system, look through the **termcap** file for others of the same brand. Often, a company will use the same control sequences from model to model. Failing that, see if the terminal will emulate an already existing **termcap** entry. At worst, you will have to read the **termcap** documentation in Section 5 of the manuals.

Putting this information to use, let's set up a **.profile** that allows for three different kinds of terminals on the system. The ports are fixed (the terminals will not move from port to port). By knowing which port the user is on, the system will know what kind of terminal she has, as you can see from the following **.profile**:

```
TTY=`tty`
if [ "$TTY" = /dev/tty0 ]
then
        TERM=vt100
elif [ "$TTY" = /dev/tty1 ]
        TERM=tv910
else
        TERM=viewpoint
fi
PATH=:/bin:/usr/bin:/usr/local:.
HOME=/us/joanna
EXINIT="set wrapmargin=10 autoindent"
export TERM HOME EXINIT PATH
```

Now if the user is on port 0, she is on a DEC VT100. On port 1 she is on a TeleVideo 910. At any other port, including the console, she is on an Adds Viewpoint terminal. This type of little program is especially handy for dialup lines, when you work from home on a different terminal from the one in your office.

Notice that a set of commands are passed into the environment to set up the visual editor, **vi**. This particular **EXINIT** environment variable tells **vi** (and **ex**) to set wraparound at 10 characters to the left screen limit and keep the auto indent feature on. But most important is the **TERM** variable. If it is not **export**ed into the environment, it will not take effect, and programs will not know what to do. On some systems, you may also have to export the location of the **termcap** file:

```
TERMCAP=/etc/termcap
export TERMCAP
```

terminfo

termcap seemed irreplaceable until AT&T introduced **terminfo** in System V Release 2. **terminfo** is a **termcap** work-alike, but it is much larger and better organized in many ways. It is located in **/usr/lib/terminfo**. There is a directory for each letter of the alphabet, and for each number one through nine. The quick way to find a terminal is to go to the directory that starts with the number or letter that corresponds to your terminal. Use the model name, not the manufacturer. Let's say you're looking for an Adds Viewpoint:

```
$ ls /usr/lib/terminfo/v | grep view
viewpoint
$
```

terminfo works in conjunction with the **curses**(3x) library. You can create your own entries and modify existing ones.

▪ Hardware Installation — From Theory to Reality ▪

There are two sides to installing computer hardware: the hardware side (making cables, setting switches) and the software side (entering data on **/etc/ttys** or **inittab** and setting other characteristics with **stty**). On large computer installations there are usually numerous hardware engineers, so the system administrator handles only the software portion of installing hardware. However, if you are on a smaller UNIX installation or if you have your own UNIX machine at home, eventually you're going to have to come to grips with the hardware. Besides, at smaller computer sites, you may be expected to do some hardware installation on the machine as well as your system administration tasks. In this section we're going to take some of what we cover in this chapter and *Appendix B — RS-232 Connections* and apply it to a real-life situation. It's one thing to talk in general terms about **/etc/ttys**, **inittab**, and **stty**, but actually installing a terminal is quite another story. We're going to "install" a terminal on a UNIX system, discussing each step as we go along.

Before we start, there are three informal hardware installation rules to remember:

1. Most terminals are switch set to default to 9600 baud. If, however, your system is heavily loaded, keep the console at 9600 baud and slow the other terminals down to 4800 or less so the system "appears" more responsive.
2. Some devices, such as modems, set themselves. A 300-baud modem is 300 baud, but a 300/1200/2400 baud incoming modem may operate at any one of those speeds. This is a job for **gettydefs**!
3. Printer baud rates depend on the speed a printer is able to receive. Normally you set it a little faster than the printer can receive *unless* you don't have hardware handshaking, in which case you set it a little slower.

Imagine that you just picked up a used Liberty 50 terminal for $150 at a computer flea market. As you take it out of your car and bring it into the house, the sweet success of getting a bargain begins to turn into concern. How much work is it going to take to interface this terminal to your UNIX system? Before you look in the hardware manual, don't forget to look at the back of the terminal, because on rare occasions the switch settings are explained in detail on the back. The Liberty 50 is one of those few, fortunately for us. The switch settings that change line speed, and hardware and software handshaking are among other things listed there.

Generally terminals are 9600 baud. Most UNIX systems are default-set at 9600 when they come out of the box. UNIX is a full duplex ASCII system that uses newlines without returns (no carriage return/linefeed pairs). You are safe to assume that the switch settings you want are full duplex with auto-linefeed off. (Refer to your hardware manual.) **stty** does not default to **xon-xoff** protocol for non-login ports, nor is it very fussy about parity. So set parity off. You have a choice, either 8 data bits transmission with 1 stop bit or 7 with 2. It's a coin toss. Using 7 guarantees that the characters received and sent are in the ASCII set. Review the plan:

baud rate	9600
parity	off
duplex	full
auto lf	off
data bits	7
stop bits	2

This is all the information you need to initialize the port and set characteristics.

Confidence high, you expect to have the terminal installed shortly. Unfortunately, your confidence dwindles when you try to find a Liberty 50 in **termcap** or **terminfo**. It isn't there. Fortunately, the good point about inexpensive terminals is that they are almost always emulators. The Liberty terminal manual shows that it emulates a number of common terminals recognized by **termcap**. One of the emulation modes in **termcap** is TeleVideo 910. If you have **terminfo** instead of **termcap**, you may not even find the TeleVideo 910, but the Liberty also emulates the Hazeltine 1420, so look for that in **terminfo**. Put the **TERM** information in the **.profile** of the users using that port.

The next logical step is to sex the terminal. Common sense tells you that a terminal should be a DTE (Data Terminal Equipment), but you can't always rely on the common sense of hardware manufacturers. For example, DEC uses male connectors on the back of their VT series instead of the standard female connectors. Now you need a spirit of adventure, a lot of patience, and a breakout box. Use Hunter's $1.98 pin tester if you have nothing else.[4] To sex the terminal, test pins 2 and 3 against pin 7. A DTE has pin 2 asserted low — otherwise pin 3 will be low (making it a DCE instead). Test the computer the same way. Chances are it will be a DCE with pin 3 low but you literally never know unless you have done it before.

If you have a conventional marriage (DTE on one and DCE on the other), you may be able to use a straight ribbon cable, 25 wires, all pins in. If this is the case, consider yourself lucky. Unfortunately, cabling is hardly ever this easy. The more sophisticated the terminal and the fussier the computer, the longer it's going to take. Attach 25 wire ribbon cables to both the computer and terminal with a breakout box in the middle. Let's say that the Liberty shows pin 2 low (DTE) and pins 4 (ready to send) and 20 (data terminal ready) high. It is telling you that it is a male (DTE) and ready to go. DTR and RTS high provides a good source of positive voltage if the computer needs a signal source. The smaller AT&T 3B computers need pins 5 and 6 pulled up, so pin 4 on the Liberty is a good source. A machine set up for easy cabling, such as the

4 Refer to *Appendix B*.

Codata 3300, is no problem — a 3 wire (2 to 2, 3 to 3, 7 to 7) cable does just fine.

Once you have your cable made, you need to get the computer ready to talk to the terminal. This is part of the software end of hardware installation. Go into **/etc** and set up the **/etc/ttys** file (old UNIX) or **/etc/inittab** for the new terminal. The baud rate is 9600, and you want to spawn a **getty**. Pick an unused port by number. If the computer is a Codata running System III, and port 4 is open, then the **/etc/ttys** entry is:

```
1dtty4
```

If it is a 3B2/300 and port 4 is open on board 1, the entry in **inittab** is:

```
14:2:respawn:/etc/getty tty14 9600
```

To get the machine to recognize the new port setting, type **init q** in System V or do a **kill -2 1** in System III.

Back to the hardware end. You still have a little more testing to do before you can make your cable. The easiest way is to borrow a functioning cable from another terminal port, but we'll assume this is your first. With a **getty** waiting patiently for a terminal to talk to, start jumpering the breakout box. With both pieces of equipment being sexed opposite (DCE to DTE) pins 2 and 3 are straight across. The ground pins, 1 (if used) and 7 are straight across as well. If both pieces of equipment are of the same sex, a null modem (pins 3 to 2, 2 to 3) is necessary. If these 3-wire connections are sufficient (as they are ninety percent of the time), the **login:** message appears on the terminal. If no login message appears, it's dart board and common sense time. Pin 4 (RTS) on the Liberty is ready to do assertion for the asking. Jumper it on the breakout box to pins 5 and/or 6 on the computer. This should get the desired results and bring on the login message. Should it fail, continue bringing up signal pins (4, 8 and 20) until data flows. Once you get your login, put your cable together and you are in business.

Back to the software part of hardware installation. Now you need to make an entry in the user's **.profile** or **.login** file for the terminal type so **vi** can work. If you have **termcap**, ask it what it thinks about 910s.

```
$ grep 910 /etc/termcap
v0|tvi910|910|televideo910:\
$
```

It will tell you that **termcap** calls your new terminal a v0. Try the same trick on System 5.2 by asking **terminfo** to talk about the Hazeltine 1420:

```
$ ls /usr/lib/terminfo/h | grep 1420
h1420
```

The Hazeltine emulation is OK, so set the emulation switches for the 1420 and go for it.

▪ Chapter Summary ▪

The UNIX system has enough versatility between **ttys** or **inittab**, **stty**, and **termcap** or **terminfo** to handle just about anything in the way of terminals or other asynchronous serial devices. A little familiarity with these files and commands goes a long way toward interfacing with the world.

C H A P T E R 11

PRINTERS ON THE UNIX SYSTEM

Getting Your Printers Running

Once your system is running smoothly, and your users start working, someone will want to print out a file. If your system is like most others, each user doesn't have the luxury of a CRT terminal with a printer attached. You probably have only one or two printers for all your users. As administrator, you have one immediate problem: how do you hook up a printer so that it can be used? You will quickly discover that your next problem is how to prevent two people from using one printer at the same time, but let's start here.

The user and the system administrator deal with the printer from different perspectives. To the user, invoking the printer seems simple, whether it's Version 7 and System III's **lpr** command or System V's **lp** command. In each case, the nomenclature (**lp** and **lpr**) refers to a *line printer*, which can range from an inexpensive matrix printer that prints one character at a time to a very large, expensive impact printer that puts an entire line at a time on paper. A user sends a file to the printer using one of two possible commands:

```
$ lpr filename        # Version 7, BSD, and System III

$ lp  filename        # System V and later
```

Although these two commands accomplish the same results in the end, the internals of **lp** and **lpr** are quite different.

As UNIX system administrator, you get to see the hidden complexities involved when dealing with the printer. Whereas pre-System V UNIX versions handle only a single printer per system, System V can run several different printers, even different printer types, on the same computer. Yet in neither case does the file go directly to the printer. Instead, it is intercepted and managed by a process known as a *spooler*.[1]

What Is a Spooler?

Daisy wheel printers and many dot matrix printers have an effective character transmission rate of 120 *c*haracters *p*er *s*econd (CPS) or less. In order for you to use the printer, you have to have direct access to that printer for as long as it takes to print out your file. In other words, the printer port has to belong to you as owner of the process, or you must have *write* permission for it. Whenever you've got to get character transmission out to a relatively slow device such as a printer, you have to wait for it to be completed before your terminal is free for other tasks. What you want to be able to do is free up your terminal so you do not have to get old waiting for the printer to finish printing your file. Of course, on UNIX you can simply put the process in the background. But let's say your system has one printer and four users, and they all start writing to the printer at once. You guessed it — everybody's output appears jumbled together on the same sheet of paper.

Here's where the spooler comes in. A spooler is a method of buffering or storing data on its way to a specific destination. The purpose of a printer spooler is to hold files to be printed until the line printer is ready to receive and process them. When the printer command (**lpr** or **lp**) is used, each file to be printed is transmitted to the printer spool buffer. It is held there until the spooler program senses that the printer is free, whereupon it sends the file, a character at a time, to the printer. The end result of all this is that the spooler does all the printing and device management, which leaves you free to do something else. On UNIX, spooling is done by copying the data to be printed into a spool area on the disk (**/usr/spool/lp**), then printing it with a *daemon*.

What Is a Daemon?

Daemon is the fanciful name given to a program that emerges to do your bidding when it's needed, and then disappears, as if by magic. In the case of the printer spooler (pre-System V), **lpr** sends its input to the **/usr/spool/lpd** directory, which then causes **/usr/lib/lpd** (sometimes found as **/etc/lpd** instead) to be activated. **/usr/lib/lpd** is the *l*ine *p*rinter *d*aemon which does nothing except go to its assigned directory, (**/usr/spool/lpd**), send every file it finds there to the file (or device) called **/dev/lp**, and then disappear.[2]

Before we take a look at some of the specifics of UNIX printer internals, you should know how to hook up a printer, tell the system it's there, and test it out. *Then* you can get fancy with the spooler.

---

1 Trivia buffs: SPOOL is an acronym for *S*imultaneous *P*eripheral *O*perations *On*-*L*ine.

2 On more advanced systems, you can use the undocumented **-P** flag, which causes a puff of smoke when the daemon disappears.

▪ Attaching a Printer to the System ▪

The first thing you do when putting a printer on the system is to find an open port for the device. Most systems utilize serial interfaces for printers, and it's generally best to put the printer on the last port of the I/O card where it has the lowest priority on most computers' interrupt structures. The reasoning behind this suggestion is that this will probably be the slowest peripheral on your system and you want it to use as little of the system resources as possible. If the I/O card has 8 ports, the printer port is 07, since numbering typically starts from 00. In a perfect world, the physical connection is an easy attachment of ribbon cable with male DB-25 connectors between the computer and the printer, and the printer baud rate set to something reasonable for both the printer and the computer. If the printer runs at 200 characters per second (CPS), a baud rate of 1200 — about 120 CPS — does not use the printer's full speed. Baud rates *over* 2400 make the computer wait for the printer most of the time. 2400 is the only *reasonable* baud rate in this situation. The rule of thumb is: CPS = baud rate divided by 10.

Unfortunately it is usually not that easy. Although in theory all that is needed to make a printer print is one wire from pin 2 (data send) of the computer hooked to pin 3 (data receive) of the printer and a common ground on pin 7, problems arise when the computer considers itself Data Terminal Equipment (DTE) and/or the printer considers itself Data Communications Equipment (DCE). Other problems are devices that need special pins (like clear-to-send) enabled. These problems are beyond the scope of this chapter, so see *Appendix B*.

Centronics parallel printer ports are found on smaller systems such as AT&T's 3B2 series. In some ways a Centronics parallel port is less difficult to work with than a serial port because the protocols and pins are all predefined. Many inexpensive printers come with a parallel port as their only method of input for this reason. The port name for the parallel port in **/dev** is generally self-descriptive (as in **/dev/centronics** or **/dev/parallel),** but we've seen some that say **/dev/lp**. Cabling is a matter of buying a Centronics parallel ribbon cable with the necessary combination of male and female fittings. Of course, you must hook it up to a printer (or plotter) with a Centronics parallel interface. No baud rates have to be set; just plug it in and go.

Once you have selected a printer port, you've got to get the system to recognize that port as a printer port when it comes up. If it is marked port 07 on the back of the computer, it is probably known as **/dev/tty7**, **/dev/serial07**, or something along that line — UNIX systems generally treat any serial device attached to the I/O card as a **tty** device. Go to your **/dev** directory and see if you already have a printer device defined as a serial port. If so, and you take a look at a long listing of **/dev/lp** and the **/dev/tty** files, you may notice that both **/dev/tty7** and **/dev/lp** have the same major and minor device numbers, let's say 4 and 7:

```
$ ls -l /dev/lp /dev/tty*

crw------- 2 daemon    4,  7 Dec  2 10:24 /dev/lp
crw-rw-rw- 1 root      1,  0 Nov 19  1982 /dev/tty
crw------- 1 root      4,  0 Dec  2 08:49 /dev/tty0
crw--w--w- 1 bruce     4,  1 Dec  2 12:33 /dev/tty1
crw------- 1 root      4,  2 Dec  2 08:49 /dev/tty2
crw------- 1 root      4,  3 Dec  2 08:49 /dev/tty3
crw------- 1 root      4,  4 Dec  2 08:49 /dev/tty4
crw------- 1 root      4,  5 Dec  2 08:49 /dev/tty5
crw------- 1 root      4,  6 Dec  2 08:49 /dev/tty6
crw------- 2 daemon    4,  7 Dec  2 10:24 /dev/tty7
```

This means that both have the same driver and port. In fact, they are simply different names for the same device. Notice also the ownership of these files. **/dev/lp** belongs to the printer daemon. Because the daemon owns and runs the printer, this is a sure indication that the system is ready to deal with **lpr**, **lpd**, and **/dev/lp** as a continuous series of "devices" that take a file from the print command **lpr** to the physical printer. As a general rule, if you have a **/dev/lp** entry defined as a device (with major and minor nodes) and its nodes do *not* match those of any **tty** devices on your system, then it's probably a Centronics printer device. If you are using a serial printer, rename **/dev/lp** to **/dev/Centronics** to save it for future use.

Creating two different names for the same device is a useful system administration technique. It is done for two main reasons: fooling the system software and making life easier for you.

Let's say you buy a used Version 7 system with poor documentation from someone, and there's no **/dev/lp** device on it. You attempt to use the spooler, having plugged a serial printer into **/dev/tty7** as we suggest:

```
$ lpr /etc/group
$ /etc/lpd: cannot open /dev/lp
```

Now what? You don't even *have* a **/dev/lp**.[3] Well, *your* printer is on **tty7**, so all you do is this:

```
# ln /dev/tty7 /dev/lp
# ls -l /dev/tty7 /dev/lp
crw-rw-rw- 2 daemon  bin      13,  7 Nov 15 21:12 /dev/tty7
crw-rw-rw- 2 daemon  bin      13,  7 Nov 15 21:12 /dev/lp
#
```

Making the link (**ln**) between **tty7** and **lp** means they are exactly the same file (device in this case). Now when you write to **/dev/lp**, you also write to **/dev/tty7**, and the output goes to your printer with no one the wiser. "No one" in

3 If you had run this as the super-user, you would have created a *file* called **/dev/lp**, which would have silently collected all the output destined for the printer until the disk filled and your system crashed!

this case includes your spooler program, which has no other way of knowing how to reach the real printer.

Is this the "right" way to do things? You bet it is! What would happen if you had the full source code to UNIX? You would proudly go to the directory with the source code for the spooler program, find the line that said "/dev/lp", change it to "/dev/tty7", recompile the program, and install the new version. Apart from the fact that this would take you at least 25 times longer than just making the link, it doesn't help you when you have to change ports for some reason or install a new word-processing program that wants to write to **/dev/lp**. By standardizing on **/dev/lp** as the name for the system default printer, it's simple for you to always make sure that **/dev/lp** addresses the real working printer on your system by linking it to the correct serial port.

This same technique should be used for each individual printer you have. It's easy to forget which of your printers is actually **/dev/lp** if you have three of them, but not if you make links for each printer name:

```
crw-rw-r-- 4 lp      bin      13,  5 Nov 15 21:12 /dev/lp
crw-rw-r-- 4 lp      bin      13,  5 Nov 15 21:12 /dev/lp0
crw-rw-r-- 4 lp      bin      13,  5 Nov 15 21:12 /dev/oki
crw-rw-r-- 4 lp      bin      13,  5 Nov 15 21:12 /dev/tty21
crw-rw-r-- 3 lp      other    13,  6 Nov 15 21:17 /dev/diablo
crw-rw-r-- 3 lp      other    13,  6 Nov 15 21:17 /dev/il
crw-rw-r-- 3 lp      other    13,  6 Nov 15 21:17 /dev/tty22
crw-rw-r-- 2 lp      other    13,  7 Nov 15 21:17 /dev/epson
crw-rw-r-- 2 lp      other    13,  7 Nov 15 21:17 /dev/tty23
```

You should also do this for your other devices. Add a **/dev/modem** link to your outgoing modem line and **/dev/tape** and **/dev/floppy** to those strange devices called **/dev/mt0** and **/dev/fdsk0**.

Making a tty Port Safe for Printers

The first thing to do is make sure logins (actually, **getty**s) to all the printer ports have been disabled, as explained in *Chapter 10*. The kernel's character device switch accesses a device driver that is usually intended for a terminal, but as mentioned earlier, the UNIX kernel is written so that **tty**-related commands can also work with printers.

Next, you must make sure each printer port has the correct characteristics, such as baud rate and tab expansion. If this is not provided for in your UNIX distribution, you must do the job yourself. It should be done at system start up from either **/etc/rc** or from another program called by **/etc/rc**, such as **lpset**. This **lpset** file usually contains a delay statement (such as **sleep 5**), which is used to give the system time to act on commands remaining in the background from **init** and **rc**, and an **stty** command. **stty** is used here to set up the characteristics for the printer port on the computer. Here is a sample **/etc/lpset** file:

```
sleep 5
stty 300  -raw -echo -nl tabs ixon ixany nl0 cr0 > /dev/lp
stty 1200 -raw -echo -nl tabs ixon ixany nl0 cr0 > /dev/tty6
```

There has to be one **stty** command for each **/dev** entry that supports a printer on a **tty** port, as illustrated above. While it may seem more efficient to do the initialization from **/etc/rc**, it is better to do it from a separate file, like **lpset**, in order to keep the internal details isolated.

Printer Troubleshooting

Testing a newly installed printer can be a suspenseful experience. Make it easy on yourself by simplifying the process at first. The way to do that is to bypass the spooler altogether and send some data directly to the printer:

```
# cat /etc/rc > /dev/lp
```

This bypasses the **lpr** command as well as **lpd**, and it's a handy shortcut when testing a new printer and/or printer cable. The output should match what you get when you **cat /etc/rc** to your terminal. But things can go wrong:

Double-spaced output: UNIX separates each line of text with a newline character (an ASCII linefeed (LF), hex code **0a**). Some operating systems use a pair of characters — a carriage return (ASCII CR, hex code **0d**) followed by a line feed — and the printer may have been set accordingly. Your printer will almost surely have a switch to take care of this condition, usually labeled something like *Auto LF* or *CR/LF*. Check the manual for your printer — sometimes the switch is internal or on a separate serial interface card. If no such switch can be found, you can fix the problem with software. Try different **stty** settings using flags such as **onlcr** or **nl**, (and their negations, **-onlcr** and **-nl**) in combination, if necessary, until the output is correct. Then incorporate the final settings in your **lpset** file.

Output all on one line: This is simply the opposite of the above problem — the printer refuses to recognize an LF code unless it is preceded by a CR. Just find the switch and flip it the other way.

Garbage output: If sending a text file to the printer produces strange graphics, alien names, or causes the paper to feed without printing, then the baud rate of the printer does not match the serial port. Check the settings, recycle power to the printer if you have changed any settings, and try again. If you still get garbage, go to the next section *Real Devices and Fooling stty*.

Missing output: Suppose you test the printer by sending it a short file, but later you find that longer printouts have some missing or garbled text. It's likely that the computer is sending data to the printer too fast. Go to the section called *Handshaking*.

No output: Check everything.

Printer switch settings:
Baud rate OK? Parity off? Seven data bits, not eight? Paper in printer properly? Printer turned on and plugged in?

Computer settings:
Baud rate OK? Parity off? Seven data bits, not eight? **/dev/lp** linked to the port the printer is plugged into? Try substituting a working terminal for the printer (set the terminal baud rate to match). Has the **getty** been disabled on the printer port? Does **daemon** (or **lp**, for System V) have write permission for **/dev/lp**?

Cable: Is the cable (or cable adapter) right for the printer? Did you try a terminal cable? Does the printer need extra pins hooked up?

Real Devices and Fooling stty

Generally, everything goes as advertised. The printers and terminals are plugged in, the baud rates are set, and everyone can start doing their work. But sometimes there are peculiarities about certain computers, devices, cables, serial ports, or even software releases that can cause headaches for the new or unwary administrator.

One example may be found on some computers running early versions of System V. Let's say you have a printer plugged in to port **tty23**, and it's set to 1200 baud. You carefully make sure that its **inittab** entry is also set to 1200 baud and doesn't force a login on that line. Now bring the system up. You send a file to the printer and get a long stream of garbage. After checking the baud rate on the printer itself, you attempt to verify that the port is indeed set to 1200 baud:

```
# stty < /dev/tty23
speed 9600 baud; -parity
brkint -inpck icrnl -ixany ixoff onlcr tab3
echo echoe echok
#
```

What's wrong? It turns out that when System V doesn't get the data from a **tty** device, it attempts to reset that **tty** line to a typical setting for the terminal. So you have to fool **stty** by holding the line open while the system comes up. The following shell script has proved to work when other simpler ones have failed. It may look like black magic, but if this is your problem, give it a try:

```
while true
do
     (sleep 60 >/dev/tty23;\
      stty clocal -echo 1200 -parity ixon -ixany tab3 opost \
        < /dev/tty23; \
      chmod 666 /dev/tty23) &
      sleep 10 >/dev/tty23
      stty clocal -echo 1200 -parity ixon -ixany tab3 opost \
        </dev/tty23
      sleep 65535 >/dev/tty23
done
```

We call our version **set_baud** and run it from **/etc/rc** with a line like this:

```
nohup set_baud &
```

Naturally, make sure to substitute the name of *your* port for **/dev/tty23**.

Handshaking

If you hook a printer rated at an honest 120 CPS to a 1200-baud line, you should be able to send data to it all day without dropping a letter. But suppose you buy a fancy new line printer that goes 800 CPS. Plug it into a 9600-baud serial port, and 960 characters per second will pour out of that port. Even if your printer has a 4 KB buffer, disaster will strike in less than 30 seconds as all of the extra characters leak out of the cable onto the floor.

The way to prevent this is for the printer to tell the computer "Slow down, please, I'm getting rather full." The technical term for this is *handshaking*, since both the computer and printer must agree on how to accomplish it. There are two methods possible on UNIX, one based on hardware and the other on software.

Hardware handshaking is the best way to prevent printer overflow. The computer may not respond fast enough to software handshaking when heavily loaded, but hardware can physically force it to stop sending characters. With serial ports, the usual way this is done is with the RTS (pin 4) and CTS (pin 5) lines (see *Appendix B*). You will have to check the manual for your printer and also verify that your computer supports these handshaking lines. Many computers do *not* support any RS-232 lines other than the few basic ones necessary to transmit data. Others have full RS-232 support on just one or two ports, usually reserved for modems. If such is your case, you are probably better off using software handshaking, as the modems need full control more than the printers do.

Software handshaking on UNIX is simple — at least in theory — because every **tty** line is set up to recognize the ubiquitous XON/XOFF[4] protocol. XON/XOFF (sometimes called flow control) is what you are using when you type Control-S (really the ASCII XOFF or DC3 code) at your terminal to temporarily halt data from coming to your screen. Typing Control-Q (ASCII XON or DC1) resumes the flow of data.

In a similar way, most serial printers automatically (or by flipping the appropriate switch) send XOFF to the computer when their input buffers are getting full and XON when the buffers are almost empty and it is again safe to send data. The trick is getting UNIX to honor the protocol, and that can be done in the file where you initialize your printers, by adding the modes **ixon** and **-ixany** to your **stty** line.

Don't try to enable *both* hardware and software handshaking at the same time. Some device is liable to get confused. If you have a UNIX Version 7 machine, you'll almost always *have* to use the hardware handshaking or lower your baud rate: XON/XOFF was not part of **stty** back then. The exceptions are machines on which the **tandem** mode was added to **stty**; this specifically enables XON/XOFF.

Testing the Spooler

If the printer was functional before, but the command line

```
# cat /etc/rc | lpr
```

doesn't work, look in **/usr/spool/lpd** for the answer. Data and lock files should exist and be readable by **daemon**. If it is a new printer installation, your cup of problems runneth over. Recheck the printer switch settings for baud rate, parity, and protocols. They must be in agreement with the parameters passed to **stty** as arguments in the printer setup file, **/etc/lpset**. If the switch settings agree with the port settings in **lpd**, then it is likely that the cable needs attention. A breakout box is unbelievably handy for this purpose. To get **stty** to give the device settings of a character special file, become super-user and invoke **stty** redirected *to* the printer port:

```
$ su
Password: achoo
# stty > /dev/lp      # Version 7 and BSD
speed 2400 baud; -cbreak tab3 -echo
#
```

Don't forget that on newer systems (System III and later) you will have to go the other way to get the same information:

```
# stty < /dev/lp      # System III, V, and later
speed 2400 baud; onlcr tab3 -echo
#
```

---

4 Trivia buffs: XON/XOFF stands for *ex*ternal device *on/off* and was used on Teletype machines to start and stop the paper tape reader.

▪ Version 7 and System III lpr Spooler Internals ▪

The spool directory where Version 7 and System III print output files are stored is called **/usr/spool/lpd**. It is an ordinary directory, and when no user printer requests are present, it is quite empty. When a printer request is made, such as

```
# cat /etc/rc | lpr
#
```

the output created by the list command is sent to a file in the **/usr/spool/lpd** directory and stored with a unique alphanumeric *c*ombination *f*ile name such as **cf00084**. Another file is created as well. It is a **lock** file and has no permissions. The purpose of this lock file is to retain the exclusive use of a device (in this case, a printer) for one user (in this case, the printer daemon). This prevents conflicts like your code listing becoming intertwined with someone else's strudel recipe. A directory listing of **/usr/spool/lpd** looks like this while the print job is running:

```
$ ls -l /usr/spool/lpd
total 26
-rw-r--r-- 1 bruce      13080    Dec 2 10:24 cf00084
-rw-r--r-- 1 bruce         50    Dec 2 10:24 df00084
---------- 1 daemon         0    Dec 2 10:24 lock
$
```

The **df00084** file is a "data file" that tells the spooler the name of the user who requested the printout and what file to print. The daemon owns the lock file, since it actually does the printing.

When the file to be printed is finally sent to the printer, the print file, data file, and lock file are removed from **/usr/spool/lpd**, and the printer is free to print something else. Usually all goes well with this arrangement, and there is nothing for the system administrator to do but enjoy a well thought-out system. Once in a while something does go wrong, and you have to open the hood on the spooler, look inside, and fix it.

Troubleshooting lpr

Imagine a scenario where a user sends a file to the printer and suddenly realizes that it is not the file he wanted to send. It is 60 pages long, so it could tie up the system's only printer for a long time. When you've got a process in deep trouble, the first thing you do is type **ps** (process status command) to get the process identification number. Then you issue a kill on the process. In our scenario, however, a kill stops the printer, but the problem is far from being solved. In fact, you are in worse trouble than ever, because the next request to the printer spooler fails to produce the expected results — namely, a printout. What happened, and what is the cure?

A lock file is present when a file is being sent to the physical printer. Its purpose is to prevent two or more files from trying to go to the printer simultaneously. When anything interrupts the process, such as a soft kill or a system crash, the lock file is left in the spool directory, and that's why the printer won't print. On pre-System V UNIX there is no way to cancel a print request; so as long as the lock file is there, nothing can be sent to the printer. As a result, printer files accumulate in the spool directory.

The cure is easy enough when the workings of the spooler are understood. You simply remove the lock file. A typical repair session looks like this:

```
$ su
Password: gesundheit
# ps -ax
   PID TTY TIME CMD
     0 ?  139:50 swapper
     1 ?    3:16 /etc/init
 27547 ?    0:00 getty -t 600 /dev/tty12 1200 h1500
 24937 co   0:10 -csh
    42 co   0:01 sh /usr/local/set_oki_baud
 24718 11   0:11 -csh
 24925 20   0:13 -csh
 24930 bi   0:15 -csh
 24717 13   0:11 -csh
    70 co   0:00 sleep 65535
 27729 ?    0:03 /usr/lib/lpd cf0084
 27774 bi   0:03 ps -ax
  3156 bi   5:09 cron
# kill 27729
# cd /usr/spool/lpd
# ls
cf0084 df0084 lock
# rm -f lock cf0084 df0084
#
```

Another possible problem is getting no output through the spooler, even though the printer works when redirecting to it. The first thing to check is that the data and lock files are being created; if they aren't, it's a sure bet that either the spool directory doesn't exist or that its permission bits prevent the daemon from writing into it. The **/usr/spool/lpd** directory should be owned by **daemon**, and the actual spooler daemon program (**/usr/lib/lpd** or **/usr/lib/lpdaemon**, or sometimes it's under **/etc** rather than **/usr/lib**) should be SUID and owned by **daemon**:

```
# chown daemon /usr/lib/lpd /usr/spool/lpd
# chmod 775 /usr/spool/lpd
# chmod 4755 /usr/lib/lpd
#
```

Another possibility is that the spooler itself (**/bin/lpr**) is not executable by the average user (it should be mode 755). Of course, the daemon should be running! Do a **ps -ax** and check for **lpd**. If you're still not getting printouts after checking all this, make sure the daemon has permission to write to the printer device. The safest way is to give ownership of the printer to the daemon:

```
# chown daemon /dev/lp
#
```

Naturally, in order for you to give ownership to the **daemon** login, it must first exist. Take a tip from System V and create the login **daemon**, with a password of VOID, and a home directory of **/usr/spool/lpd**.

Since there is no **accept/reject** command on UNIX Version 7 to stop spooler input, it is possible to queue up so much output that the spool directory overflows. You will notice this when console messages saying "no space left on device" appear, especially when you check and find the device in question is where the spool directory is, and then you go in there and see dozens of big files. There might be one user who is merrily trying to print out every file on the entire system (his login name will be apparent by the ownership of the spool files). If so, you should deal with him appropriately, considering both your company's regulations and the laws against homicide.

If the spool files being printed out are indeed useless, you can simply remove them and all will be well. On the other hand, if legitimate requests have simply gotten ahead of the printer, the best thing to do is prevent further spooling for awhile. This can be done either informally (using the **wall** program, or the telephone, to ask everyone politely to stop spooling temporarily) or by brute force (making **/bin/lpr**, the printer spooler, nonexecutable until the printer catches up).

▪ UNIX System V Printer Internals ▪

lpr, the Version 7, System III, and BSD printer spooler command, is simple enough. It accommodates one printer, one printer spooler, and one printer port. Thus, UNIX systems running these versions of UNIX are unable to spool to more than one printer. You can always get around this by plugging in a printer to one of the remaining output ports and then reach it by any file transfer command, but that is file transfer, not spooling. UNIX System V's spooler, on the other hand, is happy to deal with more printers than you can possibly afford. It's part of AT&T's answer to the complaint that "UNIX just isn't a commercial system."

Nowadays, a typical commercial computer environment, even a relatively small one, has more than one printer. One printer is usually reserved for handling most system needs, such as program printouts. A large impact printer used for speed (as opposed to print quality), is usually found in bigger installations. In small installations it is often an inexpensive, relatively fast dot matrix printer. Another printer is then reserved for handling high-quality printing tasks, usually a daisy wheel, ink-jet, or laser printer. Additional printers may also be added for various reasons. One large mainframe or supermini may service users in several buildings, so printers need to be added in each building. It is rapidly becoming the norm to find more than one printer in most computer environments. This necessitates a special printer system that is capable of dealing with a variety of printer types and printer ports.

Printers Versus Devices

In System V, AT&T makes a syntactic distinction between a *printer* and a *device* that can be confusing unless you get the terms straight. A *device* is the mechanical device that does the actual printing; say, a Diablo 630 daisy wheel printer. A *printer* is a connection to the mechanical device; specifically, the port or interface program that the file is sent to on its way to the Diablo 630. It might be considered a ''virtual'' printer.

Another term to understand is *class*. A *class* is a group of similar *printer*s that are known by one name. For example, if your system has three identical Epson MX100s (a popular dot matrix printer), they can be grouped into one **class** called **matrix**, and printing requests sent to **matrix** might reach any one of the three Epsons, depending on which was busy at a given moment.

Files to be printed are stored in **/usr/spool/lp**, and eventually they are sent either to a printer or a class. Those sent to a printer (port) continue on to a device (like the Diablo) where the actual printing process takes place. Those sent to a specific class then go on to any one of several printers, and then to the actual physical device (like one of the three Epsons) where the actual printing process takes place. All devices in a class must be similar. On the mainframe we confuse it further by creating classes for paper types that are run from separate spool areas at specified times of the day.

To the user **lp** appears to work almost the same as **lpr**, but the user can now specify a particular printer for output. If a printer is named **laser**, for instance, a file can be sent to it with the command line

```
$ lp -dlaser filename
request-id is laser-4856 (1 file)
$
```

-d is the option signifying destination. If a printer (let's say an Epson) has been declared as the default printer, it is even simpler to invoke the default printer:

```
$ lp filename
request-id is epson-4857 (1 file)
$
```

When a file is sent to the spooler, the **lp** system sends an ID number back to the user's terminal, as shown.[5] Let's say in this case the number is **epson-4857**. This ID number identifies the print ''job'', and it's necessary in case you decide that you don't want to print that file after all. As long as you know the ID number, the **cancel** command stops the file from reaching the printer. The syntax is

---

5 If you find this annoying, use the **-s** flag to **lp** to suppress the messages.

cancel *id number*

and it is used this way:

```
$ cancel epson-4857
request "epson-4857" cancelled
$
```

To fully illustrate the usefulness of the **cancel** command, let's say you accidentally sent an executable binary file to the printer rather than its documentation. If you don't cancel the request, the printer goes into a schizophrenic fit and prints a paper box full of blanks, odd characters, and graphics! **cancel** arms the average user with the necessary tool to stop any undesirable printing process. The system administrator needs more sophisticated tools, so let's take a look inside the **lp** system.

How the lp Printer Spooler Works

The **lp** system is relatively complex, and to understand it, some form of analogy is helpful. UNIX has often been compared to a set of plumbing devices, and it's an apt comparison, particularly because we are dealing with a character stream that flows throughout the entire system. Please refer to Fig. 11-1.

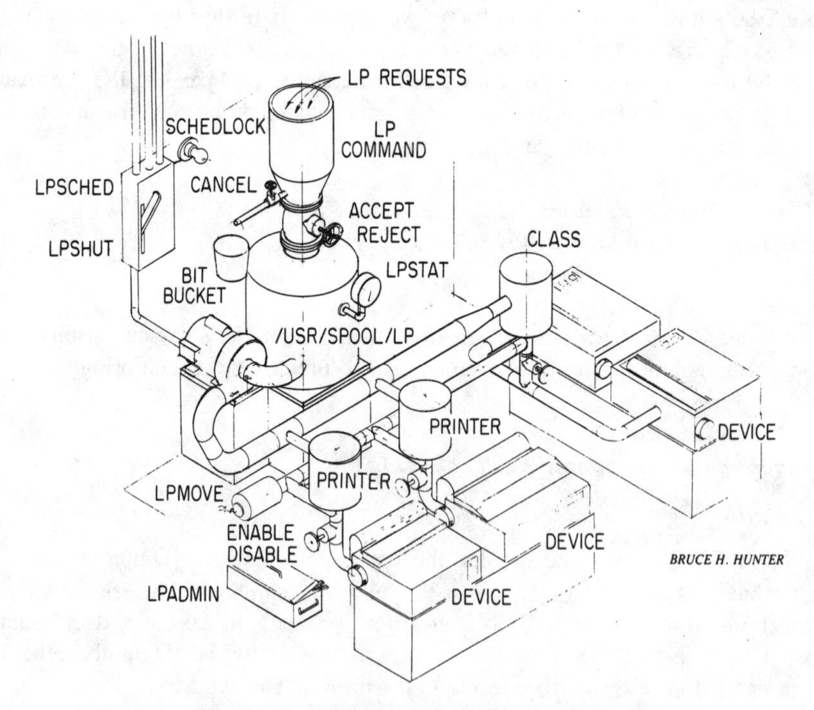

Fig. 11-1. The System V **lp** Spooler System

Requests to send a file to a printer are processed by way of the **lp** command. **lp** is represented by the hopper or funnel at the top of the spooler tank. Notice that the **cancel** command is pictured as a small, valved drain pipe that, when turned on, drains the printer request right out of the **lp** funnel. The spooler buffer, **/usr/spool/lp**, is represented by the tank. Files stored in **/usr/spool/lp** have their destinations as part of their file names. These files are queued in the spooler, waiting for an opportunity to reach the printer. If the printer is available, the file is sent immediately. Now take a look at the valve located between the spooler tank and the **lp** funnel, the position of the **accept/reject** command pair. **accept** allows a specific printer or class to accept files from the **lp** command. The off position of **accept** is **reject**. These two commands either allow or prevent the spooler from accepting any more files.

Plumbing systems have a number of pumps and valves. The main pump in the **lp** system is **lpsched**. It enables the entire process, just like turning on the power to the main pump at an industrial installation. The off position of **lpsched** is **lpshut**. It shuts off the entire system. The activation of **lpsched** is usually written into **rc**, the program called by **init** when the system is brought up. Notice the **SCHEDLOCK** flag positioned on the **lpsched/lpshut** pump. In reality **SCHEDLOCK** is a lock file, and its presence indicates the spooler daemon is (or should be) running. It prevents more than one **lpsched** from running at a time.

It's also important to control the character flow at the end of the **lp** system. A paper jam or an out-of-paper condition necessitates shutting down the device but not at the cost of rejecting files to the spooler. Under normal circumstances, the spooler should be capable of accepting any files, and the brief amount of time required to service a specific printer should not cause the spooler to fill. To keep this from happening, a set of commands at the printer end of the **lp** system is needed to control the flow of files. This command pair is **enable** and its counterpart, **disable**.

A couple of **lp** commands vital to the system administrator are **lpadmin** and **lpstat**. **lpadmin** is the system administrator's printer tool box, and it is used to configure the entire **lp** system. Although **lpstat** is pictured as a gauge located on the spooler tank, it actually gives you the status of the entire **lp** system. Imagine that you are just coming into work, and five users greet you with the information that the printers aren't working. No matter what the assumed cause, the first thing you do is an **lpstat -t**. It not only tells you of the printers' activity, it also lets you know how long the devices have been active. Perhaps its most useful purpose is telling you what is and is not enabled:

```
# lpstat -t
scheduler is running
system default destination: oki
members of class okidata:
        oki
        oki_lq
device for oki: /dev/oki
device for diablo: /dev/diablo
device for oki_lq: /dev/oki
oki accepting requests since Jun 13 15:56
okidata accepting requests since Nov 27 17:09
oki_lq accepting requests since Jun 13 15:56
diablo accepting requests since Jul  5 14:24
printer oki is idle.  enabled since Dec 25 19:59
printer oki_lq is disabled since Jun 12 18:23 -
        reason unknown
printer diablo is idle.  enabled since Jul 16 11:14
```

Notice that we have two "virtual printers" sharing the same physical device (**/dev/oki**). This technique is useful when different paper stocks (invoices, labels) are to be used with interface programs that can take advantage of them. Or, as in this case, when you want both draft output and letter-quality from the same printer. If you do something similar, it's important to remember that these are all different printers to the spooler system. Unfortunately, the system doesn't check that they all go to the same device and will happily mix your printouts together. So you should **disable** the ones not being used.

Now that you have some idea of the general structure of the **lp** system, let's put the theory into practice and discuss what you'll actually have to go through to set up **lp** on your machine.

Setting Up lp on a New Machine

Creating a functional **lp** system on a System V machine is a bit more work than enabling **lpr** on Version 7, System III, and BSD machines. This is the price of having multiple printer capabilities, yet the ability to create your own special printer drivers makes the effort worthwhile.

First of all, in order to do system administration work on the **lp** system, you must log on as **lp** (line printer administrator), not **root**, so there must be a separate **lp** login. If your system was not distributed with a login for **lp** (along with **root**, **bin**, **uucp**, and so on), you have to create one. Don't forget that **lp** needs a home directory (which should be **/usr/spool/lp**) and a password as well. The default execution path for **lp** should include **/usr/lib**, where many printer commands reside.

On machines with virtual terminals (such as UTS with Session), the **lp** login should be up whenever the machine is up. As a matter of fact, if you have a spare terminal, it is a good idea to use it to maintain an additional active **lp** login, because when errors are encountered in the operation of the printer system, the error messages are sent to **lp**'s terminal, making any necessary troubleshooting easier for you. Most installations do not have the luxury of an exclusive **lp** terminal, so when problems are encountered with the printers, you either log off and log on as **lp** or do a substitute user id (**su**) to **lp** to allow the error messages to be displayed. All subsequent commands in this chapter using the **lp:** prompt are assumed to be issued from the **lp** login.[6]

Attaching Printers to the System

You have to make the UNIX system aware of each printer that is physically attached to the system. In the following example, a printer is being added to a typical microcomputer system. The printer is attached to a serial port at **/dev/tty22.** The command to attach the printer to the system as a logical device is **lpadmin** and is executed as

```
lp: /usr/lib/lpadmin -poki -v/dev/tty22 -mdumb
```

In the above example, the printer is an Okidata 84. The argument **-mdumb** is used to let the **lp** system know that it's using the standard (''dumb'', or no special features) printer interface program. When this **-m** (for model) flag is used, **lpadmin** knows to look for a file by that name in the **/usr/spool/lp/model** directory. If you have a program in a different place, you can use the **-i** (for interface) flag, and specify the full path name of the program you want to use:

```
lp: /usr/lib/lpadmin -poki -v/dev/tty22 -i/own/dave/testprog
```

In either case, the program is copied into the directory named **/usr/spool/lp/interface.**

The **-p** flag names the printer **oki**, so subsequent **lp** commands should look like

```
$ lp -doki file1 file2
request-id is oki-4385 (2 files)
$
```

if they are meant to print on this particular printer.

You won't be able to issue many **lpadmin** commands while the daemon (**lpsched**) is active, so you'll have to run **lpshut** first. **lpadmin** will notify you of this if you forget. One thing it *won't* tell you is that after you have attached the printer, you still won't be able to use it until you run **accept** and **enable** and restart the daemon:

---

6 For reasons that will become apparent, we suggest you include the directory **/usr/lib** in **lp**'s default PATH.

```
lp: /usr/lib/lpadmin -poki -v/dev/tty22 -i/own/dave/testprog
lp: accept oki
destination "oki" now accepting requests
lp: enable oki
printer "oki" now enabled
lp: lpsched
lp:
```

Making One Printer the Default Printer

If a default printer is not specified, each invocation of the **lp** command requires that the printer be specified with the **-d** flag as mentioned above. This quickly becomes tiresome, so the most frequently used printer should be designated as the default printer. The command to create a default printer is also **lpadmin**:

```
lp: /usr/lib/lpadmin -doki
```

In the above example the printer called **oki** has been set as the default printer by use of the **-d** flag of **lpadmin**.

A Closer Look at /usr/spool/lp

The directory **/usr/spool/lp** is the heart of the **lp** printer spooling system. It is a mix of the commands and directories that make it possible to spool multiple files to multiple printers. The locations and directory names may vary from one OEM's system to another, but the purpose of these files and directories are the same on all UNIX systems. The following descriptions are thumbnail sketches of files and directories located in **usr/spool/lp**:

******Files******

SCHEDLOCK This is the lock file. If it is present when the **lpsched** command is issued, **lpsched** aborts. Its purpose is to prevent damage to a running **lp** system by reinitializing it.

FIFO This is a named pipe used by the **lp** commands to communicate with **lpsched**.

default **/usr/spool/default** holds the name of the default printer.

log **/usr/spool/lp/log** is the current log of all files sent to the printer(s). It contains the request id of the **lp** job, the login that sent it, the name of the device it went to, and the date and time.

oldlog — **/usr/spool/lp/oldlog** is the old **log** file. **log** (above) becomes **oldlog** on the next initialization of the system.

outputq — This data file is the queue (list) for all printers and classes of printers.

qstatus — This data file looks very much like **outputq** and holds the current status of the printers and printer classes.

seqfile — This file has but a single entry, the next printer request number.

******Subdirectories******

request — **/usr/spool/lp/request** has a subdirectory for each printer and printer class. Each of these is where the output files are spooled to on the way to the printers.

class — **/usr/spool/lp/class** holds information pertinent to the printer classes.

interface — This directory is the home of the executable interface programs for each printer (or printer class).

member — member contains a file for each printer or class. The brief contents of each file are the name and path of the character special file in **/dev** for each, such as **/dev/printer00e**.

model — This is where the sample interface programs are kept.

▪ Troubleshooting the lp Spooler System ▪

Imagine that your printer spooler is rapidly running out of space. Picture yourself logging on as **lp** (the printer administrator), checking the spooler, and finding out to your horror that a couple of users are printing private copies of the system manuals, while at the same time two bureaucrats-at-heart are making multiple copies of a mountain of internally generated specifications. On large UNIX systems, such as UTS on mainframes, **/usr/spool** is a separately mounted file system, and a **df** clearly shows that the remaining space is nearly exhausted. However, with this much printer activity, you don't need the sophistication of UNIX on a mainframe to tell you what is happening: the spooler has nearly filled all the remaining allocated disk space.

To add to the suspense, imagine that your other users are sending files to the printer faster than the printers can put them on green bar paper. The spooler has to be stopped from taking any more printer requests, at least for awhile. The trick is to shut off the **lp** command. The **cancel** command won't do the job. You don't want to shut off the entire **lp** system because you still want to keep the printers running. What you want to do is stop any new requests from coming into the spooler so the spooler has a chance to send its remaining output to the printer.

reject and accept

The command you want is **reject**, and here's how it's used:

```
lp: /usr/lib/reject -r"spooler full" system matrix letter
destination "system" is no longer accepting requests
destination "matrix" is no longer accepting requests
destination "letter" is no longer accepting requests
lp:
```

The above command prevents any further printer requests to the printers (or classes) named **system**, **matrix**, and **letter**. Like all printer commands, and most UNIX commands in general, **reject** has a number of flags and options. In our example, the **-r** option sends a message to the users' terminals when they attempt to use any of these printers, to tell them that the spooler is full. To reactivate that portion of the system and allow more printer requests to enter the spooler, use the **accept** command:

```
lp: /usr/lib/accept system matrix letter
destination "system" now accepting requests
destination "matrix" now accepting requests
destination "letter" now accepting requests
lp:
```

While it's not obvious, and perhaps it goes against common sense, running **reject** for an entire **class** of printers does *not* stop people from sending output to any printer in that class! For instance, if **matrix** (above) were a class of printers including **okidata**, **epson**, and **tally**, then only general requests such as

```
$ lp -dmatrix filename
```

would be rejected, though people could still successfully execute

```
$ lp -depson filename
```

disable and enable

accept and **reject** halt input *to* the spooler temporarily, but what if a printer jams or needs a paper change? Then you have to halt output *from* the spooler to the printer. For this you should use the **disable** command, which is similar in syntax to **reject**:

```
lp: disable -r"paper jammed" okidata
printer "okidata" now disabled
lp:
```

Since **disable** is used to deal with a specific printer (device), you must use the printer name, not an entire class, as an argument. When a printer is **disabled**, any file that is running on that printer will be rerun when it is **enabled**. **disable** also has an optional **-c** flag that cancels any print jobs running on the named printer(s). **enable** is the opposite command, and starts the printer going again:

```
lp: enable okidata
printer "okidata" now enabled
lp:
```

Other Problems

Suppose you can't get anything to spool or print. Here are a few things to look for:

outputq	This file must exist in the **/usr/spool/lp** directory.
permissions	Everything at the level of **/usr/spool/lp** and below it should be owned by **lp**.
SUID	All **lp** programs should have the set-user-id permission (mode 4755) on to enable them to work properly. In addition, the **lpsched** and **lpadmin** programs should be owned by root.
lpsched	This daemon *is* running, right?

In cases where file protection is especially tight, such as a file with mode 600 in a directory with mode 700, you will *not* be able to print out files with the command

```
$ lp filename
```

The result in such a case will probably be a printout with an error message such as **no permission**. To circumvent this, simply use input redirection with **lp**:

```
$ lp < filename
```

▪ Writing Printer Interface Programs ▪

One of the best features of **lp** is that you can modify the interface programs to create your own custom "printer drivers." No C programming experience is needed, because shell programs work fine. In fact, the system is generally delivered with shell interface programs. But if you plan to write your own, you have to understand some of the undocumented features.

Basic Interface Internals

When a print job is spooled, a single line of ASCII data is passed to the printer interface program, consisting of a minimum of seven fields. Some of these fields may be blank (the so-called "null string"), so you should *not* use the shell **$*** construct to examine the line, but instead get the data by position (**$1**, **$2**, etc.). Here's a guide to what you'll find for this sample command line:

```
$ lp -depson -n2 -o12 -tTitle programs
```

The data line passed to the interface program contains:

```
interface/epson epson-3126 david Title 2 12 /ch11/programs
```

Broken down, the data line looks like this:

Field 0 — This is the subdirectory (in **/usr/spool/lp**) and name of the actual interface program to which the data are being passed. If the printer name is **epson**, Field 0 contains the string **interface/epson**.

Field 1 — The **request-id** or print "job number." It might say something like **epson-3126**.

Field 2 — The login name of the person who made the **lp** request.

Field 3 — If a title for the listing was requested (via the **-t** option to **lp**), this field contains the title. Otherwise, it is empty.

Field 4 — This is the number of printout copies requested, which defaults to 1.

Field 5 — If any special options were requested (via the **-o** flag), they will *all* appear in this field, separated by spaces.

Field 6 — This is the *full* path name of the file or files to be printed. If the original command line looked like **lp filename**, then this will be the path to **filename**. If the command line was **lp -c filename** or **cat filename | lp**, then a copy was made in the spooling directory, and this field looks like

```
/usr/spool/lp/request/epson/d0-3126
```

If more than one file was requested, the other file names will follow, separated by a single space.

Three Interface Programs

With all that in mind, let's write a simple interface program:

```
shift; shift; shift; shift; shift  # get file names
                                   # to beginning of line
pr $*
exit 0
```

We *did* say simple! Are you surprised? The spooler system is set up so that when you attach a logical printer to a device using **lpadmin**, standard output from the interface program goes right to the device you want. Here's a slightly more complex example, using more of the supplied parameters. This version prints out a header page and processes the number of copies desired and any title that was requested on the **lp** command line:

```
echo ; echo ; echo
banner $2
echo ; echo ; echo
echo lp request is: $1
echo ; echo ; echo
title=$3
number=$4
shift; shift; shift; shift; shift  # get file names
                                # to beginning of line
echo $*
echo "\014\c" # formfeed to eject header page
j=1
while [ $j -le $number ]
do
        if [ -n "$title" ]
        then pr -h "$title" $*
        else pr $*
        fi
        j=`expr $j + 1`
done
exit 0
```

Our third program doesn't print headers (which are useful mostly at large installations with many people). It's meant to *follow* an invocation of the **pr** program (as in **pr file1 file2 | lp**). What's so special about it, then? It illustrates how to adapt your program for the features of a specific printer, such as pitch control. It also shows you how to print **nroff** output, by using the **termcap** database (of all things)! This program is written for the Okidata 84, but the technique involved works on any printer:

```
pitch=10
number=$4
for p in $5
do
        case "$p" in
                -12 | 12 ) pitch=12;;
                -15 | 15 ) pitch=15;;
        esac
done

case "$pitch" in
        10) echo "\036\c" ;;
        12) echo "\035\c" ;;
        15) echo "\034\c" ;;
esac

shift; shift; shift; shift; shift
files="$*"
j=1
while [ $j -le $number ]
do
        for file in $files
        do
                ul -Toki84 "$file" 2>&1
                echo "\014\c"
        done
        j=`expr $j + 1`
done
echo "\036\033\060\c" # reset to normal
exit 0
```

The **echo** commands send the octal control sequences to the printer that enable it to change to 10, 12, or 15 pitch based on the value of the **-o** flag to the **lp** command. For instance, this command prints a file in 12 pitch

```
$ pr file | lp -o12
```

whereas this is perfect for getting tiny **nroff** output:

```
$ nroff letter.file | lp -o15
```

Notice that we reset the printer at the end of the file to a known default value. While the pitch changes are pretty clear, how does this program allow printing of **nroff**?

The secret is in the use of the **ul** program. **ul**, developed at Berkeley, was meant to interface with **termcap** so that files with bold or underscore sequences could be viewed on CRT terminals that support those features. If we make up a **termcap** entry for our printer, entering the control sequences that force the printer to perform bold and underscoring, then feeding a file through **ul** automatically generates the proper control codes at the proper times. Here's the complete **termcap** entry for the Okidata:

```
ok|oki84|okidata microline 84 printer:\
        :co#136:li#66:hc:ul:so=\EH:se=\EI:us=\EC:ue=\ED:
```

If your system doesn't have **ul**, you have several alternatives. One is to ask your system supplier for either **ul** or an equivalent, such as **ncrt**. Another is write your own, but this could take a very long time.

uroff: Underline Filter for Printers

Here's a nice C program from USENET that allows most printers to underline (it won't work with CRTs). With a little work, you might be able to get it to do bold also:

```
/* uroff - produce nroff underlining for not-so-smart printers */
/* introduction */
/* uroff ---------------------------------------------------------- **
**
** uroff - produce underlining for nroff documents for printers that
**           do not do backspacing.
**
** This program works with any printer that can handle text
** followed by carriage return followed by some spaces and underscores.
**
** This program is simple-minded, but quick.  It uses buffered I/O and
** classes characters into very simple categories.
**
** usage: uroff [ file... ]
**
** If no file names are specified, it will filter standard input.
** If a file name is dash (-), standard input will be read at that
** point.
**
** Permission is granted for use and distribution, as long as you
** include the following notice:
```

```
**
** (c) 1985     Steven M. List
**              Benetics Corporation, Mt. View, CA
**              {cdp,greipa,idi,oliveb,sun,tolerant}!bene!luke!itkin
**
** ----------------------------------------------------------------- */
#include    <stdio.h>

char    *pgm;

#ifdef BSD
#define strrchr rindex
#endif
extern char *strrchr ();

/* main - control loop */
main (ac, av)
int     ac;
char    **av;
{
    register FILE    *in;              /* input stream                */

    /* ------------------------------------------------------------- */
    /* set the basename of the program name for logging              */
    /* ------------------------------------------------------------- */

    if (pgm = strrchr (av[0], '/')) pgm++;
    else pgm = av[0];

    ac--; av++;

    /* ------------------------------------------------------------- */
    /* arguments are file names - if none, use standard input        */
    /* ------------------------------------------------------------- */

    if (ac == 0)
    {
        dofile (stdin);
    }
    else while (ac--)
    {
        if (!strcmp (*av, "-"))
        {
            in = stdin;
        }
```

```
        else if (!(in = fopen (*av, "r")))
        {
            fprintf (stderr,
                "%s: cannot open %s for read\n", pgm, *(av-1));
        }

        av++;

        if (in)
        {
            dofile (in);
            if (in != stdin) fclose (in);
        }
    }

    exit (0);
}
/* dofile - process an input file */
/*
 *                                    dofile
 *
 * Read each character from the input file.  Put it into the buffer
 * appropriate for the type.  Flush the buffers on newline or eof.
 *
 ********************************************************************/
dofile (stream)
register FILE *stream;
{
    /* ------------------------------------------------------------ */
    /* some convenient defines                                      */
    /* ------------------------------------------------------------ */

#    define BUFSIZE 256
#    define BACKSPACE '\b'
#    define NEWLINE '\n'
#    define FORMFEED '\f'
#    define RETURN '\r'
#    define UNDERSCORE '_'
#    define TAB '\t'
#    define SPACE ' '
#    define NUL '\0'
```

```
register unsigned char anyund = 0;
register unsigned char backup = 0;
register char    c;
register int     i;
register char    *tp;
register char    *up;

char    tbuf[BUFSIZE];
char    ubuf[BUFSIZE];

/* ---------------------------------------------------------------- */
/* initialize BOTH buffers to all spaces                            */
/* ---------------------------------------------------------------- */

for (i = 0, tp = tbuf, up = ubuf; i < BUFSIZE; i++)
    *(tp++) = *(up++) = SPACE;
tp = tbuf; up = ubuf;

/* ---------------------------------------------------------------- */
/* process each character in the input file                         */
/* ---------------------------------------------------------------- */

while ((c = getc (stream)) != EOF)
{
    switch (c)
    {
        case    BACKSPACE:
            backup = 1;
            break;
        case    UNDERSCORE:
            if (backup) *(up-1) = c;
            else
            {
                *up = c;
                up++; tp++;
            }
            anyund = 1;
            backup = 0;
            break;
```

```
            case    NEWLINE:
                *tp = *up = NUL;
                fputs (tbuf, stdout);
                if (anyund)
                {
                    putchar (RETURN);
                    fputs (ubuf, stdout);
                }
                putchar (NEWLINE);
                anyund = 0;
                for (i = 0, tp = tbuf, up = ubuf; i < BUFSIZE; i++)
                    *(tp++) = *(up++) = SPACE;
                tp = tbuf; up = ubuf;
                break;
            case    SPACE:
            case    TAB:
            case    FORMFEED:
                *(up++) = *(tp++) = c;
                break;
            default:
                if (backup) *(tp-1) = c;
                else
                {
                    *tp = c;
                    up++; tp++;
                }
                backup = 0;
                break;
        }
    }

    if (tp != tbuf)
    {
        *tp = *up = NUL;
        fputs (tbuf, stdout);
        if (anyund)
        {
            putchar (RETURN);
            fputs (ubuf, stdout);
        }
        putchar (NEWLINE);
    }

    return;
}
```

One Last Thing

If you've made it this far, you deserve a bonus. Although it's called the **lp** spooler system, nowhere are you forced to use this wonderful invention just for printers. With a little imagination and some good interface programs, you can use the **lp** system to queue output to plotters, graphics output devices, voice synthesizers, or even your own fleet of robots!

In fact, you're not even limited to hardware. If people are overusing CPU-hogging programs such as **troff**, you could hide the actual binary file, then set up a shell interface program that would feed input to the binary, while letting the user specify an output file. After you set up a ''printer'' called **troff**, only one person is able to run **troff** at a time. Be sure that **troff** is owned by **lp** and set to mode 500. Give it a try.

▪ Handy Shell Programs ▪

lpstart

While it's true that the textbook way to initialize the System V **lp** spooler is just to run **lpsched**, this may be an oversimplification. We have found that **lpsched** doesn't always start running right away, especially when the system is heavily loaded. Worse, it can fail to initialize properly.

The **lpstart** script is designed to start up the spooler in a positive manner. It first attempts to shut down any current spooler daemons, and it loops until it does. Then it forcibly removes any lock files, runs a single instance of **lpsched**, and checks to see if it initialized properly. If so, it exits; otherwise it kills the daemon and starts again. The best way to run **lpstart** is while logged in as **lp**; to start the spooler up at boot time, add this line to your **/etc/rc** file:

```
/bin/su lp -c "/usr/local/lpstart" &
```

The reason the script is so complex is because of a defect in the **lpshut** program. **lpshut** does not actually look in the process table to ensure that all **lpsched** daemons are dead (there *can* be more than one running, despite what the manual says). The **SCHEDLOCK** file contains the process number of the daemon that created it; it's only this daemon that **lpshut** eventually kills. Since there's only room for one **SCHEDLOCK** file, other daemons might well exist. Checking the output of **ps** to find whether any are actually running is the only way to be sure.

Similarly, **lpstat -r** doesn't really tell whether the scheduler is running, but only whether the files in **/usr/spool/lp** seem to have been set up correctly. So we use both **ps** and **lpstat** to verify that the scheduler is up:

```
# lpstart
# by D. Fiedler
# the opposite of lpshut; gets the lp spooler started
# replace ps -ax by ps -e on System V

until test "$status" = "scheduler is running"
do
        /usr/lib/lpshut >/dev/null 2>&1
        while true
        do
                line=`ps -ax | grep lpsched | grep -v grep | head -1`
                if test "$line"
                then kill -9 `echo $line | cut -c1-6`
                else break
                fi
        done
        rm /usr/spool/lp/SCHEDLOCK >/dev/null 2>&1
        /usr/lib/lpsched
        line=`ps -ax | grep lpsched | grep -v grep`
        if test "$line"
        then status=`lpstat -r`
        fi
done
echo $status
```

▪ Chapter Summary ▪

Remember, whatever version of UNIX you are using, the duties of the system administrator are the same. First you get the system running, then you keep it running. Once the printer spooler is active and bug free, its maintenance is quite simple. Unlike other spooling systems, the printer spooler is self-cleaning. Once a file has been printed, it is removed! There are no **crontab** entries to create, and it's not necessary to do a periodic check of the spooler. The only time the system needs attention is when it fails to produce a printout or when you are adding new devices.

CHAPTER 12

MODEMS AND AN EVEN BIGGER WORLD

How to Talk to the World

UNIX is a communicating operating system. It is capable of extending far beyond the immediate surroundings of the basic CPU box and local terminals by reaching out to remote terminals and machines. It can extend itself via local and long-distance networks. UNIX does all this without any software other than the standard UNIX distribution.[1] Its basic communications programs, **cu** and **uucp**, come with any implementation worthy of calling itself UNIX.

It is impossible to totally cover the world of communications in one chapter, but if you set up **cu** and **uucp** on your machine, you have already laid the groundwork for the ability to talk to almost any other computer with communications capability.

cu, ct, and uucp — What They Can Do

cu is a basic communications program that lets you dial into another machine as a remote terminal on that machine. When you log on to the other machine, you are as much a part of it as any other logged-in user. You do this all using the facilities of your own computer. **cu** not only allows the local terminal to be remote but also allows data transfer in both directions. If the computer you're calling is another UNIX machine, certain protocols are followed to give the best results with little or no work on your part.

Have you ever needed help with your machine? Whether you are a novice or a guru, software support is a necessity. You pay for it when you buy your system and should expect it. With a UNIX system you can get a technician to look at your machine by having him call in via **cu** or by your attaching him via **ct**. The technician can work on your machine as if he were sitting at the terminal next to you. Although **cu** does have capabilities for file transfer (**put** and **take**), that facility falls more into the realm of **uucp**.

1 AT&T has an add-on package available now called the *Basic Networking Utilities*. This product is commonly known as *HoneyDanBer* **uucp** and will be the standard **uucp** as of System V Release 3.

ct is a program that is sort of the opposite of **cu**. Instead of letting *you* call out to another computer, **ct** calls a terminal and sends a login message to it. This can ensure security, since your system is not open to just anyone to attempt a login, but instead calls a known telephone number of a (presumably) trustworthy person.

uucp is nothing like **cu**. Whereas **cu** is a real-time communications package, **uucp** is the basis of a store-and-forward service, network protocol, and a few other things. While **uucp** is technically one command that copies files from one UNIX system to another, most people use the name **uucp** when they mean the whole range of facilities that a **uucp** link provides. **uucp** sends jobs to be executed on remote machines (**uux**), sends and receives remote mail (**rmail**), and transfers files in either direction. And it can execute these activities on a time schedule to allow complete control over your phone costs.

uucp is similar to most store-and-forward services such as CompuServe, but it stores the data in your own machine, your friend's machine, and other machine nodes along the way. The cost is lower than commercial store-and-forward services — your only cost is the phone bill.

Within your own computer installation, one machine in a network of connected machines can become the *file server*, a place to store (and back up) files for attached machines. **uucp** also allows your devices to be shared. Many devices, such as tape drives, are a necessity on almost any multiuser system, but they are not exactly giveaway items. By having one tape drive within a network, all attached machines can take advantage of this expensive device. The same applies to letter and laser printers, plotters, and high-speed printers. For instance, a single **uux** command line could run a file through **troff** and pass the output directly to a laser printer driver on another machine.

The UNIX **mail** command is a quick and convenient way to send messages and files from one terminal to another, but what if you want to send mail to someone 2,000 miles away? Remote electronic mail is almost as easy to send as local electronic mail, and it is included once you are set up for **uucp**. **uucp** is the connection method that makes remote mail possible. As we shall see, simply typing the name or path to a remote system activates the **uucp** spooling process, which transmits the mail to the other system for you.

cu and **uucp** are interrelated in some ways, however. In order to debug your modem port you need **cu** running reliably. Otherwise you don't stand much chance of getting **uucp** going. So the first thing you want to do as system administrator is set up **cu**.

▪ Getting from Here to There ▪

There are three different physical methods of connecting systems to consider when dealing with UNIX networking capabilities: direct, *LAN* (*L*ocal *A*rea *N*etwork), and *DDD* (*D*irect *D*istance *D*ialing, also known as the phone system).[2] In this book we are going to cover only two: direct lines and DDD lines. "True" networking through a LAN

2 Not to mention high-speed modems, asynchronous modems, multiplexers (MUXes), RJE, and numerous other networking protocols that are fascinating but beyond the scope of this book.

allows many things that can't be done with **uucp**, such as ''mounting'' one computer's entire file system on another, so that an attempt to access a file can actually retrieve it from another machine without any additional commands. LANs allow data transfer at anywhere from 100 KBits/second (AT&T's Starlan) to 10 MBits/second (Ethernet) or more. As a comparison, normal modem transmission operates at 1.2 KBits/second and direct hardwire lines at 9.6 KBits/second. For the same amount of data, Ethernet transmissions generally take about as much time as would a transfer to a Winchester disk.

Since any LAN involves specialized hardware as well as new system calls and commands, we can do little but make you aware of their existence. Hooking to a LAN is a nice solution for companies with many small or midsized computer systems in the same building. But it still doesn't let you talk to the big world out there.

Direct Lines

Direct lines are hardwired lines used for relatively short distances (50 feet or less on an RS-232 cable). If you have two or more computers in the same room, the same building, or even the same block, it is possible to cable them together with direct lines.

Setting up a hardwire port is one-tenth the work of setting up a modem port. The most effective method of tying together two machines in close proximity is a *null-modem hardwire connection*; a simple wire (cable) connection from one machine to another. You need to be aware of the limits in distance and speed. The maximum transmission speed is determined by the serial board's UARTs and the length of the wire. The RS-232 specification only ''allows'' transmission for 50 feet, but greater distances (up to 500 feet at 9600 baud) can often be obtained by using shielded low-capacitance cables. For even greater speed and longer distances, more costly and sophisticated methods are required, such as installing *repeaters* or *short haul modems* in the data line, which boost the signal back to standard levels.

ACU Lines

In UNIX documentation, there are often references to devices called ACUs (Automatic Calling Units). Such devices go back to the days when modems were expensive to build, and if automatic dialing was desired, it was left to a separate ACU device on another port. Some large minicomputers and mainframes still use ACUs with rack-mountable modems, but virtually all modems today have internal dialers. Part of the trick in setting up **uucp** is getting UNIX to understand that the modem and the ACU (dialer) are one and the same device.

Transmitting Data Can Be a Problem

Telephone lines are seldom perfect. We are all familiar with irritating background noise and echoes in voice transmissions, otherwise known as ''spurious signals'' that cause ''dirty lines.'' The amount of ''dirt'' is usually in direct proportion to the distance traveled and the number of switching stations along the way. Satellites are also notorious for echoes, an absolute disaster for data transmission. If you use **cu** to transmit data over a long distance, and you see curly braces mixed in with the text, the line is probably too noisy to transmit reliably.[3]

In our experience, AT&T has the best lines for long-distance data transmission. Premium discount services are better than most, but as of this writing, they are still not 100% reliable. The rule of thumb is the cheaper the service, the worse the transmission; the shorter the distance, the cleaner the line.

Data can be transmitted in several ways, but *packet transmission* has a built-in safety check. Packet transmission breaks up the data stream into packages called packets. Each packet contains a checksum, a number derived from an algorithm that adds the bit patterns of the characters going out. The receiving machine runs the same algorithm. If the checksums don't agree, the receiving machine has the sending machine resend the packet. Packet transmission is the closest thing to 100% guaranteed data transfer.

▪ Making the Initial Connections ▪

Even professional hardware engineers who do nothing all day but grapple with networks and peripheral connections have occasional problems wiring two devices together. It's an easy procedure only if you have a no-problem cable connection, such as an AT&T modem, cable, and computer, all matched with the proper AT&T RS-232 cable adapter. But you probably have a mix-and-match connection, such as installing a Prometheus modem to an AT&T 3B2/300. Mix-and-match connections are crapshoots. Expect them to take a little more time.

Setting Hardware Switches

Before you can run **cu** (or **uucp** for that matter) you have to set a few hardware switches. No data are going anywhere until the ports allow transmission. Modems have numerous hardware switches that must be set correctly to allow **cu** and **uucp** to work properly. The modem must be set to *auto-answer* if it is to receive incoming calls. The computer and **uucp** have to know if the modem is ready — in other words, the modem must send back result codes to the computer. For example, **uucp** expects a Hayes protocol modem to send back **OK** after it has sent the modem an **AT** to see if it is active. Additional switches must be set to cause this to happen. Other switches that might be set are the number of rings (to hear before answering) and redial if the line was busy (a nice idea for personal computers but almost useless to **uucp**).

Here is how one of the authors had to set up the switches on a Hayes modem. The switch settings are explained so that you can make the necessary adjustments if you have another type. Note carefully the settings with asterisks; they might have to be set differently for your machine.

For outgoing modem (dialing out with **cu** or **uucp**):

---

3 The left curly brace ({) character code corresponds to a typical noise burst on most 1200-baud modem designs.

Switch 1 — UP *	Forces the modem to hang up the phone line when the DTR (*Data Terminal Ready*) line (pin 20) is asserted low.
Switch 2 — UP	Forces the modem to send result codes to the computer as strings. If the switch is down, only digits are sent (easy to miss when parsing).
Switch 3 — DOWN	Enables the result codes to be returned to the computer. If this switch is up, you will get no result codes, overriding any setting of Switch 2.
Switch 4 — UP	Commands are echoed as they are entered. If the switch is down, you can see what you are doing.
Switch 5 — DOWN	Prevents the modem from answering calls, which is unnecessary on an outgoing-only modem.
Switch 6 — DOWN *	Forces Carrier Detect (pin 8) high (to fool the computer) so that commands can be sent *to the modem*, even before the connection is made to a distant modem.
Switch 7 — UP	Setting needed for normal installation to a single-user phone jack.
Switch 8 — DOWN	Allows the modem to recognize and execute commands.

For incoming modem (allowing logins):

Switch 1 — DOWN *	Forces DTR high to fool the modem into answering the phone, because this computer drops DTR momentarily when the modem picks up the line, which would otherwise disconnect the call.
Switch 2 — N/A Switch 3 — UP	Prevents result codes from going to the computer, since no commands are anticipated.
Switch 4 — DOWN	Commands will not be echoed.
Switch 5 — UP	Forces the modem to answer calls.
Switch 6 — UP *	Allows state of CD (Carrier Detect — pin 8) line to be passed to the computer so the **getty** program will know when a call has been received.
Switch 7 — UP	Same as for outgoing modem.
Switch 8 — UP	Prevents the modem from executing commands.

Sometimes the most important switches to set are those that "lie" to the modem. These are the ones marked with the asterisks above. RS-232 signal pins like CD and DTR allow the computer and the modem to send signals to each other to see if they are alive and if a carrier (modem on the other end) has been detected. (You may want to refer to *Appendix B — RS-232 Connections* while reading this section.) You need to make sure that each device thinks the other device is ready, and that's where the lie comes in. Simple connections do not use these signals, but if you want to take advantage of full modem control capabilities, you have to deal with these pins.

Modem Control

What is modem control, and why is it so important? As we have seen with terminals, generally only three lines (data in, data out, and ground) are necessary to send data back and forth. Modems, which operate at random intervals over phone lines, are a little more complex.

Someone can log in and work for awhile, then hang up without logging off. In such a case, you would want the fact that he broke the connection to automatically log him off, so that the next person to log in does not get the first person's shell and privileges.

Or, what if your computer places an outgoing call in the middle of the night, and the answering modem picks up the phone, yet the computer on the other end is down? You would want the phone line to be hung up after awhile, to avoid a nine-hour-long phone charge to the other side of the country, wouldn't you?

One more scenario. Another computer calls your machine, yet never gets to log in because of noise on the line. If your computer does not sense this condition, your incoming line will be tied up until someone on either end notices.

All these annoying problems can be avoided by the proper use of modem control, which simply refers to the few extra status lines that allow sensing of various phone line conditions and subsequent control of the modem by the computer. One runaway phone call can easily cost more than a modem, so pay attention!

The two main modem control lines are DTR (pin 20) and CD (pin 8). The function of DTR is to signal the modem that the computer attached to it is ready for data. If DTR is low, then the modem will hang up (if a call is already in progress) or else refuse to either answer or initiate a call. DTR is normally low if the computer is down or is turned off. It also is low (or it will go low momentarily, which is just as bad) if the computer doesn't properly support modem control.

In such a case, DTR must be held high for the modem to operate at all, whether by flipping an internal switch or by wiring the cable so that DTR is asserted high. If this is done, it will be *impossible* for the computer to hang up the line by software, so it is *unacceptable* for unattended outgoing use. The limitation on an incoming modem is that if the line is dropped, the user's shell may still be active, a potential security problem.

The CD line from the modem detects whether the remote modem has connected. CD is used on incoming lines to signal **getty** that a login message should be sent. The problem arises on outgoing lines. Since there is no remote hookup before the call takes place, CD will be low. Unless the device driver has been correctly written to ignore the CD signal when attempting to open the port for output, you have to fool the modem by wiring CD high or flipping a switch. This in turn prevents the same modem from being used for incoming calls. So in order to get away with less than two modems on your machine (one permanently incoming, one permanently outgoing) you must have one of the following:

- a correctly designed computer and operating system
- a system with the **uugetty** program or an equivalent
- a modem that ignores CD when necessary

Setting the Computer

You don't usually have to set any hardware switches at the computer end, but the I/O board may have to be ''jumpered,'' particularly if you find that you need more modem control. For example, pin 5, *Clear To Send*, allows data transmission only if it is high (or true). When it goes high, it causes pin 20 (DTR) to go high as well, thus allowing another signal to work the modem. If pin 5 (CTS) is internally true (that is, if your computer sends data with or without an external CTS high), you have to extract the board from your computer and jumper CTS to accept an external signal and act on it:

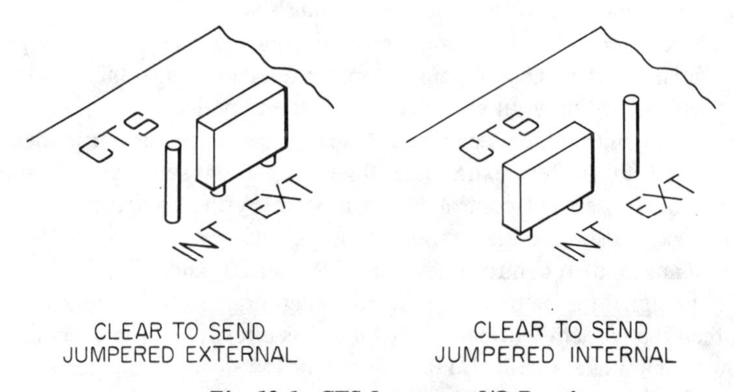

Fig. 12-1. CTS Jumper on I/O Board

By moving the shorting device or jumper from INT to EXT, the internal true signal is defeated, and the computer responds to an external signal. Now when no signal is present, no data flows. When the CTS pin goes high (true), data bits are able to flow from the computer end *if* the modem end is also ready. If DTR goes high, it allows further control as you get more sophisticated.

As you can see, even the initial stages of connecting modems can be a difficult affair. If you are a novice and you are having too many problems trying to get started, try setting all the signal pins high (switches 1 and 6 down for the Hayes). This will probably get you going. You may have to either switch the modem off manually or software-switch it to hang up, but at least you'll be transmitting data.

Once all the necessary hardware switches have been switched and jumpers have been jumped, you are ready to go to the software stage, setting ports in **/etc/ttys** or **inittab**. When you have set up the ports, it's time to start trying the connections for the first time. Modems are particularly tricky because there are more pins to deal with. So let's examine what's involved when you are trying out your first shaky modem connections.

Trying an Outgoing Modem for the First Time

Breakout box in place, queue some data on the computer port. There are different protocols for different modems. If the device is a D.C. Hayes compatible modem, type:

```
$ echo "AT" >/dev/modem
```

When you hit *return*, the prompt may fail to come back because the connection hasn't been made. Jumper the breakout box until data flows.

If the computer is a DCE, you have a crossed connection, and pin 2 must be connected to pin 3 on the opposite side. Pin 7 on the computer *always* goes to pin 7 on the modem.

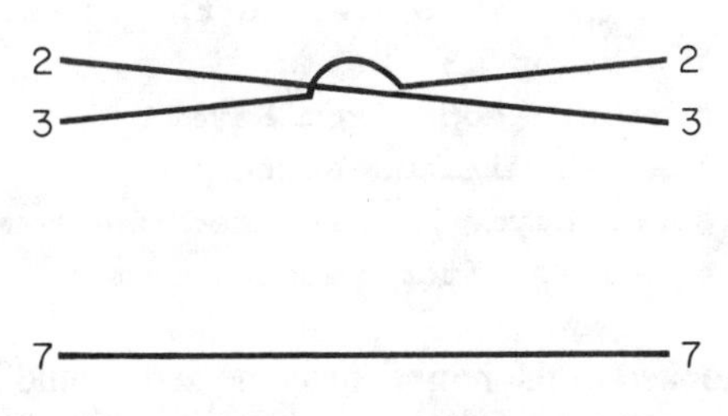

Fig. 12-2. A Minimal Modem Connection

The rest varies from machine to machine and modem to modem, but a good example is pin 8 (CD) of the modem side of the connection, going to pin 5 on the computer side to bring up *Clear To Send* and activate the computer into sending. A straight-through connection (pin 8 to pin 8, etc.) should always be tried first. When the computer has sent the message to the modem, the prompt comes back on the terminal.

Now we'll try talking to the modem with **cu**. If all goes well, you might as well make a semipermanent cable, but don't put on hoods or strain reliefs. You are probably not through yet. We have a few more factors to consider. Whereas **cu** is undemanding and simple to deal with, **uucp** is fussy, and it requires more handshaking. Plan on having to make some subtle changes in the cable connections before you finish the job.

Testing cu

Depending on your particular implementation, one of the following command lines should cause some action (dialing, the return of result codes, or at least lights blinking) on your modem:

```
$ cu
$ cu -t
$ cu -l
$ cu -l /dev/modem
$ cu -l /dev/modem -s 1200
$ cu 5551212     # use a known good modem phone number
```

If the last variation worked, and you dialed a functioning modem line, you should see a login message from the other computer appear on your screen. Otherwise, you merely made a connection to your own modem, and now you have to send your modem the command sequence to get it to dial out. In the case of the Hayes, that might look like:

```
$ cu -l
Connected       # cu has connected to the modem
AT              # wake up the Hayes
OK              # return code from Hayes
ATD5551212      # Hayes dialing sequence
CONNECT         # the Hayes has reached the remote modem
login:          # message from remote computer
```

At this point, you are hooked to the remote machine and should log in.

The first thing you should know about **cu** is how to disconnect. All **cu** commands start with the ~ character, and the disconnect sequence looks like:

```
~.
Disconnected
$
```

The $ prompt is from your own machine, since you've just exited the **cu** command. If your modem control is working, then the phone line will also disconnect when you exit **cu**. (Check the modem lights.) Otherwise, you will have to physically turn off the modem to ensure the connection has been broken. If you log off the other machine, and simply logging off drops the line, then the other system has its modem control working properly.

Using **cu**

While the actual use of **cu** is pretty well covered in the manual page, the tricky part is keeping track of the context — whether you're talking, at any given moment, to your local machine or the remote. Once in **cu**, you're generally talking to the remote. Typing a command line beginning with the characters **~!** runs that command on your local system, with the output going only to your terminal (the remote system doesn't know it was typed). Typing a command line beginning with the characters **~$** runs that command on your local system, but sends the output of the command to the remote system, as if you were typing it. So if you are logged in to a non-UNIX system and want to send it a file, put the other system in a mode where it is ready to receive, then type

```
~$cat myfile
```

and your local machine will send **myfile** — not to your terminal as usual, but to the other system. When **cat** is finished, you are talking to the other system again, automatically.

One trick that is not obvious relates to keeping a log of your remote session. While personal computer owners have to deal with ''capture buffers'' and the like, all you need on UNIX is the right command. In this case, it's **tee**:

```
$ cu 5551212 | tee save.file
Connected

Faraway login:
~.
Disconnected
$ cat save.file

Faraway login:
$
```

Direct (Computer-to-Computer) Connection

Hooking two computers back-to-back can allow data transfer up to 19200 baud. Instead of a modem, we use a null modem. A *null modem* connection is similar to a standard modem connection, only a lot simpler. It's nothing more than a cleverly wired cable. As a bare minimum, one wire is required to carry data in each direction (connecting pins 2 and 3) and one more for signal ground (connecting both pin 7s). This is the same as shown in Fig. 12-2.

If your equipment is matched, stock cables are all that is required. Two 3B2 computers are wired with stock J11 type cables with a modem adapter coupled directly to a terminal adapter:

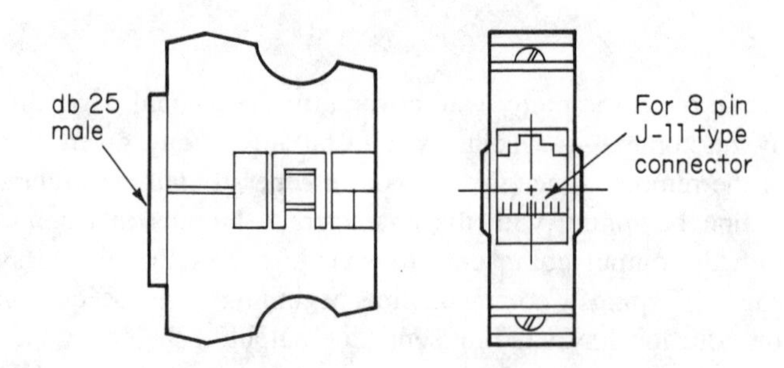

J-11 to DB25 connector for AT&T 3B2 computers internally wired for straight (terminal) or NULL modem (modem) connection

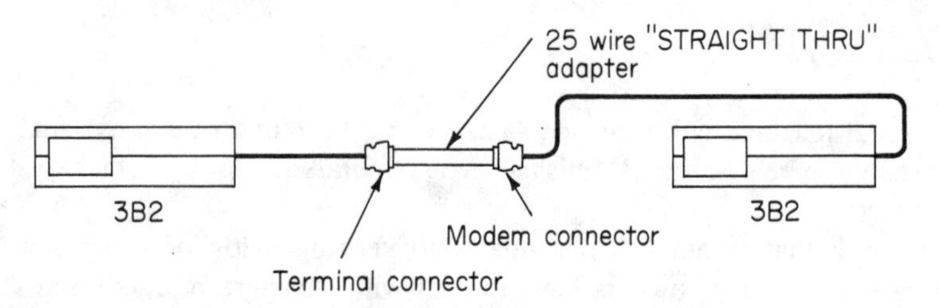

Networked 3B2 computers with stock connectors

Fig. 12-3. Connecting 3B to 3B

Mix-and-match equipment is never easy. If both computers are identical, the connections are at least symmetrical. Start with a 25-pin ribbon connector attached to the sending port of one machine and another similar cable to the receiving port of the other. As outlined in *Appendix B*, place a breakout box in the center so the connection is now port to cable to breakout box to cable to port. Then sex pins 2 and 3 on both ends. The pin asserted on the port tells the story. If pin 2 is asserted low, the port is a DTE (a terminal type). If pin 3 is asserted low, it is a DCE (communications type). If both pin 3s are low, then they are both DCE, and 2 must be crossed to pin 3 at the other machine: a null-modem connection. If they are opposite types, DCE to DTE, a straight connection fills the bill.

The plan is first to get the sending machine to retrieve a login from the receiving machine. Type in a

```
# cu -l /dev/modem
```

at the terminal of the sending machine. The prompt will not return to this terminal until the connection has been successfully made. With pins 2, 3, and 7 jumpered, the trick is to see which signal pins have to be pulled up at either end to make the connection complete. Find one of pins 4, 5, 6, 8, or 20 asserted high at either or both ends. Use it initially to pull up one or more of the unasserted signal pins until data flows. Pins 5 and/or 6 usually have to be asserted high to get things going. Pins 4 (RTS) and pin 20 (DTR) are generally high and make a good source for a signal. Once data flows, the prompt comes back on the sending machine and a login request follows, unless you have failed to set the receiving port for a **getty**. Write down the jumper connections on a work sheet. Log in on the remote machine, then drop the connection with a

```
~.
Disconnected
$
```

Now reconnect by typing your **cu** command again. If your login is still active on the remote machine, you will want to redo the cables for modem control so that an interruption of signal generates a hangup (SIGHUP) on the remote machine. As usual, the safest way is to connect all wires straight through (except for possibly having to cross pins 2 and 3), and try the connection. If this doesn't work, a typical bit of hardware engineer's magic is to take an active (asserted) pin 4 (RTS) on one machine and jumper it to an unasserted pin 5 (CTS) on the other. Similarly, you can wire pin 20 (DTR) across to the other machine's pin 8 (CD). Now when you software-disconnect, one signal pin going off or low drops the whole connection and kills the login.

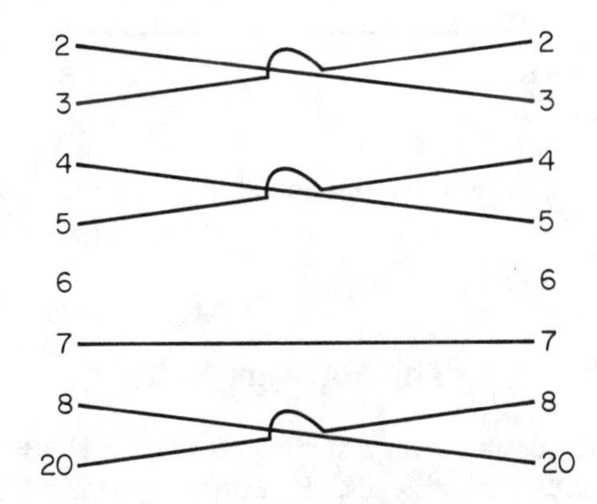

Fig. 12-4. Null Modem Cable with Modem Control

This may sound like a lot of work, but it is worth it. Since time 0 (1970) in UNIX, there has always been a problem concerning the login remaining in an active state long after a remote terminal has hung up. This ''unshakable login'' is not unique to UNIX but exists on many LANs as well. The trick is to make sure that the receiving machine (the one with the **getty**) can sense and act on a hardware hangup. Otherwise, even a sure kill (kill -9 process id number) to the stuck login cannot kill it. Only a reboot of the system clears up this problem.

The Easy Route

If you are new at cabling, you may want to take the easy route by either jumpering the cable or the I/O board so that pins like CTS and DSR are always high or true. Then a three-wire connection makes the unit work. You will not have full control, however. You may suffer with unshakable logins when using direct hardwire connections. In other words, you won't be taking advantage of the full handshaking capabilities available to you. An imperfect connection that works is better then a shaky one that doesn't, so go with whatever works for now and refine your methods as you become more experienced. If it works, make your cable without strain reliefs and hoods. Just let the pins hang out and connect it:

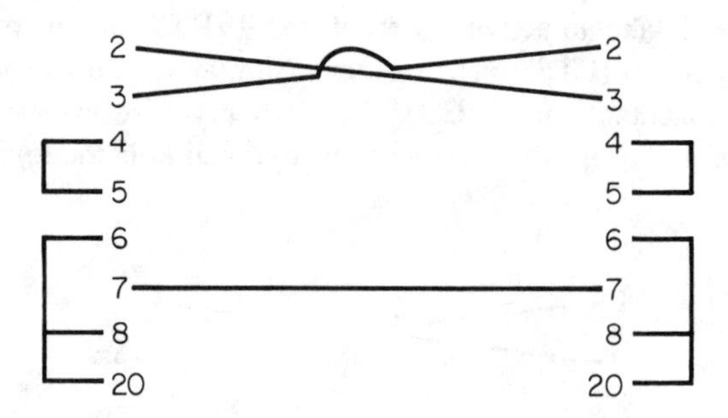

Fig. 12-5. Guaranteed Null Modem

▪ The Software Side ▪

Bidirectional logins are possible over a single port only in HDB **uucp**, using a special program called **uugetty** at both ends. If **uugetty** is available at only one end, it cannot be used. For all versions of **uucp** before HDB, two ports are required. An "in" port must have a getty, and an "out" port cannot. This is true for modem connections as well as null modems. (Later we will show you how to turn a **getty** on and off if you can only afford one modem or port). Even so, with two machines connected locally, you can have one machine call the other at 15-minute intervals all day, so it hardly matters.

A typical line speed for a hardwire connection is 9600 baud. Some machines can't handle 9600 baud reliably; if this is true with yours, try 4800. In fact, **uucp** internal overhead often limits actual transfer rates to about 750 characters per second, no matter how high the baud rate is. We recommend you set up hardwire connections at 1200 baud initially, then turn up the speed later.

The incoming port setup in **/etc/ttys** looks like this in Version 7 and earlier UNIX versions

```
19tty6
```

/etc/inittab looks like this on System III:

```
2:6:c:/etc/getty tty6 3 600
```

and like this in System V:

```
6:2:respawn:/etc/getty -t 600 tty6 1200
```

For bidirectional ports, the line in **/etc/inittab** is:

```
6:2:respawn:/usr/lib/uucp/uugetty -r -t 600 tty6 1200
```

For outgoing lines, you must turn off the **getty** in Version 7

```
09tty5
```

or System III

```
2:6:k:/etc/getty tty6 3 600
```

or, for System V,

```
5:2:off:/etc/getty tty5 1200
```

See *Chapter 10* on *terminals* for more information.

Letting UNIX Know about Your Connections

UNIX Version 7 is simple and forgiving. To add an outgoing modem, just modify **/etc/ttys** to disable the login on that port (a trivial task covered in *Chapter 10*). If there is something at the other end of the port to talk to, **cu** puts you in business.

UNIX System III and Version 7 were ill-equipped to deal with modems. If you didn't have a DEC modem, you had to rewrite **uucico**. Early Unisoft ports were so poor at handling **uucp** you could not use them to call out, and calling in was spotty at best. HDB **uucp**, available on recent releases of System V Release 2, is very tolerant, recognizing Hayes, Penril, Ventel, Rixon, and Vadic modems (among others), as well as LANs. Later, we will show you a trick that can be used to get your modem to dial out automatically even if it's not supported.

HDB **uucp** is far more stable, much more commercially oriented, but not nearly as forgiving. Before you can use **cu**, HDB wants the **/usr/lib/uucp** files to know about the port. The **Devices** file has to have an entry for each port or modem that **cu** and **uucp** use. A typical **Devices** file might look like this:

```
ACU tty11 - 1200 Hayes
ACU tty11 - 300  Hayes
hunter tty12 - 9600 direct
ACU tty13 - 1200 Hayes
ACU tty13 - 300  Hayes
```

Modem lines begin with **ACU**; direct lines begin with the node name. The port name is next. It should be the name of a device in **/dev**. Typically, you should use **tty11** if you mean **/dev/tty11**. The next field for normal connections is a ''**-**''. The fourth field is the baud rate. The last field is the name of the device. **tty11** and **tty13** have only one modem each. By putting a single modem in **Devices** at different baud rates, you can use the modem at any of those rates.

Check the file **/usr/lib/uucp/Dialers** to be sure that there is an entry for your modem. If you bought a Snark XVII, and it doesn't emulate a brand that **uucp** knows about, you'll have to enter its expect sequence here (be patient, it's just a few more paragraphs).

Believe it or not, that is about all there is to **cu** and anything short of **uucp**. For **uucp** you have completed most of the work as well. Congratulations!

Setting Up cu under HDB

On older UNIX (System III and before) **cu** had some very remarkable features that were easy to take for granted before HDB **uucp** came along. For example, **cu** could be used to address a port. By typing

```
cu -l /dev/modem
```

you talk directly to the modem port. Send the port the modem dialing sequence, and if all goes well, you are in the communications business. A user or administrator can use **cu** to talk to a printer, a **tty**, or any device attached to a port. This flexibility is highly advantageous, because it allows you to easily test devices attached to ports, thus making system administration easier.

UNIX 5.2 allows you to talk to a port only on a direct line. If you have a modem on a port, it is customary to use **cu** to ''direct dial'' as in

```
cu -l /dev/tty14 12015551234
```

or

```
cu machine
```

The **-l** option specifies **line** (port), which has UNIX dial the named machine for you. With a conventional setup in **/usr/lib/uucp/Devices**, you can no longer talk directly to the modem port. An attempt to reach the port such as

```
cu -l /dev/tty14
```

will be met with the error message

```
DEVICE NOT AVAILABLE
```

and an understandable amount of frustration. The way to circumvent the problem is to make an entry for the modem port as a direct device as well as an ACU. In the following example from **/usr/lib/uucp/Devices**, port 13 is set up as a conventional **uucp** port for an ACU, port 12 is a hardwire port, and port 14 is set up for a direct connection to the modem:

```
ACU tty14 - 1200 hayes
Direct tty14 - 1200 direct \D
Direct tty12 - 9600 direct \D
hunter tty12 - 9600  direct
ACU tty13 - 1200 hayes
```

Note the two entries for tty14, one **Direct** and the other **ACU**. By adding this extra **Direct** entry, a user or administrator can **cu** directly to the port and thus to the modem, manipulate the device on the port before dialing, and then process as if it were a modem connection in the mode of Version 7.

L-devices

The corresponding file to **Devices** in the old **uucp** is called **L-devices**. It is quite similar and looks like this:

```
DIR tty5 0 1200
DIR tty5 0 300
ACU cul0 cua0 1200
```

The two entries for **tty5** allow you to run the modem at either speed. The entries **cul0** (that's *ell zero*, not *one zero*) and **cua0** are a Version 7 anachronism. As we mentioned earlier, dialers used to be known as ACUs, and they were separate physical devices from modems. If your modem dials out in response to commands, you have to fool the system into recognizing the old names as being the same as your modem device. To do this, simply make links in your **/dev** directory, like this:

```
# cd /dev
# ln tty5 modem
# ln tty5 cua0
# ln tty5 cul0
# ls -l tty5 modem cu?0
crw-rw-rw- 4 nuucp   staff    13,  5 Nov 23 12:30 cua0
crw-rw-rw- 4 nuucp   staff    13,  5 Nov 23 12:30 cul0
crw-rw-rw- 4 nuucp   staff    13,  5 Nov 23 12:30 modem
crw-rw-rw- 4 nuucp   staff    13,  5 Nov 23 12:30 tty5
#
```

Now any program that tries to access any of these old names will simply talk to your real modem on **/dev/tty5**.

▪ Setting Up uucp ▪

uucp is a magnificent tool for both networking and communications. Until recently, however, its splendor was unavailable to most UNIX system owners simply because installing it was extremely difficult. It is said that installing **uucp** takes a day and a half the first time and 15 minutes each time after. That is pretty close to the truth. Systems with menu-driven administration like AT&T's "simple administration" make installing **uucp** nearly painless. In fact, on their UNIX PC, you don't even realize you're setting it up. We will address bringing up **uucp** the long way.

Definitions

All UNIX machines have a *node* name. In this context, the word node means a link in the communications network; it's simply the name by which your computer will be known to others. On many UNIX System III and previous systems, the node name of the machine is entered in **/usr/lib/uucp/SYSTEMNAME**, where it may be easily changed. You may be unlucky, and it has been compiled right into the kernel! If that's the case, look for an entry in a file like **/usr/sys/name.c** or **/usr/include/whoami.h** that corresponds to **sysname** or **nodename**, and edit accordingly. Then you have to recompile the kernel, a procedure which is different for every system.

In case you're wondering, no, you don't have to have a source license to do this. Suppliers that allow recompiling the kernel have made it possible for you to not only change the node name but also add or take away drivers and otherwise reconfigure your system. Such people are good to deal with. On the other hand, if you can't reconfigure the kernel, you will have to manually patch a copy of the **/unix** file. Since this is rather a trick, we've included a **sysname** program at the end of this chapter that does all the hard work for you.

On System V, the node name can be displayed with the **uname** command:

```
$ uname -n          # the n stands for node
infopro
$
```

And on an AT&T 3B2 it can be changed as easily as this:

```
# uname -n
netsuke
# uname -S hunter
# uname -n
hunter
#
```

On some machines, the equivalent is provided by the command **setuname -n nodename**. Other computers have the **uuname** command rather than **uname**. **uuname -l** displays the node name of your machine, while simply typing **uuname** reveals the names of all other computers that your system can call.

When you initiate a data call to another machine, that is known as *polling* the other machine. As delivered, use of any of the **uucp** commands, or remote mail, forces immediate polling of the other machine. We'll show you a way to stop that from happening, which you will surely appreciate when your phone bill arrives.

The way **uucp** works is fascinating. Space restrictions preclude a full description, but we will attempt to touch on some highlights. The **uucico** (*U*NIX-*to*-*U*NIX-*c*opy-*i*n-*c*opy-*o*ut) program is the one that actually performs polling. When the remote picks up the phone, your machine takes any strings that the remote machine puts out. It is expecting a login message. When it gets a substring that is acceptable to the *expect-send* sequence in the **Systems** file, it sends the *send* message, which is the login name.

Pause here and remember that the data coming and going between the two machines, modems, and all that phone equipment, satellites, and switching gear are very "noisy" and will probably interject stray characters. This is an important consideration when expecting to transfer files on a nonpacketizing system like **cu**.

Once a logname is sent and acknowledged, **uucico** sends the password. If the login is accepted, the real fun begins. The link has been set up and both machines can communicate. Unless told otherwise, the sending machine completes any queued-up business first. The operation then shifts to the work directory, **/usr/spool/uucp**. In pre-HDB **uucp**, files have the name of the remote system imbedded in the file name, such as **D.infoproB0856**. In HDB **uucp**, each node has its own directory. Now all files to be transferred, all remote mail to be sent, and all remote commands to be executed go out. Next the process reverses and the called machine does the same, sending files, mail, and commands for remote execution. When all work is complete, **uucico** hangs up the phone, writes to the log file, and goes away.

The **Systems** File

If you have followed all the steps outlined in the previous sections, you are close to getting **uucp** working. Now you need to create your **uucp** system file. This tells **uucp** what machines it can call, and how to call them. On HDB **uucp** it is **/usr/lib/uucp/Systems**, and it looks like this:

```
dragon  Any hunter 9600   - in:--in: bruce word: reptile
infopro Any ACU 1200 12015551234 in:--in: Uhunter word: Unique
hunter  Any ACU 1200 3334321 in:--in: uucp word: karen
```

In older UNIX the corresponding file is **/usr/lib/uucp/L.sys**, and here's how it looks:

```
infopro Any tty5 1200 tty5 12015551234 ogin-EOT-ogin Uhunter \
?sword: Unique
hunter1 Any tty5 1200 tty5 5559876     ogin-EOT-ogin bruce \
?sword: hi,bruce
```

The node names above are **infopro**, **hunter1**, **dragon**, and **hunter**. The second field in the **Systems** file is the time of day that calls are allowed to that machine. For reasons of cost, security, or whatever, you may want to limit call time, and this is the field in which to do it. An entry of **Never** or **None** prevents all calls to that machine, so *they* have to poll *you*. **Any** allows calls at any time. Days are entered as one or more of

```
Su Mo Tu We Th Fr Sa Wk
```

where **Wk** stands for every day, Monday through Friday. Time may be entered as a range as a further modifier on which days to call. The classic 9-to-5 is entered on a 24-hour clock basis so that 0900-1700 is the equivalent of 9:00 AM to 5:00 PM. Thus the entry

```
SaSu0615-1800
```

means Saturday/Sunday dialouts only from 6:15 AM to 6:00 PM. The most inexpensive time to call is late evening to early morning, which can be entered as:

```
Any2301-0759
```

The third field is the type of device that **uucp** must deal with. If the device is a modem, it is called **ACU**. If it is a network, use a name that is recognized by the **Dialers** file like **micom** or **devcon**. If the connection is direct, use the system node name (a link to **dragon** has **dragon** in this field). The word **Direct** is not applicable in this field since even a direct line has to be to a machine with a node name. On machines with an **L.sys** file, you may need to enter the **tty** line as shown.

The next field is class or speed. It normally has the baud rate or (line) speed of the ACU or line. It may also have a letter as well, such as **D1200** or **C1200**. The letter is a reference to the **Devices** file and stands for a type of PBX such as [D]imension or [C]entrex.

The fifth field is the phone number. The phone number can be straightforward, such as

```
12135559876
```

which translates into

```
1 (213) 555-9876
```

in human. Or, it may use substitute strings from another file, **/usr/lib/uucp/Dialcodes**. An example is

```
LA5559876
```

where **LA** was defined in **Dialcodes** as:

```
1 213
```

L.sys files have an extra field before the phone number, where you should again put the **tty** line.

The rest of the line is a bit tricky. It consists of a sequence of entries that are subfields and have the format:

expect send

An *expect-send* sequence looks like

```
ogin: uucp
```

The *expect* is a substring. Thus **Login:** or **login:** satisfies the substring **ogin:** Once received, the logname **uucp** is sent by **uucico**. This is all fine in theory, but in practice a single *expect-send* won't work. The reason is that machines send a lot of garbage when a login starts like

```
Welcome to Mos Eisley 5 with Unisys 3.1
```

so a series of repetitive *expect-sends* must go out. This is especially true if more than one baud rate may be used on the machine being called. A pair of hyphens (**--**) causes the *expect-send* to repeat, so

```
ogin:--ogin:
```

repeats the *expect* sequence after about 30 seconds if it isn't received properly the first time. The *send* is the full logname expected by the **getty** at the other end. The password sequence, if any, is entered with an *expect-send* as well. A typical entry is:

```
ogin:--ogin: bond sword: jb007
```

There are a number of escape characters that can be sent for convenience. They are:

\N	null
\b	backspace
\c	suppress newline (like **echo**)
\d	a two-second delay
\p	pause (around 1/4 to 1/2 second)
\n	newline
\r	return
\s	a space or 020 hex
\t	tab
****	an escaped ****
EOT	ASCII EOT (end of transmission or Control-D)
\ddd	a sequence of octal digits like **\006** for ACK
BREAK	a *break*

Not all of the above work on all machines, but give them a try. Another string that is handy is **BREAK** or **BREAK1**. This sends out the *break* character, useful for switching baud rates on machines that use more than one. If the first **expect-send** pair is not satisfied, you might be at the wrong baud rate, and this can start it over again:

```
gold Any tty2 1200 5551212 ?login:-BREAK1--?login: uucp
```

Fooling uucico

If your modem isn't directly supported, then **uucico** won't know how to send out the proper dialing sequences. But since the **L.sys** file sends out arbitrary strings on the basis of other received strings, you can put the dialing sequence right in the **L.sys** file. Here's how a typical entry looks when used with a Hayes modem:

```
hunter Any tty2 1200 tty2 ATDT5551234 ?login:--?login: uucp
```

Very simply, **uucico** sends out the Hayes ATDT dialing sequence once the line to the modem is opened. This technique has proved successful on many systems with different modem brands.

uucp Logins

The password file **/etc/passwd** has to be modified. It requires an entry for **uucp**, and traditionally for **nuucp**, as well as for any users that are allowed to dial in through **cu**. Here we see some entries from a **passwd** file:

```
uucp:4gq5h:5:4:UUCP:/usr/spool/uucppublic:/usr/lib/uucp/uucico
Uinfopro:yS75hb:5:4::/usr/spool/uucppublic:/usr/lib/uucp/uucico
Uintel:f13d8h:5:4::/usr/spool/uucppublic:/usr/lib/uucp/uucico
nuucp:iZ3W4Nf(CWhaIeg:4:4:uucp Administrator:/usr/lib/uucp:
david:zCQrpnUP1s22:23:22:David Fiedler:/us/david:/bin/csh
```

Notice that the **nuucp** entry hasn't a conventional shell but rather uses **/usr/lib/uucp/uucico** as a shell. This is imperative. **uucico** is the work-horse program of **uucp** and must be brought up when **uucp** logs in. **uucp**'s home directory (top line, sixth field) should be **/usr/spool/uucppublic** on most systems, since that's the default place to put files received by **uucp**.

For security reasons, it's a good idea to give every computer that calls you its own **uucp** login. If everybody uses the login name **uucp**, it's hard to track specific machine logins. Don't even try to make the **uucp** login name the same as the system node name; terrible things will happen. Use a leading **U** or **u** as we've done. Notice that all **uucp** login entries can share the same **uid** and **gid** numbers. Many systems are set up so that **nuucp** is the **uucp** login name, and **uucp** is the administrative login. Either way will work; we advise that you set up your system the way the supplier intended.

Saving Big Bucks

As delivered, the **uux** and **uucp** programs usually activate **uucico** immediately, meaning your system will attempt to dial out every time mail or a file is sent. To alter this method of operation, there is a **-r** flag option to these programs (undocumented on most systems) that stops **uucico** from being automatically executed. In this way, you can run **uucico** from the **cron** at regular intervals, so that all mail queued within that interval goes out at once. If you don't have the source code for **uucp**, the only way to change the operation of **uux** is to create a ''phony'' **uux** that calls the real one with the flags you want:

```
# ls -l /bin/uux
-rwsr-xr-x 1 nuucp   sys    28130 Dec  4  1984 /bin/uux
# mkcmd /usr/local/uux
exec /bin/UUX -r $*
^D
# ls -l /usr/local/uux
-rwxr-xr-x 1 root    bin       20 Dec 11 15:36 /usr/local/uux
# mv /bin/uux /bin/UUX
# cp /usr/local/uux /bin/uux
#
```

Now the "real" executable **uux** program is safely stored as **/bin/UUX**, and your shell version passes to it any flags it was called with, *plus* the **-r** flag you want. Now, you must make sure **uucico** is executed every hour or so in a manner that causes it to only dial out to systems with work pending. For this, we recommend the following lines (or their equivalent), in a file called **/usr/lib/uucp/uudemon.hr** to be run every hour from **cron**:

```
cd /usr/lib/uucp
/usr/bin/uulog
exec uucico -r1
```

The **uulog** command serves to consolidate any pending log information, and executing **uucico** with the **-r1** flag performs the necessary phone calls.

▪ Using uucp ▪

Copying Files to Another System

The simplest use of the **uucp** command is to transfer a file from your system to a remote system. Once you have established a reliable connection with another system you should try transferring a file:

```
$ uucp /etc/group remote!/usr/spool/uucppublic
```

Running this **uucp** command does not actually transfer the file directly. It creates a "workfile" in the same spooling directory used by **uux**. When a **uucp** command is issued, it executes **uucico** to perform the actual phone call. If your system returns a prompt as indicated above, then your **/etc/group** file has been queued for copying to the remote system. This illustrates one of the problems of the **uucp** facility: unless you take certain steps, the security of your system can be compromised. Meanwhile, if an error message occurs, do this instead:

```
$ cp /etc/group /usr/spool/uucppublic
$ cd /usr/spool/uucppublic
$ chmod o+r group
$ uucp group remote!/usr/spool/uucppublic
```

Now go into the proper spooling directory for the system called **remote** (**/usr/spool/uucp/remote** for HDB versions, or **/usr/spool/uucp** for all others). You will see the workfile there, with a **C** prefix:

```
$ cd /usr/spool/uucp
$ ls -lt
total 169
-rw-r--r-- 1 nuucp   uucp      72 Dec 11 15:48 C.remoten4KAd
---------- 1 nuucp   uucp       0 Dec 11 15:48 dummy
-rw-rw-rw- 1 nuucp   uucp    8013 Dec 11 15:48 LOGFILE
-rw-r--r-- 1 nuucp   mail      56 Dec 11 14:50 D.infoproX4KAT
-rw-r--r-- 1 nuucp   mail     108 Dec 11 14:50 C.btyA4KAW
-rw-r--r-- 1 nuucp   mail     665 Dec 11 14:50 D.btyB4KAV
-rw-r--r-- 1 nuucp   uucp      75 Dec 11 08:12 AUDIT
-rw-r--r-- 1 nuucp   uucp    1837 Dec 11 05:14 SYSLOG
-rw-rw-r-- 1 nuucp   uucp   13168 Dec 10 23:57 Sys-WEEK
-rw-rw-r-- 1 nuucp   uucp   53145 Dec 10 23:57 Log-WEEK
-rw-r--r-- 1 nuucp   mail      59 Dec 10 21:33 D.infoproX4K91
-rw-r--r-- 1 nuucp   mail    2633 Dec 10 21:33 D.pclesB4K93
-rw-r--r-- 1 nuucp   mail     114 Dec 10 21:33 C.pclesA4K94
-rw-r--r-- 1 nuucp   mail     114 Dec 10 21:33 C.pclesA4K4O
-rw-r--r-- 1 nuucp   mail      59 Dec 10 21:33 D.infoproX4K4L
-rw-r--r-- 1 nuucp   mail    1531 Dec 10 21:33 D.pclesB4K4N
$ cat C.remoten4KAd
S  /usr/spool/uucppublic/group /usr/spool/uucppublic david \
-dc D.0 644
```

The contents of the workfile tell **uucico** that the file **/usr/spool/uucppublic/group** must be sent to the directory **/usr/spool/uucppublic**, that the originator of the request is **david**, and that the mode of the file is 644.

Because our system has been set up for delayed calling (as explained in *Saving Big Bucks*), this workfile sits around waiting until we poll the system called **remote** (or they poll us). If all goes well the file is transferred and the workfile is removed.

Why do we continually specify the **/usr/spool/uucppublic** directory for file transfers? On most systems, this is the **uucp** "public directory" (*PUBDIR* in some of the documentation) that can always be assumed to permit file transfers into or out of a UNIX-based computer system. With proper security, this is the only one your system should use as well. Because the name is so long, it can be shortened to a single tilde character in **uucp** commands, as in the following:

```
$ uucp file.c remote!~
$
```

This saves a great deal of typing. If you are using the C shell, you have to ''backslash'' the **!** character, like this:

```
% uucp file.c remote\!~
%
```

Copying Files from Other Systems

If you can have a **uucp** connection to another machine with normal security levels, a regular user can ordinarily perform the following tasks:

- copy files from the PUBDIR area of the local machine to the PUBDIR area of the remote machine
- copy files from the PUBDIR area of the remote machine to the PUBDIR area of the local machine (except on HDB releases)
- send mail to a user on the remote machine
- queue mail to the remote machine for transmission to more distant machines that the remote connects to

Electronic Mail

Apart from file transfer, you will find the **uucp** system most useful for sending electronic mail to remote computers. Suppose you are user **ralph** on a machine with the node name **kramden**, and you want to send mail to your friend **ed** on a machine called **norton**. Normally, to send mail to another user on the *same* machine, you type **mail someone**, where **someone** is their login name. Assuming there is a direct **uucp** connection between **kramden** and **norton**, all you have to do here is use a slightly different syntax:

```
$ mail norton!ed
How about coming to the lodge meeting?
.
$
```

The *electronic mail address* (or simply *address*) for **ed** is thus **norton!ed**, which is pronounced *norton bang ed*. The exclamation mark, or *bang*, separates the machine's node name (**norton**) from the user's login name (**ed**).

When mail to a remote system is initiated, the **mail** program automatically invokes **uux** to do the job. When sending mail, **uux** actually operates by queueing a job on the remote machine that will execute the **rmail** program there. **rmail** (meaning *r*emote *mail*) is simply a link to **mail** that performs only the *sending* of mail for security purposes. When the mail arrives and **ed** reads it, it looks something like this:

```
From ralph Fri Jan 10 20:04:05 1986 remote from kramden
To: norton!ed
How about coming to the lodge meeting?
```

If there is no entry for the remote system in the **L.sys** or **Systems** file, you get an error message when sending mail:

```
$ mail mood!alice
Baby, you're the greatest!
.
bad system name: mood
uux failed. code 101
mail: saved in dead.letter
$
```

The **mail** program will attempt to save your carefully-typed mail in a file called **dead.letter** in the current directory. If you don't have permission to create files in the current directory, it will then save the mail in your home directory. Presumably, you made a mistake when typing the name of the remote system, and can simply resend it correctly:

```
$ mail moon!alice < dead.letter
$
```

Once you send the mail, it doesn't actually get to the user on the other system until the two systems next "talk," or connect via **uucp**, as we've seen.

If you want to send mail to a user on a computer that your machine *doesn't* talk directly to, you have to find a *mail path*, or sequential list of machines that talk to yours, his, and possibly some in the middle. Let's say that your machine is still **kramden**, and it has direct connections with machines known as **norton**, **moon**, and **lodge**. You want to send mail to **vulcan!spock**, and you know that the machine **vulcan** talks to **moon**. So by routing your mail to **moon!vulcan!spock**, you stand a pretty good chance of getting it where you want it.

Your mail will not reach **spock** until **moon** talks to **vulcan** *after* **moon** talks to **kramden**. However, you are spared the cost of the rather expensive communications link between **vulcan** and **moon**. Your machine only needs to call **moon**. For this reason, it's a good idea to set up connections with as many close-by machines as possible. As you find more people with computers that are willing to talk to yours, keep track of which machines each of them talks to, and you will gradually expand the universe of machines — and people — that you can exchange electronic mail with. To find other UNIX users in the area, try contacting a local computer club, UNIX user group, or even your local university.

Why would anyone want to let your machine talk to theirs? As we've noted, **uucp** works both ways. Eventually, your machine may become a good one for others to talk to, especially if you make a good number of connections. Setting up even a simple mail connection like this one, however, means a certain amount of tacit agreement. Etiquette demands that either party will pass mail to its other connections with some expectation of privacy. If you expect the other machine to make phone calls on behalf of your mail users, they should also expect you to poll your other connections when they route mail through your machine. Further, once you have set up the connection and have tested it in both directions, you shouldn't need to look at mail passing through.

Over the past decade or so, over 5000 sites worldwide have joined this informal *UUCP-Net* by simply agreeing to pass mail to one or more other machines. The power of this is amazing. By just knowing the correct mail path, you can reach people *all over the world* for the price of a local phone call.

How do you find the right path? One of your connections will probably have a machine-readable copy of a network map, which you can use to figure out paths to distant machines. Another thing that helps is being able to read other people's net addresses. For instance, given the information above, here is **ralph**'s full net address:

```
{lodge, moon, norton}!kramden!ralph
```

This means that **ralph** is a user on the **kramden** machine, and you can reach **kramden** directly via **lodge**, **moon**, and **norton**. This syntax, very much like that of the C shell, is simply shorthand for the equivalent three paths

```
lodge!kramden!ralph
moon!kramden!ralph
norton!kramden!ralph
```

Sometimes you will also see an address like **ralph@kramden** or **ralph@kramden.UUCP**, which are equivalent to **kramden!ralph**. Such address forms assume that you (or your mail software) can figure out how to reach the **kramden** machine. The second form specifies that the message is to be sent over the UUCP-Net, rather than one of the other available networks such as *BITNET*, *ARPANET*, or *CSNET*.

Naturally, you're not limited to UUCP-Net for your electronic mail. It's relatively simple to set up your own private network among offices across the street or across the country by doing essentially the same thing as outlined above but keeping your connections private.

USENET: Anarchy and Chaos?

If the relative informality of UUCP-Net is to your liking, you may be interested in *USENET*. USENET is a loose collection of systems that do far more than pass mail back and forth. They send collections of "articles" to each other, organized by "newsgroups" about various subjects. These articles are written and contributed by any of the thousands of people on the net. It's sort of like a daily newspaper with different columns — sports, music, technical discussions, and so on — except that anyone can write for the net. As you might expect, this means that a great variety of material, in both quantity and quality, can be found on USENET.

Most newsgroups have generally understandable names such as **net.aviation** and **net.unix**. Others are more cryptic, such as **net.news.sa** (which is for system administrators), but still tend to be easier to figure out than the names of some UNIX commands. The useful public domain programs in groups like **net.sources** and **mod.sources** make joining the net worthwhile for many sites. Some programs that have been distributed this way include spreadsheets, a 68000 disassembler, a complete B-tree implementation, dozens of C-related programming tools, printer drivers for Epsons and the HP LaserJet, and screen-oriented mail programs.

The disadvantage of USENET is that *all* the news is passed from computer to computer. This generally amounts to about one megabyte *per day*, and may add up to 7 to 15 megabytes, depending on how long you retain older news articles. Your *news feed* (the machine that sends the news data to your machine) can be instructed to delete certain newsgroups, but if you feed other sites in turn, etiquette requires that you feed them the newsgroups that they want.

Etiquette is particularly important on USENET, since "posting" an article to the wrong newsgroup causes a chain reaction where thousands of computers pass incorrect data all over the world, costing them a certain amount of time and money. Certain taboos, if broken, will result in the culprit being "flamed," or sent complaining mail messages from perhaps dozens of people. USENET exists by the good graces of the companies who find it worth their time and money to pass this data around. So it's especially recommended not to post commercial advertising messages. The few who have tried taking advantage of USENET for such purposes have found the bad publicity — and flames — not worth the "free advertising." At the same time, news and information of importance passes quickly on the net.

Posting articles is not for those whose egos are easily bruised, and your first posting is likely to be a traumatic event. It's best to read the articles on the net for several weeks before deciding to join in.

Connecting to USENET is a bit harder than hooking up to UUCP-Net. While any two UNIX machines can create a mail link, it's necessary to get the complete set of news software from an existing USENET site before you can begin. As before, you will have to ask around; part of the admission to the "club" is the ability to do some research. Actual news transmission is done by **uucp**, but it's fed into a program called **rnews** that puts it into the proper directory on your machine. Sometimes the news articles are batched together, or even compressed, for more convenient transfer.

Because the news software is constantly undergoing change, and it must be modified for your machine, it's hard to give any more than general hints past the documentation that comes with the software. You must set up a news spooling directory (usually **/usr/spool/news**) and a program directory (**/usr/lib/news**), compile and install all the programs, and poll the site that is feeding you news. By watching the log file (use **tail -f /usr/lib/news/log**), you will see the inevitable errors as they occur. Most beginning errors are the result of missing files, directories, or incorrect permissions, and the log file will be your best guide.

For many administrators of large systems, it will be necessary to find someone else to run the news system, although it tends to stabilize in a month or two. The biggest problem with USENET is disciplining yourself and your users to *not* read all those thousands of sometimes fascinating articles.

kermit and xmodem

kermit is not standard UNIX. It is a communications protocol developed to make file transfer possible between minis, micros, and mainframes. It will go places that **cu** and **uucp** will not. **cu** will talk to anything, even a toaster, if it has a RS-232 port and an I/O board. It does not packetize data, however, and is not practical on long or "dirty" lines. **kermit** will go anywhere as long as there is a **kermit** program at the other end, and it does packetize data, which greatly increases data reliability. **kermit** is a public domain program and available from sources such as Columbia University in New York City for the price of the tape and handling, as well as on the USENET network. With the exception of Ward Christensen's **modem7** program, few communications programs have spread as quickly.

modem7 is a program written many years ago to enable personal computer users to transmit files to one another with some degree of error checking. While originally written in assembler language for the 8080, it was ported to many different architectures and languages, including C. **xmodem** is a UNIX implementation of the **modem7** protocol which gets you into the act. It is also available on USENET. Most PC owners have one or another of the corresponding programs.

The use of **kermit** or **xmodem** is simplicity itself. It requires that you ascertain that the identical program is present on the remote site, and know the device name of your outgoing modem. Once you have made the initial connection (using **kermit** or even **cu**), you just type **xmodem s filename** on the sending computer, and **xmodem r filename** on the receiving computer. The two programs ''sync up'' with each other, and the file is transferred. There are several different implementations of both **kermit** and **xmodem** (the program you actually run may be called **ckermit** or **umodem**), but the general idea is the same for all these programs. Some have batch transfer capabilities, so you can type **kermit s *.c** and send all the C programs in a directory. One version of **kermit** allows you to set up a mail system using **kermit** to transfer the files rather than **uucp**.

Transmission without Tears

An important consideration in **uucp** file transmission is the use of packet transmission. We already mentioned that ''noisy'' phone lines can make data transmission difficult.

To review packet transmission: Data are sent in packets, small bundles of characters that are put together by the sending machine and taken by the remote machine. Each packet contains a checksum, a number generated by adding the actual bit patterns of the characters sent. The receiving machine uses the same checksum algorithm. If they don't agree, something is wrong; ''dirt'' has entered the line. The packet is then rejected and resent. Watch **uucp** working by observing the send and receive lights on your modem. In the first phase when your machine is sending, the send light stays on for a few seconds, and then the receive light flickers. In the second phase when receiving, the receive light stays on, and the send light flickers. The flicker is the transmission of the checksum from the receiving machine.

For short transmissions, such as on a local (direct) line that is shielded and of a reasonably short length or a local call on a very clean dialup line, **cu** *may* get your data across in one piece. If it is ASCII text, like a letter or memo, it may be OK. Code or data usually isn't worth risking. Use a packet transmission method like **uucp**, **xmodem**, or **kermit**.

There is more to the overall **uucp** system than **uucico**. Polling must be taken care of in an orderly manner. Unsent packages and old logfiles must be swept up and thrown out with the trash. We will look at these tasks and how to automate them next.

The cron Files

Two transactions must be handled automatically on a regular basis for **uucp** to function well. These are polling and cleaning up **/usr/spool/uucp**. The following is a **crontab** excerpt from HDB:

```
#        root
#
41,11 8-17 * * * /bin/su uucp -c "/usr/lib/uucp/uudemon.poll" \
> /dev/null 2>&1
45,15 * * * * /bin/su uucp -c "/usr/lib/uucp/uudemon.hour" \
> /dev/null 2>&1
50 23 * * * /bin/su uucp -c "/usr/lib/uucp/uudemon.cleanup" \
> /dev/null 2>&1
```

The first entry states, "At 11 and 41 minutes after the hour from 8 AM to 5 PM any day, set up polling to those systems in listed in **/usr/lib/uucp/Poll**." **uudemon.hour** runs **uucico** for any systems with outstanding work (including systems set up to be polled by **uudemon.poll**). The last entry states, "At ten minutes to midnight every day, clean up logs and directories that are over three days old." (This is accomplished within the shell procedure called **uudemon.cleanup**). If you have regular file transmissions on Fridays, you may want to use a different schedule.

Many of these functions can be performed manually. **uudemon.cleanup** cleans up but you have the option of saying when and how old. **uucico** and **Uutry** can be used to force polling.

The shell program **uudemon.admin** may be run once per day (before **uudemon.cleanup**) to have daily statistics about the **uucp** system mailed to the administrative login **uucp**.

One or Two Modems?

In the past all serious UNIX systems with communications ran on a minimum of two modems: one for incoming calls, one for outgoing. Under HDB, the **uugetty** command makes it possible to run with one modem since a port can now be bidirectional.

With the old UUCP it is possible to switch the ports programatically by a script or C program that changes the definition of the port in **/etc/ttys** and resets the modem for incoming or outgoing calls. Here is a shell script to do that:

```
#           modem
# adds or removes getty from modem port and
# switches echo on or off
#
if test $# -eq 0
then
   echo "   usage:  modem -in for incoming data calls"
   echo "           modem -out for outgoing data calls"
fi
case $1 in
  -in)
   ed /etc/ttys > /dev/null <<EOF
   1,$s/09tty5/19tty5/
   w
   q
EOF
   echo "ATE0\r" > /dev/tty5
   echo "ATQ1\r" > /dev/tty5
   kill -1 1
   stty 1200 even odd*>/dev/tty5
   chmod 666 /dev/tty5
   chown nuucp /dev/tty5
   ;;
  -out)
   ed /etc/ttys > /dev/null <<EOF
   1,\$s/19tty5/09tty5/
   w
   q
EOF
   echo "ATE1\r" > /dev/tty5
   echo "ATQ0\r" > /dev/tty5
   kill -1 1
   sleep 2
   stty 1200 even odd -raw cbreak \
   -nl -lcase echo -tabs > /dev/tty5
   chmod 666 /dev/modem
   ;;
  *)
   echo "no $1 option"
   exit 1
   ;;
esac
```

Note that this script is a kludge, not a cure-all. It must be called each time the direction of a modem port has to be changed.

Naturally, if you have System V but not **uugetty**, you can still turn a modem from incoming to outgoing by setting up the appropriate entries in **/etc/inittab** and switching **init** levels. But modem control problems might still preclude this.

Uugoodies

There are a number of UNIX programs (commands) that make life easier for the **uucp** user and the system administrator. Many are available as public domain software and on the USENET network. They are quite handy, but be forewarned that they may not compile on your machine. Many are BSD (Berkeley software) programs and make reference to header files that may not be available on your system. Here are some of the more interesting commands from the standard AT&T UNIX distribution:

uucheck	checks the system for necessary uucp files
uulog	prints out data from the **uucp** log files
uuname	set or get the system name (node name)
uuto	like **uucp** but deliberately restricted
uupick	accepts or rejects files sent to user
Uutry	try **uucico** with debugging messages

Some of the more interesting public domain programs are:

uuq	manipulate the **uucp** queue
uusub	monitor the **uucp** network
uuhosts	extract and interpret network maps from the **mod.map** newsgroup
pathalias	figure out optimum path to any machine from network maps and builds database
msg	screen-oriented mail program; can automatically send mail using **pathalias** database

▪ Handy Shell Programs ▪

uul

This will quickly show you the contents of the spool directory, in time order.

```
ls -lt /usr/spool/uucp
```

uufol

A must when watching **uucp** connections. This sits on the log file and shows you every new entry, until it is killed.

```
tail -f /usr/spool/uucp/LOGFILE
```

On HDB you can use **uulog -f system** instead.

uutail

A quick command to see the last few **uucp** transactions and file transfers.

```
cd /usr/spool/uucp
tail LOGFILE
tail SYSLOG
```

On HDB **uulog -10** gives the same effect.

uurmst

This is a useful when things appear stuck. It removes all the old **status** files that may be preventing your system from dialing out.

```
rm -f /usr/spool/uucp/ST*
```

For HDB users the equivalent is

```
rm -f /usr/spool/uucp/.status/*
```

poll

This is an absolute must for testing new connections. **poll** should only be used when no other **uucp** activity is in progress (especially outgoing). It forcibly removes any old **lock** and **status** files, and polls the system named on the command line.

The **-x9** flag can be used if desired.

```
if $# < 1
then echo usage: $0 system [-x9] ; exit 1
fi
rm -f /usr/spool/uucp/STST.$1 /usr/spool/uucp/LCK*
/usr/lib/uucp/uucico -r1 -s$1 $2
rm -f /usr/spool/uucp/STST.$1
```

On HDB you can use **Uutry -r system** instead.

sysname

This marvelous C program, by Pat Wood, actually changes the node name compiled into your kernel, so you can set your node name even if your kernel isn't reconfigurable. It doesn't actually change the file **/unix**, **/xenix**, or whatever your kernel is called (this should be set in the program on the line that starts **#define UNIX**), but rather changes the in-memory copy while it's running. This means that if you need this program, you should run it every time the system is rebooted (probably from **/etc/rc**). Just type

 # sysname *newname*

where *newname* is the name you want your system to be known as, e.g.,

```
# sysname kramden
```

```
#include <types.h>
#include <sys/utsname.h>
#include <fcntl.h>

#define KMEM "/dev/kmem"          /* kernel memory */

main (argc, argv)
int argc;
char *argv[];
{
    struct utsname uts;
    int memory;
    unsigned long nameloc;
    unsigned long unixname();

    if (argc != 2) {
        printf ("%s:  needs system name\n", argv[0]);
        exit(1);
    }
    if (strlen (argv[1]) > 8) {
        printf ("%s:  system name must be <= 8 chars\n", argv[0]);
        exit(1);
    }
```

```
    nameloc = unixname ();
    if (nameloc == 0) {
        printf ("%s:  cannot get address for utsname\n", argv[0]);
        exit(1);
    }
    if ((memory = open(KMEM, O_RDWR)) == -1){
        printf ("%s:  cannot open %s\n", argv[0], KMEM);
        exit(1);
    }

    lseek (memory, nameloc, 0);
    read (memory, &uts, sizeof (uts));
    strcpy (uts.sysname, argv[1]);
    strcpy (uts.nodename, argv[1]);
    lseek (memory, nameloc, 0);
    write (memory, &uts, sizeof (uts));
}

/*
**  unixname -- look up name in UNIX namelist
**  argument is a string to look up in UNIX
**  returns address
*/

#define ATTSV       /* define if running System V or V.2 */
/* #define BSD      /* define if running BSD */
/* #define V7       /* define if running V7 SYS3 or XENIX */

/*
** name of the "utsname" structure changed
** as of System V from _utsname to utsname
*/
#ifdef ATTSV
# define UTSNAME "utsname"
#else
# define UTSNAME "_utsname"
#endif

/*
** define UNIX to be name of unix object file,
** e.g., /unix, /vmunix, /xenix.
*/
#define UNIX "/unix"

#if defined(ATTSV) || defined(BSD)
# include <nlist.h>
#else
# include <a.out.h>
#endif
```

```
unsigned long unixname ()
{
    struct nlist list[2];
    static char *name = UTSNAME;
/*
** the following #ifdef is necessary due to a change of
** the definition of the n_name element from an array
** to a pointer
*/
#ifdef ATTSV
    /* set up name list array */
    char array1[10];
    list[0].n_name = name;
    list[1].n_name = "";
#else
    /* set up name list array */
    strcpy (list[0].n_name, name);
    list[1].n_name[0] = 0;
#endif

    /* get name list entry for "name" */
    if (nlist (UNIX, list) == -1)
        return (0L);
    return ((long) list[0].n_value);
}
```

▪ Chapter Summary ▪

Times change. For a generation large computing meant large computers. It was the heyday of Sperry, Honeywell, and IBM. Joining the ranks of big computers now are Amdahl, Cray, Fujitsu, and several other manufacturers. More and more frequently, the way to increased computing power is networking. This means connecting a mixed bag of computers large, medium, and small into a loosely coupled giant spreading both power and versatility to everyone in that network.

A variation on the theme of networking several machines into a larger working entity is called *clustering*. Clustering smaller machines to match the power of larger machines is extremely cost effective. So much so that, when cleverly done, cost effectiveness can be at a factor of 10 to 1 or even 50 to 1 against the cost of a mainframe.[4] While a small computer cannot match the mainframe's speed of execution, a heavily loaded mainframe can be far slower than a lightly loaded supermicro. Clustering has additional advantages. When a mainframe or a large minicomputer goes down every one is out of work. When a single element in a network of clustered machines goes down only those people directly attached to that machine are down, and if the cluster has a file server, those people can go to another terminal and pick up where they left off. Redundancy is the prime virtue in a system where reliability is important, and clustering is redundancy exemplified.

---

4 This is based on the following: One 100-user Amdahl costs $3,000,000 (base price), while ten 10-user supermicros cost $150,000 (base price), yielding a ratio of 20 to 1.

Today's office relies on "personal" computers. These little micros have become as prolific as typewriters. Their potential as a part of a larger system has been ignored, largely for a lack of communications software and the knowledge of networking. AT&T and many others, seeing the potential of the myriad of PCs, has created the means of easily networking them to UNIX machines of all sizes. Thus the PC-DOS/UNIX bridge is in place to join this sea of small computers into extensions of even greater computational power. With the advent of commercial electronic mail systems that accept **uucp** protocol, such as AT&T Mail, UNIX users now have the ability to exchange electronic mail and files with millions of personal computer users as well as people on other UNIX systems.

C H A P T E R

13

SHELL PROGRAMMING

▪ Introduction to the Bourne Shell ▪

A comprehensive Bourne shell tutorial is beyond the scope of this book. However, because Bourne shell scripts are such a vital part of commercial UNIX system administration, we are going to cover some Bourne shell basics. Then we jump right into some system administration shell scripts and examine how they work, why they work, and when you should use them.

At this writing, the Bourne shell is considered the official UNIX system shell interpreter. The C shell (BSD) is also a shell interpreter, and it's very popular. The syntax is C-like, much more elegant in appearance than the Bourne shell. But don't let appearances fool you. The Bourne shell runs 4 to 20 times faster than the C shell, and the C shell passes scripts to the Bourne shell unless deliberately told to do otherwise. The Bourne shell is a bit clunky to use. It is also rather difficult to learn because of its somewhat clumsy syntax. But it is extremely powerful, and once you get the hang of it you can move programmatic mountains. Even if you prefer the C shell, we recommend that you save the C shell for personal use and rely on the Bourne shell for official system administration use. This gives you the additional advantage of ensuring the portability of your system administration scripts from machine to machine.

The Bourne shell is a command interpreter language. Most users use only a few operating system commands during the course of the day, and they think of them as isolated messages to the operating system. System administrators must not only communicate with the operating system but manipulate it as well. That's where command interpreter languages enter the picture. The Bourne shell is a sophisticated interpreter language, an excellent vehicle for UNIX system administrators.

Command interpreters are not new, nor are they exclusive to UNIX. IBM has EXECs and REX. CP/M has SUBMIT. Minis such as Data General have macros (not to be confused with the programming term *macro*). They all serve the same purpose — they take in command names and arguments and act upon them. However, the Bourne shell comes close to being a fully developed programming language. Not only that, all UNIX commands and utilities are also at its disposal. Thus any feature the Bourne shell lacks can be picked from one of the outstanding UNIX utilities such as **awk**, **grep**, and **sed**.

▪ Levels of Shell Programming ▪

Shell programs vary in complexity. They can be a simple series of standard UNIX commands entered into a file by an editor, or they can be complex with nested programs and loops. All the major programming constructs are at your disposal as a shell programmer. There are **if**s, **if-then-else**s, and **elif**s (else-ifs). There are both **for** and **while** loops and an elegant case structure. The shell is extremely powerful, and it's a tremendous time-saver. A complex two-page shell script could require almost a thousand lines of C code to duplicate it. It is not absolutely necessary to know C to run a UNIX system, but it *is* necessary to be able to program in shell script.

The for Loop

Programs of any kind are most often written to perform repetitive tasks, and looping is the ideal construct for this. The most common loop forms are **for** loops and **while** loops. The **for** loop works as long as an argument list exists. The loop exits once the argument list is exhausted.

Following is a simple shell program that writes a list of names to the screen:[1]

```
$ cat simple
for name in root bruce karen david susan
do
        echo $name
done
$ simple
root
bruce
karen
david
susan
$
```

When the program executes, it takes the list following **in** and assigns each word in turn to the variable **name**, executing the **echo** once for each word. The **$name** is replaced by the string (in this case a name) stored in the variable **name**.

Notice the structure of the **for** loop:

1 All shell scripts must be made executable with **chmod** (e.g., **chmod +x simple**) before they can be used as a command.

```
for variable in list
do
        command(s)
done
```

The *command(s)* are executed once for each word in *list*, with the shell variable *variable* assigned to a different one each time.

Getting Mileage out of the **for** Loop

The argument list in the program above need not be built into the program. It also can be passed to the program from the command line or generated by other means. Consider the following script:

```
$ cat for_demo
for arg
do
        echo $arg
done
```

The shell gets just a bit tricky here. No argument list is explicitly specified to the **for** loop. The command-line argument list when you type in the program name is used instead. Notice the arguments (**1 2 3 4 5 6 7 8**):

```
$ for.demo 1 2 3 4 5 6 7 8
1
2
3
4
5
6
7
8
$
```

The **for** loop takes the argument list (here the numbers 1 through 8) and assigns them in turn to the variable **arg**.

Positional Parameters

Positional parameters is a fancy term for the items in an argument list. The shell maintains ten special variables, **0** through **9**, which are each assigned an argument from the command line. Here's an example:

```
$ cat echo.prog
echo $0
echo $1
echo $2
echo $3
$
```

The program above runs like this:

```
$ echo.prog one two three
echo.prog
one
two
three
$
```

The positional parameters are **0**, **1**, **2**, and **3**. Thus, **$1** is replaced by the first argument, **$2** the second, and so on. The argument **$0** is special and refers to the actual name of the executing program. Some other special shell variables are **$#**, the number of arguments and **$$**, the process id (*pid*) number of the shell itself. We show these below.

▪ The while Loop ▪

The **while** loop is similar to the **for** loop except it uses the exit status of a command to determine when to quit looping. It also lacks the **for** loop's connotation of being incremented. The **while** loop is usually used with the **test** command. Its form is

```
while test expression
do
        command(s)
done
```

and it looks like this in use

```
$ cat printall
while test $# != 0
do
        echo printing $1
        lp $1
        shift
done
$ printall file1.c file2.c file3.c
printing file1.c
```

```
request-id is laser-1442 (1 file)
printing file2.c
request-id is laser-1443 (1 file)
printing file3.c
request-id is laser-1444 (1 file)
$
```

test is testing the variable, **$#**, the number of arguments. As long as it isn't zero, there are still arguments to process, and this script sends **$1** to the printer. Note the word **shift**. This is a shell programming device that shifts the positional arguments down. **$3** becomes **$2**, **$2** becomes **$1**, and **$1** goes away; **$#** is also decremented by one. When it exhausts the argument list, the **while** loop finishes, as **$#** will be zero.

Another Look at test

Don't expect the shell to perform like a high-powered programming language such as C or PL/I. The shell has most of the programming constructs of any language, but it has two failings. First, it is exceptionally picky about syntax and whitespace. Second, it needs some hand holding.

The shell needs the help of **test** or some other program or command that returns a valid exit status:

```
while test $# != 0
while test $1 != templ
while grep "UNIX" $1
```

The use of **test** might offend some programmers. Fortunately, you can change the first two lines above to

```
while [ $# != 0 ]
while [ $1 != templ ]
```

The left bracket ([) means **test**; the right bracket (]) balances the statement.

Here is a partial list of useful **test** options:

-r *filename*	true if the file exists and is readable.
-w *filename*	true if the file exists and is writable.
-f *filename*	true if the file exists and is a regular file.
-d *filename*	true if the file exists exists and is a directory.
-s *filename*	true if the file exists and is greater than zero length.
-z *s1*	true if the length of string *s1* is zero.

-n *s1*	true if the length of the string *s1* is nonzero.
s1 = *s2*	true if the strings *s1* and *s2* are equal.
s1 != *s2*	true if the strings *s1* and *s2* are not equal.
s1	true if *s1* is not a null string.
n1 **-eq** *n2*	true if the integers *n1* and *n2* are algebraically equal. Other comparison operators **-ne**, **-gt**, **-ge**, **-lt**, and **-le**
-a	logical AND operator
-o	logical OR operator
(*expr*)	parentheses for grouping.

Note: **-a** has higher precedence than **-o**.

The **if-then-else** Construct

The shell has a fully developed **if-then-else** construct. It also has an **elif** (else-if) construct. There are several variations:

IF THEN

```
if test expression
then
        command(s)
fi
```

IF THEN ELSE

```
if test expression
then
        command(s)
else
        command(s)
fi
```

IF THEN ELSE IF

```
if test expression
then
        command(s)
elif test expression
        command(s)
else    optional
        command(s)
fi
```

Here's a simple example of the use of **if**:

```
$ cat if.test
if [ "$1" = yes ]
then
        echo You typed in yes
else
        echo You did not type in yes
fi
$ if.test yes
You typed in yes
$ if.test no
You did not type in yes
$ if.test
You did not type in yes
$
```

You can combine the **if** with other constructs, like the **while**:

```
while test $# != 0
do
        if test -s "$1"
        then
                echo printing $1
                lp $1
        fi
        shift
done
```

This shell script is just like **printall** except it tests to see if the specified file(s) exist and contain data (**-s** option to **test**) before printing them.

As with the **while** statement, you don't have to use **test**; any command that returns a valid exit status may be used:

```
$ cat if1.test
if grep UNIX "$1" > /dev/null
then
        echo "$1 contains UNIX"
else
        echo "$1 doesn't contain UNIX"
fi
$ if1.test intro
intro contains UNIX
$ if1.test junk
junk doesn't contain UNIX
$
```

▪ The case Statement ▪

The **case** construct, a multiple branch, goes all the way back to FORTRAN. Many programmers prefer to use the **case** over an **if-else** construct because the **case** is more straightforward. The **case** is particularly useful when doing multiple branching on a string. Its form is

case *word* **in**
    pattern 1)
        command list 1;;
    pattern 2)
        command list 2;;

        . . .

    pattern N)
        command list N;;
esac

If *pattern 1* matches *word*, then *command list 1* is executed; otherwise, if *pattern 2* matches *word*, then *command list 2* is executed, and so on. A *pattern* is any string, and may include shell file name expansion characters, *****, **?**, and **[]**. A *pattern* may be a composite of other patterns separated by the vertical bar (pipe symbol, **|**), which implies a logical ORing of the *patterns*.

Here's a simple example of the **case** construct. It displays different messages depending upon what you type in:

```
$ cat case.test
case "$1" in
        bh)
                echo "Hi Bruce!  How are ya?";;
        kh)
                echo "Hi Karen!  How are ya?";;
        df)
                echo "Hi Dave!  How are ya?";;
        sf)
                echo "Hi Susan!  How are ya?";;
        *)
                echo "Who are you?";;
esac
$ case.test bh
Hi Bruce!  How are ya?
$ case.test sf
Hi Susan!  How are ya?
$ case.test pw
Who are you?
$
```

$1 is used as the string to match against the patterns in the **case**. It is quoted (more on those later) to make sure it doesn't get misinterpreted if it contains a blank or if it's empty. Notice the use of ***** as a pattern. This is like saying, ''if nothing else matches, I will.''

▪ Quoting ▪

An executing shell program reads (parses) each character and token and interprets them. Some characters have special meaning to the shell. A few of them are

```
# * ? \ [ ] { } ( ) < > " ' ` | ^ & ; $
```

One of the first shell script tricks you learn is keeping these characters from being misinterpreted. You do this by quoting, and there are four different ways to quote. Deciding on which one to use is one of the most confusing shell programming techniques. At first it seems like a cross between art and alchemy. But it gets easier after you use them for a while.

We're going to dive directly into some shell quoting specifics. We will not get into quoting complete to the last detail but will cover only what is necessary for our purposes. First the quoting devices themselves:

" double quote	Prevents all the shell's special characters from being interpreted *except for* **$**, **`**, *and in certain cases* ****.
' single quote	Prevents all the shell's special characters from being interpreted
\ backslash	Prevents the character following it from being interpreted. It works the same as putting the character inside single quotes.
` accent grave	Is replaced by the result of any command(s) trapped within them.

To get a feel for quoting try the following experiments.

EXPERIMENT #1:

```
$ echo hi          there
hi there
$ echo "hi          there"
hi         there
```

The double quotes removed the special meaning associated with the space character (word separation).

EXPERIMENT #2:

```
$ echo "$PATH"
/bin:/usr/bin:/usr/local:.
```

The double quotes allowed the shell to interpret **$PATH** as the contents of a variable.

EXPERIMENT #3:

```
$echo '$PATH'
$PATH
```

The single quotes *prevented* the shell from interpreting **$PATH** as the contents of a variable.

EXPERIMENT #4:

```
$ echo pwd
pwd
```

This is straightforward. But look at the next experiment.

EXPERIMENT #5:

```
$ echo `pwd`
/us/bruce/work
```

The expression **`pwd`** allows **pwd** to execute as a command and pass its results back to **echo**.

EXPERIMENT #6:

```
$ echo $PATH
/bin:/usr/bin:/usr/local:.
$ echo \$PATH
$PATH
```

Here, the **** removed the special meaning of the **$**.

A good example of the difficulties that can be encountered with shell quoting is the following line out of a script called **rml+f**:

```
if [ "lost+found" != `basename \`pwd\` ` ]
```

The script has to compare the **basename** of the current directory with the string **lost+found.**[2] Trapping a command between grave accents returns the output of the

---

2 **basename** is a command that returns the last portion of a qualified file name (i.e., the name to the right of the last **/**). The **basename** of **/usr/spool/crontab/cron** is **cron**.

command. But what happens when you need to execute a command within a command such as **pwd** executed within **basename**, and all of that within a shell script? You must prevent the inner **`pwd`** from being interpreted too early. To preserve the command, the `s are quoted with backslashes. The result is the syntax above.

expr

expr is a useful command that can be used inside grave accents to perform integer arithmetic with the shell. The arguments given to **expr** are dealt with as an expression in **expr**'s own peculiar way. There is a lot of escaping with the backslash character, since **expr** uses some of the shell's special characters as operators (like ***** for multiplication). Below is a brief description of the most useful operators and keywords for **expr**:

expr relop expr	where *relop* stands for one of **=**, **>**, **<**, **<=**, **>=**, or **!=**. The action yields "1" if the indicated comparison is true, "0" if false. The comparison is numeric if both *expr* are integers, otherwise lexicographic.
expr **+** *expr* *expr* **-** *expr*	The **+** and **-** operators perform addition or subtraction of the arguments.
expr ***** *expr* *expr* **/** *expr* *expr* **%** *expr*	The multiplication, division, or remainder operators are as straightforward as the addition and subtraction operators, performing multiplication division and the modulus (remainder) of the arguments.
(*expr* **)**	Parentheses may be used for grouping.

A few examples of **expr** should show you how it works:

```
$ expr 5 + 21
26
$ expr 17 - 2
15
$ expr 23 \* 22
506
$ expr \( 23 + 22 \) \* 2
90
```

In the last two examples above, the *****, **(**, and **)** operators were quoted with a backslash to keep the shell from interpreting them.

Here's a simple shell program that increments a variable inside a **while** loop:

```
$ cat expr.test
j=1
while test $j -le 10
do
        echo $j
        j=`expr $j + 1`
done
$ expr.test
1
2
3
4
5
6
7
8
9
10
$
```

Putting **basename** to Work

The system administrator has the unending task of removing files from the system where they tend to accumulate unnoticed. An active system that crashes from time to time quickly fills the many **lost+found** directories attached to each mounted file system. Those that fill fastest are **/usr/spool** and **root**. That is because of the many invisible **tmp** files created. They never show unless the processes are interrupted. The **rml+f** program was written to remove all of those files (after restoring those that are found to be necessary to the users). It has one argument, the date. Normally today's date is used unless the crash occurred yesterday and the night operator didn't clean up the mess. Operators are not always system programmers and should not be expected to clean up the system; they just do their best to keep it alive and inform you of problems.

Notice this script is bulletproofed. You have to be in **lost+found** to execute it or it will exit. This is to keep you from firing it up in any other directory where it would clobber the contents and send you back to last night's backup:

```
#            rml+f
#  removes file from lost + found
#           bhh 8/2/85
#         modified by phw
#
if [ "lost+found" != `basename \`pwd\`` ]
then
        echo "you must be in lost+found"
        exit
fi
```

```
if [ $# -ne 1 ]
then
        echo "usage:  rml+f date"
        echo "as in rml+f \"Jul 24\" "
        echo "used to remove all lost+found"
        echo "files except those dated Jul 24"
        exit
fi

echo "files found: \c"
ls | wc -l

rm -f `ls -l | grep -v "$1" | cut -c55-`

echo "files left: \c"
ls | wc -l
```

Notice the heavy use of quoting. **pwd** is executed within **basename**, as we discussed earlier. The grave accents must be quoted. Thus

```
`basename \`pwd\``
```

Also note that quotes are required around **$1** in the **grep**; otherwise, the shell will interpret a date such as **Jul 24** as two arguments, and **grep** will go looking for the string **Jul** in the file **24**.

An Example: the ptr Script

We are going to show you a shell script called **ptr**. First the script tests to see if there are command-line arguments. If there are none, it takes that as an opportunity to show the user how to use the script before exiting. Then the script goes into a **case** to set up the processing command (**pr** or **cat**) and the printing command and arguments.[3] Next it goes through the files and buffers them to a printer file buffer. Finally it sends the entire buffer to the printer of choice.

Whereas small systems usually have only one *line* printer, most larger systems have several *offline* printers. Handling a number of dissimilar printers can be a chore. System V has an **lp** command that handles a number of printer spoolers, but in most commercial installations, system programmers develop their own printer commands to handle the built-in idiosyncrasies of the equipment and user needs in their installations. This script, for example, was written for an installation that has numerous printers located in buildings a street or two away from the computer. A complete printer program should be equipped to deal with multiple files as arguments.

3 Although this script uses the **opr** command to print out files, we encourage you to modify it to work with *your* line printer command, be it **lpr**, **lp**, or something else.

Now for a look at the entire script:

```
#                           ptr
#                 Bruce Hunter and Pat Wood
#      a program to run multiple files to the printer of choice
#                     created 02/23/86

if test $# -eq 0
then
    echo \
"Usage: $0 [-m2] [-m3] [-l] [-z] [-w] [-ww] [-n] [-q] [-f] [-i] file(s)
use -m2 option for matrix 2
use -m3 for matrix 3
use -l  for letter printer
use -z  for the laser printer
use -w  for 8.5 by 11 white paper
use -ww for 11 by 17 white paper
use -n  for no page formatting
use -q  for mm documents, letter ptr 8 1/2 x 11
use -f  for std. forms on letter 1
use -i  for printing on DP system printer"
    exit
fi

oprcmd="opr -v system -c a"
prcmd="pr"
for arg
do
    case $1 in
        -m2) oprcmd="opr -v rscs -t matrix2";;
        -l)  oprcmd="opr -v rscs -t letter1";;
        -m3) oprcmd="opr -v rscs -t matrix3";;
        -n)  prcmd="cat";;
        -w)  oprcmd="opr -v system -c c";;
        -ww) oprcmd="opr -v system -c w";;
        -q)  oprcmd="opr -v rscs -t letter1"
             prcmd="pr -w76";;
        -z)  oprcmd="opr -v system -c l";;
        -f)  oprcmd="opr -v system -c f";;
        -i)  oprcmd="opr -v rscs -t 'inform v1'";;
        -*)  echo "$0 no option $1";;
             exit ;;
    esac
    shift
done

if [ $# -eq 0 ]
then
    echo "$0: needs file"
    exit
fi

trap 'rm -f /tmp/head.$$ /tmp/ptr.$$; echo terminated; exit 1' 1 2 3 15
```

```
logname | banner >>/tmp/head.$$
binno | banner >>/tmp/head.$$           # UTS specific command
echo "\014" >> /tmp/head.$$             # page eject

for file
do
    if [ ! -s "$file" ]
    then
        echo "$file does not exist or is an empty file"
        continue
    fi
    $prcmd $file >> /tmp/ptr.$$
    echo "\014" >> /tmp/ptr.$$      # page eject
done

if [ -s /tmp/ptr.$$ ]
then
    $oprcmd /tmp/head.$$ /tmp/ptr.$$
fi

# cleanup
rm -f /tmp/head.$$ /tmp/ptr.$$
```

Let's take this script apart and see how it works. First, it uses **test** to determine whether there are command-line arguments. If none are present, it shows how to use the program. After all, UNIX scripts can be user-friendly. It assumes that the user knows how to use the printer command, but if he doesn't, the program is ready with a brief, helpful review:

```
if test $# -eq 0
then
        echo \
"Usage: $0 [-m2] [-m3] [-l] [-z] [-w] [-ww] [-n] [-q] [-f] [-i] file(s)
use -m2 option for matrix 2
use -m3 for matrix 3
use -l  for letter printer
use -z  for the laser printer
use -w  for 8.5 by 11 white paper
use -ww for 11 by 17 white paper
use -n  for no page formatting
use -q  for mm documents, letter ptr 8 1/2 x 11
use -f  for std. forms on letter 1
use -i  for printing on DP system printer"
        exit
fi
```

Notice how multiple lines may be specified to **echo**. As long as they are enclosed in quotes, **echo** receives them as one big argument and prints them, including the newlines.

Now for a really, reeaaally big **case**:

```
for arg do
        case $1 in
                -m2) oprcmd="opr -v rscs -t matrix2";;
                -l)  oprcmd="opr -v rscs -t letter1";;
                -m3) oprcmd="opr -v rscs -t matrix3";;
                -n)  prcmd="cat";;
                -w)  oprcmd="opr -v system -c c";;
                -ww) oprcmd="opr -v system -c w";;
                -q)  oprcmd="opr -v rscs -t letter1"
                     prcmd="pr -w76";;
                -z)  oprcmd="opr -v system -c l";;
                -f)  oprcmd="opr -v system -c f";;
                -i)  oprcmd="opr -v rscs -t 'inform v1'";;
                -*)  echo "$0 no option $1";;
                     exit ;;
        esac
        shift
done
```

The **for** loop takes each of the command-line arguments and passes them to the **case** until none are left with a preceding hyphen. Note that the **for** statement, **for arg**, does not specify where the available **arg** is coming from. The default is the command-line argument list.

As each **case** is satisfied, the variable **oprcmd** (and sometimes **prcmd**) is set to an entire command. You'll see how it's used in a bit. After the **case** is finished, the arguments are shifted, so that when all options have been handled, we're left with just the files to print out.

The argument list is checked to see if it is empty (someone may have used **ptr** with just options but no file names), and if it is, an error message is given:

```
if [ $# -eq 0 ]
then
        echo "$0: needs file"
        exit
fi
```

Operating systems must deal with interrupts constantly, and so do humans. When you are getting ready to go out, and one of your children runs up to you and tells you she has a bloody nose, that is a human interrupt. When you are acting as system administrator, and a user tells you he just lost an entire file tree, that is an human interrupt. When the interrupt character (*delete* or *break*) is pressed in the middle of a script, the process stops, and that is a UNIX computer interrupt. When the phone line on the modem hangs up (literally) it sends a hangup interrupt to the system. The system acts accordingly and drops the calling program in response to the interrupt.

Most of the time we act responsibly and deal with human-type interrupts right away, but sometimes we just don't feel like it. When the phone rings and you are in the middle of a shower, that's definitely an interrupt you want to ignore! Operating systems and the shell are able to treat interrupts selectively as well. Mature shell scripts must be able to deal with interrupts from the system. Some need to be ignored, and others must be acted on.

If **ptr** receives an interrupt, it makes sure it doesn't leave temporary files behind to clutter up the system. The **ptr** script must handle interrupts properly. It must act on the interrupt by removing the temporary file first before exiting. This is accomplished by an ingenious little mechanism called a **trap**:

```
trap 'rm -f /tmp/head.$$ /tmp/ptr.$$; echo terminated; exit 1' 1 2 3 15
```

It says, "Trap interrupts 1, 2, 3, and 15. If any one of these specific interrupts is received, erase the printer buffers in **/tmp** and send error messages to the bit bucket. Then send the message **terminated** to the user's screen and exit."[4]

logname and **banner** are UNIX utilities; **binno** is a UTS utility that returns the bin number of the invoking user. **logname** returns the name of the logged-on user. **banner** expands text into characters about an inch and a half high. Linked together they give a headline size representation of the user's name and bin number. The results are written to the file **/tmp/head.$$**. The shell expands **$$** into the process number of the currently running shell. This gives us a unique file name that another program won't inadvertently clobber. Finally, a form feed (octal 14) is written to the file to separate the header from the body of the files to be printed.

Next a **for** loop is used to look at each argument, decide if it is a valid file, and append the file to the output file:

```
for file
do
    if [ ! -s "$file" ]
    then
        echo "$file does not exist or is an empty file"
        continue
    fi
    $prcmd $file >> /tmp/ptr.$$
    echo "\014" >> /tmp/ptr.$$
done
```

Notice that instead of using **cat** or **pr**, **$prcmd** is the command that copies the file to **/tmp/ptr.$$**. This shell variable is set in the **case** at the beginning of the script. It starts out as **pr**, but the **-q** option sets it to **pr -w76**, and the **-n** option sets it to **cat**. Here the shell simply replaces **$prcmd** with whatever string it contains and then parses the command line from there.

---

4 See **signal** (2) in the manual for more information on interrupts.

Once the file(s) have been processed, **/tmp/ptr.$$** is tested to see if it contains any data. If none of the input files existed or contained data, **/tmp/ptr.$$** will be empty. (There's always the possibility that a user may misspell a file name.) If it does indeed contain data, the header file **/tmp/head.$$** and **/tmp/ptr.$$** are sent to the appropriate printer:

```
$oprcmd /tmp/head.$$ /tmp/ptr.$$
```

As with **$prcmd** above, **$oprcmd** is set in the **case**.

▪ Special sh Commands for Programming ▪

Some shell programming commands don't exactly fit into any specific category, but they are too important to ignore, even in our brief treatment of the shell. These commands are **break**, **continue**, and **exec**.

break and continue

break and **continue** are right out of the C language. Both are used in **for** and **while** loops. The **break** command causes an immediate exit from a loop. The **continue** command causes the program execution to continue on the next iteration of a loop. In pseudocode they look like this:

```
for names in name_list
do
        if name = "Uncle Harry"
        then
                continue
        fi
        if evaluate money_left = 0
        then
                break
        fi
        print invitation
done
```

Here we are looping through a list of names and printing invitations. If the name of the infamous, unpopular *Uncle Harry* comes up, the program execution goes back to the **for** loop without sending him an invitation. If the amount of money left for the party drops to 0, then the **break** command has the program leave the **for** loop altogether.

Both **break** and **continue** take an optional integer argument:

```
break 3

continue 2
```

Use these in nested loops to tell **continue** or **break** how many nested loop structures it must deal with.

exec

The **exec** command causes the command used as its argument to be executed in place of the current shell rather than spawning a new shell.

▪ File System Manipulation ▪

The find Command

find is used to search a directory hierarchy and perform some action on the various files and directories that are found. **find**'s syntax is

find *dir(s) search-options*

where *dir(s)* is one or more directories to search, and *search-options* is a list of options telling **find** what it should do with each file found.

Most often, **find** is simply used to list *every* file in a directory and all its subdirectories; this is performed with the **-print** option:

```
# find / -print
/
/unix
/dev
/dev/console
/dev/syscon
    . . .
#
```

The above example will list every file on the system.

find's search may be limited to certain types of files with the **-type** option. **-type** is followed by a single character that specifies what type of file is to be found. Valid characters are

f regular file

d directory

p FIFO (named pipe)

c character-special (device file)

b block-special (device file)

So if you want to list the names of all the directories on your system you can use **find** with the **-type d** option:

```
# find / -type d -print
/
/dev
/dev/dsk
/dev/rdsk
/dev/mt
/dev/rmt
/etc
/bin
/tmp
/bck
/lib
/lost+found
/usr
/usr/bin
  . . .
```

Note that the **-print** *is still required to list the file names* and that it comes *after* **-type d**. This is due to the way **find** works internally: it combines the various options *from left to right*; therefore, **-type** is used before **-print** to filter out all nondirectories before requesting to print them. Reversing their order will cause a file to be listed *before* it is tested to see if it's a directory.

The following are the most often used **find** options:

-print	Print the found file's name.
-type *char*	Find files of type *char*.
-name *name*	Find files named *name*.
-atime *num* **-mtime** *num* **-ctime** *num*	Find files accessed, modified, or that had their inodes changed in *num* days. **+***num* means more than *num* days, and **-***num* means less than *num* days.
-size *num*	Find files *num* blocks in size. *num* may be preceded by a **+** or a **-** as above.
-user *name*	Find files owned by the user *name*.
-group *name*	Find files owned by the group *name*.

-exec *command* Execute *command* for each file found. Whenever the string **{}** is encountered in *command*, it is replaced by the found file's name. The command must be terminated with a semicolon (**;**). Since the shell interprets **;**, it should be quoted.

-cpio *device* Write out all found files to *device* in **cpio** format.

The above options may be grouped together inside parentheses (**()**), preceded by a **!** to get the logical negation of an option, and combined with **-o** to logically OR options.

Here are a few examples of **find**.

List all files in the current directory structure larger than 10 blocks:

```
find . -size +10 -print
```

List all directories on the system owned by **root**:

```
find / -type d -user root -print
```

Remove all files owned by the user **jim**:

```
find / -user jim -exec rm -f {} \;
```

cpio all files owned by **root**, **bin**, and **adm** to tape drive zero in medium density (1600 bpi):

```
find / -user root -o -user bin -o -user adm -cpio /dev/rmt/0m
```

Remove all **core** and **dead.letter** files older than one day:

```
find / \( -name core -o -name dead.letter \) -mtime +1 \
        -exec rm -f {} \;
```

The xargs Command

find can be combined with the **xargs** command to reduce the number of times a command is executed on found files. For example, the two **find**s above that use **rm** run it once for each found file, which could be a lot of invocations. **xargs** takes a list of arguments on its *standard input* and constructs a command based on these and its own command line arguments. For example

```
ls | xargs rm -f
```

removes all the files in the current directory. It takes the output of **ls** and runs **rm -f** on it. The difference between this and

```
rm -f `ls`
rm -f *
```

is that after the shell performs all of its expansions on `*` or `` `ls` ``, the size of the command line may cause an error. **xargs** generates command lines (from standard input) of manageable size, running the specified command as few times as possible without overflowing the maximum command line size. So the two **find**s mentioned above can be rewritten as follows:

```
find / -user jim -print | xargs rm -f
find / \( -name core -o -name dead.letter \) -mtime +1 \
        -print | xargs rm -f
```

and **xargs** will run **rm** as few times as possible on the found files.

fs, File Search

If you have been working on a UNIX system for a couple of years, you have accumulated a lot of programs, scripts, and files. Scores of directories and hundreds of files attest to the fact that you have been on the system long enough to make a permanent mark. So one of these days you are bound to need a file you created a few years ago but now can't remember where it is. The **fs** script was written not only to find elusive files but also to tell you what sort of files they are once they are found.

Here's the code:

```
#
# fs -- find file(s) on system
# fs file ...
#
if [ $# -eq 0 ]
then
        echo "Usage: fs f1 ... fn"
else
        names="( -name $1"
        shift
        for flist
        do
                names="$names -o -name $flist"
        done
        names="$names )"
        file `find / $names -print 2> /dev/null` |
                pr -t -e25
fi
```

First the code tests to see if there are no arguments:

```
if test $# -eq 0
then
        echo "Usage: fs f1 ... fn"
```

If there are none, it shows you how to use the script correctly.

Notice that the program is built around the UNIX **find** and **file** commands. **find** finds the files and **file** tells what they are. When you write a script that builds on commands with other commands, you are using the traditional UNIX building block principle.

There are a couple of lines in this script that bear further explanation. The code builds up a **find** argument that looks for several files at the same time. Its form is

(-name *file1* **-o -name** *file2* **-o . . .)**

So the command

```
find / \( -name fred -o -name john \) -print
```

will look for any files named **fred** or **john** on the system and prints their full path names, and

```
for flist
do
        names="$names -o -name $flist"
done
```

builds up an argument comprised of an arbitrary number of file names to look for.

```
find / $names -print 2> /dev/null
```

looks for all the specified files.

The **pr -t -e25** formats the output with tab stops every 25 columns, instead of every 8. Since **file** uses tabs in its output, the fields are aligned in columns 1 and 26:

```
$ fs tt up
/us/Script/tt            ascii text
/us/Script/up            ascii text
/us/Sysad/Bourne/up      ascii text
$
```

ds, Directory Block-usage Reporter

Trees are major UNIX file systems. **/usr** is an example of a tree. Subtrees are anything less than a tree but larger than a directory. **ds** is written to give a block-usage report of each directory in a tree, subtree, or directory. The standard UNIX **df** command does somewhat the same thing, but for trees (mounted file systems) only. When it comes time to clean out your system to gain back some disk space, this program is invaluable. Now for the code:

```
# ds
# prints block usage by directory within a tree
# Robert E. Singer 11/06/84
# modified by phw 2/23/86

if [ $# -ne 1 ]
then
        echo "usage: ds directory_name"
        echo "for best results use a fully qualified path name"
        exit 1
fi

echo "Blocks  Directory"
echo "------  ---------"
du $1 | sort +1 | sed "s/^I.*\//^I/"
```

The **sort +1** sorts the output of **du** on the second field (fields in **sort** start at zero), the full path name. The **sed** simply strips the leading path from the file name. You may want to remove this, since seeing the full path name can be useful from time to time. (^I is a Control-I or *tab* character).

Here is some typical **ds** output:

```
$ ds /us
Blocks  Directory
------  ---------
3975    us
34      AT+T
8       admin
24      Amdahl
1       cmd
187     C
1       Cbook
237     Cj
72      Doc
36      HCR
198     Bourne
135     Uts
145     bruce
```

```
4       3B
18      bin
1       misc
4       src
2       cmd
1       include
1       tmp
19      uucp
$
```

ts, Tree Search

The **ts** script searches a mounted file system (tree), subtree, or directory, separates out each directory, notes its name and qualified path, and then presents its contents via a long listing:

```
#       ts      the tree search
#       singer/wood

if test $# -gt 1
then
        echo "Usage:  ts [dir]"
        exit
fi
if test $# -eq 1
then
        pwdir=$1
else
        pwdir=`pwd`
fi

echo
for dir in `find $pwdir -type d -print`
do
        echo
        echo "$dir"
        ls -lsi $dir
        echo
done
```

▪ System Administration Scripts ▪

System administration scripts aid the system administrator in her day-to-day chores. They may be created out of necessity or convenience, but many of these scripts end up being an integral part of a working UNIX system.

monitor, for System Diagnoses and Statistics

Systems running at less than 60% CPU capacity are in little danger of displaying the infamous symptoms of the "fully loaded" syndrome. But over 60%, it's panic city. An operating system must take a percentage of its available CPU time for itself. UNIX spends its time in the kernel just trying to keep the system's sanity and handle the workload. The more the system is used, the more the overhead. Kernel time goes up exponentially at the expense of user time.

When a system becomes overloaded, all sorts of nasty bugs come crawling out of the woodwork. A system that never crashed before crashes daily in the midst of prime time. Paging becomes so rapid that nothing seems to get done. Trivial response (the time it takes to get the screen to react) goes from milliseconds to seconds. Disk usage gets so high that the read/write heads don't settle. They lag behind I/O requests and create "contention."

Even before you start to remedy the overloading situation, you have to diagnose precisely where your problems are. There are many UNIX system diagnostics, but which one should you use and how often? The following script, called **monitor**, calls most of the system diagnostic commands. The results are written out to a special directory created especially for holding system statistics. **monitor** is called from **cron (/user/spool/cron/crontabs/root)**. It is fired every 10 minutes, 5 days a week, during prime working hours. Its output is then analyzed for trouble areas like commands taking too much CPU time, excessive contention, high page rates, abnormal user activity, and other nasty side effects:

```
# monitor
#       a program to monitor
#       number of users and response time
#       bhh 05/13/856
#       added active processes 06/05/85
#       tmp 06/24/85 - modified for UTSA
#
FILE="/sys/monitor/dat/mon`date +%m%d%y`"
echo "**********************************">>$FILE
echo>>$FILE
date >> $FILE
users=`who | wc -l`
echo "$users users">>$FILE
processes=`ps -a | wc -l`
echo "$processes active user processes">>$FILE
time mkdir /tmp/mon.$$ 2>>$FILE
```

```
time ls /tmp/mon.$$ >/dev/null 2>>$FILE
time rmdir /tmp/mon.$$ 2>>$FILE
smart d dasd %cnt | grep UTS>>$FILE  # these lines
iostats>>$FILE                       # are specific
stats >>$FILE                        # to UTS
ind >>$FILE                          #
sar>>$FILE
ps -af >>$FILE
```

The script is straightforward. There are no decision-making or branching constructs, only a straight run from top to bottom.

Worthy of notice is the way the file name is created from the **date** command with the **%m%d%y** notation:

```
FILE="/sys/monitor/dat/mon`date +%m%d%y`"
```

The constant **FILE** is used throughout the code to cut down on code density.

When trying to diagnose the problems causing an overloaded system, one of the main items to watch is response time (trivial response). Three trivial responses are recorded: the time required to create a directory, the time it takes to **ls** that directory, and the time it takes to remove the directory.

```
time mkdir /tmp/mon.$$ 2>>$FILE
time ls /tmp/mon.$$ >/dev/null 2>>$FILE
time rmdir /tmp/mon.$$ 2>>$FILE
```

Note that here the standard error (file descriptor 2) is being written to **$FILE** because **time** writes the execution time of the specified command to standard error. On a happy system the time required to create, remove, or **ls** an empty directory is less than the **time** command's unit of granularity, 1/10 of a second. Thus any measurable time is trivial response, the delay caused by the system's inability to respond. We look at the response time for a few commands to get enough samples to avoid any random fluctuations in response time.

Cleaning Up the Script

The original **monitor** script above was born of necessity and created on the fly as a quick and dirty program. Because it turned out to be a valuable tool, it was kept as a permanent part of the system. But the continuous writes to **$FILE** make the program run much slower than it has to. The script was cleverly modified to make just one major write, thus maximizing efficiency:

```
# monitor     a program to monitor number of users
#             and response time
#             bhh 05/13/85
#             added active processes 06/05/85
#             tmp 06/24/85 - modified for UTSA
#             made pretty 8/20/85 Lou & Bob

FILE="/sys/monitor/dat/mon`date +%m%d%y`"

(
echo
echo "*****************************************"
echo
date
users=`who | wc -l`
echo "$users users"
processes=`ps -a | grep " 6.. " | wc -l`
echo "$processes active user processes"
time mkdir /tmp/mon.$$
time ls /tmp/mon.$$ > /dev/null
time rmdir /tmp/mon.$$
smart d dasd %cnt | grep %CNT
smart d dasd %cnt | grep UTS
ind
stats
iostats
sar
ps -af
) >>$FILE 2>&1
```

Notice the ingenious use of parentheses to trap all the executable commands into a single shell:

```
(command;command;command,...command)>>$FILE
```

Its output is put to the file in one fell swoop.

The **time** command used to measure trivial response time sends its output to standard error. Unless something is done to capture standard error, the results of the time will be lost. The notation

```
2>&1
```

takes the standard error (file descriptor 2) and joins it to the standard output (file descriptor 1).

pwdchk

The following shell script looks up entries in the password and group files.

```
#           pwdchk
# test tentative login data for previous entries
# bhh  7/29/85
# phw 2/23/86
#
if [ $# -eq 0 ]
then
   echo \
"usage:  $0 [login] [-l login] [-u UID] [-g GID]
use -l to specify login name (default)
use -u to specify UID number
use -g to specify GID number"
   exit
fi

flag=login
for data in $*
do
   case $data in
      -l) flag=login;;
      -u) flag=uid;;
      -g) flag=gid;;
      -*) echo "$0: $data is not a valid option";;
       *) echo "$flag = $data:"
          case $flag in
             login) grep "^$data:" /etc/passwd
                    grep "^[^:]*:[^:]*:[^:]*.*[:,]$data" /etc/group;;
             uid)   grep "^[^:]*:[^:]*:$data:" /etc/passwd;;
             gid)   grep "^[^:]*:[^:]*:$data:" /etc/group
                    grep "^[^:]*:[^:]*:[^:]*:$data:" /etc/passwd;;
          esac;;
   esac
done
$ pwdchk root
login = root:
root:JV3Oxc30vuylA:0:0:The Super User:/:/bin/ksh
root:x:0:root
$ pwdchk -g 51
gid = 51:
dave::51:dave,bruce,les
dave:EWFFochOFmBdI:201:51:davef:/us/dave:
bruce:GZbLL4w26mFTQ:202:51:bhh:/us/bruce:
```

die

The **die** program can be used to kill a user's processes quickly, without consulting **ps** or **who**. It sends a HANGUP signal (number 1) to the specified user's processes, waits five seconds, and then sends a KILL signal. It uses the fact that when **kill** is given a process number of -1, it sends the given signal to all of the processes owned by the calling user. **su** is used to first change identity to the specified user, and then **kill** is called with the appropriate arguments. **die** also has an ''immediate''mode (**-k** option) where a KILL signal is sent post-haste.

```
#       die [-k] user
# kills all processes owned by specified user
# sends HUP signal first to allow programs
# like vi to attempt to preserve files and exit
# lists processes after the first kill and sends
# a KILL signal (can't be caught) five seconds later
# (the su command is killed as well)
# The -k option may be used to immediately send a
# KILL signal to that user's processes.
# Note that any user may run this command, but only
# root will NOT be prompted for the user's password
#        pat wood
#        02/20/86

if [ $# -eq 0 ]
then
        echo "Usage: $0 username"
fi

if [ "x$1" != "x-k" ]
then
        echo "Sending hangup to $1's processes"
        su $1 -c "kill -1 -1"
        ps -fu $1
        echo "Sending kill to $1's processes,"
        echo "DEL to abort (5 seconds)"
        sleep 5
else
        shift
fi

su $1 -c "kill -9 -1"
```

▪ Chapter Summary ▪

Although we've taken a brief look at the Bourne shell, there is much more we could cover. Most UNIX system administration programming is done in shell, but be aware that C is usually used to translate permanent shell scripts into faster and more flexible programs. C code is substantially longer, but it runs ten times as fast. However, exploring the extensive realm of C programming is beyond this scope of this book.

C H A P T E R

14

ASSORTED ADMINISTRATION TIPS

Administration Philosophy

Managing a commercial UNIX system — or any system, for that matter — is an awesome responsibility. Poor planning culminated by a careless move can lose the system as well as all of the user data. Mistakes that cause major downtime or massive data loss are not tolerable on commercial systems. This is a heavy note to start on, but it is a fact. The hacking so long associated with computers in the 1970s and 1980s is no longer a viable system administration technique.

Planning

There is no substitute for good planning. An endeavor executed ''by the seat of the pants'' may succeed on occasion, but will more likely cause untold harm. An example of a major undertaking is the creation of a new system. The place to start the new machine is in **vi**, the visual editor. Write down everything you do. Leave nothing out. Record the space requirements, the number of spindles (disks), as well as disk subdivisions, source, and destination. All of this is important.

Before picking up a tape, start by making a map of the new system. Plot where and how the user trees are to be located and how big they will be. Don't settle for default areas on a disk. Figure how much room you are going to need and use that much, no more or less. If software is to be installed, find out where it must go. If it does not have to be located somewhere specific, such as **/usr** or **/usr/bin**, find a home for it where it can be maintained away from UNIX proper.

A large virtual machine created by one of the authors was made from six smaller machines. It took nearly three gigabytes and used all of the resources of a large mainframe. The plan from which the machine was blueprinted was 20 pages long. It was not neat, nor was it even closely checked for spelling, but each address, device, and specification was checked twice by three system programmers before starting. The creation of this gigamachine went well and would have been without mishap except that a system programmer carelessly left the **/etc/passwd** file open in the editor for over an hour. This caused the system to lose track of **root**'s *uid*, and the machine went down, never to come up on its own again. The system was repaired by attaching it to another system. The cost: three work days and hundreds of user hours lost and unrecoverable.

Carefully written plans have two purposes. The first is to outline each move before it is made. It is far easier to examine the sequence of events and criticize them *before* execution. If any changes are decided upon, they should be added in writing to the master plan. The second advantage is that there is a written record of what was done after the plan was executed. In the case of a machine creation, the plan of its creation is also a map of its construction. It should be updated whenever the system is, and will always serve as a future planning aid.

▪ Creating a New System ▪

Most new UNIX systems start out as standard distribution copies, and then user files are added to **/usr**. As we mentioned in earlier chapters, adding groups to **/usr** seems to make sense until you find out that backing up that kind of system can be a nightmare. When it is issued, **/usr** is a very large directory, containing **src**, the source directories; **man**, the manual pages; **spool**, the system's closet (buffer); **games**, the system's playpen; **learn**, the system's grade school; and other major directory trees. It is already the largest file tree in UNIX proper, yet novice UNIX system administrators often insist on putting more trees in it. With this in mind, let's go over some common sense rules of system creation.

Common Sense Rules of System Creation

1. Add user trees to root (**/**), not **/usr**. If you want all user trees to have a common base directory (on a small system), have them attached directly to root such as **/us** or **/users**. Never attach user trees to **/usr**.

2. Use **/usr/local** for locally created commands only. If the system was shipped with commands in **/usr/local** from the OEM or VAR, move them to **/usr/bin**. **/usr/local** is for homegrown commands only and should be part of the system's backup list.

3. Do not mix UNIX proper with the system's "home" files. To keep the mounting of directory trees and system backups as sane as possible, never mix the distributed portion of UNIX with the parts that are unique to your system. User trees, **/usr/local**, and major add-on software such as a DBMS should be backed up separately. This is not possible if they are intermixed with UNIX proper like fruit in a fruitcake. For maximum efficiency, they should also be separately mounted to their own "minidisks."

The central principle is that you want to keep the distributed part of UNIX (the part that came on the original binary distribution tape) separate, or at least separable from what you are going to add. As stressed in earlier chapters, there are many good reasons for this. Backups are the first. With the exception of a few files in **/etc** that are modified by the system programmers, **passwd**, **ttys**, mount and device lists, there is no need to continually back up the distributed portion of UNIX as long as you have it on the original distribution tape (or diskette) and another backup. If you modify the kernel (through **sysgen**) or any other parts of UNIX proper, make a dated separate tape.

The installation of a new version of the operating system is usually done from an ''install'' tape or diskette. If this is a major revision, areas like **/bin**, **/usr/src**, **/usr/man**, and others will be overwritten. If you have homegrown files mixed in, they will be lost.

File System Maintenance

Remember that major file system maintenance should be done in either single-user mode or in multiuser mode with all other users locked out of the system. At this time all file systems are left unmounted except those being worked on. It is best to have systems such as **/usr/bin**, **/usr/src**, **/usr/man**, **/usr/spool**, and **/usr/games** as separately mounted file trees. Imagine having the problem of **/usr** not allowing any new directories to be added. **fsck**, **dcheck**, **icheck** and all of the other system diagnostics may or may not have found inconsistencies, but the directory remains obstinate about not allowing any new additions. The fix is to bring up the system with only the root file system, **/bin,** **/dev**, and **/etc** mounted, if possible. Mount **/usr** only, and make a **tar** copy of it. If this is done with **/usr/bin** and the others mentioned above mounted, they will be on the tape and that is not what you want.

The next step is analogous to a frontal lobotomy. Do a complete backup, check it, then unmount **/usr** and format its disk. Then make a file system (**mkfs**). Mount the blank **/usr**, and read the tape back to it. The result should be a new, clean, and healthy **/usr**, like the phoenix rising from its own ashes. If **/usr** is inseparable from **/usr/***, all of it will have to be restored, making the job much more difficult and time-consuming. It gets worse at the extremes, a mainframe with slow tape (800 to 1600 bpi 50-100 ips), or at the other end, a supermicro with floppy disk backup.

Writing Down Everything as You Do It

The SA is usually the system guru as well. It is easy to find his desk or office by the line that is constantly queued before it. With users, programmers, and operators constantly parading in and out, it is very easy to lose your concentration on daily tasks. The sequence of making new file systems, formatting, **mkfs**, making **lost+found** directories for one tree after another is tedious. If you don't write down each move, you may find yourself in the middle of a disaster later.

For example, the system crashes and as a part of crash recovery you run **fsck**. A file is in need of a link, and you agree to let **fsck** repair it. The problem is you were distracted while making **lost+found**, and you failed to "catch" the file in need of a name. The work is irrevocably lost. The user's supervisor may well want to have your hide! A side benefit of writing down every move is that once done and filed away, you can reconstruct the moves should the work be lost for any reason. This is another good argument for a hardcopy console device.

System Tuning

If you want to create a tuned system, there are other considerations. In order for a system to be fast, head and channel contention must be anywhere from minimal to nonexistent. You won't get this by praying or wishing. You must fine tune the file structure by placing each separate file system by its usage so that those disk partitions using a large number of seeks are allocated disk space closer to the center of each of the hard disk's head travel path, and those with fewer accesses are geometrically further away from the center. This technique requires that each file tree be sized and then located by real addressing on the disk as an exact calculated location. Tuning is painfully tedious to map out, but the results are outstanding and worth the effort if you find that your system's resources are being taxed. At least try to keep UNIX proper on a different physical disk than the user's files.

Analyze Mishaps and Disasters

When a disaster befalls the system — a crash in particular — write down the scenario preceding the crash and what the results were. If you don't learn from a disaster, you will repeat it. An example is losing a system because the spooler filled up. Why did the spooler fill? In one case that comes to mind, the crash was caused by a rash of loading files up and down, which left file images behind in **/usr/spool/rdr** on a UTS system. The crash was so disastrous it took down three virtual machines on the same piece of 470 hardware because they all shared the same manual and source directories. Examining the scenario, it was decided that the only way to avoid this in the future was to write a shell script that would destroy all but the last five files written into the reader spool, should it be found filling rapidly. The script is run at five-minute intervals around the clock by **cron**.

▪ Protect the root Password with Your Life ▪

Never risk losing the **root** password to anyone, not even a close friend. People who have to know the **root** password are the system administrator, the machine operators, and system programmers — no one else. Keep it locked in your desk drawer. If any of these people leave the company for any reason, *change the password*!

The **passwd** file is open for reading to all users. It is accessed constantly by numerous commands and processes. The login portion of **getty**, the **passwd** command, **adduser** scripts, **chown**, **su**, and other commands constantly read

/etc/passwd. A sure invitation to disaster is holding the **/etc/passwd** file open for writing in an editor for a minute or more on a busy system. If any other person uses the **passwd** program before you write the file out, the data will get scrambled. This is not only guaranteed to crash the system, it will probably never come up again. Once the system fails to access **passwd**, it can't log on **root**. Then it's all over. The simple solution is to create the **/etc/ptmp** lock file before you start editing, and remove it when you are done (see the **adduser** program in *Chapter 7*).

The password file should have the nonpeople listed first. Nonpeople are users like **root**, **bin**, **lpadmin**, **sys**, **adm**, **rje**, **uucp**, and **nuucp**. The users come next. If you have employee numbers, use them for uids (user identification numbers). This will save much grief if you have to merge password files from two or more machines when making a large machine. Sort the users by lognames. Remember, *RULE #1 is: Don't work directly on the* **/etc/passwd** *file!* Anything more than trivial work should be done on a copy of the **passwd** file. Do whatever you need to do to the copy, examine it, and if it looks good, copy it to **/etc/passwd**.

Move Slowly

Don't let anyone rush you on any system work. Users can exert more pressure than used-car salesmen. Don't yield. A typical example: A user finds that after a system rollover his files don't all belong to him. You are in the midst of cleaning up **/etc/group** and **/usr/mail** and don't want to be disturbed. The user knows that if he makes a nuisance out of himself he'll get your attention. You yield and move off to his base directory and type in something like

```
# chown schwartz * .* */* */*/* */*/*/*
```

The **.*** is to be sure that you get **.profile** and **.login**. Now doing an **ls -al** you find that he owns all of his files. He also now owns half the files on the system (since the dot directories are **.** and **..** as well), the users' base directory, and the one below that. Mistakenly, you also typed **.*/*** as part of your **chown** command. You rushed and now have a cleanup task that is ten times the work that you would have had if you stopped to make a plan. How to do it the right way?

```
# cd /group1
# ls
schwartz
ziggy
# cd schwartz
# pwd
/group1/schwartz
# find . -print | xargs chown schwartz
# ls -al
```

Again: move slowly, plan carefully, and check what you have done.

▪ The System Log ▪

Whether you are working with or without the aid of a hardware tech or field engineer, be sure to maintain a log. Every physical change or addition to the hardware should be recorded. The following data are critical to have logged and stored:

- switch settings
- board jumper settings
- cable wiring
- terminal ports and locations
- printer ports
- modem phone numbers

Any time the hardware is changed, it should be entered in the log. You had a set of switch settings on the Ventel modem that worked pretty well, but they were changed and now the modem won't hang up. What were they before you changed them? If the old settings are in the log and dated, you are in business.

▪ Tricks of the Trade ▪

Full-time system administrators and system programmers develop a number of "tricks" over the years to make their jobs easier and faster. System administrators are not necessarily smarter or more clever than other computer users — they just have more experience. Most often they have a number of UNIX systems to maintain and have very little time for textbook techniques. Most system administration techniques are initially created on the fly and refined through continuous use. Here are a number of rules, tricks, and techniques that have come into being after years of computer administration.

Testing and Repairing the File System

Test and repair the file systems on each booting of the system. Any time the system is brought down through a crash or other mishap, there is a good chance the file systems were damaged by the system not having time to do the last **sync**.

It is a fatal error to do a **sync** and immediately bring the system down before the **sync** has had a chance to take effect. Scripts that include a **sync** command should be followed by a **sleep 5** to give the system time to let the **sync** take effect. It is nearly a tradition to do two or three **sync** commands successively. It gives time for the final disk writes of the super blocks and directories. Many UNIX systems run 24 hours a day, 7 days a week, and if they are not brought down on a periodic basis, they can suffer damage to the file systems and never have the damage diagnosed until it is too late. A system administrator should make it a point to take her machines down at least once a week to check the file systems while they are quiescent.

Once a file system has sustained damage, following Murphy's Law, it is bound to receive successive and compound damage. If left unchecked, in time the system becomes so damaged that it has to be reconstructed. This is yet another good argument for saving backup tapes for at least a week without writing over them. Extensive repair work on full-time machines is almost impossible on large sites. You must wait until evening when most of the users are gone; the machine is quiet and no one will be disturbed. Repair work can be done either at the site or by modem.

To give you an idea what can happen if you don't take the time to check your files for consistency, consider this true story. A large UNIX engineering machine was up for a month without ever being taken down for PM (preventative maintenance). There was no free modem available at the time to attach to the system, so evening maintenance was impossible without driving down to the site. Within a month the machine became so ''brain-damaged,'' it was nearly unusable. A lengthy session with **fsck** made the system minimally operable, but it eventually had to be reconstructed on another disk pack before it was ''healthy'' again.

Scheduled Weekly Maintenance

Maintaining the system should never be left to chance. Select a day or an evening once a week to perform system maintenance. If you have several virtual machines, it is good practice to bring down one machine at a time, testing and repairing its file system. Remember that major file system maintenance should be done in either single-user mode or in multiuser mode with all other users locked out of the system. At this time all file systems should be left unmounted except those being worked on. Here are some maintenance tasks that should be done:

1. Check the file systems for room.
2. Test the file systems for consistency.
3. Test all of the system's spoolers.

A **df** on each file system shows if a mounted system is running out of room. On most pre-System V systems a filled root disk or spooler crashes the system. Testing file systems for consistency goes without question.

If the system has accounting and it is enabled, this is the time to gather the system's *use statistics* and interpret them. Look for users who are potentially abusing the system. This is done by testing for inconsistencies. Here's one profile you need to watch for. Look for a user with extremely high CPU time, very little in the way of reads and writes, and few commands issued. In all likelihood, this user is up to some intellectual fool's errand like using **dc** to find *pi* out to 1000 places. Using the system for ''fun'' programs like this may be the norm on university computers, but it is intolerable in commercial environments. He could also be trying to break the encryption on the **/etc/passwd** file!

Test all of the system's spoolers. Directories like **/usr/spool/uucppublic**, **/usr/spool/uucp**, **/usr/spool/lp[d]**, **/usr/spool/rdr**, and **/usr/spool/mail** are supposed to be *temporary* holding places. If they fill, they jeopardize the system. Check them often, and empty them if full. Better yet, create small maintenance shell programs to test spoolers and empty them when full. Maintenance programs (such as our **rmtrash**) can be run automatically by **cron**. Test for users who do not read or empty their mailboxes. If they refuse to empty the mailboxes, send their mail to the printer, empty their **/usr/spool/mail** files, and have the printout put on their desks.

Changing Shells

You can change to the other shell by typing

```
% sh
```

in the C shell or

```
$ csh
```

in the Bourne shell. You may also go from one shell to a new shell of the same type by typing in the shell command again as in

```
$ sh
```

for a second Bourne shell or

```
% csh
```

for an additional C shell.

Why would you want to? Each shell has its own environment. When a new shell is created (spawned) the new shell (child) takes on its own environment without disturbing that of its parent's. If you are in your home directory and have to go off to a work area for a while, you can generate a new shell by typing **sh**. Once in the new shell, you can change directories to that of the work area and do whatever you have to. When done, simply do a Control-D to exit the new shell, and you will be back in your home directory with the old environment. The old shell or parent shell simply ''went to sleep'' while you used the new or child shell. The Control-D killed the child shell and woke up the parent shell, leaving you exactly where you were just before the new shell was created. If you want to switch shells until the next time you log in, it is slightly cheaper (in terms of system resources) to **exec** the new shell:

```
$ exec csh
%
```

▪ Removable Secondary Storage ▪

How UNIX Sees Secondary Storage

UNIX sees disk and tape drives attached to it as peripherals that require device drivers, just like any other type of device. The only major differences are that tape and disks have to be both character devices as well as block devices. Thus they must have two sets of drivers. Additionally, the drivers for disks must have a ''strategy'' routine to take care of ''gap'' or ''skewing,'' the mechanically required offset from sector to sector for efficient reading. Having a device driver, it has a node in **/dev**, and that is how UNIX will talk to it.

Talking Directly to a Device

Devices deal with data streams. Data streams can be directed anywhere, which is the principle behind pipes and redirection. A simple demonstration redirects a few characters to a terminal other than your own:

```
# echo "HI" > /dev/tty1
```

Dealing with a disk device is no different, except that we usually want data on that device to be treated as a file rather than a stream of characters without any handle. Thus we use file commands:

```
$ cp letters /floppy
```

Tape is an exception, since it separates ''files'' by gaps. Unarchived files on tape are just a contiguous stream of data separated from the next by a short piece of tape with nothing written on it. Since nothing special is needed to archive the data, the device can be directly addressed:

```
$ cp letters /dev/rmt0
```

The above copy command sends the file **letters** directly out to the machine's tape device. More typically, you send data to the tape without a file copy command if data streams are required:

```
dd if=foo of=/dev/rmt0 conv=ucase
```

Here we are sending a file from the system's hard disk to the tape device while translating all ASCII alpha characters into uppercase.

Most users never need to know the not-too-subtle differences between dealing with devices directly or indirectly, but the system administrator must. When using the **tar** command (see *Chapter 8 — Backups*), he sends the archived file directly to a device, not to a file system:

```
# tar cvf /dev/rmt0 /us
```

Here the tape archiver **tar** has sent the file tree **/us** directly to the tape device **rmt0** by using tar's **f** option. There are no commands under standard UNIX that work exclusively with tape.

Mounting a Tape

On the majority of UNIX systems, the tape drive is already mounted as the machine comes up. It does not have to be mounted like a disk drive (as a part of the **rc** script). The exceptions are very large systems with multiple tape drives like UTS UNIX running over VM. The difference is subtle; the tape is attached from VM:

```
ATT 632 TO UTS AS 181
```

Then tapes are dealt with in the normal manner:

```
# tar cvf /dev/tape/181 /usr/everyone/
```

Tape Handling

Cartridge tapes are streaming tapes. They have no provisions for manipulating the tape other than to mechanically rewind it and to write or read the tape as a continuous device. Tapes are inserted into the tape drive with the window, the little trapdoor at the top right of the case, in first. The drive automatically looks for the beginning of the tape, which is marked by two holes punched through the tape. Cartridge tape can be write-protected by turning the drum in the upper-left corner of the tape so that a window faces the drive.

Reel-to-reel tape requires that you manually mount the tape on the tape drive spindle. The first step is to decide if the tape is to be writable. If it is, a write ring must be inserted around the hub in the channel provided for it. The most expensive drives use vacuum to pull the tape down into the tape channel. The tape is placed on the hub, and then a few inches of tape is dropped down to allow the vacuum to pull it into the tape machinery. The other extreme is the tape drive that requires you to manually take the tape leader and thread it over the read/write heads and on to the take-up reel, like a stereo tape.

Floppy Disks

The advent of the floppy disk gave birth to the microcomputer. Floppy disks are cheap and easy to use. Floppies were foreign to UNIX systems, but the smaller machines were manufactured by microcomputer manufacturers who automatically used them. They are practical from a cost point of view. But they are limited in that their capacity is around a megabyte, and few UNIX systems have less than 10 MB to back up. On the other hand, if they are all that is available, then floppies are what you have to use.

Floppy disks are a rotating removable media. That is a distinct advantage because they are treated by the system as any other form of a drive. They are mounted and unmounted, copied to and from, and in all respects are a disk device. The two big differences from hard disks are their smaller capacity and slower speed.

Finding the Floppy Disk in /dev

Floppy disks have strange names in **/dev**, like **ifdsk06** (AT&T) for the floppy as a block device, or **rifds06** as a character device. Character devices for tape and disk traditionally start with "r" to signify raw. Unisoft ports make it simpler, calling the floppy **fd** so that **fdl** is a block device and **rfdl** is a raw device. Look for a link to a more manageable or recognizable name, like floppy or diskette:

```
$ cd /dev
$ ls -l flop* disk*
flop* not found
brw-------   6 root     sys      17,134 Jul  4 17:51 diskette
```

The key here is **17,134**: the major and minor device names. Now we can find all of the aliases of the device:

```
$ ls -l /dev | grep "17,134"
brw-------   6 root     sys      17,134 Jul  4 17:51 diskette
brw-------   6 root     sys      17,134 Jul  4 17:51 ifdsk06
brw-------   6 root     sys      17,134 Jul  4 17:51 install
crw-------   6 root     sys      17,134 Apr  1 04:54 rdiskette
crw-------   6 root     sys      17,134 Apr  1 04:54 rifdsk06
crw-------   6 root     sys      17,134 Apr  1 04:54 rinstall
crw-------   6 root     sys      17,134 Apr  1 04:54 rsave
brw-------   6 root     sys      17,134 Jul  4 17:51 save
```

Notice which are character devices and which are raw. **ifdsk06** is the block device. You have to use this to mount the device to use it for conventional file work. The raw device is used for formatting. Note that this will not work on all systems, because the major and minor device numbers do not always match. To be sure, you can search for **/dev/r***.

Formatting Floppy Disks

Formatting is not a standard UNIX function, so the command name to format the floppy disk will vary with the distribution. On XENIX, it's called **format**. The AT&T floppy format command is **fmtflop**. Just insert a diskette in the drive and do this:

```
# /etc/fmtflop /dev/rifdsk06
```

It is not necessary to mount the device, since you're not dealing with a file system.

Writing Directly to Floppy

It is not necessary to mount a diskette and make a file system (**mkfs**) for simple tasks like archiving and backup. Both take time, and time is not a surplus commodity in system administration work. Insert a formatted floppy disk in the machine's drive, and then take advantage of one of UNIX's archivers. The archiving utility currently in vogue in UNIX is **cpio**. It has replaced **tar**.

cpio

cpio takes a list of files for its input from the standard input (**stdin**) and sends it to the standard output (**stdout**). It is not an easy command to use at first, and the manual is less than lucid. The file list sources for the standard input are usually the **ls** command or **find.** Either

```
$ ls . | cpio -o > /usr/archive
```

or

```
$ find . -print -cpio > /usr/archive
```

sends the contents of the current directory to an archive directory created in **/usr**.

There is a *p* option to **cpio** that stands for "pass" and allows mass copying. A good use for **cpio** with the *p* option is to copy an entire user area (for backup) to a floppy disk:

```
$ cd /us/susan
$ find . -depth -print | cpio -pdlv /floppy
```

The entire directory is copied to the floppy disk exactly as it exists in **/us/susan**.

Using Floppies as Conventional Storage

Conventional disk storage requires that the device be attached to a directory by the **mount** command. This presupposes that the disk has a file system on it. Thus, a series of tasks must be performed before putting the floppy to use:

- format
- make a file system (**mkfs**)
- mount the disk (**/etc/mount**)
- make the **lost+found** directory

In practice, it looks like:

```
$ su
Password: teguface
# /etc/fmtflop /dev/rdiskette
# mkfs /dev/diskette 1422:192
# mount /dev/diskette /floppy
# cd /floppy
# mkdir lost+found
# cd /us/work.dir
# find . -depth -print | cpio -pdlv /floppy
```

▪ Chapter Summary ▪

Whose system is it? You are the administrator, and more than any one individual, it is your machine. But in the long run, it is for the users. You are the guardian of the cookie jar. Ration out the cookies, but do not let any hand but yours get into the jar. You are the guardian of UNIX's standard distribution and all local **bin**s and documentation. The users are given disk areas to work in, and the disk areas are theirs to use, but not abuse. If they run out of room, it is their problem to pick out the trash to be archived and removed. If they need room and none is available on the system, it is the users' collective job to get appropriations for more storage.

In essence you are the samurai of the system. Yours is to serve, preserve, and protect. You serve the users, preserve the system software and their data, and protect the users from outsiders and from themselves.

We have come a long way from learning how to bring up a UNIX system. Although we have seen more of UNIX than most UNIX users will ever see, we've only just begun to explore UNIX system administration. The rest of the adventure is up to you!

APPENDIX A

WHERE TO LEARN MORE

Useful Resources

There are many companies involved in UNIX training, consulting, and software. However, few specialize in UNIX system administration. Mentioned below are the most prominent ones that do, as well as a few other interesting addresses.

AT&T Technologies, Inc.
Corporate Education Center
PO Box 1000
Hopewell, NJ 08525
(800) 221-1647

AT&T's current classes are the broadest and perhaps the best in the industry today.

The Gawain Group
47 Potomac Street
San Francisco, CA 94117
(415) 626-7581

The Gawain Group, run by Jim Joyce, arranges training courses on a large variety of UNIX and C topics including system administration. They are noted for finding some of the most well-known people in the field as instructors.

InfoPro Systems
3108 Route 10
Denville, NJ 07834
(201) 989-0570
{astrovax,clyde,harpo,topaz}!infopro!{bruce,david}

InfoPro Systems is owned and operated by David and Susan Fiedler. Authors David Fiedler and Bruce Hunter can be reached through IPS. IPS publishes *UNIQUE*, the premier newsletter covering the UNIX system, as well as *The C Journal*, the magazine for C programmers, and distributes the O'Reilly books mentioned in the *Bibliography*. IPS also offers training, consulting, and related services (including dial-up checks of your machine) on system administration and security.

Institute for Advanced Professional Studies
55 Wheeler Street
Cambridge, MA 02138
(617) 497-2075

IAPS is one of the oldest and most respected UNIX training organizations. They specialize in in-house courses geared to a company's specific computer system.

IQ Technologies, Inc.
11811 N.E. First Street
Bellevue, WA 98005
(206) 451-0232
(800) 232-8324

IQ Technologies makes the Smart Cable, which obviates the need to play around with signal pins. If you have trouble getting a serial device to work, try one of these.

Lachman Associates, Inc.
645 Blackhawk Drive
Westmont, IL 60559
(312) 986-8840
(800) LAI-UNIX

Lachman Associates is one of the leading general consulting firms in the UNIX business, providing wizards of all kinds for a variety of tasks.

UNITECH Software, Inc.
Suite 800
8330 Old Courthouse Road
Vienna, VA 22180
(703) 734-9844

Unitech sells two software packages of interest to administrators. *UBACKUP* controls all system backups with verification and audit trails, and provides an online catalog of data storage. *USECURE* provides a menu system for all directory and file access, as well as management reports.

USENIX Association
PO Box 7
El Cerrito, CA 94530
(415) 528-8649
{decvax,ucbvax}!usenix!office

USENIX is the original organization of UNIX users, and many top technical people can be counted among its members. They hold two conferences a year, and publish an excellent newsletter.

/usr/group
4655 Old Ironsides Drive, #200
Santa Clara, CA 95054
(408) 986-8840

/usr/group is an association geared more towards end users and industry than is USENIX. They produce the UniForum trade show and conference each year, and also publish a magazine of great interest.

A P P E N D I X

B

TALKING TO THE OUTSIDE WORLD

▪ The RS-232 Blues ▪

When a peripheral has to be added to your machine, such as a terminal, printer, plotter, or modem, you have to either find a hardware technician to cable the device to the machine or do it yourself. Cable connections are expensive to have made, and they can be very frustrating to create yourself. Either way, you're looking at some aggravation. We remember one shocking news story about a new computer owner who asked the manager of the computer store to cable a device to the new computer he just bought because he couldn't do the job himself. The bill was over $100.00. The customer was so angry, he shot and killed the store manager! Most of us will never become that frustrated over a cable connection, but we may come close.

Naturally, we cannot possibly cover everything you need to know about the RS-232 specification in one chapter, but we hope to lay down some vital concepts that you may wish to supplement with further reading.

Basic Definitions

Before we start, let's go over a few basic definitions. It's difficult to talk about the RS-232 specification without mentioning *handshaking*. Loosely defined, handshaking is having two pieces of equipment tell each other they are both ready to move data.

All electrical devices that transmit intelligence work around a ground reference. That ground is said to be at 0 potential (voltage). A pin is said to be *asserted* when it has a positive or negative voltage on it. These voltages run approximately +12 V (high) or -12 V (low). A positive voltage ''asserts the pin high.'' A negative voltage ''asserts the pin low.''

When you *pull up* a pin, you take the positive voltage from another pin already asserted high and use it to pull the voltage up on the unasserted pin.

Breakout boxes help you do all the tricky work needed to make a cable connection. They are somewhat similar to an old-fashioned telephone switch board allowing connections to be made by plugging in wires from here to there. Whenever you attach peripheral equipment to your UNIX system, unless you want to pay someone to make the cable, you will probably need a breakout box to do the job.

▪ The RS-232 Specification ▪

The RS-232 specification was created primarily for modem type communication. It has turned into a fits-all, do-all concept, and like so many other universal solutions, it doesn't fit everything perfectly. Still, it is good enough to become an industry standard.

The first important RS-232 terms to learn are *DTE* and *DCE*. DTE stands for data terminal equipment, DCE for data communications equipment. Unfortunately, DTE was intended for terminals, and DCE was intended for modems, so problems crop up because they now also have to apply to printers, plotters, and computers. Bear in mind that now DTE means something like "it looks a little like a terminal because data goes out on pin 2," and DCE means "it looks a little like a modem because data goes out on pin 3."

DB-25 Pin Connectors

RS-232 connections make use of the DB-25 pin connector. 25 pins translates into 50 potential problems, 25 at each end, but sometimes connections can be made with as few as 3 pins. Of the 25, we need only be concerned with nine, and by breaking these pins down into groups, some of the mystery can be removed.

Pin	Abbreviation	Description
1	FG	Frame Ground
2	TD	Transmit Data
3	RD	Receive Data
4	RTS	Request To Send
5	CTS	Clear To Send
6	DSR	Data Set Ready
7	SG	Signal Ground (Common)
8	CD	Carrier Detect
20	DTR	Data Terminal Ready

Ground Pins

The first group are the ground pins:

pin 1	frame ground	FG (optional)
pin 7	signal ground	SG

The *frame ground* allows both devices to have their chassis at the same potential (voltage). The *signal ground* guarantees a ground reference for the remaining 7 critical pins.

Data Pins

The next two pins transmit data:

pin 2	send data	TD
pin 3	receive data	RD

Pin 2 sends data, and pin 3 receives data. But there's a catch. The send/receive relationship is established by the data terminal equipment (DTE) device standard. Most terminals are DTEs. Most modems are DCEs, so that takes care of modems and terminals, but what about computers? There is no standard. Some are DTEs and other are DCEs. You're going to have to ''sex'' the computers to find out if they are DTEs or DCEs. We will call DTEs males and DCEs females.

Pins That Send Condition Signals

Of the nine pins used for most connections, 5 deal with signals that are neither data nor ground pins. There are no hard and fast rules on which pins send and which receive the signals in all cases. In practice, those that send signals are found to be asserted. Those that receive signals are normally not asserted. Be aware that this is a generalization and does not hold true in all cases.

Two pins are supposed to tell how the equipment is doing. They tell you if the device is ready to go to work:

pin 4	request to send	RTS
pin 20	data terminal ready	DTR

When pin 20 goes high (+) it signals to whatever it's connected to that the DTE is ready to go to work. Pin 4, RTS, was intentionally set to signal the DCE, most often a modem, that the device is ready to transmit. In practice, it can signal that any device is ready, such as emitting a signal from the computer showing that it is alive.

Pins That Receive Signals

On DCEs, pins 5 and 6 are mostly used to take signals from other pins such as 4, 8, or 20. They cause the piece of equipment to which they are attached to either receive or transmit data:

pin 5	clear to send	CTS
pin 6	data set ready	DSR

In the IEEE RS-232 specification, all pins are treated as functional, but in actual practice, this is seldom true. For example, the *clear to send* pin is defined as a terminal pin (DTE) which when pulled up tells the terminal it's OK to go about its business. However, in practice, terminals seldom need pin 5 high. Only some computers, such as the AT&T 3B2, will not work unless pin 5 is high. Pin 6, *data set ready*, has a similar function, but it was intended to show that the modem was connected to a communications device and not in test mode. No matter what the original intentions were, the signal send/receive pins 4, 5, 6, 8 and 20 seldom do what they were originally designed to do. Remember that the IEEE RS-232 specifications are for terminal to modem connections, and seldom followed completely on small machines. The most common connections are terminal-to-computer, modem-to-computer and computer-to-printer.

▪ From Theory to Practice ▪

Now let's walk through a typical cabling session. RS-232 theory is not enough. You need to know what's involved in a real-life situation.

The Breakout Box and Hunter's $1.98 Pin Tester

A breakout box deals dynamically with the connection between the two devices. It has switches, sockets and jumpers, and it is laid out like a RS-232 work sheet. The breakout box is cabled between the two pieces of equipment to be attached, usually the computer and a peripheral, and various combinations are tried until data can be successfully transmitted.

Breakout boxes come in many flavors. Inexpensive breakout boxes (about $100) have LEDs on only a few pins. On the DTE side, the LEDs are on TD, RTS and DTR (as a minimum). On the DCE side, there are diagnostic LEDs on RD, CTS, DSR and CD. This is hardly ideal, but it will do the job. The best breakout boxes ($250 and up) have LEDs on most pins and use tri-states rather than red LEDs. These glow red when a pin is high and green when the pin is held low, making it easier to envision what's going on. They also have bisexual connectors, capable of handling both male and female connectors. There are 24 switches capable of closing the circuits of each pin, and 50 pins can be wire-jumpered to one another.

Good breakout boxes are not cheap, but a single, custom-installed cable can cost you as much or more. Serious interfacing work cannot be done without one. However, in order to start your connections, you need to test each pin individually. You can do this with an inexpensive breakout box, but it's a minor hassle. Only expensive, tri-state breakout boxes instantly tell you the condition of every single pin. If you have an inexpensive breakout box, Hunter's $1.98 pin tester can save a lot of time. For a couple of dollars you can construct a handy dandy pin tester that is ideal for the initial pin testing work. It is a simple device using a tri-state light emitting diode (LED), a 470-ohm resistor and a couple of RS-232 pins.

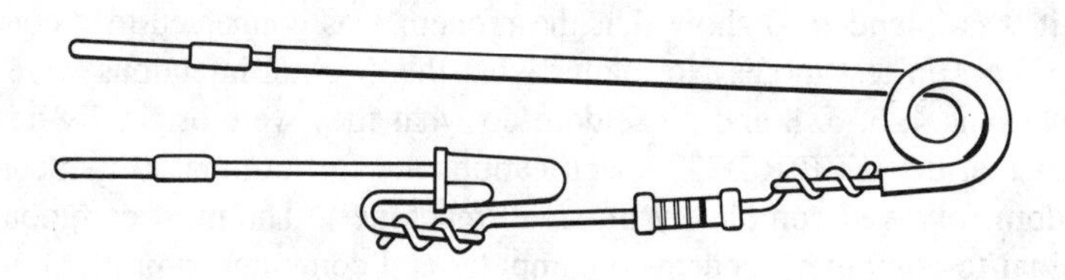

Fig. B-1. Hunter's $1.98 Pin Tester

Be sure to attach the wire to the side of the LED with a flat. The opposite pin should be directly soldered or crimped to an RS-232 pin. Two of these $1.98 pin testers are even more useful, one with male pins and one with female pins. The male version is used more often, but some equipment, such as DEC VT100 terminals, have male pins and require female testers.

The First Step

Test pins 2, 3, 4, 5, 6, 8 and 20 to see if they are asserted (is there a voltage on the pin?). Plug the negative lead (the pin without a wire) into pin socket 7, the signal ground. Then walk the wired end from pin to pin. Active pins cause the LED to light up. Pins that are low (-) cause the LED to glow green. Pins that are high (+) cause the LED to glow red. The pins on either side (DTE and DCE) should be tested and the results written down on a work sheet. Then you analyze the data.

```
                RS-232 Work Sheet

           DTE                         DCE


      TD  | |                       ->| | 2


      RD  | |<-                       | | 3


     RTS  | |                       ->| | 4


     CTS  | |<-                       | | 5


     DSR  | |<-                       | | 6


      CD  | |<-                       | | 8


     DTR  | |                       ->| | 20
```

Sexing A Device

Like turning a puppy over to find out whether it's Max or Maxine, you have to sex the equipment. When RD (pin 3) or TD (pin 2) are active, they are low (-). If pin 2 glows green when tested, the device is a DTE. If pin 3 causes the LED to glow green, it is a DCE. It is just that simple. Write the information on the work sheet.

Testing The Remaining Pins

Once you have tested pins 2 and 3, it is time to go on to 4, 5, 6, 8 and 20. Test each and note the results. These pins are the signal pins (2 and 3 are data pins and 1 and 7 are ground pins). Knowing the condition of them is critical to making the final working connection. Those that are high (+) are going to assert other pins. Those that are low (-) may have to be asserted high or go high to signal ready. For example, on the AT&T 3B2/300, you pull up pins 5 & 6 and pin 20 goes from low to high.

First Pass Jumpering

If you haven't already, connect the breakout box to the two devices. You're going to need feedback from the breakout box and your computer to verify the connection. Wiring pin 1 to pin 1 (*chassis ground*) and pin 7 to pin 7 (*signal ground*) is standard operational procedure. Many people ignore pin one, but this is not a good practice, as it can permit excess voltage to build up between the equipment. Even so, many manufacturers connect pin 1 to pin 7 internally, so the minimum connection still uses pins 2, 3, and 7.

Now refer to your work sheet. Terminal type equipment (DTE) sends data on pin 2 and receives it on pin 3. Modem-type equipment (DCE) takes data on pin 2 and sends it on pin 3. The simplest connection is when one piece of equipment like a terminal is clearly a DTE with pin 2 asserted negative. The other (the computer) is clearly a DCE with pin 3 asserted negative. If the terminal is dumb and the computer isn't fussy about signal pins, an off-the-shelf ribbon cable with all pins in makes a good connection.[1] Even a cable with pins 2, 3 and 7 straight-wired will do the job. However, if both devices are the same type, DTE to DTE or DCE to DCE, a *null-modem* connection is required (pin 2 tied to pin 3 and pin 3 tied to pin 2):

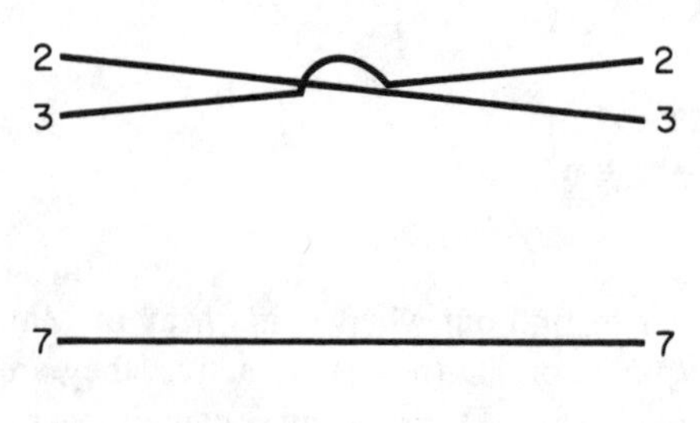

Fig. B-2. Simple Null Modem

In some rare instances this is enough to get data moving. However, if any sort of handshaking is wanted, you're going to need at least a fourth wire. The **cu** command allows you to talk directly to the port, but some machines like the AT&T 3B2/300[2] time the port out if it fails to make a connection in a few seconds. It is simpler to redirect data to the port. For example:

```
$ ls / > /dev/tty5
```

The computer now buffers the data until the connection can be made.

1 Some OEMs ship their computers with the I/O board jumpered so that CTS is internally true. As a result CTS does not respond to external signals. The good news is that terminals can be wired quickly with either straight cables or 3 wire cables. The bad news is that hardware handshaking is impossible without rejumpering the I/O board.

2 If you have the new HDB **uucp**, be sure to enter the port in **/usr/lib/uucp/Devices** as a direct device (even if it is also listed as an ACU) to debug your cable connection.

The Next Stage

Now the scenario is set. With data buffered, your breakout box in place, and the ground and data lines connected, it is time to start the pin guessing game. At the computer end, pins 5 (CTS) and/or 6 (DSR) frequently have to be asserted to get data flowing. Take the voltage from any convenient pin (refer to your work sheet). Pins 4 and 20 are frequently asserted positive, so one of them may be available for this purpose. On modem connections, pin 8 has to be pulled up as well.

At the other end, the nature of the device determines (to some extent) the pins to pull up. Printers want to turn off when their buffers are filled. They will frequently need to have pin 4 or 5 (RTS or CTS) asserted to make them work. Modems are wire-intensive devices. Pin 8, CD, must be wired to gain reasonable control of the device.

The Dart Board Game

Taking voltage from any reasonable source, apply it sequentially to pins 5, 6 and (in the case of modems) 8. Try this on both sides until data starts to flow. When the screen of the sending terminal redisplays the prompt, you know you're in business.

Common-Sense Rewiring

Once data have successfully moved, write down the asserted pins on the work sheet and start thinking about better places from which to channel the asserting voltage. If, for example, you have used pin 4 to pull up pin 6 on the same side of the connection, you may well want to look at taking pin 20 (*data terminal ready*) from the opposite side to pull it up. The reason for this is to have DTR (*data terminal ready*) on the one side signal DSR (*data set ready*) on the other when it is ready. If the sending device fails or gets disconnected, the receiving end shuts down with this combination.

There are many possible wiring combinations. Experience is your best teacher. You work with 9 pins on each side for a possible 18, but only two are normally asserted to signal a device to be ready, RTS and DTR. At most, three have to be asserted when the other end is ready, CTS, DSR and CD.

Now You Can Finally Make the Cable

Once the breakout box connection works, you already know a minimal way to wire the cable. At that point, if you think there's a better way to wire it to get the same results, look for it. In our previous example we mentioned that if you used pin 4 on one device (one side of the breakout box) to pull up pin 6 on the same device, it's a good idea to get the source of the asserting voltage from the other device (the other side of the breakout box). If you take it from the other side, should that piece of equipment fail, it causes a break in transmission, instead of allowing the device to sit there telling itself (with its own line) that everything is okay.

Installing a peripheral device to your UNIX system involves more than merely establishing a cable connection between the system and the device. You still need to take care of the software end. In other words, UNIX not only needs to know that the device is there, it needs to know several specifics about the device as well. For this, we refer you to the text.

▪ Other Possibilities ▪

There is also a diagnostic device available that you can place between any two RS-232 connectors that simply has LEDs on the most important pins to show their status. Such a device generally costs $40 or so and is a good compromise.

Another possibility is a so-called ''intelligent cable''. This consists of a small plastic box with a few lights and switches, and RS-232 connectors on both ends. For about $90, simply follow the directions, plug it into whatever you want to connect, and the cable figures out how to detour the signals all by itself. This will save you a great deal of time, and may be the best idea in the long run for some people.

A P P E N D I X

C

A TYPICAL UUCP CONNECTION

Using the -x9 Option

When initially setting up **uucp**, it is most helpful to be able to watch the action of the phone dialing and the strings being passed back and forth for logins. Using the **poll** shell program given in *Chapter 12*, along with the **-x9** option to **uucico**, it is possible to see a great deal of information. While some of this is only of interest to those working with the innermost secrets of the program, using the maximum debugging information available is recommended the first few times you run **uucp**. After you feel more comfortable with the program, you can use **-x4** or **-x1** for less data, and finally you can turn off debugging completely.

The annotated log was collected by executing

```
$ poll attunix -x9
```

which is the equivalent of executing

```
$ /usr/lib/uucp/uucico -r1 -sattunix -x9
```

directly. One mail message (consisting of two actual files) has been queued up to be sent to **attunix**. The system (InfoPro Systems' Cadmus) is connected to a Hayes Smartmodem 1200, and the trick outlined in *Chapter 12* for dialing directly from the **L.sys** file is being used. The following is the entry in L.sys for this machine:

```
attunix Any tty23 1200 tty23 ATDT12015226805\r \
?login:-\r-?login:-\r-?login: attunix\r
```

This particular machine has a slightly different **L.sys** format from normal. Here, a newline (denoted by the **\r**) is sent if the **login:** string is not received within the timeout period. The messages you get from your machine, of course, may be quite different, but they should be recognizably similar. Any mismatch of strings, or failure to log in, will become immediately apparent with this level of debugging.

Now follows the log itself:

```
finds called
getto called
call: no. tty23 for sys attunix login called
send them <ATDT12015226805\r>
expect <login:>
```

Here **uucico** has found the **L.sys** entry, it has sent the dialing command string to the modem, and it is waiting for the **login:** message:

```
ATDT12015226805___CONNECT__got ?
send them <\r>
expect <login:>
```

The modem echoes the command string, then reports a **CONNECT**. Since a string has been received that did not correspond to the expected string, a newline is sent:

```
___login:got that
send them <attunix\r>
```

The **login:** string has been received, and the actual login name is sent to the remote machine:

```
enter us_sst, status is : 11
Enter us_open, file: /usr/lib/uucp/L_stat
normal return from us_open.c
s.sysname : hunter
s.sysname : whuxcc
s.sysname : bty
s.sysname : topaz
s.sysname : clyde
s.sysname : harpo
s.sysname : tmmnet
s.sysname : pcles
s.sysname : attunix
enter ub_sst, status is : 0
Rmtname: attunix
Enter us_open, file: /usr/lib/uucp/L_sub
normal return from us_open.c
```

On the **infopro** machine, the status files are opened to keep track of the connection. The software searches through past records until it finds the correct one for the machine being polled:

```
imsg >\341tt\365\356ix\215\12UN\311\330\240S\371\363te\355
\240V\240\322ele\341\363e\240\262.0.\264\2403B\262\240
Ver\363io\356\240\262\215\12\341tt\365\356ix\215\12\303o
\366e\344\215\12\20<
Shere=attunix\  0 imsg >\ 20 <
```

We get the login message from the remote machine. It is garbled with numbers and backslashes because some bytes have their parity bit set, but a few strings are readable. Sometimes you will see a long **/etc/motd** message here. Once control is passed to the **/usr/lib/uucp/uucico** program on the *remote* machine (analogous to finally getting into your shell), the **Shere=attunix** message appears. Once the **uucico** on the calling machine sees this **Shere**, the connection has officially started up. Some machines only echo the **Shere** without their actual node name.

```
ROK\  0 msg-ROK
Rmtname attunix, Role MASTER,  Ifn - 4, Loginuser - root
rmesg - 'P' imsg >\ 20 <
Pg\  0 got Pg
wmesg 'U'g
send 73
rec h->cntl 73
send 61
state - 1
rec h->cntl 61
send 53
state - 3
rec h->cntl 53
state - 10
Proto started g
protocol g
```

The remote computer has been identified as **attunix**, and the ''g'' protocol has been selected (this is the only protocol in use, actually).

```
enter us_sst, status is : 09
Enter us_open, file: /usr/lib/uucp/L_stat
normal return from us_open.c
s.sysname : hunter
s.sysname : whuxcc
s.sysname : bty
s.sysname : topaz
s.sysname : clyde
```

```
s.sysname : harpo
s.sysname : tmmnet
s.sysname : pcles
s.sysname : attunix
```

Again, a traversal is made through the status files.

```
*** TOP ***  -  role=1, wrktype - S
wmesg 'S' D.attunixB4M4F D.attunix
send 210
rmesg - 'S' rec h->cntl 41
state - 10
rec h->cntl 211
send 41
got SY
PROCESS: msg - SY
```

A determination has been made to send the first queued-up file.

```
SNDFILE:
send 221
send 331
send 341
sent data 117 bytes 0 secs
rmesg - 'C' rec h->cntl 42
state - 10
rec h->cntl 43
state - 10
rec h->cntl 44
state - 10
rec h->cntl 224
send 42
got CY
PROCESS: msg - CY
```

The file has been sent and acknowledged. The **CY** received from the remote means all went well with the transfer.

```
RQSTCMPT:
*** TOP ***  -  role=1, wrktype - S
wmesg 'S' D.infoproX4M4D X.infopro
send 252
rmesg - 'S' rec h->cntl 45
state - 10
rec h->cntl 235
send 43
got SY
PROCESS: msg - SY
SNDFILE:
send 263
send 373
send 303
sent data 72 bytes 0 secs
rmesg - 'C' rec h->cntl 46
state - 10
rec h->cntl 47
state - 10
rec h->cntl 40
state - 10
rec h->cntl 240
rec h->cntl 240
send 24
got CY
PROCESS: msg - CY
```

The second file has been accepted by the remote.

```
RQSTCMPT:
*** TOP ***  -  role=1,
enter us_rrs, cfile: C.attunixA4M4G  request status: 3000
Enter us_open, file: /usr/lib/uucp/R_stat
normal return from us_open.c
```

The transfer of both files has been logged in the **R_stat** file.

```
jobn : 4
wmesg 'H'
send 214
rmesg - 'H' rec h->cntl 40
send 44
state - 10
```

```
rec h->cntl 41
state - 10
rec h->cntl 251
send 45
got HY
PROCESS: msg - HY
```

No more work is available, so the machines prepare to hang up.

```
HUP:
wmesg 'H'Y
send 225
send 10
send 10
cntrl - 0
enter us_sst, status is : 00
Enter us_open, file: /usr/lib/uucp/L_stat
normal return from us_open.c
s.sysname : hunter
s.sysname : whuxcc
s.sysname : bty
s.sysname : topaz
s.sysname : clyde
s.sysname : harpo
s.sysname : tmmnet
s.sysname : pcles
s.sysname : attunix
send OO 0,imsg >\ 20 <
```

The log file is closed and the hangup message is transferred.

```
\11 \210 \252 "\11 \20 \2 \25 \250 \262 \15 HY\0 imsg ><\200
\201 \1 2\0 \0 \37 \12 \0 \0 \0 \0 \0 \0 \0 \0 \0
\0 \0 \0 \0 \0 \0 \360 \200 \210 \205 \264 \300 \2
\22 x\300 \2 \22 \210 @\0 \2 \210 \300 \2 \22 h\300
\11 \242 \252 \10 \11 \20 \11 \242 \252
\10 \11 \20 OOOOOO\ 0 imsg >\20 <
OOOOOO\  0 exit code 0
```

The connection has been broken, but initially only by logging off from **attunix**. Once the **exit code 0** message is printed, the RS-232 line DTR is forced to a low voltage state (''dropped'') to force the outgoing modem to hang up.

BIBLIOGRAPHY

AT&T Bell Laboratories Technical Journal. 63, no. 8, part 2 (special issue, October 1984).

Comer, D. *Operating System Design: The Xinu Approach.* Englewood Cliffs, NJ: Prentice-Hall, Inc., 1984.

Kernighan, Brian W., and Rob Pike. *The UNIX Programming Environment.* Englewood Cliffs, NJ: Prentice-Hall, Inc., 1984.

Kochan, Stephen G., and Patrick H. Wood. *UNIX Shell Programming.* Hasbrouck Heights, NJ: Hayden Book Co., 1985.

Sobell, Mark G. *A Practical Guide to UNIX System V.* Menlo Park, CA: The Benjamin/Cummings Publishing Co., 1985.

Strang, John. *Reading and Writing Termcap Entries.* Newton, MA: O'Reilly and Associates, Inc., 1985

Todino, Grace, and Tim O'Reilly. *Managing UUCP and Usenet.* Newton, MA: O'Reilly and Associates, Inc., 1986

Wood, Patrick H., and Stephen G. Kochan. *UNIX System Security.* Hasbrouck Heights, NJ: Hayden Book Co., 1985.

INDEX

ACU. *See* Modems
ADDS Viewpoint, 178-179
adduser (/etc), 107
adduser (shell program), 115-116
Altos, 6, 8
Amdahl, 3, 10
  470 V7a, 6
  4070, 8
  UTS UNIX, 4, 50, 54, 86, 267
Applications software, 6-7
Argument list, shell programming, 253-254
Arithmetic, shell programming, 261-262
Assembly language
  device drivers, 51
  and portability, 3-4
at, 59, 62
AT&T
  3B series, 3, 6, 8, 86, 180, 181, 185, 223, 231, 304
  help from, 9
  long-distance, 217
  resources, 295
  UNIX PC, 8

Backspace, 174
backup (shell program), 134-135
Backups, 7, 117-144
  archive vs. copy programs, 126
  checking, 127
  cpio, 133-137
  dd, 131-133
  deleted users, 112-114
  dump and restor, 130-131
  floppy disks, 121
  full, 118-119
  importance, 117-118
  incremental, 119-120
  media, 122-126
    write protection, 125-126, 290-294
  partial, 119-120
  restoring data, care required, 126-127
  schedules, 120-122
  shell programs, 129, 134-135, 140-144
  tapes, number, 121
  volcopy, 138-140
  see also tar
banner, 267
basename, shell programming, 260-263
Baud rates, 66
  optimizing, 179-180
  printer, 185
  terminals, 170
bcheckrc (/etc), 47
/bin, 48, 49-50
  /login, 72-73
Blocks, 20-22, 87-89
  breakage, 21
  checking, fsck, 33-40
  free, 43, 94-96
    list, 38-40
  logical cf. physical, 41
  size, 83, 132
  spacing, 86-89
  usage, directories, 274-275
Block special files, 51-52
Booting system, 13
  failures, 26-27
Bourne shell. *See* Shell; Shell programming (Bourne)
BREAK, 170, 234
break (shell programming), 268-269
Breakout box, 224, 298-299, 301-306
Bringing up UNIX, 12-19, 72

Cadmus, 8, 68, 296, 307
  graphics terminal, 177
cancel, 195-196, 201
Capture buffers, 223
case (shell programming), 258-259, 266
CD, 218-221; *see also* RS-232
Centronics parallel ports, 185
Channel, 102
Character special files, 51-52
checkall (shell program), 47
checksure (shell program), 164-165
/chgrp, 147
chmod, 147-149
chown, 111, 113, 146-147, 153, 286
C language
  device drivers, 51
  header files, 49
  and portability, 3-4
Class, 195
clri, 24-25, 40
Clustering, 249
Codata, 6, 8, 181
Command line arguments, shell programming, 265
Command log, 58
Commands, using output for subsequent input, 74
Comments, 66
Communications, 5-6, 214-215
  direct links, 215
  log files, 68
  telephone (DDD), 215
  see also cu; Modems; Networks; uucp
Connectivity, checking, 37
continue (shell programming), 268-269
Core dumps, file maintenance, 61
cp, 21
cpio, 52, 117, 133-137
  floppy disks, 293
  cf. tar, 137-138
CP/M, 2, 251
CPU-intensive tasks, 107
crash, 105
Crashes, 32, 104-105
  analyzing, 285
  head, 120
  recovery from, 99, 105
    editor files, 70-71
create (shell program), 28

cron
  calling monitor, 276-278
  delayed calling, 235-236
  log files, cleaning, 78
  uucp, 243
crontab (/usr/lib), 56-59, 71
  security considerations, 153-154
crypt, 161-162
C shell. *See* Shell
.cshrc, 7
ct, 214-215
CTS, 220, 221; *see also* RS-232
cu, 214-215, 225
  log files, 223
  testing modem, 221-222
curses(3x) library, 179
Customizing, 98
  rc, 67-69, 71-72
Cylinder, 89

Daemon, 53, 93, 194, 203
  defined, 184
Data encryption, 161-162
Data General, AOS, 3, 251
date, 14-15, 17
  testing response time, 277
Date, setting, 14-15
DB-25 pin connectors, 299-301; *see also* RS-232
dcheck, 24-25
dd, 52, 117, 131-133
DEC
  MicroVAX II, 8
  PDP-7, 168
  PDP-11, 4
  RK07 cartridge drive, 133
  VAX 11/780, 3, 8
  VMS, 3
  VT100, 168, 177, 302
deluser, 112
/dev, 48, 50-54
  security considerations, 163
  special file structure, 51-52
  terminals, 169
Development tools, 4-5
Device drivers, 2, 50-54
  disk, 83, 132
  and portability, 3-4
  source code modification, 53-54
Devices
  hung, 103-104
  numbers, 52
  vs. printers, 194-196
  raw, 52
  talking directly to, 290-291
df, 41, 43, 46, 84, 91, 94
dfsck, 47
diction, 6
Dictionary. *See* Spelling checker
die (shell program), 280
Direct lines, 216, 223-227
Directories
  block usage, 274-275
  checking, fsck, 33-35
  empty, 85
  entries, file, 22
  home, 63, 110, 113
  large, finding, 76-77
  lost+found, 25, 25-26, 37, 40, 105
    cleaning, shell program, 262-263
    slotting, 28-29
  misaligned, 35
  ownership, 146
  parent, 85
  printing, script, 11
  root (/). *See* root
  shell programming, cleaning, 262-263
  tree structure, 19, 30, 275
  UNIX proper, listed, 48-49
  user, creating, 111
  see also lost+found directories
Disks/disk drives, 20, 87-89
  cartridge, 124
  device driver, 83
  drivers, 132
  floppy, 13, 86, 121, 123, 131-132, 291-294
  head crash, 120
  -intensive tasks, 107
  packs, removable, 124
  partitions, 83, 84-85
    backing up, 133
    creating, 86-89
  usage, security considerations, 166-167
dmesg, 59
dospell, 77-78
ds (shell program), 274-275
DTE/DCE, 180-181, 185, 299-301, 303
DTR, 218, 219-221, 224, 312; *see also* RS-232
dump, 117, 130-131
/dump, 48, 61

EBCDIC, 131
echo (shell programming) 265
ed, 161-162
Editor files
  data encryption, 161-162
  saving, 70-71
Electronic mail. *See* Mail; mail
Error log, 59, 61
/etc, 49, 62-73
  /adduser, 107
  /bcheckrc, 72
  /brc, 72
  /getty. *See* getty
  /group, 64, 110-111
  /init. *See* init (/etc)
  /inittab, 65, 171-172, 227
  /login, 72-73
  /mnttab, 93
  /motd, 98
  /passwd. *See* passwd file (/etc)
  /rc, 17, 47, 67-69, 71-72, 81
  /shutdown, 97-98
  /termcap, 176-177
  /ttys, 169-170, 226, 227
  /update, 31
exec (shell programming), 268-269
Execute permission, 147-149
expr (shell programming), 261-262

f77, 56
Fetch commands (UTS), maintenance, 61
fickle finger (shell program), 115
file, 101-102
Files
  creating empty, 28
  names, substitution, 137
  ownership, 146
  printing, script, 11
  searching for, 79, 272-273
File server, 215
File system, 2, 19-26
  background theory, 82-83
  checking, 16, 17, 30-47, 72
    importance, 30
    root directory, 47
    shell programs, 47
    see also fsck
  communications between, 82
  consistency programs, 24-25
  creation and implementation, 84-85
  directory entries, 22
  file type, determining, 73-76
  hierarchical (tree) structure, 19, 30, 275
  maintenance, 284, 288-289
  manual repair, 40-46
  mounted, 82-83
  mounting, 90-94
  permissions, 52
  removing files, 77
  shell programming, 28-29, 269-271
    mounting/unmounting, 93-96
  stacked, 82
  structure
    blocks, 20-22
    inodes, 22
  super-block, 30-31
  sync, 31
  testing and repairing, 287-289
  unmounting, 92-94
  update, 31
  as volume, 138
File transfer, uucp, 236-238
  find, 117
  -cpio option, 112-113
  piping command to cpio, 133-134
  shell programming, 269-271

findbig (shell program), 76-77
Floppy disks, 13, 86, 131-132, 121, 123, 291-294
fmtflop, 292
for loop (shell programming), 252-253, 267
format, 86, 292
free (shell program), 94-96
Free list, checking, fsck, 38-40
fs (shell program), 272-273
fsck, 16, 17, 22-23, 24, 26, 32-40, 52, 105
  flags, 23
  phases, 22
    blocks and sizes, 33-35
    connectivity, 37
    free list, 38-39
    free list, salvage, 39-40
    path names, 36
    reference counts, 37-38
  predecessors to, 24-25
  root file system, 39-40
  slotting /lost+found, 28-29
  tips, 40
fsdb, 40-46
fsize, 40-46
fuser, 103

Gap, disk, 87-89
getty, 12, 66-67, 72-73, 171, 172, 219, 225, 226
  -c option, 173-174
gettydefs, 73, 172-174
  gid, 63, 109
Granularity, 277
grep, 69, 176-177
Groups, 64
  entries, looking up, 279
  id (GID), 63, 109
    set (SGID), 151, 154
  passwords, 156-159

Handshaking, 190-191
Hardware upgrade, 71
Hayes modems, 221-222, 234, 307
Hazeltine 1420, 180, 181
HDB, 226-229, 304
help, 8, 9
Host operating system, 86
Hung devices/processes, 102-104
Hunter's $1.98 pin tester, 180-181, 301-302

IBM, 10, 251
  4300, 8
  MVS, 3
  PC, 4
  PC/AT, 8
  terminals, 103
icheck, 24-25
Idris, 4
if-then-else (shell programming), 256-257

init (/etc), 13, 64-67
  level 2 (multiuser), 16-17, 65-66, 81
  level s (single-user), 15-16, 65-66, 81
  soft kill, 97
  terminal considerations, 171
inittab (/etc), 65, 171-172, 227
Inodes, 22
  free, 43
  initializing, 86-87
  and ncheck, 24
  testing, 24
  see also fsck
Intelligent cable, 306
Interleaving, 87, 89
Interrupts (shell programming), 266-267
isize, 40-46

Joe, 155
Jumpering, 220, 304

kermit, 55, 242
Kernel, 2-3, 54
  changing name, 247-249
  name, 13
  recompiling, 230
kill, 97, 103

LANs, 5-6, 215-217
learn, 8
  file maintenance, 60-62
Lee Data terminals, 103
Liberty 50 terminal, 179-182
Libraries, 55-56
  curses(3x), 179
Links, 21, 22
  checking, fsck, 37-38
  lost, 24-25
  printers, 186-187
  testing, 24
lint, 5
ln, 21, 22
Lock files, 68, 71, 193
Log files
  cleaning, 78
  commands, 58
  communications, 59, 68, 223
  cpio, 136
  error messages, 59
  file maintenance, 61-62
  lp, 200-201
  system activity, 56
Login
  as lp, 198-199
  name, global removal, 114
  unshakable, 225
login:, 12
.login, 181
/login (/etc or /bin), 72-73
logname, 267

Log, system, 287
lost+found directories, 25-26, 37, 40, 105
  cleaning, shell program, 262-263
  slotting, 28-29
lp (System V print spooler), 7, 11, 183, 184, 194-212
  accept/reject, 197, 199, 202
  attaching printers, 199-200
  custom drivers, 204-212
  disable/enable, 197, 199, 202-203
  interface programs, 204-212
  login as, 198-199
  lpadmin/lpstat, 197, 199
  lpsched/lpshut, 197, 199
  non-printer uses, 212
  shell programs, 212-213
  troubleshooting, 201-203
  /usr/spool/lp, 200-201
lpr (version 7 and System III print spooler), 11, 183, 184, 192-194
lpset, 175
lpstart (shell program), 212-213
ls, 21, 22
  piping commands to cpio, 133-134

Macros, 251
Mail
  file maintenance, 60-62
  new users, 112
  path, 239
  uucp, 236-238
mail, 5, 71, 72, 164
Mainframes, 8
Maintenance, scheduled, 288-289; *see also* File system, checking
make, 5
mall (shell program), 165-166
Memory management, 2
Microcomputers, 4, 8
Minicomputers, 8
mkcmd (shell program), 11
mkfs, 81, 86-89
mnttab (/etc), 93
Modems, 214-230
  as ACU, 216
  baud rates, 179
    direct connection, 226
  bidirectional, 172, 226, 243-245
  control, 219-221
  hardware switches, 217-219
  hung, 104
  null (direct line), 172, 216, 223-229, 304
  short-haul, 216
  testing, 221
  see also Communications; specific programs
monitor (shell program), 276-278
morning (shell program), 73

Motorola 68000, 4, 6, 7
mount, 90-94
Mount (shell program), 93-94
MS-DOS (PC-DOS), 2, 6, 10
  -UNIX bridge, 250
mtab, 68
MULTICS, 168
Multitasking, 2
Multiuser mode, 16
  failures, 26-27
mv, 21, 35, 85
MVS, 3, 10

ncheck, 24
Networks, 5-6, 215
  clustering, 249
  LANs, 215-217
newcron (shell program), 78
newgrp, 147
New systems, creating, 283-285
Niceness, 101
  negative, 101
Node name, 230-231, 309
  changing, 247-249
nroff, 5, 6, 55, 56
  underline filter, 207-211
NULL, 170
Null modem, 172, 216, 223-229, 304

Octal bits, 148
od, 53
Okidata 84, 199
Operating system
  definition, 1-2
  host, 86
Overloaded systems, 276-278

pack, 161
Packet transmission, 217, 242-243
Parallel ports, 51-52
  Centronics, 185
Parent directories, 85
Parity, 180
passwd command, 108
passwd file (/etc), 63, 235
  adding users, 107-110
  close file quickly, 107, 110, 285-286
  group passwords, 158-159
  sorting, 115
  typical entry, 108-110
  security considerations, 151
Passwords, 18-19, 63, 72-73, 155-159
  aging, 109, 156
  changing, 114
  entries, looking up, 279
  group, 64, 156-159
  guidelines, 155-156
  installing, 107-110
  Joe, 155
  record, 63
  root, protecting, 285-286
Path
  mail, 239
  names, checking, fsck, 36
PATH, 79
PC-DOS (MS-DOS), 2, 6, 10
  -UNIX bridge, 250
Permissions, 52
  default, 149-150
  lp, 203
PID, 99
Pipes, 53
  lp, 200
  sideways, 73-76
poll (shell program), 246-247
Polling, 231
Portability, 3-4
  Bourne shell, 2
  and device drivers, 3-4
  and program development, 5
Ports
  bidirectional, 243-245
  parallel cf. serial, 51-52
  serial, 71
  see also Modems; Printers; Terminals
Positional parameters (shell programming), 253 -254
PPID, 101
print all (shell program), 11
Printers, 183-213
  attaching, 185-191
  baud rates, 179,185
  class, 195
  default, 200
  vs. devices, 195-196
  handshaking, 190-191
  killed, 104
  multiple files, shell program, 263-269
  multiple names, 186-187
  ports, 185
  bug in, 71
  stty, fooling, 189-190
  troubleshooting, 188-189
  tty port, 187-188
  user perspective, 183-184
  virtual, 198
Printer spooler, 71, 184
  bypassing, 188
  testing, 191
  see also lp; lpr
Printing terminals, 40
Privilege, 145-149
Processes, 99-104
  hung, 102-104
  killing, 280
  owner, 99
  parent, 99
.profile, 7, 110, 111
  permissions, 150
  terminal considerations, 178, 181
`program`, 73
Programmers Workbench, The, 5
Programming tools, 4-5
PROM, 13, 86
Prompt, 172
Protection bits, 147-149
  read, write, execute, 147-149
  SGID, 151, 154
  sticky bit, 151, 154-155
  SUID, 151-153
ps, 99, 103, 162
pwdchk (shell program), 279

Quotes
  backwards cf. forwards, 73
  shell programming, 259-262, 263

rc (/etc), 17, 47, 67-69, 71-72, 81
Read permission, 147-149
Redirection, 53
  lp, 203
Reference counts, checking, fsck, 37
Remote job execution. *See* uux
renice, 101
Resources, 295-297
respawn, 171-172
Response time, testing, 276-278
restor, 130-131
Restoring data. *See* Backups
Restricted shell, 159-161
rm, 25, 113-114
rmail, 215
rmtrash (shell program), 58, 62, 77
rmuser, 112
roff, 5
Rollovers, 126
root, 17-19, 164
  checking, 39-40, 47
  cleaning, 262-263
  displaying, 44
  killing processes, 99
  password, protecting, 285-286
RS-232, 298-306
  direct links, 216
  intelligent cable, 306
  specification, 299-301
rsh, 159-161
RTS, 224

SCCS, 5
Scheduler, 2
Sector skewing, 87, 89
Security, 18, 59, 66, 82, 114, 145-167
  crontab, 153-154
  data encryption, 161-162
  /dev and /src, 163
  and maintenance, 288-289
  ownership, changing, 146-147
  passwords, 155-159
  privilege, 145-146
  protection bits, 147-149, 151-155
  restricted shell, 159-161

Security, *(continued)*
- shell programs, 164-167
- sticky memory, 155
- sushi, 152-154
- terminals, 163-164
- uucp file transfer, 237-238
- *see also* Passwords

Serial ports, 51-52, 71; *see also* Printers; Terminals
setuid, 164
setuname, 231
SGID, 151, 154
Shared text, 101
Shell, 2, 13, 63, 64, 106, 110
- Bourne, 2, 63, 251
  - cf. C, 251
- C, 2, 63, 238
- changing, 289
- restricted, 159-161

Shell programming (Bourne)
- basename, 260-263
- break, continue, exec, 268-269
- case, 258-259, 266
- creating, 11
- ds, 274-275
- echo, 265
- expr, 261-262
- find, 269-271
- for loop, 252-253, 267
- fs, 272-273
- if-then-else, 256-257
- interrupts, 266-267
- positional parameters (argument list), 253-254
- quoting, 259-262
- sample ptr script (multiple file printing), 263-268
- system administration, 276-280
- test command, 254-256
  - abbreviation with [, 255
  - command-line arguments, 265
- ts, 275
- while loop, 254-255
- xargs, 271-272

shutdown (/etc), 97-98
Shutting down system, 97-105
Single-user mode, 15-16, 18, 81
Sizes, checking, 33-35
Soft kill, 97
sortpw (shell program), 115
Source code directories, 49
- security considerations, 163

Special files, device drivers, 51-52
spellcount (shell program), 77-78
Spelling checker, 5
- file maintenance, 60-62
- updating dictionary, 78

Spoolers
- file maintenance, 60-62
- and maintenance, 288-289
- *see also* lp; lpr; Print spoolers

/src, security considerations, 163
sticky (shell program), 165
Sticky bit, 151, 154-155
- finding, 165

strip, 76
stty, 53, 174-176, 189-190
style, 6
su, 18-19, 59
SUID, 151-153
- lp, 203

Super-block, 30-31, 38
- dump, 41-43
- manual repair, 40-46
- structure, 42-43

Supermicros, 8
Super-user, 17-19, 111
- passwd, 109
- shell, interactive (sushi), 152-154

Sushi, 152-154
swap, 64
swapper, 13
Symbol tables, removing, 76
sync, 31, 68, 287
- and crashes, 104-105

sysname.c (C program), 247-249
System
- accounting, 55, 59, 68
  - file maintenance, 60-62
  - security considerations, 166-167
- activity, logs, 56
- calls, 2-3
- crashes. *See* Crashes
- programs, 2
- -specific
  - commands, 49-50
  - directories, 49, 54, 55

System administration
- crashes, analyzing, 285
- file system maintenance, 284
- new systems, 283-285
- planning, 282-283
- resources, 295-297
- scripts, 276-280

System administrator
- role, 7-8
- workload, 8-9

SZ, 101

Tabs, 56, 172, 176
tail, 136
Tape, 290-291
- cartridge, 123
- handling, 291
- reel-to-reel, 123

tapefit (shell program), 142-144
tape_mount, tape_copy, tape_print (shell programs), 141-142
tar, 117, 127-130
- cf. cpio, 137-138
- flags, 128-129
- restoring data, 129-130
- script, 129

Telephone links, 215-217
- noise, 216
- *see also* Modems

TeleVideo 910, 180
Temporary files, maintenance, 61
termcap (/etc), 176-177
Terminals, 56, 168-182
- defining characters, 174-175
- emulation, 180
- hardware installation, 179-182
- ports
  - initializing, 169-176
  - printers on, 187-188
- screen control, 176-179
- security considerations, 163-164
- tabs, 172, 176
- turning off/resetting, 103
- versatility of UNIX, 168

terminfo (/usr/lib), 178-179
test (shell programming), 254-256
- abbreviation with [, 255
- command line arguments, 265

tfree, 43
Thompson, Ken, 168
Timeout, 66
Time, setting, 14-15
time, testing response time, 278
TIMEZONE, 15
tinode, 43
/tmp, 49, 61-62
tm, 141
Training, 295-297
Trees, 19, 30, 275
troff, 5, 6, 55, 56
- as printer, 212

Trojan horse, 114
Troubleshooting, 26-27
ts (shell program), 275
type (shell program), 73-76
Typesetting, 5, 55, 56
TZ, 15

UID, 63, 101, 109
- new, 107-108

umask, 149-150
umount, 92-94
uname, 230-231
Underline filter, printers, 207-211
Unisoft UNIX, 175
UNIX
- advantages, 1
- availability, 3, 4
- bringing up, 12-29
- customizing, 50, 67-69, 71-72, 98
- history, 168
- microcomputer versions, 4
- overview, 1-11
- -PC-DOS bridge, 250
- software, 6-7
- source code, 3-4, 53, 60
- structure, 3
- system sizes, 8
- versatility, 168

/unix, 12, 13

UNIX versions
  Berkeley, 10, 176
  init, compared, 65-67
  -specific directories, 49
  standardization, 10
  System III, 6
  System V, 6
    release II (UNIX 5.2), 10
  terminal considerations, 169-172
Unmount (shell program), 94, 98
update (/etc), 31, 68
uroff.c (sample program), 207-211
USENET, 9, 56, 87, 240-242
  file maintenance, 61-62
Users
  adding, 106-112
  directories, cf. /usr, 54
  directory, creating, 111
  home directory, 63, 110, 113
  id (UID), 63
    set (SUID), 151-153
  names, clarity, 107
  printers, perspective on, 183-184
  removing, 112-114
  -related shell programs, 115-116
  shell, 106, 110
/usr
  /adm, 49, 61
  /bin, 49, 54
  /include, 49
  /lbin, 49
  /lib, 55-56
    /crontab. *See* crontab
    /terminfo, 178-179
    /uucp. *See* uucp
  /local, 49
    /bin, 49, 55
    /rmtrash, 58
  /spool, 60-62
    cleaning, 262-263
    /mail, new users, 112
    see also lp; lpr; printer spoolers; Spoolers
  /src, 53, 60
    and subdirectories, UNIX proper, listed, 49
    cf. user directories, 54
utmp, 68
uucico, 227, 231, 234, 235
uucp, 5, 7, 55, 56, 63, 71, 215, 230-250
  delayed calling, 235-236
  Devices and Dialers files, 227-228
  Dialcodes, 233
  file maintenance, 61
  file transfer, 236-238
  HDB, 226-229, 304
  L-devices, 228-230
  log files, 59
  logins, 235
  L.sys, 232
    dialing from, 234, 307
  mail, 238-240
  packet transmission, 242-243
  polling, 231
  setting up, 230-236
  shell programs, 246-249
  Systems, 232
  typical connection, 307-312
  -x9 option, 307
UUCP-Net, 240
uufol (shell program), 246
uugetty, 172, 220, 226, 243-245
uul (shell program), 246
uuname, 231
uurmst (shell program), 246
uutail (shell program), 246
uux, 215, 235-236, 238-240

VENIX, 4, 155
vi, 55
  data encryption, 161-162
Virtual machines, 282-283, 288
Virtual memory, 101
  security considerations, 154
VMS, 3, 10
/vmunix, 13
volcopy, 52, 117, 138-140

wall, 98, 165
Warm start, 32
whatis, 55
where.c (sample program), 79-80
whereis, 50, 55, 79
which, 50, 79
while (shell program), 254-255
who, 102, 107
write, 5
Write permission, 147-149
Write protection, 125-126
Writers, 5
Writer's Workbench, The, 5, 6, 56
Wyse 50 terminal, 164

xargs (shell programming), 271-272
XENIX, 4, 6, 10, 133, 292
xmodem, 242
Xon/Xoff protocol, 180
xroff, 5

Zombie, 100

UNIX is a trademark of AT&T Bell Laboratories.

HAYDEN BOOKS UNIX System Library

UNIX SHELL PROGRAMMING

By STEPHEN G. KOCHAN and PATRICK H. WOOD. A complete, easy-to-understand introduction to UNIX shell programming that covers the standard shell, C shell, restricted shell, and the newer Korn shell. It also shows how to tailor the UNIX environment to individual requirements, and how to customize UNIX commands.
#6309-1; $24.95 paper
#8301-7; $34.95 cloth

UNIX SYSTEM SECURITY

By PATRICK H. WOOD and STEPHEN G. KOCHAN. This practical guide to UNIX system security describes available programs for administering passwords, security auditing, checking file permissions, securing terminals, DES data encryption, and setting up a restricted environment. Includes sources for the programs described.
#6267-2; $34.95 cloth

EXPLORING THE UNIX SYSTEM

By STEPHEN G. KOCHAN and PATRICK H. WOOD. An indispensable hands-on guide produced with AT&T Bell Laboratories' support, this complete introduction to the UNIX environment covers the file system, shell programming, program development, screen editing, and system administration.
#6268-0; $22.95 paper
#8302-5; $34.95 cloth

PROGRAMMING IN C

By STEPHEN G. KOCHAN. This introduction to the C language contains over 90 complete program examples and covers all the latest language features. "Kochan's book, simply, is the BEST introduction to C."—*UNIX Review.* "An excellent book for anyone who wants to learn C for use in writing applications programs. ...Well organized, accurate, and filled with good examples and exercises."—*Microcomputing.*
#6261-3; $23.95 paper
#8300-9; $34.95 cloth

HAYDEN BOOKS **A Division of Howard W. Sams & Company**
4300 W. 62nd Street, Indianapolis, IN 46268

Please send the quantities and titles indicated on the right. (Add $2.50 per book for postage & handling plus applicable sales tax.) I enclose $______ (check or money order) or charge my order:

____UNIX Shell Programming (6309-1) @ $24.95 p
____UNIX Shell Programming (8301-7) @ $34.95 cl
____UNIX System Security (6267-2) @ $34.95 cl
____Exploring the UNIX System (6268-0) @ $22.95 p
____Exploring the UNIX System (8302-5) @ $34.95 cl
____Programming in C (6261-3) @ $23.95 p
____Programming in C (8300-9) @ $34.95 cl

VISA #____________ Name____________
MasterCard #____________ Address____________
Signature____________ City____________
Exp.____________ State____________Zip____________